THE ASSOCIATED PRESS

STYLEBOOK

AND LIBEL MANUAL

With Appendixes on
PHOTO CAPTIONS
FILING THE WIRE

Edited by Howard Angione

THE ASSOCIATED PRESS
50 Rockefeller Plaza
New York, N.Y. 10020
(212) 262-4000

Published by
THE ASSOCIATED PRESS
50 Rockefeller Plaza
New York, N.Y. 10020

Library of Congress Catalog Card Number: **77-7007**
ISBN: **0-917360-01-X**

Printed in the United States of America
Composition by Catherine Graphics Inc., New York
Printed by George Banta Inc.

First Printing — August 1977
Second Printing — October 1977
Third Printing — November 1977
Fourth Printing — April 1978
Fifth Printing — August 1978
Sixth Printing — November 1978

CONTENTS

FOREWORD

Work on this revised Stylebook began almost two years ago. The orders were: Make clear and simple rules, permit few exceptions to the rules, and rely heavily on the chosen dictionary as the arbiter of conflicts.

As work progressed we became convinced that while style would remain the chief purpose, there were many factual references we should include to make things a bit easier for busy editors.

So we have a Stylebook, but also a reference work.

As for the "style" itself, we thought at the outset that it wouldn't be possible to please everyone. Of course, we were right.

Journalists approach these style questions with varying degrees of passion. Some don't really think it's important. Some agree that basically there should be uniformity for reading ease if nothing else. Still others are prepared to duel over a wayward lowercase.

We encountered all three types and, in their special ways, all were helpful.

It is customary at this place to thank those whose aid and counsel produced the volume that follows.

That list is long. It ranges from the staff of The Associated Press to editors and writers on member newspapers, to other individuals and groups with special interests in some subjects. In particular we sought and received member views on a variety of difficult questions so that this book could reflect what members wanted.

We are particularly grateful to those newspaper editors who agreed to review the final draft and give us their comments as well as those of their staffs. The completed book incorporates many of their suggestions.

We have tried to make the Stylebook current and trust it will be a lasting work. But language changes, and we will review entries annually, making necessary changes by wire notes during the review period.

Finally, we are indebted to Howard Angione, a member of the AP General Desk in New York who directed this project for us with noteworthy energy, skill and, not least of all, persistence.

And we are indebted to Eileen Alt Powell, also of the General Desk, for her work in seeing the book through final editing and publication.

LOUIS D. BOCCARDI
Vice President and
Executive Editor
July 1977

STYLEBOOK

STYLEBOOK KEY

This updated and revised version of The Associated Press Stylebook has been organized like a dictionary. Need the acronym for a government agency? Look under the agency's name. Should you capitalize a word? Check the word itself or the **capitalization** entry. What's the format for baseball boxes? See **baseball**.

Following is a key to the entries:

airport Capitalize as part of a proper name: *La Guardia Airport, Newark International Airport.*

The first name of an individual and the word *international* may be deleted from a formal airport name while the remainder is capitalized: *John F. Kennedy International Airport, Kennedy International Airport* or *Kennedy Airport.* Use whichever is appropriate in the context.

Do not make up names, however. There is no *Boston Airport*, for example. The *Boston airport* (lowercase *airport*) would be acceptable if for some reason the proper name, *Logan International Airport*, were not used.

airtight

airways The system of routes that the federal government has established for airplane traffic.

See the **airline, airlines** entry for its use in carriers' names.

Alabama Abbrev.: *Ala.* See **state names**.

Entry words, in alphabetical order, are in **boldface**. They represent the accepted word forms unless otherwise indicated.

Text explains usage.

Examples of correct and incorrect usage are in *italics*.

Many entries simply give the correct spelling, hyphenation and/or capitalization.

Abbrev. indicates the correct abbreviation of a word.

Related topics are in **boldface**.

Other abbreviations used in the Stylebook:

n. : noun form
v. : verb form

adj.: adjectives
adv. : adverbs

a, an Use the article *a* before consonant sounds: *a historic event, a one-year term* (sounds as if it begins with the letter w), *a united stand* (sounds like you).

Use the article *an* before vowel sounds: *an energy crisis, an honorable man* (the h is silent), *an NBA record* (sounds as if it begins with the letter e), *an 1890s celebration.*

a- The rules in **prefixes** apply, but in general, no hyphen. Some examples:

achromatic   atonal
amoral

A&P Acceptable in all references for *Great Atlantic & Pacific Tea Co. Inc.*

abbreviations and acronyms The notation *abbrev.* is used in this book to identify the abbreviated form that may be used for a word in some contexts.

A few universally recognized abbreviations are required in some circumstances. Some others are acceptable depending on the context. But in general, avoid alphabet soup.

The same principle applies to acronyms — pronounceable words formed from the initial letters in a series of words: *ALCOA, NATO, radar, scuba,* etc.

Guidance on how to use a particular abbreviation or acronym is provided in entries alphabetized according to the sequence of letters in the word or phrase.

Some general principles:

BEFORE A NAME: Abbreviate the following titles when used before a full name outside direct quotations: *Dr., Gov., Lt. Gov., Mr., Mrs., Rep., the Rev., Sen.* and certain military designations listed in the **military titles** entry. Spell out all except *Dr., Mr.* and *Mrs.* when they are used before a name in direct quotations.

For guidelines on how to use titles, see **courtesy titles; legislative titles; military titles; religious titles;** and the entries for most commonly used titles.

AFTER A NAME: Abbreviate *junior* or *senior* after an individual's name. Abbreviate *company, corporation, incorporated* and *limited* when used after the name of a corporate entity. See entries under these words and **company names.**

In some cases, an academic degree may be abbreviated after an individual's name. See **academic degrees.**

WITH DATES OR NUMERALS: Use the abbreviations *A.D., B.C., a.m., p.m., No.* and abbreviate certain months when used with the day of the month.

Right: *In 450 B.C.; at 9:30 a.m.; in room No. 6; on Sept. 16.*

Wrong: *Early this a.m. he asked for the No. of your room.* The abbreviations are correct only with figures.

Right: *Early this morning he asked for the number of your room.*

See **months** and individual entries for these other terms.

IN NUMBERED ADDRESSES: Abbreviate *avenue, boulevard* and *street* in numbered addresses: *He lives on Penn-*

sylvania Avenue. He lives at 1600 Pennsylvania Ave.

See **addresses.**

STATES AND NATIONS: The names of certain states, the *United States* and the *Union of Soviet Socialist Republics* (but not of other nations) are abbreviated with periods in some circumstances.

See **state names; datelines;** and individual entries.

ACCEPTABLE BUT NOT REQUIRED: Some organizations and government agencies are widely recognized by their initials: *CIA, FBI, GOP.*

If the entry for such an organization notes that an abbreviation is acceptable in all references or on second reference, that does not mean that its use should be automatic. Let the context determine, for example, whether to use *Federal Bureau of Investigation* or *FBI.*

See **second reference.**

AVOID AWKWARD CONSTRUCTIONS: Do not follow an organization's full name with an abbreviation or acronym in parentheses or set off by dashes. If an abbreviation or acronym would not be clear on second reference without this arrangement, do not use it.

Names not commonly before the public should not be reduced to acronyms solely to save a few words.

SPECIAL CASES: Many abbreviations are desirable in tabulations and certain types of technical writing. See individual entries.

CAPS, PERIODS: Use capital letters and periods according to the listings in this book. For words not in this book, use the first-listed abbreviation in Webster's New World Dictionary.

If an abbreviation not listed in this book or in the dictionary achieves widespread acceptance, use capital letters. Omit periods unless the result would spell an unrelated word.

ABC Acceptable in all references for *American Broadcasting Cos.* (the plural is part of the corporate name).

Divisions are ABC News, ABC Radio and ABC-TV.

ABCs

able-bodied

ABM, ABMs Acceptable in all references for *anti-ballistic missile(s)*, but the term should be defined in the story.

Avoid the redundant phrase *ABM missiles.*

A-bomb Use *atomic bomb* unless a direct quotation is involved.

See **Hiroshima.**

aboveboard

absent-minded

absent without leave *AWOL* is acceptable on second reference.

academic degrees If mention of degrees is necessary to establish someone's credentials, the preferred form is to avoid an abbreviation and use instead a phrase such as: *John Jones, who has a doctorate in psychology.*

Use an apostrophe in *bachelor's degree, a master's,* etc.

Use such abbreviations as *B.A., M.A., LL.D.* and *Ph.D.* only when the need to identify many individuals by degree on first reference would make the preferred form cumbersome. Use these abbreviations only after a full name — never after just a last name.

When used after a name, an academic abbreviation is set off by commas: *Daniel Moynihan, Ph.D., spoke.*

Do not precede a name with a courtesy title for an academic degree and follow it with the abbreviation for the degree in the same reference:

Wrong: *Dr. Sam Jones, Ph.D.*

Right: *Dr. Sam Jones, a chemist.*

When in doubt about the proper abbreviation for a degree, follow the first listing in Webster's New World Dictionary.

See **doctor.**

academic departments Use lowercase except for words that are proper nouns or adjectives: *the department of* *history, the history department, the department of English, the English department.*

academic titles Capitalize and spell out formal titles such as *professor, dean, president, chancellor, chairman,* etc., when they precede a name. Lowercase elsewhere.

Lowercase modifiers such as *history* in *history Professor Oscar Handlin* or *department* in *department Chairman Jerome Wiesner.*

See **doctor** and **titles.**

academy See **military academies.**

Academy Awards Presented annually by the Academy of Motion Picture Arts and Sciences. Also known as the *Oscars.*

Lowercase *the academy* and *the awards* whenever they stand alone.

accept, except *Accept* means to receive.

Except means to exclude.

accommodate

accused A person is *accused of,* not *with,* a crime.

To avoid any suggestion that an individual is being judged before a trial, do not use a phrase such as *accused slayer John Jones.* Instead, use *John Jones, accused of the slaying.*

For guidelines on related words, see **allege; arrest;** and **indict.**

Ace A trademark for a brand of elastic bandage.

acknowledgment

acre Equal to 43,560 square feet or 4,840 square yards. The metric equivalent is .4 (two-fifths) of a hectare or 4,047 square meters.

To convert to hectares, multiply by .4 (5 acres x .4 = 2 hectares).

See **hectare.**

acronyms See the **abbreviations and acronyms** entry.

act Capitalize when part of the name for pending or implemented legislation: *the Taft-Hartley Act.*

acting Always lowercase, but capitalize any formal title that may follow before a name: *acting Mayor Peter Barry.*

See **titles.**

act numbers Use Arabic figures and capitalize *act: Act 1; Act 2, Scene 2.* But: *the first act, the second act.*

actor (man) **actress** (woman)

Actors Equity Association Headquarters is in New York.

A.D. Acceptable in all references for *anno Domini:* in the year of the Lord.

Because the full phrase would read *in the year of the Lord 96,* the abbreviation *A.D.* goes before the figure for the year: *A.D. 96.*

Do not write: *The fourth century A.D. The fourth century* is sufficient. If *A.D.* is not specified with a year, the year is presumed to be A.D.

See **B.C.**

-added Follow this form in sports stories: *The $50,000-added sweepstakes.*

addresses Use the abbreviations *Ave., Blvd.* and *St.* only with a numbered address: *1600 Pennsylvania Ave.* Spell them out and capitalize when part of a formal street name without a number: *Pennsylvania Avenue.* Lowercase and spell out when used alone or with more than one street name: *Massachusetts and Pennsylvania avenues.*

All similar words (*alley, drive, road, terrace,* etc.) always are spelled out. Capitalize them when part of a formal name without a number; lowercase when used alone or with two or more names.

Always use figures for an address number: *9 Morningside Circle.*

Spell out and capitalize *First* through *Ninth* when used as street names; use figures with two letters for *10th* and above: *7 Fifth Ave., 100 21st St.*

Abbreviate compass points used to indicate directional ends of a street or quadrants of a city in a numbered address: *222 E. 42nd St., 562 W. 43rd St., 600 K St. N.W.* Do not abbreviate if the number is omitted: *East 42nd Street, West 43rd Street, K Street Northwest.*

See **highway designations.**

adjectives The abbreviation *adj.* is used in this book to identify the spelling of the adjectival forms of words that frequently are misspelled.

The **comma** entry provides guidance on punctuating a series of adjectives.

The **hyphen** entry provides guidance on handling compound modifiers used before a noun.

ad-lib (n., v., adj.)

administration Lowercase: *the administration, the president's administration, the governor's administration, the Carter administration.*

See the **government, junta, regime** entry for distinctions that apply in using these terms and *administration.*

administrative law judge This is the federal title for the position formerly known as hearing examiner. Capitalize it when used as a formal title before a name.

To avoid the long title, seek a construction that sets the title off by commas: *The administrative law judge, John Williams, disagreed.*

administrator Never abbreviate. Capitalize when used as a formal title before a name.

See **titles.**

admiral See **military titles.**

admissible

admit, admitted These words may in some contexts give the erroneous connotation of wrongdoing.

A person who announces that he is a homosexual, for example, may be ac-

knowledging it to the world, not admitting it. *Said* is usually sufficient.

ad nauseam

adopt, approve, enact, pass Amendments, ordinances, resolutions and rules are *adopted* or *approved.*

Bills are *passed.*

Laws are *enacted.*

Adrenalin A trademark for the synthetic or chemically extracted forms of epinephrine, a substance produced by the adrenal glands.

The non-proprietary terms are *epinephrine hydrochloride* or *adrenaline.*

Adventist See **Seventh-day Adventist Church.**

adverbs The abbreviation *adv.* is used in this book to identify the spelling of adverbial forms of words frequently misspelled.

See the **hyphen** entry for guidelines on when an adverb should be followed by a hyphen in constructing a compound modifier.

adverse, averse *Adverse* means unfavorable: *He predicted adverse weather.*

Averse means reluctant, opposed: *She is averse to change.*

adviser Not *advisor.*

advisory

Aer Lingus The headquarters of the airline is in Dublin, Ireland.

Aeroflot The headquarters of this airline is in Moscow.

Aeromexico This airline formerly was known as Aeronaves de Mexico. Headquarters is in Mexico City.

aesthetic

affect, effect *Affect,* as a verb, means to influence: *The game will affect the standings.*

Affect, as a noun, is best avoided. It occasionally is used in psychology to describe an emotion, but there is no need for it in everyday language.

Effect, as a verb, means to cause: *He will effect many changes in the company.*

Effect, as a noun, means result: *The effect was overwhelming. He miscalculated the effect of his actions. It was a law of little effect.*

AFL-CIO Acceptable in all references for the *American Federation of Labor and Congress of Industrial Organizations.*

A-frame

African Of or pertaining to Africa, or any of its peoples or languages. Do not use the word as a synonym for *Negro.*

In some countries of Africa, *colored* is used to describe those of mixed white and black ancestry. In other societies *colored* is considered a derogatory word.

Because of the ambiguity, avoid the term in favor of a phrase such as *mixed racial ancestry.* If the word cannot be avoided, place it in quotation marks and provide its meaning.

See **colored**.

after- No hyphen after this prefix when it is used to form a noun:
aftereffect	afterthought

Follow *after* with a hyphen when it is used to form compound modifiers:
after-dinner drink	after-theater snack

afterward Not *afterwards.*

Agency for International Development *AID* is acceptable on second reference.

agenda A list. It takes singular verbs and pronouns: *The agenda has run its course.*

The plural is *agendas.*

agent Lowercase unless it is a formal title used before a name.

In the FBI, the formal title is *special agent.* Use *Special Agent William Smith* if appropriate in a special context. Otherwise, make it *agent William Smith* or *FBI agent William Smith.*

See **titles**.

ages Always use figures. When the context does not require *years* or *years old,* the figure is presumed to be years.

Ages expressed as adjectives before a noun or as substitutes for a noun use hyphens.

Examples: *A 5-year-old boy,* but *the boy is 5 years old. The boy, 7, has a sister, 10. The woman, 26, has a daughter 2 months old. The law is 8 years old. The race is for 3-year-olds. The woman is in her 30s* (no apostrophe).

See also **boy; girl; infant;** and **youth**.

See **comma** for punctuation guidelines.

ages of history See the **historical periods and events** entry.

agnostic, atheist An *agnostic* is a person who believes it is impossible to know whether there is a God.

An *atheist* is a person who believes there is no God.

aid, aide *Aid* is assistance.

An *aide* is a person who serves as an assistant.

aide-de-camp, aides-de-camp A military officer who serves as assistant and confidential secretary to a superior.

ain't A dialectical or substandard contraction. Use it only in quoted matter or special contexts.

air base Two words. Follow the practice of the U.S. Air Force, which uses *air force base* as part of the proper name for its bases in the United States and *air base* for its installations abroad: *Lackland Air Force Base, Texas,* but *Clark Air Base, Philippines.*

On second reference: *the Air Force base, the air base,* or *the base.*

Do not abbreviate, even in datelines: *LACKLAND AIR FORCE BASE, Texas (AP)* — . . .
CLARK AIR BASE, Philippines (AP) — . . .

Air Canada Headquarters is in Montreal.

air-condition, air-conditioned (v. and adj.) The nouns are: *air conditioner, air conditioning.*

aircraft names Use a hyphen when changing from letters to figures; no hyphen when adding a letter after figures.

Some examples for aircraft often in the news: *B-1, BAC-111, C-5A, DC-10, FH-227, F-4, Phantom II, F-86 Sabre, L-1011, MiG-21, Tu-144, 727-100C, 747, 747B, VC-10.*

This hyphenation principle is the one used most frequently by manufacturers and users. Apply it in all cases for consistency. For other elements of a name, use the form adopted by the manufacturer or user. If in doubt, consult Jane's All the World's Aircraft.

NO QUOTES: Do not use quotation marks for aircraft with names: *Air Force One, the Spirit of St. Louis, Concorde.*

PLURALS: *DC-10s, 727s.* But: *747B's.* (As noted in **plurals**, the apostrophe is used in forming the plural of a single letter.)

SEQUENCE: Use Arabic figures to establish the sequence of aircraft, spacecraft and missiles: *Apollo 10.* Do not use hyphens.

aircraft terms Use *engine,* not *motor,* for the units that propel aircraft: *a twin-engine plane* (not *twin-engined*).

Use *jet plane* or *jetliner* to describe only those aircraft driven solely by jet engines. Use *turboprop* to describe an aircraft on which the jet engine is geared to a propeller. Turboprops sometimes are called *propjets.*

Jet planes in commercial use include the *BAC-111; Boeing 707, 727, 737, 747; the Convair 880;* the *DC-8, DC-9* and *DC-10;* the *L-1011;* and the *VC-10.*

See the **engine, motor** entry.

air force Capitalize when referring to U.S. forces: *the U.S. Air Force, the Air Force, Air Force regulations.* Do not use the abbreviation *USAF.*

Use lowercase for the forces of other nations: *the Israeli air force.*

This approach has been adopted for consistency, because many foreign nations to not use *air force* as the proper name.

See the **military academies** and **military titles** entries.

air force base See **air base**.

Air Force One The Air Force applies this name to any aircraft the president of the United States may be using.

In ordinary usage, however, *Air Force One* is the name for the airplane normally reserved for the president's use.

Air France Headquarters is in Paris.

Air-India The hyphen is part of the formal name.

Headquarters is in Bombay, India.

Air Jamaica Headquarters is in Kingston, Jamaica.

airline, airlines Capitalize *airlines, air lines* and *airways* when used as part of a proper airline name.

Major airlines are listed in this book separately by name.

Companies that use *airlines* include Alitalia, Allegheny, American, Continental, Eastern, Frontier, Hawaiian, National, North Central, Northwest Orient, Trans World, United and Western.

Companies that use *air lines* include Delta, Japan and Ozark.

Companies that use *airways* include Braniff, British, Pan American World, Qantas and Southern.

Companies that use none of these include Aer Lingus, Aeromexico, Air Canada, Air France, Air-India, Air Jamaica, Hughes Airwest, Iberia, KLM and Western Alaska.

On second reference, use just the proper name (*Delta*), an abbreviation if applicable (*Pan Am, TWA*), or *the airline*. Use *airlines* when referring to more than one line.

Do not use *air line, air lines* or *airways* in generic references to *an airline*.

airmail

airman See **military titles**.

Air National Guard

airport Capitalize as part of a proper name: *La Guardia Airport, Newark International Airport*.

The first name of an individual and the word *international* may be deleted from a formal airport name while the remainder is capitalized: *John F. Kennedy International Airport, Kennedy International Airport* or *Kennedy Airport*. Use whichever is appropriate in the context.

Do not make up names, however. There is no *Boston Airport*, for example. The *Boston airport* (lowercase *airport*) would be acceptable if for some reason the proper name, *Logan International Airport*, were not used.

airtight

airways The system of routes that the federal government has established for airplane traffic.

See the **airline, airlines** entry for its use in carriers' names.

Alabama Abbrev.: *Ala.* See **state names**.

a la carte

a la king, a la mode

Alaska Do not abbreviate. Largest land area of the 50 states — 586,432 square miles.

See **state names**.

Alaska-Hawaii Standard Time The time zone used in Hawaii and most of Alaska.

There is an *Alaska Daylight Time*, but there is no daylight time in Hawaii.

Bering time applies in some far western sections of Alaska. *Yukon time* is used in a small section south of the Yukon border. *Pacific time* applies in most of the area that borders British Columbia, including the city of Juneau.

See **time zones**.

Alberta A province of western Canada. Do not abbreviate.

See **datelines**.

albino, albinos

ALCOA, Alcoa The acronym *ALCOA* is acceptable on second reference for *Aluminum Company of America*.

Alcoa is a city in Tennessee.

alcoholic Use *recovered*, not *reformed*, in referring to those previously afflicted with the disease of alcoholism.

alderman Do not abbreviate. See **legislative titles**.

alert See **weather terms**.

Al Fatah A Palestinian guerrilla organization. Drop the article *Al* if preceded by an English article: *the Fatah statement, a Fatah leader*.

align

Alitalia Airlines Headquarters is in Rome.

all- Use a hyphen:

all-around	all-out
(not all-round)	all-star
all-clear	

See **all right** and the **all time, all-time** entry.

All-America, All-American The Associated Press recognizes only one All-America football team. This is Walter Camp's selection through 1924, and

AP selections after that. Do not call anyone an *All-America player* unless he is listed on either the Camp or AP roster.

Similarly do not call anyone an *All-America basketball player* unless an AP selection. The first All-America basketball team was chosen in 1948.

An individual team member may be called an *All-American*, but use *All-America* in all other uses: *He is an All-American. He is an All-America player.*

The same rules apply to the Little All-America teams in both football and basketball.

allege The word must be used with great care.

Some guidelines:

—Avoid any suggestion that the writer is making an allegation.

—Specify the source of an allegation. In a criminal case, it should be an arrest record, an indictment or the statement of a public official connected with the case.

—Use *alleged bribe* or similar phrase when necessary to make it clear that an unproved action is not being treated as fact. Be sure that the source of the charge is specified elsewhere in the story.

—Avoid redundant uses of *alleged.* It is proper to say: *The district attorney alleged that she took a bribe.* Or: *The district attorney accused her of taking a bribe.* But not: *The district attorney accused her of allegedly taking a bribe.*

—Do not use *alleged* before an event that is known to have occurred when the dispute is over who participated in it. Do not say: *He attended the alleged meeting* when what you mean is: *He allegedly attended the meeting.*

—Do not use *alleged* as a routine qualifier. Instead, use a word such as *apparent, ostensible* or *reputed.*

For guidelines on related words, see **accuse**; **arrest**; and **indict**.

Allegheny Airlines Headquarters is in Washington.

Allegheny Mountains Or simply: *the Alleghenies.*

alley Do not abbreviate. See **addresses**.

allies, allied Capitalize *allies* or *allied* only when referring to the combination of the United States and its Allies during World War I or World War II: *The Allies defeated Germany. He was in the Allied invasion of France.*

allot, allotted, allotting

all right (adv.) Never *alright.* Hyphenate only if used colloquially as a compound modifier: *He is an all-right guy.*

all time, all-time *An all-time high,* but *the greatest runner of all time.*

Avoid the redundant phrase *all-time record.*

allude, refer *To allude* to something is to speak of it without specifically mentioning it.

To refer is to mention it directly.

allusion, illusion *Allusion* means an indirect reference: *The allusion was to his opponent's war record.*

Illusion means an unreal or false impression: *The scenic director created the illusion of choppy seas.*

alma mater

almost never Do not use the phrase. Instead use *seldom* or *hardly ever.*

also-ran (n.)

altar, alter An *altar* is a tablelike platform used in a church service.

To alter is to change.

Aluminum Company of America *ALCOA* is acceptable on second reference.

Headquarters is in Pittsburgh.

alumnus, alumni, alumna, alumnae Use *alumnus* (*alumni* in the plural) when referring to a man who has attended a school.

Use *alumna* (*alumnae* in the plural) for similar references to a woman.

Use *alumni* when referring to a group of men and women.

AM Acceptable in all references for the *amplitude modulation* system of radio transmission.

a.m., p.m. Lowercase, with periods. Avoid the redundant *10 a.m. this morning.*

Amalgamated Clothing and Textile Workers Union of America The shortened forms *Amalgamated Clothing Workers* and *Clothing Workers union* are acceptable in all references.
Headquarters is in New York.

Amalgamated Transit Union Use this full name on first reference.
Headquarters is in Washington.

ambassador Use for both men and women. Capitalize as a formal title before a name.
See **titles.**

ambassador-at-large But: *ambassador extraordinary, ambassador plenipotentiary.*

amendments to the Constitution Use *First Amendment, 10th Amendment,* etc.
Colloquial references to the Fifth Amendment's protection against self-incrimination are best avoided, but where appropriate: *He took the Fifth seven times.*

American Do not limit the description to citizens or residents of the United States. It also may be applied to any resident or citizen of nations in North or South America.

American Airlines Headquarters is in New York.

American Automobile Association *AAA* is acceptable on second reference. Also: *the automobile association, the association.*
Headquarters is in Falls Church, Va.

American Baptist Association See **Baptist churches.**

American Baptist Churches in the U.S.A. See **Baptist churches.**

American Bar Association *ABA* is acceptable on second reference. Also: *the bar association, the association.*
Headquarters is in Chicago.

American Broadcasting Cos. See **ABC.**

American Civil Liberties Union *ACLU* is acceptable on second reference.
Headquarters is in New York.

American Federation of Government Employees Use this full name on first reference to prevent confusion with other unions that represent government workers.
Headquarters is in Washington.

American Federation of Labor and Congress of Industrial Organizations *AFL-CIO* is acceptable in all references.
Headquarters is in Washington.

American Federation of Musicians Use this full name on first reference.
The shortened form *Musicians union* is acceptable on second reference.
Headquarters is in New York.

American Federation of State, County and Municipal Employees Use this full name on first reference to prevent confusion with other unions that represent government workers.
Headquarters is in Washington.

American Federation of Teachers Use this full name on first reference to prevent confusion with other unions that represent teachers.
Headquarters is in Washington.

American Federation of Television and Radio Artists *AFTRA* is acceptable on second reference.
Headquarters is in New York.

American Hospital Association *AHA* is acceptable on second reference. Also: *the hospital association, the association.*
Headquarters is in Chicago.

Americanisms Words and phrases that have become part of the English language as spoken in the United States are listed in Webster's New World Dictionary with a star ★.
Most Americanisms are acceptable in news stories, but let the context be the guide.
See **word selection**.

American Legion Capitalize also *the Legion* in second reference. Members are *Legionnaires,* just as members of the Lions Club are *Lions.*
Legion and *Legionnaires* are capitalized because they are not being used in their common noun sense. A *legion* (lowercase), is a large group of soldiers or, by derivation, a large number of items: *His friends are legion.* A *legionnaire* (lowercase) is a member of such a legion.
See the **fraternal organizations and service clubs** entry.

American Medical Association *AMA* is acceptable on second reference. Also: *the medical association, the association.*
Headquarters is in Chicago.

American Motors Corp. *AMC* is acceptable on second reference.
Headquarters is in Southfield, Mich.

American Newspaper Publishers Association *ANPA* is acceptable on second reference. Also: *the newspaper publishers association, the publishers association, the association.*
Headquarters is in Reston, Va.

American Petroleum Institute *API* is acceptable on second reference.
Headquarters is in Washington.

American Postal Workers Union This union represents clerks and similar employees who work inside post offices.

Use the full name on first reference to prevent confusion with the National Association of Letter Carriers. The shortened form *Postal Workers union* is acceptable on second reference.
Headquarters is in Washington.

American Press Institute *API* is acceptable on second reference.
Headquarters is in Reston, Va.

American Society for the Prevention of Cruelty to Animals This organization is limited to the five boroughs of New York City. *ASPCA* is acceptable on second reference.
See **Society for the Prevention of Cruelty to Animals**.

American Society of Composers, Authors and Publishers *ASCAP* is acceptable on second reference.
Headquarters is in New York.

American Stock Exchange In second reference: *the American Exchange, the Amex,* or *the exchange.*

American Telephone & Telegraph Co. *AT&T* is acceptable on second reference.
AT&T has adopted the proper name *Bell System* (not *Bell Telephone Co.*) to describe the corporate complex composed of itself; its manufacturing unit, Western Electric Co.; its research and development unit, Bell Laboratories; and the telephone companies it owns in whole or in part.
Headquarters is in New York.

American Veterans of World War II, Korea and Vietnam *AMVETS* is acceptable in all references.
Headquarters is in Washington.

Americas Cup (golf)   **America's Cup** (yachting)

Amex See **American Stock Exchange**.

amid Not *amidst.*

amidships

ammunition See **weapons**.

amnesty See the entry that reads **pardon, parole, probation**.

amok Not *amuck*.

among, between The maxim that *between* introduces two items and *among* introduces more than two covers most questions about how to use these words: *The funds were divided among Ford, Carter and McCarthy.*

However, *between* is the correct word when expressing the relationships of three or more items considered one pair at a time: *Negotiations on a debate format are under way between the network and the Ford, Carter and McCarthy committees.*

As with all prepositions, any pronouns that follow these words must be in the objective case: *among us, between him and her, between you and me.*

ampersand (&) Use the ampersand when it is part of a company's formal name: *Baltimore & Ohio Railroad, Newport News Shipbuilding & Dry Dock Co.*

The ampersand should not otherwise be used in place of *and*.

amplitude modulation *AM* is acceptable in all references.

Amtrak This acronym, drawn from the words *American travel by track*, may be used in all references to the *National Railroad Passenger Corp.* Do not use *AMTRAK*.

The corporation was established by Congress in 1970 to take over intercity passenger operations from railroads that wanted to drop passenger service. All except Southern Railway, Denver and Rio Grande Western Railroad, and the Chicago, Rock Island and Pacific Railroad elected to do so. Amtrak contracts with railroads for the use of their tracks and of certain other operating equipment and crews.

Amtrak is subsidized in part by federal funds appropriated yearly by Congress and administered through the Department of Transportation.

Amtrak should not be confused with *Conrail* (see separate entry). However, the legislation that established Conrail provided for Amtrak to gradually take over ownership of certain trackage in the Boston-Washington corridor and from Philadelphia to Harrisburg.

Amtrak headquarters is in Washington.

AMVETS Acceptable in all references for *American Veterans of World War II, Korea and Vietnam.*

anemia, anemic

anesthetic

Anglican Communion This is the name for the worldwide association of the 22 separate national Anglican churches.

Each national church is independent. A special position of honor is accorded to the archbishop of Canterbury, as the pre-eminent officer in the original Anglican body, the Church of England.

The test of membership in the Anglican Communion traditionally has been whether a church is in communion with the See of Canterbury. No legislative or juridical ties exist, however.

BELIEFS: Anglicans believe in the Trinity, the humanity and divinity of Christ, the virginity of Mary, salvation through Christ, and everlasting heaven and hell.

Baptism and the Lord's Supper are recognized as sacraments, although belief in the degree to which Christ is present in the Eucharist may vary.

Together with Scripture, the Book of Common Prayer serves as the principal guide to belief and practice.

A principal difference between Roman Catholics and Anglicans is still the dispute that led to the formation of the Church of England — refusal to acknowledge that the pope, as bishop of Rome, has ruling authority over other bishops.

The communion also contends that its clergy have a direct link to Christ's apostles that is traceable through an unbroken series of ceremonies in which authority was passed down by a laying-on of hands. The Roman Catholic Church, which claims the same type of historic succession for its clergy, has held that 16th century Anglican practice broke the continuity of apostolic succession among its clergy.

Among individual Anglican (or *Episcopal* in the United States) parishes, practices fall into one of three categories — high, broad or low. A high parish stresses the sacraments and extensive ritual in worship. A low parish favors simpler services and emphasizes the preaching of the Gospel. A broad parish embraces portions of high and low worship practices, while tending to be activist on social questions and flexible in matters of church government.

The term *Anglo-Catholic* occasionally is used to describe high Anglican practice. See **catholic, catholicism**.

ANGLICAN CHURCHES: Members of the Anglican Communion, in addition to the Church of England, include the Scottish Episcopal Church, the Anglican Church of Canada, and in the United States, the Protestant Episcopal Church.

See **Episcopal Church**.

Anglo- Always capitalized. No hyphen when the word that follows is in lowercase:

Anglomania	Anglophobe
Anglophile	

Use a hyphen when the word that follows is capitalized:

Anglo-American	Anglo-Indian
Anglo-Catholic	Anglo-Saxon

angry *At* someone or *with* someone.

animals Do not apply a personal pronoun to an animal unless its sex has been established or the animal has a name: *The dog was scared; it barked. Rover was scared; he barked. The cat, which was scared, ran to its basket. Susie the cat, who was scared, ran to her basket. The bull tosses his horns.*

Capitalize the name of a specific animal, and use Roman numerals to show sequence: *Bowser, Whirlaway II.*

For breed names, follow the spelling and capitalization in Webster's New World Dictionary. For breeds not listed in the dictionary, capitalize words derived from proper nouns; use lowercase elsewhere: *basset hound, Boston terrier.*

anno Domini See **A.D.**

annual An event cannot be described as *annual* until it has been held in at least two successive years.

Do not use the term *first annual.* Instead, note that sponsors plan to hold an event *annually*.

annual meeting Lowercase in all uses.

anoint

another *Another* is not a synonym for *additional*; it refers to an element that somehow duplicates a previously stated quantity.

Right: *Ten women passed, another 10 failed.*

Wrong: *Ten women passed, another six failed.*

Right: *Ten women passed, six others failed.*

antarctic, Antarctica, Antarctic Ocean

ante- The rules in **prefixes** apply, but in general, no hyphen. Some examples:

antebellum	antedate

anthems See **composition titles**.
Lowercase the term *national anthem*.

anti- Hyphenate all except the following words, which have specific meanings of their own:

antibiotic	antipasto
antibody	antiperspirant
anticlimax	antiphon
antidote	antiphony
antifreeze	antiseptic
antigen	antiserum
antihistamine	antithesis
antiknock	antitoxin
antimatter	antitrust
antimony	antitussive
antiparticle*	

*And similar terms in physics such as *antiproton.*

This approach has been adopted in the interests of readability and easily remembered consistency.

Hyphenated words, many of them exceptions to Webster's New World, include:

anti-aircraft	anti-labor
anti-bias	anti-slavery
anti-inflation	anti-social
anti-intellectual	anti-war

See **Antichrist, anti-Christ.**

anti-aircraft See **weapons.**

Antichrist, anti-Christ *Antichrist* is the proper name for the individual the Bible says will challenge Christ.

The adjective *anti-Christ* would be applied to someone or something opposed to Christ.

anticipate, expect *Anticipate* means to expect and prepare for something; *expect* does not include the notion of preparation:

They expect a record crowd. They have anticipated it by adding more seats to the auditorium.

Antiochian Orthodox Christian Archdiocese of North America Formed in 1975 by the merger of the Antiochian Orthodox Christian Archdiocese of New York and All North America and the Antiochian Orthodox Arch-

diocese of Toledo, Ohio, and Dependencies in North America. It is under the jurisdiction of the patriarch of Antioch.

See **Eastern Orthodox churches.**

anybody, any body, anyone, any one One word for an indefinite reference: *Anyone can do that.*

Two words when the emphasis is on singling out one element of a group: *Any one of them may speak up.*

AP Use in logotypes. Acceptable on second reference for *The Associated Press.*

Do not capitalize *the* when it precedes *AP.*

apostolic delegate, papal nuncio An *apostolic delegate* is a Roman Catholic diplomat chosen by the pope to be his envoy to the church in a nation that does not have formal diplomatic relations with the Vatican.

A *papal nuncio* is the pope's envoy to a nation with which the Vatican has diplomatic relations.

apostrophe (') Follow these guidelines:

POSSESSIVES: See the **possessives** entry.

OMITTED LETTERS: *I've, it's, don't, rock 'n' roll. 'Tis the season to be jolly. He is a ne'er-do-well.* See **contractions.**

OMITTED FIGURES: *The class of '62. The Spirit of '76. The '20s.*

PLURALS OF A SINGLE LETTER: *Mind your p's and q's. He learned the three R's and brought home a report card with four A's and two B's. The Oakland A's won the pennant.*

DO NOT USE: For plurals of numerals or multiple-letter combinations. See **plurals.**

Appalachia In the broadest sense, the word applies to the entire region along the Appalachian Mountains, which extend from Maine into northern Alabama.

In a sense that often suggests economic depression and poverty, the reference is to sections of eastern Tennessee, eastern Kentucky, southeastern Ohio and the western portion of West Virginia.

The Appalachian Regional Commission, established by federal law in 1965, has a mandate to foster development in 397 counties in 13 states — all of West Virginia and continguous parts of Alabama, Georgia, Kentucky, Maryland, Mississippi, New York, North Carolina, Ohio, Pennsylvania, South Carolina, Tennessee and Virginia.

When the word *Appalachia* is used, specify the extent of the area in question.

Appalachian Mountains Or simply: *the Appalachians*.

appeals court See **U.S. Court of Appeals**.

apposition A decision on whether to put commas around a word, phrase or clause used in apposition depends on whether it is essential to the meaning of the sentence (no commas) or not essential (use commas).

See the **essential phrases, nonessential phrases** entry for examples.

approve See the entry that reads **adopt, approve, enact, pass**.

April See **months**.

April Fools' Day

Aqua-Lung A trademark for an underwater breathing apparatus.
See **scuba**.

Arabian American Oil Co. *Aramco* is acceptable on second reference.

Headquarters is in Dhahran, Saudi Arabia

Arabic names In general, use an English spelling that approximates the way a name sounds in Arabic.

If an individual has a preferred spelling in English, use that. If usage has established a particular spelling, use that.

Problems in transliteration of Arabic names often are traceable to pronunciations that vary from region to region. The *g,* for example, is pronounced like the *g* of *go* in Northern Africa, but like the *j* of *joy* in the Arab Peninsula. Thus it is *Gamal* in Egypt and *Jamal* in nations on the peninsula. Follow local practice in deciding which letter to use.

Arabs commonly are known by two names (*Fuad Butros*), or by three (*Ahmed Zaki Yamani*). Follow the individual's preference on first reference. On second reference, use only the final name in the sequence.

The articles *al-* or *el-* should be used on first reference only when they are the individual's preference (*Ahmed Hassan el-Bakr, Rashid bin Said al-Maktum*). On second reference: *Bakr* and *Maktum*.

The Arabic word for *son* (*ibn* or *bin* depending on personal preference and the nation) is sometimes part of a name (*Rashid bin Humaid*). On second reference, use only the final word in the name: *Humaid*.

The word *abu*, meaning *father of*, occasionally is used as a last name (*Abdul Mohsen Abu Maizer*). Capitalize and repeat it on second reference: *Abu Maizer*.

The titles *king, emir, sheik* and *imam* are used, but *prince* usually replaces *emir*. Some Arabs are known only by the title and a given name on first reference (*King Hussein*). Others are known by a complete name (*Sheik Sabah al-Salem al-Sabah*). Follow the common usage on first reference. On second reference, drop the title, using only the given name if it stood alone (*Hussein*) or the final name in the sequence if more than one was used on first reference (*Sabah*). Make an exception to this procedure for second reference if an individual commonly is known by some other one of the names used on first reference.

Arabic numerals The numerical figures *1, 2, 3, 4, 5, 6, 7, 8, 9, 10*.

In general, use Arabic forms unless denoting the sequence of wars or establishing a personal sequence for people and animals. See **Roman numerals**.

Separate entries list more details and examples. For a full list, see the **numerals** entry.

arbitrate, mediate Both terms are used in reports about labor negotiations, but they should not be interchanged.

One who *arbitrates* hears evidence from all persons concerned, then hands down a decision.

One who *mediates* listens to arguments of both parties and tries by the exercise of reason or persuasion to bring them to an agreement.

arch- No hyphen after this prefix unless it precedes a capitalized word:

archbishop   arch-Republican
archenemy   archrival

archbishop See **Episcopal Church**; **Roman Catholic Church**; and **religious titles**.

archbishop of Canterbury In general, lowercase *archbishop* unless it is used before the name of the individual who holds the office.

Capitalize *Archbishop of Canterbury* standing alone only when it is used in a story that also refers to members of Britain's nobility. See the **nobility** entry for the relevant guidelines.

archdiocese Capitalize as part of a proper name: *the Archdiocese of Chicago, the Chicago Archdiocese*. Lowercase when it stands alone.

See the entry for the particular denomination in question.

archery Scoring is usually in points. Use a basic summary. Example:

(After 3 of 4 Distances)
1, Darrell Pace, Cincinnati, 914 points.
2, Richard McKinney, Muncie, Ind., 880.
3, Etc.

arctic, Arctic Circle, arctic fox, Arctic Ocean

are A unit of surface measure in the metric system, equal to 100 square meters.

An are is equal to approximately 1,076.4 square feet or 119.6 square yards.

See **hectare** and **metric system**.

area codes See **telephone numbers**.

Arizona Abbrev.: *Ariz.* See **state names**.

Arkansas Abbrev.: *Ark.* See **state names**.

Armenian Church of America The term encompasses two independent dioceses that cooperate in some activities: the Eastern Diocese of the Armenian Church of America, for areas outside California, and the Western Diocese of the Armenian Church of America, which serves California.

See **Eastern Orthodox churches**.

Armistice Day It is now *Veterans Day*.

army Capitalize when referring to U.S. forces: *the U.S. Army, the Army, Army regulations*. Do not use the abbreviation *USA*.

Use lowercase for the forces of other nations: *the French army*.

This approach has been adopted for consistency, because many foreign nations do not use *army* as the proper name.

See **military academies** and **military titles**.

arrest To avoid any suggestion that someone is being judged before a trial, do not use a phrase such as *arrested for killing*. Instead, use *arrested on a charge of killing*.

For guidelines on related words, see **accuse; allege**; and **indict**.

arrive It requires the preposition *at*. Do not omit, as airline dispatchers often do in: *He will arrive La Guardia.*

artifact

artillery   See **weapons**.

art works   See **composition titles**.

as   See **like, as**.

ashcan, ashtray

Ash Wednesday The first day of Lent, 46 days before Easter.
See **Easter** and **Lent**.

Asian, Asiatic Use *Asian* or *Asians* when referring to people.
Some Asians regard *Asiatic* as offensive when applied to people.

Asian flu

Asian subcontinent In popular usage the term applies to Bangladesh, Bhutan, India, Nepal, Sikkim and the island nation of Sri Lanka (formerly Ceylon) at the southeastern tip of India.
For definitions of terms that apply to other parts of Asia, see **Far East; Middle East**; and **Southeast Asia**.

as if The preferred form, but *as though* is acceptable.

assassin, killer, murderer An *assassin* is a politically motivated killer.
A *killer* is anyone who kills with a motive of any kind.
A *murderer* is one who is convicted of murder in a court of law.
See **execute** and the **homicide, murder, manslaughter** entry.

assassination, date of A prominent person is shot one day and dies the next. Which day was he assassinated? The day he was attacked.

assault, battery Popularly, *assault* almost always implies physical contact and sudden, intense violence.

Legally, however, *assault* means simply to threaten violence, as in pointing a pistol at an individual without firing it. *Assault and battery* is the legal term when the victim was touched by the assaulter or something the assaulter put in motion.

assembly Capitalize when part of the proper name for the lower house of a legislature: *the California Assembly*. Retain capitalization if the state name is dropped but the reference is specific: *SACRAMENTO, Calif. (AP) — The state Assembly . . .*
If a legislature is known as a general assembly: *the Missouri General Assembly, the General Assembly, the assembly. Legislature* also may be used as the proper name, however. See **legislature.**
Lowercase all plural uses: *the California and New York assemblies.*

assemblyman, assemblywoman Do not abbreviate. See **legislative titles.**

assets Everything a company or individual owns or is owed.
Assets may be categorized further as:
—*Current assets:* cash, investments, money due to a corporation, unused raw materials and inventories of finished but unsold products.
—*Fixed assets:* buildings, equipment and land.
—*Intangible assets:* patents and good will.

assistant Do not abbreviate. Capitalize only when part of a formal title before a name: *Assistant Secretary of State George Ball.* Wherever practical, however, an appositional construction should be used: *George Ball, assistant secretary of state.*
See **titles.**

associate Never abbreviate. Apply the same capitalization norms listed under **assistant.**

Associated Press, The A news-gathering cooperative dating from 1848.

Use *The Associated Press* on first reference (the capitalized article is part of the formal name).

On second reference, *AP* or *the AP* (no capital on *the*) may be used.

The address is 50 Rockefeller Plaza, New York, N.Y. 10020. The telephone number is (212) 262-4000.

association Do not abbreviate. Capitalize as part of a proper name: *American Medical Association.*

astronaut It is not a formal title. Do not capitalize when used before a name: *astronaut John Glenn.*

Astroturf A trademark for a type of artificial grass.

Atchison, Topeka & Santa Fe Railway A subsidiary of Santa Fe Industries.

Headquarters is in Chicago.

atheist See the **agnostic, atheist** entry.

athlete's foot, athlete's heart

athletic club Abbreviate as *AC* with the name of a club, but only in sports summaries: *Illinois AC.* See the **volleyball** entry for an example of such a summary.

athletic teams Capitalize teams, associations and recognized nicknames: *Red Sox, the Big Ten, the A's, the Colts.*

Atlanta The city in Georgia stands alone in datelines.

Atlantic Coast Conference Clemson, Duke, Maryland, North Carolina, North Carolina State, Virginia, Wake Forest.

Atlantic Ocean

Atlantic Richfield Co. *Arco* is acceptable on second reference.

Headquarters is in Los Angeles.

Atlantic Standard Time, Atlantic Daylight Time Used in the Maritime Provinces of Canada and in Puerto Rico. See **time zones**.

at large Usually two words for an individual representing more than a single district: *congressman at large, councilman at large.*

But it is *ambassador-at-large* for an ambassador assigned to no particular country.

Atomic Age It began Dec. 2, 1942, at the University of Chicago with the creation of the first self-sustaining nuclear chain reaction.

Atomic Energy Commission It no longer exists. See **Nuclear Regulatory Commission**.

attache It is not a formal title. Always lowercase.

attorney, lawyer In common usage the words are interchangeable.

Technically, however, an *attorney* is someone (usually, but not necessarily, a lawyer) empowered to act for another. Such an individual occasionally is called an *attorney in fact.*

A *lawyer* is a person admitted to practice in a court system. Such an individual occasionally is called an *attorney at law.*

Do not abbreviate. Do not capitalize unless it is an officeholder's title: *defense attorney Perry Mason, attorney Perry Mason, District Attorney Hamilton Burger.*

See **lawyer**.

attorney general, attorneys general Never abbreviate. Capitalize only when used as a title before a name: *Attorney General Griffin B. Bell.*

See **titles**.

augur A transitive verb. Do not follow it with the preposition *for: The tea leaves augur a time of success.*

August See **months**.

author A noun, used for both men and women. Do not use it as a verb.

automaker, automakers

automatic See **pistol** and **weapons** entries.

automobiles Capitalize brand names: *Buick, Ford, Mustang, MG, Impala*. Lowercase generic terms: *a Volkswagen van, a Mack truck*.

auto racing Follow the form listed below for summaries.
Example:

> HAMPTON, Ga. (AP) — The finish of Sunday's $151,900 Atlanta 500 NASCAR Grand National stock car race with type of car, laps completed and winner's average speed:
> 1. David Pearson, Mercury, 328 laps, 128.094 mph.
> 2. Benny Parsons, Chevrolet, 328.
> 3. Etc.

In international events, insert the name of the driver's country after his name or, for a U.S. driver, his hometown, as in:

> 4. Mario Andretti, Nazareth, Pa., Ford, 328.

For point leaders:

> World Driver Leaders
> (Points on 9-6-4-3-2-1 basis)
> 1, Nicki Lauda, Austria, 47 points. 2, Emerson Fittipaldi, Brazil, 53. 3, Etc.

Auto-Train Corp. A private company that hauls passengers and their cars, leasing rails and equipment owned by other companies.
Headquarters is in Washington.

autoworker, autoworkers One word when used generically.
But *Auto Worker* when referring specifically to the membership and the activities of the United Automobile, Aerospace and Agricultural Implement Workers of America.

autumn See **seasons**.

avenue Abbreviate only with a numbered address. See **addresses**.

average, mean, median, norm
Average refers to the result obtained by dividing a sum by the number of quantities added together: The average of 7, 9, 17 is 33 divided by 3, or 11.
Mean commonly designates a figure intermediate between two extremes: The mean temperature of the day with a high of 56 and a low of 34 is 45.
Median is the middle number of points in a series arranged in order of size: The median grade in the group of 50, 55, 85, 88, 92 is 85. The average is 74.
Norm implies a standard of average performance for a given group *The child was below the norm for his age in reading comprehension.*

average of The phrase takes a plural verb in a construction such as: *An average of 100 new jobs are created daily.*

averse See **adverse, averse**.

Avianca The headquarters of this airline is in Bogota, Colombia.

aviator Use for both men and women.

awards and decorations Capitalize them: *Bronze Star, Medal of Honor*, etc.
See **Nobel Prize** and **Pulitzer Prize**.

awe-struck

awhile, a while *He plans to stay awhile.*
He plans to stay for a while.

AWOL Acceptable on second reference for *absent without leave*.

ax Not *axe*.
The verb forms: *ax, axed, axing*.

Axis The alliance of Germany, Italy and Japan during World War II.

B

baby-sit, baby-sitting, baby sitter

baccalaureate

bachelor of arts, bachelor of science *A bachelor's degree* or *bachelor's* is acceptable in any reference.

See **academic degrees** for guidelines on when the abbreviations *B.A.* or *B.S.* are acceptable.

backboard, backcourt, backfield, backhand, backspin, backstop, backstretch, backstroke Some are exceptions to Webster's New World, made for consistency in handling sports stories.

back up (v.) **backup** (n. and adj.)

backward Not *backwards*.

back yard (n.) **backyard** (adj.)

bad, badly *Bad* should not be used as an adverb. It does not lose its status as an adjective, however, in a sentence such as *I feel bad*. Such a statement is the idiomatic equivalent of *I am in bad health*. An alternative, *I feel badly*, could be interpreted as meaning that your sense of touch was bad.

See the **good, well** entry.

badminton Games are won by the first player to score 21 points, unless it is necessary to continue until one player has a two-point spread. Most matches go to the first winner of two games.

Use a match summary. See **racquetball** for an example.

Bahamas In datelines, give the name of the city or town followed by *Bahamas*:

NASSAU, *Bahamas (AP)* —

In stories, use *Bahamas, the Bahamas* or *the Bahama Islands* as the construction of a sentence dictates.

Identify a specific island in the text if relevant.

bail *Bail* is money or property that will be forfeited to the court if an accused individual fails to appear for trial. It may be posted as follows:

—The accused may deposit with the court the full amount or its equivalent in collateral such as a deed to property.

—A friend or relative may make such a deposit with the court.

—The accused may pay a professional bail bondsman a percentage of the total figure. The bondsman, in turn, guarantees the court that it will receive from him the full amount in the event the individual fails to appear for trial.

It is correct in all cases to say that an accused *posted bail* or *posted a bail bond* (the money held by the court is a form of *bond*). When a distinction is desired, say that the individual *posted his own bail*, that *bail was posted by a friend or relative*, or that *bail was obtained through a bondsman*.

Bakelite A trademark for a type of plastic resin.

baker's dozen It means 13.

Bakery and Confectionery Workers' International Union of America The shortened form *Bakery Workers union* is acceptable in all references. Headquarters is in Washington.

balance of payments, balance of trade The *balance of payments* is the difference between the amount of money that leaves a nation and the amount that enters it during a period of time.

The balance of payments is determined by computing the amount of money a nation and its citizens send abroad for all purposes — including goods and services purchased, travel, loans, foreign aid, etc. — and subtracting from it the amount that foreign nations send into the nation for similar purposes.

The *balance of trade* is the difference between the monetary value of the goods a nation imports and the goods it exports.

An example illustrating the difference between the two:

The United States and its citizens might send $10 billion abroad — $5 billion for goods, $3 billion for loans and foreign aid, $1 billion for services and $1 billion for tourism and other purposes.

Other nations might send $9 billion into the United States — $6 billion for U.S. goods, $2 billion for services and $1 billion for tourism and other purposes.

The United States would have a *balance-of-payments deficit* of $1 billion but a *balance-of-trade surplus* of $1 billion.

ball carrier

ballclub, ballpark, ballplayer, ballroom

ball point pen

baloney Foolish or exaggerated talk.

The sausage or luncheon meat is *bologna.*

Baltimore The city in Maryland stands alone in datelines.

Band-Aid A trademark for a type of adhesive bandage.

Bank of America Acceptable in all references for *Bank of America National Trust & Savings Association.*

The parent company is BankAmerica Corp. of San Francisco.

bankruptcy The legal sense of the word applies only if a court has told an individual or organization to liquidate assets and distribute the proceeds to creditors.

The action may be involuntary, as the result of a suit by creditors, or it may be a voluntary effort to deal with bills that cannot be paid.

Often a company with financial problems announces that it is seeking to reorganize under federal bankruptcy laws. In such a case, it is incorrect to describe the company as *bankrupt.*

A story that announces such a filing should specify the chapter of the Federal Bankruptcy Act under which the reorganization is sought and describe the basic provisions.

Under Chapter 11, the most frequently used, a company obtains a federal court order that frees it from the threat of creditors' lawsuits until it can develop a plan to put its finances in order. While the reorganization proceeds, the activities of management must be approved by the court. The ultimate reorganization plan must be accepted by a majority of the creditors. It may involve various options, including a full or partial payment of debts.

Chapter 10, which is used occasionally, takes away management from the existing officers and turns it over to an independent trustee. Under a Chapter 10 reorganization, stockholders could lose their entire investment. By contrast, under a Chapter 11 reorganization, it is possible for stockholders to retain something even if creditors are not paid in full.

Some other chapters apply to specific types of companies or situations.

If a reorganization plan fails, a company may be forced into bankruptcy.

baptism See **sacraments.**

baptist, Baptist A person who baptizes is a *baptist* (lowercase). A *Baptist* (uppercase) is a person who is a member of the Protestant denomination described in the next entry.

Baptist churches It is incorrect to apply the term *church* to any Baptist unit except the local church.

The ultimate governing power rests with members of the local congregation. Majority rule prevails.

This emphasis on the authority of the individual churches helps account for the existence of more than 20 Baptist bodies in the United States.

The largest, the Southern Baptist Convention, has more than 12 million members, most of them in the South, although it has churches in 50 states.

The largest Northern body is American Baptist Churches in the U.S.A., with about 1.5 million members.

Blacks predominate in three other large Baptist bodies, the National Baptist Convention of America, the National Baptist Convention U.S.A. Inc., and the Progressive National Baptist Convention Inc.

The roster of Baptist bodies in the United States also includes the Baptist General Conference, the Conservative Baptist Association of America, the General Association of Regular Baptist Churches, the General Association of General Baptists, and the North American Baptist General Conference.

The Baptist World Alliance, a voluntary association of Baptist bodies throughout the world, fosters communication among its members, provides a forum for discussion of doctrine and practice, and organizes the Baptist World Congress meetings generally held every five years. Headquarters is in Washington.

BELIEFS: Baptists are free to interpret Scripture as their consciences dictate.

In general, however, Baptists believe that no one can be validly baptized without first giving a personal confession of faith in Christ as his savior. They also believe that the baptism should be by immersion.

In addition to belief in original sin and the need of redemption, Baptists generally believe in the Trinity, the humanity and divinity of Christ, salvation through Christ, and everlasting heaven and hell.

CLERGY: All members of the Baptist clergy may be referred to as *ministers. Pastor* applies if a minister leads a congregation.

On first reference, use *the Rev.* before the name of a man or woman. On second reference, use only the last name of a man; use *Miss, Mrs.* or *Ms.* before the last name of a woman depending on her preference.

See **religious titles.**

See **religious movements** for definitions of some descriptive terms that often apply to Baptists but are not limited to them.

barbiturate

barmaid

bar mitzvah The Jewish religious ritual and family celebration that marks a boy's 13th birthday. Judaism regards the age of 13 as the benchmark of religious maturity. *Bar mitzvah* translates as "one who is responsible for the Commandments."

Conservative congregations have instituted the *bas mitzvah* or *bat mitzvah,* a similar ceremony for girls.

baron, baroness See **nobility**

barrel A standard barrel in U.S. measure contains 31.5 gallons.

A standard barrel in British and Canadian measure contains 36 Imperial gallons.

In international dealings with crude oil, a standard barrel contains 42 U.S. gallons or 35 Imperial gallons.

See the **oil** entry for guidelines on computing the volume and weight of petroleum products.

barrel, barreled, barreling

barrel-chested, barrelhouse Also: *double-barreled shotgun.*

barrister See **lawyer**.

barroom

baseball The spellings for some frequently used words and phrases:

backstop	passed ball
ballclub	put out (v.)
ballpark	putout (n.)
ballplayer	pinch hit (v.)
base line	pinch-hit (n., adj.)
bullpen	pinch hitter (n.)
center field	pitchout
center fielder	play off (v.)
designated hitter	playoff (n., adj.)
double-header	RBI (s., pl.)
double play	rundown (n.)
fair ball	sacrifice
fastball	sacrifice fly
first baseman	sacrifice hit
foul ball	shoestring catch
foul line	shortstop
foul tip	shut out (v.)
ground-rule double	shutout (n., adj.)
home plate	slugger
home run	squeeze play
left-hander	strike
line drive	strike zone
line up (v.)	Texas leaguer
lineup (n.)	triple play
major league(s) (n.)	twi-night double-
major-league (adj.)	header
major-leaguer (n.)	wild pitch
outfielder	

NUMBERS: Some sample uses of numbers: *first inning, seventh-inning stretch, 10th inning; first base, second base, third base; first home run, 10th home run; first place, last place; one RBI,*

10 RBI. The pitcher's record is now 6-5. The final score was 1-0.

LEAGUES: Use *American League, National League, American League West, National League East,* etc. On second reference: *the league, the pennant in the West, the league's West Division,* etc.

BOX SCORES: A sample follows.

The visiting team always is listed on the left, the home team on the right.

Only one position, the last he played in the game, is listed for any player.

Figures in parentheses are the player's total in that category for the season.

Use the *First Game* line shown here only if the game was the first in a double-header.

One line in this example — *None out when winning run scored.* — could not have occurred in this game as played. It is included to show its placement when needed.

First Game

CINCINNATI	ab r h bi	SAN DIEGO	ab r h bi
Rose 3b	5 0 1 0	Almon ss	4 0 1 0
Griffey rf	5 2 2 0	Grubb cf	2 0 2 0
Morgan 2b	2 1 1 0	Melendez rf	0 1 0 0
TPerez 1b	5 0 1 2	Rttmund lf	2 1 1 0
Driessen lf	3 0 0 1	Valentine lf	2 1 0 0
Armbrstr lf	0 0 0 0	MChmpn 2b	0 1 0 0
Geronimo cf	4 0 0 0	Ivie 1b	3 1 2 2
Plummer c	3 0 1 0	Fuentes 2b	2 0 1 0
Flynn ss	3 0 0 0	Turner ph	1 0 0 0
Gullett p	3 0 1 0	WDavis cf	0 0 0 0
Alcala p	0 0 0 0	DoRader 3b	3 0 1 2
Lum ph	0 0 0 0	Kendall c	4 0 0 1
		TGriffin p	3 0 0 0
		Metzger p	0 0 0 0
Totals	33 3 7 3	Totals	26 5 8 5

Cincinnati　　　　002 010 000— 3
San Diego　　　　000 200 03x— 5
None out when winning run scored.

E—Fuentes. DP—Cincinnati 2. LOB—Cincinnati 10, San Diego 6. 2B—Fuentes, T. Perez, Rettenmund. 3B—DoRader. HR—Ivie (3). SB—Griffey, Morgan, Geronimo. S—Grubb, Fuentes, Rettenmund. SF—Driessen.

	IP	H	R	ER	BB	SO
Gullett	7	5	2	2	4	2
Alcala (L,11-4)	1	3	3	3	1	1
T.Griffin (W,8-6)	8	7	3	3	6	4
Metzger	1	0	0	0	0	0

Save—Metzger (4). HBP—by Gullett (Grubb). WP—Gullett. Balk—Alcala. PB—Kendall. T—2:19. A—8,230.

LINESCORE: When a bare linescore summary is required, use this form:

```
Los Angeles        100 020 000—3  8 3
San Francisco      002 311 00x—7 10 3
  Sutton, Downing (6) and Yeager; Ha-
licki and Rader. W—Halicki, 9-11. L—Sut-
ton, 16-12. HRs—Los Angeles, Cey (3).
San Francisco, Joshua 2 (6), Montanez
(10).
```

LEAGUE STANDINGS: The form:

```
            NATIONAL LEAGUE
                East
                 W    L   Pct.  GB
Pittsburgh      92   69   .571   —
Philadelphia    85   75   .531  6½
Etc.
                West
                 W    L   Pct.  GB
Cincinnati     108   54   .667   —
Los Angeles     88   74   .543  20
Etc.
        (Night games not included)
            Monday's Results
Chicago 7, St. Louis 5
Atlanta at New York, rain.
            Tuesday's Games
            (All Times EDT)
Cincinnati (Gullett 14-2 and Nolan 4-4)
at New York (Seaver 12-3 and Matlack 6-
1) 2, 6 p.m.
            Wednesday's Games
Cincinnati at New York
Chicago at St. Louis, night
Only games scheduled.
```

In subheads for results and future games, spell out day of the week as: *Tuesday's Games,* instead of *Today's Games.*

basic summary

This format for summarizing sports events lists winners in the order of their finish. The figure showing the place finish is followed by an athlete's full name, his affiliation or hometown, and his time, distance, points, or whatever performance factor is applicable to the sport.

If a contest involves several types of events, the paragraph begins with the name of the event.

A typical example:

```
    60-yard dash—1, Steve Williams, Flori-
da TC, 6.0. 2, Hasley Crawford, Phila-
delphia Pioneer, 6.1. 3, Mike McFarland,
Chicago TC, 6.2. 4, Etc.
    100—1, Steve Williams, Florida TC, 10.1.
2, Etc.
```

Additional examples are provided in the entries for many of the sports that are reported in this format.

Most basic summaries are a single paragraph per event, as shown. In some competitions with large fields, however, the basic summary is supplied under a dateline with each winner listed in a single paragraph. See the **auto racing** and **bowling** entries for examples.

For international events in which U.S. or Canadian competitors are not among the leaders, add them in a separate paragraph as follows:

```
    Also: 14, Dick Green, New York, 6.8.
17, George Bensen, Canada, 6.9. 19, Etc.
```

In events where points, rather than time or distance, are recorded as performances, mention the word *points* on the first usage only:

```
    1, Jim Benson, Springfield, N.J., 150
points. 2, Jerry Green, Canada, 149. 3,
Etc.
```

basketball

The spellings of some frequently used words and phrases:

backboard	half-court pass
backcourt	halftime
backcourtman	hook shot
baseline	jump ball
field goal	jump shot
foul line	layup
foul shot	man-to-man
free throw	midcourt
free-throw line	pivotman
frontcourt	play off (v.)
full-court press	playoff (n., adj.)
goaltending	zone

NUMBERS: Some sample uses of numbers: *in the first quarter, a second-quarter lead, nine field goals, 10 field goals, the 6-foot-5 forward, the 6-10 center. He is 6 feet 10 inches tall.*

LEAGUE: In general, spell out *National Basketball Association* on first reference. A phrase such as *NBA playoffs* may be used on first reference, however, to avoid a cumbersome lead.

For subdivisions: *the Atlantic Division of the Eastern Conference, the Pacific Division of the Western Con-*

ference, etc. On second reference: *the NBA East, the division, the conference,* etc.

BOX SCORE: A sample follows.

The visiting team always is listed first.

In listing the players, begin with the five starters — two forwards, center, two guards — and follow with all substitutes who played.

Figures after each player's last name denote field goals, free throws, free throws attempted and total points.

Example:

```
ATLANTA (85)
  Brown 2 2-3 6, Hawkins 1 1-2 3, Jones 3
2-2 8, Henderson 6 0-0 12, Hudson 7 0-0 14,
Etc. Totals 36-13-19 85.
LOS ANGELES (107)
  Calhoun 4 1-1 9, Warner 4 3-3 11, Abdul-
Jabbar 10 3-4 23, Allen 5 2-3 12, Goodrich
6 2-2 14, Etc. Totals 45-17-24 107.
Atlanta          21 27 17 20— 85
Los Angeles      29 22 30 26—107
  Fouled out—Goodrich, Henderson. Total
fouls—Atlanta 24, Los Angeles 24. Techni-
cal—Brown, Los Angeles bench. A—
10,969.
```

In **college boxes,** the score by periods is omitted because games are divided only into halves. The bottom of the box looks like this:

```
  Halftime—UCLA   45,  Minnesota   36.
Fouled out—Jones, Smith. Total fouls—
UCLA 22, Minnesota 19. Technical—
Smith, UCLA Coach Bartow, Minnesota
bench 2, UCLA fans. A—19,450.
```

STANDINGS: The format for **professional standings:**

	W	L	Pct.	GB
Eastern Conference				
Atlantic Division				
Boston	43	22	.662	—
Philadelphia	40	30	.571	5½
Etc.				

The format for **college conference standings:**

	Conference			All Games		
	W	L	Pct.	W	L	Pct.
Missouri	12	2	.857	24	4	.857
Etc.						

battalion Capitalize when used with a figure to form a name: *the 3rd Battalion, the 10th Battalion.*

battlefield Also: *battlefront, battleground, battleship.* But *battle station*

Bavarian cream

bay Capitalize as an integral part of a proper name: *Hudson Bay, San Francisco Bay.*

Capitalize also *San Francisco Bay area* or *the Bay area* as the popular name for the nine-county region that has San Francisco as its focal point.

bazaar A fair. *Bizarre* means unusual.

B.C. Acceptable in all references to a calendar year in the period *before Christ.*

Because the full phrase would be in *the year 43 before Christ,* the abbreviation *B.C.* is placed after the figure for the year: *43 B.C.*

See **A.D.**

because, since Use *because* to denote a specific cause-effect relationship: *He went because he was told.*

Since is acceptable in a causal sense when the first event in a sequence led logically to the second but was not its direct cause: *He went to the game, since he had been given the tickets.*

before Christ See **B.C.**

Belize The former British Honduras.

Bell System See **American Telephone & Telegraph Co.**

bellwether

benefit, benefited, benefiting

Benelux Belgium, the Netherlands and Luxembourg.

If *Benelux* is used, explain that it is an inclusive word for these three nations.

Ben-Gurion International Airport
Located at Lod, Israel, about 10 miles
south of Tel Aviv.
See **airport.**

Benzedrine A trademark for a type
of pep pill or stimulant.

**Bering Standard Time, Bering
Daylight Time** Used in the far western
section of Alaska, including Nome.
See **time zones.**

Berlin Stands alone in datelines.
When a distinction must be made between sections of the city, do so in the
body of the story, using such phrases as
*the Communist sector, the eastern sec-
tor* or *the western sector.*
Use *East Berlin* or *West Berlin* only in
direct quotations.

Berlin Wall On second reference, *the
wall.*

**Bermuda collar, Bermuda grass,
Bermuda shorts**

beside, besides *Beside* means at
the side of.
Besides means in addition to.

besiege

best seller (n.)

betting odds Use figures and a
hyphen: *The odds were 5-4, he won
despite 3-2 odds against him.*
The word *to* seldom is necessary, but
when it appears it should be hyphenated
in all constructions: *3-to-2 odds, odds of
3-to-2, the odds were 3-to-2.*

bettor A person who bets.

between See the **among, between**
entry.

bi- The rules in **prefixes** apply, but in
general, no hyphen. Some examples:

bifocal   bimonthly
bilateral   bipartisan
bilingual

biannual, biennial *Biannual* means
twice a year and is a synonym for the
word *semiannual.*
Biennial means every two years.

Bible Capitalize, without quotation
marks, when referring to the Scriptures
of the Old Testament or the New Testament. Capitalize also related terms such
as *the Gospels, Gospel of St. Mark, the
Scriptures, the Holy Scriptures.*
Lowercase *biblical* in all uses.
Lowercase *bible* as a non-religious
term: *My dictionary is my bible.*
Do not abbreviate individual books of
the Bible.
The books of the Old Testament, in
order, are: Genesis, Exodus, Leviticus,
Numbers, Deuteronomy, Joshua,
Judges, Ruth, 1 Samuel, 2 Samuel,
1 Kings, 2 Kings, 1 Chronicles,
2 Chronicles, Ezra, Nehemiah, Esther,
Job, Psalms, Proverbs, Ecclesiastes,
Song of Solomon, Isaiah, Jeremiah,
Lamentations, Ezekiel, Daniel, Hosea,
Joel, Amos, Obadiah, Jonah, Micah,
Nahum, Habakkuk, Zephaniah, Haggai,
Zechariah, Malachi.
The books of the New Testament, in
order: Matthew, Mark, Luke, John,
Acts, Romans, 1 Corinthians, 2 Corin-
thians, Galatians, Ephesians, Philip-
pians, Colossians, 1 Thessalonians,
2 Thessalonians, 1 Timothy, 2 Timothy,
Titus, Philemon, Hebrews, Epistles of
James, 1 Peter, 2 Peter, 1 John, 2 John,
3 John, Jude, Revelation.
Citations listing the number of chap-
ter and verse(s) use this form: *Matthew
3:16, Luke 21:1-13, 1 Peter 2:1.*

Bible Belt Those sections of the
United States, especially in the South
and Middle West, where fundamentalist
religious beliefs prevail. Use with care,
because in certain contexts it can give
offense.
See **religious movements.**

bicycle

big-bang theory The theory that the universe began with the explosion of a superdense primeval atom and has been expanding ever since.

The **oscillating theory**, another hypothesis, maintains that expansion eventually will stop, followed by contraction to a superdense atom, followed by another big bang.

The **steady-state theory**, an alternate hypothesis, maintains that the universe always has existed and that matter constantly is being created to replace matter that constantly is being destroyed.

Big Board Acceptable on second reference for the *New York Stock Exchange.*

big brother One's older brother is a *big brother. Big Brother* (capitalized) means under the watchful eye of big government, from George Orwell's "1984."

Capitalize *Big Brother* also in references to members of **Big Brothers Inc.**, an organization that encourages adult men to spend time with boys who need guidance. Headquarters is in New York.

Big Eight Conference Colorado, Iowa State, Kansas, Kansas State, Missouri, Nebraska, Oklahoma, Oklahoma State.

Big Ten Conference Illinois, Indiana, Iowa, Michigan, Michigan State, Minnesota, Northwestern, Ohio State, Purdue, Wisconsin.

Big Three automakers General Motors, Ford, Chrysler.
Big Four: The Big Three plus American Motors.

bigwig

billiards Scoring is in points.
Use a match summary. Example:

Minnesota Fats, St. Paul, Minn., def. Pool Hall Duke, 150-141.

billion A thousand million.
For forms, see the **millions, billions** entry.

Bill of Rights The first 10 amendments to the Constitution.

bimonthly Means every other month. *Semimonthly* means twice a month.

birthday Capitalize as part of the name for a holiday: *Washington's Birthday.* Lowercase in other uses.

bishop See **religious titles** and the entry for the denomination in question.

biweekly Means every other week. *Semiweekly* means twice a week.

bizarre Unusual. A fair is a *bazaar.*

black Acceptable in all references for *Negro.*
Do not use *colored* as a synonym. See the **colored** entry.

Black Muslims See **Moslem.**

blackout, brownout A *blackout* is a total power failure over a large area or the concealing of lights that might be visible to enemy raiders.

The term *rotating blackout* is used by electric companies to describe a situation in which electric power to some sections temporarily is cut off on a rotating basis to assure that voltage will meet minimum standards in other sections.

A *brownout* is a small, temporary voltage reduction, usually from 2 to 8 percent, implemented to conserve electric power.

blast off (v.) **blastoff** (n. and adj.)

Blessed Sacrament, Blessed Virgin

blizzard See **weather terms.**

bloc, block A *bloc* is a coalition of persons, groups or nations with the same purpose or goal.

Block has more than a dozen definitions, but a political alliance is not one of them.

blond, blonde Use *blond* as a noun for males and as the adjective for all applications: *She has blond hair.*
Use *blonde* as a noun for females.

bloodhound

Bloody Mary A drink made of vodka and tomato juice. The name is derived from the nickname for Mary I of England.

blue blood (n.) **blue-blooded** (adj.)

blue chip stock Stock in a company known for its long-established record of making money and paying dividends.

B'nai B'rith See the **fraternal organizations and service clubs** entry.

board Capitalize only when an integral part of a proper name. See **capitalization.**

board of aldermen See **city council.**

board of directors, board of trustees Always lowercase. See the **organizations and institutions** entry.

board of supervisors See **city council.**

boats, ships A *boat* is a watercraft of any size. A *ship* is a large, seagoing vessel, big enough to carry smaller boats.
The word *boat* is used, however, in some words that apply to large craft: *ferryboat, PT boat, gunboat.*
Use Arabic or Roman numerals in the names of boats and ships: *the Queen Elizabeth 2* or *QE2; Titan I, Titan II.*
The reference for military ships is Jane's Fighting Ships; for non-military ships, Lloyd's Register of Shipping.

bobsledding, luge Scoring is in minutes, seconds and tenths of a second. Extend to hundredths if available.
Identify events as *two-man, four-man, men's luge, women's luge.*
Use a basic summary. Example:

Two-man—1, Jim Smith and Dick Jones, Alaska Sledders, 4:28.77. 2, Tom Winner and Joe Finisher, Mountaineers, 4:31.15. 3, Etc.

Boeing Co. Formerly Boeing Aircraft Co.
Headquarters is in Seattle.

boldface Use boldface type for the slug lines, bylines and underlines for bylines atop a story, and for separate subhead lines if needed within a story.
Do not use boldface for individual words within a paragraph.

bologna The sausage. *Baloney* is foolish or exaggerated talk.

bona fide

bonbon

bond ratings The two most popular are prepared by Moody's Investors Service Inc. and Standard & Poor's Corp.
Moody's uses nine ratings. The range, from the designation for top-quality issues to the one for those judged the greatest risk, is: Aaa, Aa, A, Baa, Ba, B, Caa, Ca and C.
Standard & Poor's uses seven basic grades. The range, from top to bottom, is: AAA, AA, A, BBB, BB, B and D. Occasionally it adds a plus or minus sign on grades AA through BB.

bonds See **loan terminology.**

boo-boo

book titles See **composition titles.**

book value The difference between a company's assets and liabilities.
The *book value per share of common stock* is the figure obtained by dividing the total number of common shares out-

standing into the book value of the company as a whole.

The book value of a stock may have little or no significant relationship to the selling price.

borscht Exception to Webster's New World.

Bosporus, the Not *the Bosporus Strait.*

Boston The city in Massachusetts stands alone in datelines.

Boston brown bread, Boston cream pie, Boston terrier

boulevard Abbreviate only with a numbered address. See **addresses.**

boundary

bowlegged

bowl games Capitalize them: *Cotton Bowl, Orange Bowl, Rose Bowl,* etc.

bowling Scoring systems use both total points and won-lost records.

Use the basic summary format in paragraph form. Note that a comma is used in giving pinfalls of more than 999. Examples:

> ST. LOUIS (AP)   Second-round leaders and their total pinfalls in the $100,000 Professional Bowlers Association tournament:
> 1. Bill Spigner, Hamden, Conn., 2,820.
> 2. Gary Dickinson, Fort Worth, Texas, 2,759.
> 3. Etc.

> ALAMEDA, Calif. (AP)   The 24 match play finalists with their won-lost records and total pinfall Thursday night after four rounds   26 games   of the $65,000 Alameda Open bowling tournament:
> 1. Jay Robinson, Los Angeles, 5-3, 5,937.
> 2. Butch Soper, Huntington, Beach, Calif., 3-5, 5,932.
> 3. Etc.

boxing Some frequently used terms and their definitions:

The weight classes:

flyweight A boxer weighing no more than 112 pounds.

bantamweight 113 to 118 pounds.
featherweight 119 to 126 pounds.
lightweight 127 to 135 pounds.
welterweight 136 to 147 pounds.
middleweight 148 to 160 pounds.
light heavyweight 161 to 175 pounds.
heavyweight 176 or more pounds.

Some other terms:

kidney punch A punch to an opponent's kidney when the puncher has only one hand free. An illegal punch. If the puncher has both hands free, a punch to the opponent's kidney is legal.

knock out (v.) **knockout** (n. and adj.) A fighter is *knocked out* if he takes a 10-count.

If a match ends early because one fighter is unable to continue, say that the winner *stopped* the loser. In most boxing jurisdictions there is no such thing as a *technical knockout.*

outpointed Not *outdecisioned.*

rabbit punch A punch behind an opponent's neck. It is illegal.

SUMMARIES: Use a match summary. Some examples, with the fighters' weights after their names and the number of rounds at the end.

> Randy Jackson, 152, New York, outpointed Chuck James, 154, Philadelphia, 10.
> Muhammad Ali, 220, Chicago, knocked out Pierre Coopman, 202, Belgium, 5.
> George Foreman, 217½, Hayward, Calif., stopped Joe Frazier, 214, Philadelphia, 2.

TALE OF THE TAPE: An example:

> SAN JUAN, Puerto Rico (AP) — The tale of the tape for the Jean Pierre Coopman-Muhammad Ali world heavyweight championship fight Friday night:

	Coopman	Ali
Age	29	34
Weight	202	220
Height	6-0	6-3
Reach	75	80
Chest normal	43	44
Chest expanded	45½	46
Biceps	15	15
Forearm	13	13½
Waist	34½	34
Thigh	25½	26
Calf	15	17
Neck	17	17½
Wrist	7½	8
Fist	12½	13
Ankle	9	9½

SCORING BY ROUNDS: An example:

```
NEW YORK (AP) — Scorecards for the
Muhammad Ali-Joe Frazier heavyweight
title fight Friday night:
   Scoring by rounds:
         Referee Tom Smith
AAA FFF AAA AFA FFF—A8-7
         Judge Bill Swift
AAA FFF FFF AFA FFF—F10-5
         Judge Ralph Cohen
AAA FFF FFF FFF AFF—F11-4
   Scoring by points system:
         Referee Tom Smith
A  10 10 10 10 10 10 10 10 10 10 10  9  9  9  9 10
F  10  9  9  9  9  9  9 10 10  9 10 10 10 10 10
   Total—Ali 146, Frazier 143.
         Judge Bill Swift
A  10 10 10  9  9  9  9 10  9  9  9 10  9 10   9
F   9  9  9 10 10 10 10 10 10 10  9 10  9 10
   Total—Frazier 145, Ali 141.
         Judge Ralph Cohen
A  10  9 10 10 10 10 10 10 10 10 10  9  9  9   9
F   9 10 10  9  9  9  9  9 10 10  9 10 10 10 10
   Total—Ali 145, Frazier 143.
```

box office (n.) **box-office** (adj.)

boy Applicable until 18th birthday is reached. Use *man* or *young man* afterward.

boycott, embargo A *boycott* is an organized refusal to buy a particular product or service, or to deal with a particular merchant or group of merchants.

An *embargo* is a legal restriction against trade. It usually prohibits goods from entering or leaving a country.

boyfriend, girlfriend

Boy Scouts The full name of the national organization is *Boy Scouts of America*. It also uses the name *Scouting-USA*. Headquarters is in New Brunswick, N.J.

Cub Scouting is for boys 8 through 10. Members are *Cub Scouts* or *Cubs*.

Boy Scouting is for boys 11 through 17. Members are *Boy Scouts* or *Scouts*.

Exploring is a separate program open to boys and girls from high school age through 20. Members are *Explorers,* not *Explorer Scouts*. Members of units that stress nautical programs are *Sea Explorers*.

See **Girl Scouts** for programs that a separate organization runs for girls.

bra Acceptable in all references for *brassiere*.

brackets They cannot be transmitted over news wires. Use parentheses or recast the material.

See **parentheses**.

Brahman, Brahmin *Brahman* applies to the priestly Hindu caste and a breed of cattle.

Brahmin applies to aristocracy in general: *Boston Brahmin*.

brand names When they are used, capitalize them.

Brand names normally should be used only if they are essential to a story.

Sometimes, however, the use of a brand name may not be essential but is acceptable because it lends an air of reality to a story: *He fished a Camel from his shirt pocket* may be preferable to the less specific *cigarette*.

When a company sponsors an event such as a golf tournament to obtain publicity, use a generic term for the event in first and subsequent references. Provide the name of the sponsor in a separate paragraph that can be deleted if a newspaper wishes.

Brand name is a non-legal term for *service mark* or *trademark*. See entries under those words.

brand-new (adj.)

Braniff Airways Headquarters is in Dallas.

break in (v.) **break-in** (n. and adj.)

break up (v.) **breakup** (n. and adj.)

breeds See **animals**.

Bricklayers, Masons and Plasterers' International Union of America The shortened form *Bricklayers union* is acceptable in all references.

Headquarters is in Washington.

bride, bridegroom, bridesmaid
Bride is appropriate in wedding stories, but use *wife* or *spouse* in other circumstances.

brigadier See **military titles.**

Bright's disease After Dr. Richard Bright, the London physician who first diagnosed this form of kidney disease.

Brill's disease After Nathan E. Brill, a U.S. physician. A form of epidemic typhus fever in which the disease recurs years after the original infection.

Britain Acceptable in all references for *Great Britain,* which consists of England, Scotland and Wales.
See **United Kingdom.**

British, Briton(s) The people of Great Britain: *the English, the Scottish, the Welsh.*

British Airways The successor to British European Airways and British Overseas Airways Corp.
Headquarters is in Hounslow, England.

British Broadcasting Corp. *BBC* is acceptable in all references within contexts such as a television column. Otherwise, do not use *BBC* until second reference.

British Columbia The Canadian province bounded on the west by the Pacific Ocean. Do not abbreviate.
See **datelines.**

British Commonwealth See **Commonwealth, the.**

British Petroleum Co. Ltd. *BP* is acceptable on second reference.
Headquarters is in London.

British thermal unit The amount of heat required to increase the temperature of a pound of water one degree Fahrenheit. *Btu* (the same for singular and plural) is acceptable on second reference.

British ton See **ton.**

British Virgin Islands Use with a community name in datelines on stories from these islands. Do not abbreviate.
Specify an individual island in the text if relevant.
See **datelines.**

broadcast The past tense also is *broadcast,* not *broadcasted.*

Broadway, off-Broadway, off-off-Broadway When applied to stage productions, these terms refer to distinctions made by union contracts, not to the location of a theater.
Actors Equity Association and unions representing craft workers have one set of pay scales for *Broadway* productions (generally those in New York City theaters of 300 or more seats) and a lower scale for smaller theaters, classified as *off-Broadway* houses.
The term *off-off-Broadway* refers to workshop productions that may use Equity members for a limited time at substandard pay. Other unions maintain a hands-off policy, agreeing with the Equity attitude that actors should have an opportunity to whet their talents in offbeat roles without losing their Equity memberships.

broccoli

Bromo Seltzer A trademark for a brand of bicarbonate of soda.

Bronze Age The age characterized by the development of bronze tools and weapons, from 3500 to 1000 B.C. Regarded as coming between the Stone Age and the Iron Age.

brother See **Roman Catholic Church.**

Brotherhood of Railway, Airline and Steamship Clerks, Freight Handlers, Express and Station Employees The shortened form *Railway Employees union* is acceptable in all references.
Headquarters is in Rosemont, Ill.

brothers Abbreviate as *Bros.* in formal company names: *Warner Bros.*

For possessives: *Warner Bros.'* profits.

brownout See the **blackout, brownout** entry.

brunet, brunette Use *brunet* as a noun for males, and as the adjective for both sexes.

Use *brunette* as a noun for females.

brussels sprouts

Btu The same in singular and plural. See **British thermal unit.**

Budapest The capital of Hungary. In datelines, follow it with *Hungary.*

Buddha, Buddhism

Bufferin A trademark for buffered aspirin.

bug, tap A concealed listening device designed to pick up sounds in a room, an automobile, etc. is a *bug.*

A *tap* is a device attached to a telephone circuit to pick up conversations on the line.

building Never abbreviate. Capitalize the proper names of buildings, including the word *building* if it is an integral part of the proper name: *the Empire State Building.*

build up (v.) **buildup** (n. and adj.)

bullet See **weapons.**

bullfight, bullfighter, bullfighting

bullpen One word, for the place where baseball pitchers warm up, and for a pen that holds cattle.

bull's-eye

bureau Capitalize when part of the formal name for an organization or agency: *the Bureau of Labor Statistics, the Newspaper Advertising Bureau.*

Lowercase when used alone or to designate a corporate subdivision: *the Washington bureau of The Associated Press.*

burglary, larceny, robbery, theft Legal definitions of *burglary* vary, but in general a *burglary* involves entering a building (not necessarily by breaking in) and remaining unlawfully with the intention of committing a crime.

Larceny is the legal term for the wrongful taking of property. Its non-legal equivalents are *stealing* or *theft.*

Robbery in the legal sense involves the use of violence or threat in committing larceny. In a wider sense it means to plunder or rifle, and may thus be used even if a person was not present: *His house was robbed while he was away.*

Theft describes a larceny that did not involve threat, violence or plundering.

USAGE NOTE: You *rob* a person, bank, house, etc., but you *steal* the money or the jewels.

bus, buses Transportation vehicles. The verb forms: *bus, bused, busing.* See **buss.**

bushel A unit of dry measure equal to four pecks or 32 dry quarts. The metric equivalent is approximately 35.2 liters.

To convert to liters, multiply by 35.2 (5 bushels x 35.2 = 176 liters). See **liter.**

business editor Capitalize when used as a formal title before a name. See **titles.**

business names See **company names.**

buss, busses Kisses. The verb forms: *buss, bussed, bussing.* See **bus.**

by- The rules in **prefixes** apply, but in general, no hyphen. Some examples:

byline byproduct
bypass bystreet

By-election is an exception. See the next entry.

by-election A special election held between regularly scheduled elections. The term most often is associated with special elections to the British House of Commons.

Byelorussian Soviet Socialist Republic See **Russia, Soviet Union.**

bylaw

bylines Use only if the reporter was in the dateline community to gather the information reported.

Nicknames should not be used unless they specifically are requested by the writer.

cabinet Capitalize references to a specific body of advisers heading executive departments for a president, king, governor, etc.: *The president-elect said he has not made his Cabinet selections.*

The capital letter distinguishes the word from the common noun meaning cupboard, which is lowercase.

See **department** for a listing of all the U.S. Cabinet departments.

Cabinet titles Capitalize the full title when used before a name; lowercase in other uses: *Secretary of State Cyrus R. Vance,* but *Juanita M. Kreps, secretary of commerce.*
See **titles.**

cactus, cactuses

cadet See **military academies.**

Caesarean section

caliber The form: *.38-caliber pistol.* See **weapons.**

California Abbrev.: *Calif.* See **state names.**

call letters Use all caps. Use hyphens to separate the type of station from the basic call letters: *WBZ-AM, WBZ-FM, WBZ-TV.*

Until summer 1976, the format for citizens band operators was three letters and four figures: *KTE9136.* Licenses issued since then use four letters and four figures: *KTEM1234.*

Shortwave stations, which operate with greater power than citizens band

stations and on different frequencies, typically mix letters and figures: *K2LRX.*

See **channel; citizens band; radio station;** and **television station.**

call up (v.) **call-up** (n. and adj.)

Cambodia Use this name rather than *Democratic Kampuchea* in datelines. When *Kampuchea* is used in the body of a story, it should be identified as the formal name of Cambodia.

Cameroon Not *Camerouns* or *Cameroun.* See **geographic names.**

campaign manager Do not treat as a formal title. Always lowercase.
See **titles.**

Canada *Montreal, Ottawa, Quebec* and *Toronto* stand alone in datelines. For all other datelines, use the city name and the name of the province or territory spelled out.

The 10 provinces of Canada are Alberta, British Columbia, Manitoba, New Brunswick, Newfoundland (includes Labrador), Nova Scotia, Ontario, Prince Edward Island, Quebec and Saskatchewan.

The two territories are the Yukon and the Northwest Territories.

The provinces have substantial autonomy from the federal government.

The territories are administered by the federal government, although residents of the territories do elect their own legislators and representatives to Parliament.

See **datelines**.

Canada goose Not *Canadian goose*.

Canadian Broadcasting Corp. *CBC* is acceptable in all references within contexts such as a television column. Otherwise, do not use *CBC* until second reference.

canal Capitalize as integral part of a proper name: *the Suez Canal.*

Canal Zone Do not abbreviate. See **Panama Canal Zone**.

cancel, canceled, canceling, cancellation

cannon, canon A *cannon* is a weapon. See the **weapons** entry.

A *canon* is a law or rule, particularly of a church.

cannot

canoeing Scoring is in minutes, seconds and tenths of a second. Extend to hundredths if available.

Use a basic summary. Example:

> Canoeing, Men
> Kayak Singles, 500 meters
> Heat 1—Rudiger Helm, East Germany, 1:56.06. 2, Zoltan Sztanity, Hungary, 1:57.12. 3 Etc.
> Also: 6, Henry Krawczyk, New York, 2 04.64.
> First Repechage—1, Ladislay Soucek, Czechoslovakia, 1:53.20. 2, Hans Eich, West Germany, 1:54.23. 3, Etc.

cant The distinctive stock words and phrases used by a particular sect or class.

See **dialect**.

can't hardly A double negative is implied. Better is: *can hardly.*

cantor See **Jewish congregations**.

Canuck It means a French Canadian, and often is considered a deroga-

tory racial label. Avoid the word except in formal names (*the Vancouver Canucks,* a professional hockey team) or in quoted matter.

See the **nationalities and races** entry.

canvas, canvass *Canvas* is heavy cloth.

Canvass is a noun and verb denoting a survey.

cape Capitalize as part of a proper name: *Cape Cod, Cape Hatteras.* Lowercase when standing alone.

Although local practice may call for capitalizing *the Cape* when the rest of the name is clearly understood, always use the full name on first reference in wire copy. On second reference in wire copy, either repeat the full name or use *the cape* in lowercase.

Cape Canaveral, Fla. Formerly Cape Kennedy. See **John F. Kennedy Space Center**.

capital The city where a seat of government is located. Do not capitalize.

When used in a financial sense, *capital* describes money, equipment or property used in a business by a person or corporation.

capital gain, capital loss The difference between what a capital asset cost and the price it brought when sold.

capitalization In general, avoid unnecessary capitals. Use a capital letter only if you can justify it by one of the principles listed here.

Many words and phrases, including special cases, are listed separately in this book. Entries that are capitalized without further comment should be capitalized in all uses.

If there is no relevant listing in this book for a particular word or phrase, consult Webster's New World Dictionary. Use lowercase if the dictionary lists it as an acceptable form for the sense in which the word is being used.

As used in this book, *capitalize* means to use uppercase for the first letter of a word. If additional capital letters are needed, they are called for by an example or a phrase such as *use all caps.*

Some basic principles:

PROPER NOUNS: Capitalize nouns that constitute the unique identification for a specific person, place or thing: *John, Mary, America, Boston, England.*

Some words, such as the examples just given, are always proper nouns. Some common nouns receive proper noun status when they are used as the name of a particular entity: *General Electric, Gulf Oil.*

PROPER NAMES: Capitalize common nouns such as *party, river, street* and *west* when they are an integral part of the full name for a person, place or thing: *Democratic Party, Mississippi River, Fleet Street, West Virginia.*

Lowercase these common nouns when they stand alone in subsequent references: *the party, the river, the street.*

Lowercase the common noun elements of names in all plural uses: *the Democratic and Republican parties, Main and State streets, lakes Erie and Ontario.*

Among entries that provide additional guidelines are:

animals	holidays and
brand names	holy days
buildings	legislature
committee	months
congress	monuments
datelines	nationalities
days of the week	and races
directions	nicknames
and regions	organizations and
family names	institutions
food	planets
foreign govern-	plants
mental bodies	police
foreign legis-	department
lative bodies	religious
geographic names	references
governmental bodies	seasons
heavenly bodies	trademarks
historical periods	unions
and events	

POPULAR NAMES: Some places and events lack officially designated proper

names but have popular names that are the effective equivalent: *the Combat Zone* (a section of downtown Boston), *the Main Line* (a group of Philadelphia suburbs), *the South Side* (of Chicago), *the Badlands* (of North Dakota), *the Street* (the financial community in the Wall Street area of New York).

The principle applies also to shortened versions of the proper names for one-of-a-kind events: *the Series* (for the World Series), *the Derby* (for the Kentucky Derby). This practice should not, however, be interpreted as a license to ignore the general practice of lowercasing the common noun elements of a name when they stand alone.

DERIVATIVES: Capitalize words that are derived from a proper noun and still depend on it for their meaning: *American, Christian, Christianity, English, French, Marxism, Shakespearean.*

Lowercase words that are derived from a proper noun but no longer depend on it for their meaning: *french fries, herculean, manhattan cocktail, malapropism, pasteurize, quixotic, venetian blind.*

SENTENCES: Capitalize the first word in a statement that stands as a sentence. See **sentences** and **parentheses**.

In poetry, capital letters are used for the first words of some phrases that would not be capitalized in prose. See **poetry**.

COMPOSITIONS: Capitalize the principal words in the names of books, movies, plays, poems, operas, songs, radio and television programs, works of art, etc. See **composition titles; magazine names**; and **newspaper names**.

TITLES: Capitalize formal titles when used immediately before a name. Lowercase formal titles when used alone or in constructions that set them off from a name by commas.

Use lowercase at all times for terms that are job descriptions rather than formal titles.

See **academic titles; courtesy titles; legislative titles; military titles; nobility titles; religious titles**; and **titles**.

ABBREVIATIONS: Capital letters apply in some cases. See the **abbreviations and acronyms** entry.

capitol Capitalize *U.S. Capitol* and *the Capitol* when referring to the building in Washington: *The meeting was held on Capitol Hill in the west wing of the Capitol.*

Follow the same practice when referring to state capitols: *The Virginia Capitol is in Richmond. Thomas Jefferson designed the Capitol of Virginia.*

captain See **military titles** for military and police usage.

Lowercase and spell out in such uses as *team captain Carl Yastrzemski.*

carat, caret, karat The weight of precious stones, especially diamonds, is expressed in *carats.* A carat is equal to 200 milligrams or about 3 grains.

A *caret* is a writer's and proofreader's mark.

The proportion of pure gold used with an alloy is expressed in *karats.*

carbine See **weapons.**

cardinal See **Roman Catholic Church.**

cardinal numbers See **numerals.**

CARE Acceptable in all references for *Cooperative for American Relief Everywhere Inc.*

Headquarters is in New York.

carefree

caretaker

Caribbean See **Western Hemisphere.**

carmaker, carmakers

car pool

carry-over (n. and adj.)

cash on delivery *c.o.d.* is preferred in all references.

caster, castor *Caster* is a roller.

Castor is the spelling for the oil and the bean from which it is derived.

catalog, cataloged, cataloger, cataloging, catalogist

Caterpillar A trademark for a brand of crawler tractor.

Use lowercase for the wormlike larva of various insects.

catholic, catholicism Use *Roman Catholic Church, Roman Catholic* or *Roman Catholicism* in first references to those who believe that the pope, as bishop of Rome, has the ultimate authority in administering an earthly organization founded by Jesus Christ.

Most subsequent references may be condensed to *Catholic Church, Catholic* or *Catholicism. Roman Catholic* should continue to be used, however, if the context requires a distinction between Roman Catholics and members of other denominations who often describe themselves as Catholic. They include some high church Episcopalians (who often call themselves *Anglo-Catholics),* members of Eastern Orthodox churches, and members of some national Catholic churches that have broken with Rome. Among churches in this last category are the Polish National Catholic Church and the Lithuanian National Catholic Church.

Lowercase *catholic* when used in its generic sense of general or universal, meanings derived from a similar word in Greek.

Those who use *Catholic* in a religious sense are indicating their belief that they are members of a universal church that Jesus Christ left on Earth.

cats See **animals.**

cattle See **animals.**

Caucasian

cave in (v.) **cave-in** (n. and adj.)

CB See **citizens band radio.**

CBS Acceptable in all references for *CBS Inc.,* the former Columbia Broadcasting System.

Divisions include CBS News, CBS Radio and CBS-TV.

cease-fire, cease-fires (n. and adj.) The verb form is *cease fire.*

celebrant, celebrator Reserve *celebrant* for someone who conducts a religious rite: *He was the celebrant of the Mass.*

Use *celebrator* for someone having a good time: *The celebrators kept the party going until 3 a.m.*

cellophane Formerly a trademark, now a generic term.

Celsius Use this term rather than *centigrade* for the temperature scale that is part of the metric system.

The Celsius scale is named for Anders Celsius, a Swedish astronomer who designed it. In it, zero represents the freezing point of water, and 100 degrees is the boiling point at sea level.

To convert to Fahrenheit, multiply a Celsius temperature by 9, divide by 5 and add 32 (25 × 9 = 225, divided by 5 = 45, plus 32 = 77 degrees Fahrenheit).

When giving a Celsius temperature, use these forms: *40 degrees Celsius* or *40 C* (note the space and no period after the capital *C*) if degrees and Celsius are clear from the context.

See **Fahrenheit** and **metric system** entries.

cement *Cement* is the powder mixed with water and sand or gravel to make concrete. The proper term is *concrete* (not *cement*) *pavement, blocks, driveways,* etc.

censer, censor, censure A *censer* is a container in which incense is burned.

To censor is to prohibit or restrict the use of something.

To censure is to condemn.

centerfold

Center for Disease Control The center, located in Atlanta, is the U.S. Public Health Service's national agency for control of infectious and other preventable disease. It works with state health departments to provide specialized services that they are unable to maintain on an everyday basis.

The normal form for first reference is the *national Center for Disease Control. CDC* is acceptable on second reference.

centi- A prefix denoting one-hundredth of a unit. Move a decimal point two places to the left in converting to the basic unit: 155.6 centimeters = 1.556 meters.

centigrade See **Celsius**.

centimeter One-hundredth of a meter.

There are 10 millimeters in a centimeter.

A centimeter is approximately the width of a large paper clip.

To convert to inches, multiply by .4 (5 centimeters × .4 = 2 inches).

See **meter; metric system;** and **inch**.

Central America See **Western Hemisphere**.

Central Conference of American Rabbis See **Jewish Congregations**.

Central Intelligence Agency *CIA* is acceptable in all references.

The formal title for the individual who heads the agency is *director of central intelligence.* On first reference: *Director George Bush of the CIA, Director of Central Intelligence George Bush,* or *CIA Director George Bush.*

Central Standard Time (CST), Central Daylight Time (CDT) See **time zones**.

cents Spell out the word *cents* and lowercase, using numerals for amounts less than a dollar: *5 cents, 12 cents.* Use the $ sign and decimal system for larger amounts: *$1.01, $2.50.*

Numerals alone, with or without a decimal point as appropriate, may be used in tabular matter.

century Lowercase, spelling out numbers less than 10: *the first century, the 20th century.*

For proper names, follow the organization's practice: *20th Century Fox, Twentieth Century Fund, Twentieth Century Limited.*

Ceylon It is now *Sri Lanka,* which should be used in datelines and other references to the nation.

The people may be referrred to as *Ceylonese* (n. or adj.) or *Sri Lankans.* The language is *Sinhalese.*

cha-cha

Chagas' disease After Charles Chagas, a Brazilian physician who identified the chronic wasting disease caused by a parasite that is carried by insects.

chairman, chairwoman Capitalize as a formal title before a name: *company Chairman Henry Ford, committee Chairwoman Margaret Chase Smith.*

Do not capitalize as a casual, temporary position: *meeting chairman Robert Jones.*

Do not use *chairperson* unless it is an organization's formal title for an office. See **titles.**

chamber of deputies See **foreign legislative bodies.**

chancellor The translation to English for the first minister in the governments of West Germany and Austria. Capitalize when used before a name.

See the **premier, prime minister** entry and **titles.**

changeable

changeover

change up (v.) **change-up** (n. and adj.)

channel Capitalize when used with a figure; lowercase elsewhere: *He tuned to Channel 3. No channel will broadcast the game.*

Also: *the English Channel,* but *the channel* on second reference.

chapters Capitalize *chapter* when used with a numeral in reference to sections of a book or legal code. Always use Arabic figures: *Chapter 1, Chapter 20.*

Lowercase when standing alone.

character, reputation *Character* refers to moral qualities.

Reputation refers to the way a person is regarded by others.

charismatic groups See **religious movements.**

Charleston, Charlestown, Charles Town *Charleston* is the name of the capital of West Virginia and of a port city in South Carolina.

Charlestown is a section of Boston.

Charles Town is the name of a small city in West Virginia.

chauffeur

chauvinism, chauvinist The words mean unreasoning devotion to one's race, sex, country, etc., with contempt for other races, sexes, countries, etc.

The terms come from Nicolas Chauvin, a soldier of Napoleon I, who was famous for his devotion to the lost cause.

check up (v.) **checkup** (n.)

Chemical Mace A trademark, usually shortened to *Mace,* for a brand of tear gas that is packaged in an aerosol canister and temporarily stuns its victims.

chess In stories, the names and pieces are spelled out, lowercase: *king, queen, bishop, pawn, knight, rook, kingside, queenside, white, black.*

Examples: *White was unable to defend his kingside bishop. The black pieces were cramped. Black brought pressure on the queenside knight file. White took black's kingside bishop's pawn.*

The news services use the descriptive notation in providing tabular summaries. Capital letters represent the pieces and files: *B* for bishop, *K* for king, *N* for knight, *Q* for queen, *R* for rook, *P* for pawn. Each file is given the name of the piece originally posted on it, and the ranks are numbered from *1* to *8* away from the player. Each rank thus has a dual designation, depending on which player makes the move.

The initial of the moving piece comes first, followed by a hyphen, followed by the designation of the square moved to. Thus, moving a pawn to the fourth rank of the queen's bishop file would be noted: *P-QB4*.

The castle, a move involving two pieces, is noted by lowercase *o*'s separated by a hyphen. The kingside castle: *o-o*; the queenside castle: *o-o-o*.

To note a capture, a lowercase *x* is substituted for the hyphen. Thus, if a pawn takes another pawn it would be noted: *PxP*.

The initials *ch* are used to indicate a check.

The word *mate* is used for checkmate.

Indication of queenside *Q* or kingside *K* are omitted when no ambiguity would result.

The form, taken from the first modern international tournament in London in 1851:

White Anderson	Black Kieseritzki
1. P-K4	P-K4
2. P-KB4	PxP
3. B-B4	P-QN4
4. BxNP	Q-R5ch
5. K-B1	N-KB3
6. N-KB3	Q-R3
7. P-Q3	N-R4
8. N-R4	P-QB3
9. N-B5	Q-N4
10. P-KN4	N-B3
11. R-N1	PxB
12. P-KR4	Q-N3
13. P-R5	Q-N4
14. Q-B3	N-N1
15. BxP	Q-B3
16. N-B3	B-B4

White Anderson	Black Kieseritzki
17. N-Q5	QxP
18. B-Q6	BxR
19. P-K5	QxRch
20. K-K2	N-QR3
21. N-Pch	K-Q1
22. Q-B6ch	NxQ
23. B-K7	mate

Chevy Not *Chevie* or *Chevvy*. This nickname for *Chevrolet* should be used only in automobile features or in quoted matter.

Chicago The city in Illinois stands alone in datelines.

Chicano, Chicanos Although not always derogatory, *Chicano* should be avoided as a routine description for U.S. citizens or residents of Mexican descent. *Mexican-Americans* is preferred.

Some say *Chicano* resulted from Indian attempts to pronounce *Mexicano*. Others say its origin is a derisive description that Mexicans used for what they regarded as the chicanery of bureaucrats during the French rule of Mexico.

Chicano has been adopted by some social activists of Mexican descent, and may be used when activists use it to describe themselves. To apply it to all Spanish-surnamed citizens would be roughly the same as calling all blacks Muslims.

See the **nationalities and races** entry.

chief Capitalize as a formal title before a name: *He spoke to Police Chief Michael Codd. He spoke to Chief Michael Codd of the New York police.*

Lowercase when it is not a formal title: *union chief Walter Reuther.*

See **titles**.

chief justice Capitalize only as a formal title before a name: *Chief Justice Warren Burger.* The officeholder is the chief justice of the United States, not of the Supreme Court.

See **judge**.

chief petty officer See **military titles.**

chief warrant officer See **military titles.**

Chile The nation.

chili, chilies The peppers.

chilly Moderately cold.

China When used alone, it refers to the mainland nation. Use it in datelines and other routine references.

Use *People's Republic of China, Communist China, mainland China* or *Red China* only in direct quotations or when needed to distinguish the mainland and its government from Taiwan.

For datelines on stories from the island of Taiwan, use the name of a community and *Taiwan.* In the body of a story, use *Nationalist China* or *Taiwan* for references to the government based on the island. Use the formal name of the government, *the Republic of China,* when required for legal precision.

Chinaman A patronizing term. Confine it to quoted matter.

Chinese names Drop the apostrophes sometimes used: *Chiang Kai-shek,* not *K'ai-shek.* Note that the name following the hyphen is not capitalized.

The family name usually comes first: *Mao* in second reference to *Mao Tse-tung.* If you are unsure which is the family name, a good rule of thumb is that surnames are never hyphenated, while given names often are.

Some Chinese have westernized their names, putting their given names or the initials for them first: *P.Y. Chen, Jack Wang.*

When translating a name into English, use letters that yield the closest phonetic equivalent in English. If an individual has a preferred English spelling, use it.

chitchat

chop suey

Christian Church (Disciples of Christ) The parentheses and the words they surround are part of the formal name.

The body owes its origins to an early 19th century frontier movement to unify Christians.

The Disciples, led by Alexander Campbell in western Pennsylvania, and the Christians, led by Barton W. Stone in Kentucky, merged in 1832.

The local church is the basic organizational unit.

National policies are developed by the General Assembly, made up of representatives chosen by local churches and regional organizations. The regional units certify the standing of ministers and provide help and counsel to ministers and congregations.

The church lists more than 1 million members.

BELIEFS: The church allows for varied opinions and stresses freedom of interpretation, based on the historic conviction that there is no creed but Christ and no saving doctrines except those of the New Testament.

CLERGY: All members of the clergy may be referred to as *ministers. Pastor* applies if a minister leads a congregation.

On first reference, use *the Rev.* before the name of a man or woman. On second reference, use only the last name of a man; use *Miss, Mrs.* or *Ms.* before the last name of a woman depending on her preference.

See **religious titles.**

Christian Methodist Episcopal Church See **Methodist churches.**

Christian Science Church See **Church of Christ, Scientist.**

Christmas, Christmas Day Dec. 25. The federal legal holiday is observed on Friday if Dec. 25 falls on a Saturday, on Monday if it falls on a Sunday.

Never abbreviate *Christmas* to *Xmas* or any other form.

church Capitalize as part of the formal name of a building, a congregation or a denomination; lowercase in other uses: *St. Mary's Church, the Roman Catholic Church, the Catholic and Episcopal churches, a Roman Catholic church, a church.*

Lowercase in phrases where *the church* is used in an institutional sense: *He believes in separation of church and state. The pope said the church opposes abortion.*

See **religious titles** and the entry for the denomination in question.

Churches of Christ Approximately 18,000 independent congregations with a total U.S. membership of more than 2 million cooperate under this name. They sponsor numerous educational activities, primarily radio and television programs.

Each local church is autonomous and operates under a governing board of elders. The minister is an evangelist, addressed by members as *Brother*. The ministers do not use clergy titles. Do not precede their names by a title.

The churches do not regard themselves as a denomination. Rather, they stress a non-denominational effort to preach what they consider basic Bible teachings. The churches also teach that baptism is an essential part of the salvation process.

See **religious movements**.

churchgoer

Church of Christ, Scientist This denomination was founded in 1879 by Mary Baker Eddy, who attributed her recovery from an illness to insights she gained from reading Scripture.

The Mother Church in Boston is the international headquarters. Its board of directors guides all of the approximately 3,200 branch churches throughout the world.

A branch church, governed by its own democratically chosen board, is named First Church of Christ, Scientist, or Second Church, etc. according to the order of its establishment in a community.

The terms *Christian Science Church* or *Churches of Christ, Scientist,* are acceptable in all references to the denomination.

BELIEFS: Christian Science describes God as the source of all real being, so that nothing except what he has created can ultimately be real. Death, disease and sin are regarded as having no real existence because they are not created by God. Scripture is cited as evidence that a true understanding of God heals sickness as well as sin.

The principal beliefs are contained in "Science and Health With Key to the Scriptures," the denominational textbook written by Mrs. Eddy.

The word *Christian* is used because New Testament writings are an integral element of the denomination's teachings. The word *science* denotes the concept that reality can be understood and proved in Christian experience.

A distinction is made between Christ, regarded as the divine nature or godliness of Jesus, and Jesus, regarded as the human Wayshower and Exemplar of man's sonship with God.

CLERGY: The church is composed entirely of lay members and does not have clergy in the usual sense. Either men or women may hold the three principal offices — *reader, practitioner* or *lecturer.*

Readers are elected from congregations to conduct worship services. *Practitioners* devote full time to the public healing ministry of the church. *Lecturers,* appointed by the directors of the Mother Church, give public lectures on Christian Science.

The preferred form for these titles is to use a construction that sets them off from a name with commas. Capitalize them only when used as a formal title immediately before a name. Do not continue use of the title in subsequent references.

The terms *pastor* and *minister* are not applicable. Do not use *the Rev.* in any reference.

See **religious titles**.

Church of England See **Anglican Communion.**

Church of Jesus Christ of Latter-day Saints Note the capitalization and punctuation of *Latter-day*. *Mormon Church* is acceptable in all references, but always include the proper name in a story dealing primarily with church activities.

The church is based on revelations that Joseph Smith said were brought to him in the 1820s by heavenly messengers.

After Smith's death in 1844, his followers split into factions, the largest of them the Church of Jesus Christ of Latter-day Saints. Led west by Brigham Young, they founded Salt Lake City, Utah, in 1847.

Today, the church headquarters there directs more than 6,500 congregations with more than 3 million members worldwide.

Church hierarchy is composed of men known as general authorities. Among them, the policy-making body is the First Presidency, made up of a president and two or more counselors. It has final authority in all spiritual and worldly matters.

The Council of the Twelve Apostles, primarily an advisory body, helps the First Presidency direct church activities. When the church president dies, the First Presidency is dissolved and the Council of the Twelve Apostles selects a new president, traditionally the man who is the senior apostle in the council. He then chooses his counselors.

Other general authorities include the church patriarch, a spiritual adviser; a three-member Presiding Bishopric, which administers temporal affairs; and the First Quorum of Seventy, in charge of missionary work. Women may not become general authorities.

The church's basic geographical units are called stakes. They are governed by a stake presidency, made up of a president and two counselors, and a stake high council. Individual congregations within a stake are called wards. Missions, which oversee members where there are no stakes, are headed by a president and may include one or more congregations known as branches.

BELIEFS: Mormons believe that Jesus Christ established one church on earth, that it was taken away upon his death and not restored until the revelations to Smith. They believe that Jesus came to America after his Resurrection, visiting its people, who had immigrated to the continent in ancient times.

Among the revelations were directions to gold plates that Smith said he found on Hill Cumorah, near Palmyra, N.Y. He taught that the plates, left by a prophet who lived some time after Jesus, contained the records of the people Jesus had visited in America and the true word of God.

The "Book of Mormon," written by Smith, contains what members believe are his translation of the hieroglyphics on the plates. The plates were later returned to Moroni, the heavenly messenger who led Smith to them. Smith also wrote the "Book of Doctrine and Covenants" and the "Pearl of Great Price." These three books and the Bible are the key church documents, although revelation is considered to continue today through members of the First Presidency.

CLERGY: All faithful male members over the age of 11 are members of the priesthood and may attain positions of leadership in the all-lay clergy. Younger members go through a series of ranks from deacon to teacher to priest before becoming elders sometime after their 18th birthdays. They may later become seventies or high priests. A high priest may become a bishop or one of two bishop's counselors, who lead local congregations.

The only formal titles are *president* (for the head of the First Presidency), *bishop* (for members of the Presiding Bishopric and for local bishops) and *elder* (for other general authorities and church missionaries). Capitalize these formal titles before a name on first reference; use only the last name on second reference.

The terms *minister* or *the Rev.* are not used.

See **religious titles.**

SPLINTER GROUPS: The term *Mormon* is not properly applied to the other Latter Day Saints churches that resulted from the split after Smith's death.

The largest is the Reorganized Church of Jesus Christ of Latter Day Saints (note the lack of a hyphen and the capitalized *Day*), with headquarters in Independence, Mo. It was founded by Smith's son Joseph III and claims to be the continuation of the original church. It has about 1,000 churches and 150,000 members.

CIA Acceptable in all references for *Central Intelligence Agency*.

cigarette

Cincinnati The city in Ohio stands alone in datelines.

CIO See **AFL-CIO**.

Citibank The former First National City Bank. The parent holding company is Citicorp of New York.

cities and towns Capitalize them in all uses. See **datelines** for guidelines on when they should be followed by a state or country name.

Capitalize official titles, including separate political entities such as *East St. Louis, Ill.,* or *West Palm Beach, Fla.*

The preferred form for the section of a city is lowercase: *the west end, northern Los Angeles.* But capitalize widely recognized names for the sections of a city: *South Side* (Chicago), *Lower East Side* (New York).

Spell out the names of cities unless in direct quotes: *A trip to Los Angeles,* but: *"We're going to LA."*

See **city**.

citizen, resident, subject, national, native A *citizen* is a person who has acquired the full civil rights of a nation either by birth or naturalization. Cities and states in the United States do not confer citizenship. To avoid confusion, use *resident,* not *citizen,* in referring to inhabitants of states and cities.

Subject is the term used when the government is headed by a monarch or other sovereign.

National is applied to a person residing away from the nation of which he is a citizen, or to a person under the protection of a specified nation.

Native is the term denoting that an individual was born in a given location.

citizens band Without an apostrophe after the *s,* an exception to Webster's New World based on widespread practice.

CB is acceptable on second reference.

The term describes a group of shortwave radio frequencies set aside by the Federal Communications Commission for local use at low power by individuals or businesses.

Until summer 1976, the format for call letters was three letters and four figures: *KTE9136.* Licenses issued since then use four letters and four figures: *KTEM1234.*

city Capitalize *city* as part of a proper name: *Kansas City, New York City, Oklahoma City, Jefferson City.*

Lowercase elsewhere: *a Texas city; the city government; the city Board of Education;* and all *city of* phrases: *the city of Boston.*

Capitalize when part of a formal title before a name: *City Manager Francis McGrath.* Lowercase when not part of the formal title: *city Health Commissioner Frank Smith.*

See **city council** and **governmental bodies**.

city commission See the next entry.

city council Capitalize when part of a proper name: *the Boston City Council.*

Retain capitalization if the reference is to a specific council but the context does not require the city name: *BOSTON (AP) — The City Council . . .*

Lowercase in other uses: *the council, the Boston and New York city councils, a city council.*

Use the proper name if the body is not known as a city council: *the Miami City Commission, the City Commission, the commission; the Louisville Board of Aldermen, the Board of Aldermen, the board.*

Use *city council* in a generic sense for plural references: *the Boston, Louisville and Miami city councils.*

city editor Capitalize as a formal title before a name. See **titles**.

city hall Capitalize with the name of a city, or without the name of a city if the reference is specific: *Boston City Hall, City Hall.*

Lowercase plural uses: *the Boston and New York city halls.*

Lowercase generic uses, including: *You can't fight city hall.*

citywide

Civil Aeronautics Board *CAB* is acceptable on second reference.

civil cases, criminal cases A *civil case* is one in which an individual, business or agency of government seeks damages or relief from another individual, business or agency of government. Civil actions generally involve a charge that a contract has been breached or that someone has been wronged or injured.

A *criminal case* is one that a state or the federal government brings against an individual charged with committing a crime.

Civil War

claptrap

clean up (v.)   **cleanup** (n. and adj.)

clear-cut (adj.)

clerical titles See **religious titles**.

Cleveland The city in Ohio stands alone in datelines.

clientele

cloak-and-dagger

Clorox A trademark for a brand of bleach.

closed shop A *closed shop* is an agreement between a union and an employer that requires workers to be members of the union before they may be employed.

A *union shop* requires workers to join the union within a specified period after they are employed.

An *agency shop* requires that the workers who do not want to join the union pay the union a fee instead of union dues.

A *guild shop,* a term often used when the union is The Newspaper Guild, is the same as a *union shop.*

See the **right-to-work** entry for an explanation of how some states prohibit contracts that require workers to join unions.

close-up (n. and adj.)

cloture Not *closure,* for the parliamentary procedure for closing debate.

Whenever practical, use a phrase such as *closing debate* or *ending debate* instead of the technical term.

clue Not *clew.*

co- Retain the hyphen when forming nouns, adjectives and verbs that indicate occupation or status:

co-author	co-pilot
co-chairman	co-respondent
co-defendant	(in a divorce suit)
co-host	co-signer
co-owner	co-star
co-partner	co-worker

(Several are exceptions to Webster's New World in the interests of consistency.)

Use no hyphen in other combinations:

coed	cooperate
coeducation	cooperative
coequal	coordinate
coexist	coordination
coexistence	

Cooperate, coordinate and related words are exceptions to the rule that a hyphen is used if a prefix ends in a vowel and the word that follows begins with the same vowel.

Co. See **company.**

coach Capitalize only when used without a qualifying term before the name of the person who directs an athletic team: *General Manager Red Auerbach signed Coach Tom Heinsohn to a new contract.*

If *coach* is preceded by a qualifying word, lowercase it: *third base coach Frank Crosetti, defensive coach George Perles, swimming coach Mark Spitz.*

Lowercase *coach* when it stands alone or is set off from a name by commas: *The coach, Tom Heinsohn, was charged with a technical.*

The capitalization of *coach* is based on the general rule that formal titles used directly before an individual's name are capitalized. See **titles.**

coast Lowercase when referring to the physical shoreline: *Atlantic coast, Pacific coast, east coast.*

Capitalize when referring to regions of the United States lying along such shorelines: *the Atlantic Coast states, a Gulf Coast city, the West Coast, the East Coast.*

Do not capitalize when referring to smaller regions: *the Virginia coast.*

Capitalize *the Coast* when standing alone only if the reference is to *the West Coast.*

coastal waters See **weather terms.**

coast guard Capitalize when referring to the U.S. force: *the U.S. Coast Guard, the Coast Guard, Coast Guard policy, the Guard.* Do not use the abbreviation *USCG.*

Use lowercase for similar forces of other nations.

This approach has been adopted for consistency, because many foreign nations do not use *coast guard* as the proper name.

See **military academies.**

Coast Guardsman Note spelling. Capitalize as a proper noun when referring to an individual in a U.S. Coast Guard unit: *He is a Coast Guardsman.*

Lowercase *guardsman* when it stands alone.

See **military titles.**

coastline

coattails

Coca-Cola, Coke Trademarks for a brand of cola drink.

cocaine The slang term *coke* should appear only in quoted matter.

c.o.d. Acceptable in all references for *cash on delivery* or *collect on delivery.* (The use of lowercase is an exception to the first listing in Webster's New World.)

Cold War Capitalize when referring specifically to the rivalry between the United States and the Soviet Union.

collateral Stock or other property that a borrower is obliged to turn over to a lender if unable to repay a loan.

See **loan terminology.**

collective nouns Nouns that denote a unit take singular verbs and pronouns: *class, committee, crowd, family, group, herd, jury, orchestra, team.*

Some usage examples: *The committee is meeting to set its agenda. The jury reached its verdict. A herd of cattle was sold.*

PLURAL IN FORM: Some words that are plural in form become collective nouns and take singular verbs when the group or quantity is regarded as a unit.

Right: *A thousand bushels is a good yield.* (A unit.)

Right: *A thousand bushels were created.* (Individual items.)

Right: *The data is sound.* (A unit.)

Right: *The data have been carefully collected.* (Individual items.)

collectors' item

college Capitalize when part of a proper name: *Dartmouth College.*

Consult special sections of the Webster's New World for lists of junior colleges, colleges and universities in the United States and Canadian colleges and universities.

See the **organizations and institutions** entry.

College of Cardinals See **Roman Catholic Church.**

collide, collision Two objects must be in motion before they can *collide.* An automobile cannot *collide* with a utility pole, for example.

colloquialisms The word describes the informal use of a language. It is not local or regional in nature, as dialect is.

Webster's New World Dictionary identifies many words as colloquial with the label *Colloq.* The label itself, the dictionary says, "does not indicate substandard or illiterate usage."

Many colloquial words and phrases characteristic of informal writing and conversation are acceptable in some contexts but out of place in others. Examples include *bum, giveaway* and *phone.*

Other colloquial words normally should be avoided because they are substandard. Webster's New World notes, for example, that *ain't* is colloquial and not automatically illiterate or substandard usage. But it also notes that *ain't* is "a dialectical or substandard contraction." Thus it should not be used in news stories unless needed to illustrate substandard speech in writing.

See the **dialect** and **word section** entries.

colon The most frequent use of a colon is at the end of a sentence to introduce lists, tabulations, texts, etc.

Capitalize the first word after a colon only if it is a proper noun or the start of a complete sentence: *He promised this: The company will make good all the losses.* But: *There were three considerations: expense, time and feasibility.*

EMPHASIS: The colon often can be effective in giving emphasis: *He had only one hobby: eating.*

LISTINGS: Use the colon in such listings as time elapsed (*1:31:07.2*), time of day (*8:31 p.m.*), biblical and legal citations (*2 Kings 2:14*; *Missouri Code 3:245-260*).

DIALOGUE: Use a colon for dialogue. In coverage of a trial, for example:
Bailey: What were you doing the night of the 19th?
Mason: I refuse to answer that.

Q AND A: The colon is used for question-and-answer interviews:
Q: Did you strike him?
A: Indeed I did.

INTRODUCING QUOTATIONS: Use a comma to introduce a direct quotation of one sentence that remains within a paragraph. Use a colon to introduce longer quotations within a paragraph and to end all paragraphs that introduce a paragraph of quoted material.

PLACEMENT WITH QUOTATION MARKS: Colons go outside quotation marks unless they are part of the quotation itself.

MISCELLANEOUS: Do not combine a dash and a colon.

colonel See **military titles**.

colonial Capitalize *Colonial* as a proper adjective in all references to *the Colonies.* (See the next entry.)

colonies Capitalize only for the British dependencies that declared their independence in 1776, now known as the United States.

Colorado Abbrev.: *Colo.* See **state names.**

colorblind

colored In some societies, including the United States, the word is considered derogatory and should not be used.

In some countries of Africa, it is used to denote individuals of mixed racial ancestry. Whenever the word is used, place it in quotation marks and provide an explanation of its meaning.

Columbia Broadcasting System
It no longer exists. See **CBS**.

Columbia Lippincott Gazetteer of the World, The
The reference, after Webster's New World Dictionary, for geographic names not covered in this book.

Columbus Day
Oct. 12. The federal legal holiday is the second Monday in October.

combat, combated, combating

comedian Use for both men and women.

comma The following guidelines treat some of the most frequent questions about the use of commas. Additional guidelines on specialized uses are provided in separate entries such as **dates** and **scores**.

For more detailed guidance, consult "The Comma" and "Misused and Unnecessary Commas" in the Guide to Punctuation section in the back of Webster's New World Dictionary.

IN A SERIES: Use commas to separate elements in a series, but do not put a comma before the conjunction in a simple series: *The flag is red, white and blue. He would nominate Tom, Dick or Harry.*

Put a comma before the concluding conjunction in a series, however, if an integral element of the series requires a conjunction: *I had orange juice, toast, and ham and eggs for breakfast.*

Use a comma also before the concluding conjunction in a complex series of phrases: *The main points to consider are whether the athletes are skillful enough to compete, whether they have the stamina to endure the training, and whether they have the proper mental attitude.*

See the **dash** and **semicolon** entries for cases when elements of a series contain internal commas.

WITH EQUAL ADJECTIVES: Use commas to separate a series of adjectives equal in rank. If the commas could be replaced by the word *and* without changing the sense, the adjectives are equal: *a thoughtful, precise manner; a dark, dangerous street.*

Use no comma when the last adjective before a noun outranks its predecessors because it is an integral element of a noun phrase, which is the equivalent of a single noun: *a cheap fur coat* (the noun phrase is *fur coat*); *the old oaken bucket; a new, blue spring bonnet.*

WITH NON-ESSENTIAL CLAUSES: See the **essential clauses, non-essential clauses** entry.

WITH NON-ESSENTIAL PHRASES: See the **essential phrases, non-essential phrases** entry.

WITH INTRODUCTORY CLAUSES AND PHRASES: A comma normally is used to separate an introductory clause or phrase from a main clause: *When he had tired of the mad pace of New York, he moved to Dubuque.*

The comma may be omitted after short introductory phrases if no ambiguity would result: *During the night he heard many noises.*

But use the comma if its omission would slow comprehension: *On the street below, the curious gathered.*

WITH CONJUNCTIONS: When a conjunction such as *and, but* or *for* links two clauses that could stand alone as separate sentences, use a comma before the conjunction in most cases: *She was glad she had looked, for a man was approaching the house.*

As a rule of thumb, use a comma if the subject of each clause is expressly stated: *We are visiting Washington, and we also plan a side trip to Williamsburg. We visited Washington, and our senator greeted us personally.* But no comma when the subject of the two clauses is the same and is not repeated in the second: *We are visiting*

Washington and plan to see the White House.

The comma may be dropped if two clauses with expressly stated subjects are short. In general, however, favor use of a comma unless a particular literary effect is desired or it would distort the sense of a sentence.

INTRODUCING DIRECT QUOTES: Use a comma to introduce a complete, one-sentence quotation within a paragraph: *Wallace said, "She spent six months in Argentina and came back speaking English with a Spanish accent."* But use a colon to introduce quotations of more than one sentence. See **colon**.

Do not use a comma at the start of an indirect or partial quotation: *He said his victory put him "firmly on the road to a first-ballot nomination."*

BEFORE ATTRIBUTION: Use a comma instead of a period at the end of a quote that is followed by attribution: *"Rub my shoulders," Miss Cawley suggested.*

Do not use a comma, however, if the quoted statement ends with a question mark or exclamation point: *"Why should I?" he asked.*

WITH HOMETOWNS AND AGES: Use a comma to set off an individual's hometown when it is placed in apposition to a name: *Mary Richards, Minneapolis, and Maude Findlay, Tuckahoe, N.Y., were there.* However, the use of the word *of* without a comma between the individual's name and the city name generally is preferable: *Mary Richards of Minneapolis and Maude Findlay of Tuckahoe, N.Y., were there.*

If an individual's age is used, set it off by commas: *Maude Findlay, 48, Tuckahoe, N.Y., was present.* The use of the word *of* eliminates the need for a comma after the hometown if a state name is not needed: *Mary Richards, 36, of Minneapolis and Maude Findlay, 48, of Tuckahoe, N.Y., attended the party.*

WITH PARTY AFFILIATIONS, ACADEMIC DEGREES, RELIGIOUS AFFILIATIONS: See separate entries under each of these terms.

NAMES OF STATES AND NATIONS USED WITH CITY NAMES: *His journey will take him from Dublin, Ireland, to Fargo, N.D., and back. The Selma, Ala., group saw the governor.*

Use parentheses, however, if a state name is inserted within a proper name: *The Huntsville (Ala.) Times.*

WITH YES AND NO: *Yes, I will be there.*

IN DIRECT ADDRESS: *Mother, I will be home late. No, sir, I did not do it.*

SEPARATING SIMILAR WORDS: Use a comma to separate duplicated words that otherwise would be confusing: *What the problem is, is not clear.*

IN LARGE FIGURES: Use a comma for most figures higher than 999. The major exceptions are: street addresses (*1234 Main St.*), broadcast frequencies (*1460 kilohertz*), room numbers, serial numbers, telephone numbers, and years (*1976*). See separate entries under these headings.

PLACEMENT WITH QUOTES: Commas always go inside quotation marks. See **semicolon**.

commander See **military titles**.

commander in chief Capitalize only if used as a formal title before a name. See **titles**.

commissioner Do not abbreviate. Capitalize when used as a formal title. See **titles**.

commitment

committee Do not abbreviate. Capitalize when part of a formal name: *the House Appropriations Committee.*

Do not capitalize *committee* in shortened versions of long committee names: the Special Senate Select Committee to Investigate Improper Labor-Management Practices, for example, became the *rackets committee.*

See **subcommittee**.

commodity When used in a financial sense, the word describes the products of mining and agriculture before they have undergone extensive processing.

Common Market Acceptable in all references for *European Economic Community.*

The nine members, as of 1977: Belgium, France, West Germany, Italy, Luxembourg, Netherlands (the original six), Denmark, Ireland, United Kingdom.

common stock, preferred stock An ownership interest in a corporation.

If other classes of stock are outstanding, the holders of common stock are the last to receive dividends and the last to receive payments if a corporation is dissolved. The company may raise or lower common stock dividends as its earnings rise or fall.

When preferred stock is outstanding and company earnings are sufficient, a fixed dividend is paid. If a company is liquidated, holders of preferred stock receive payments up to a set amount before any money is distributed to holders of common stock.

commonwealth A group of people united by their common interests.

See **state**.

Commonwealth, the Formerly the British Commonwealth. The members of this free association of sovereign states recognize the British sovereign as head of the Commonwealth. Some also recognize the sovereign as head of their states; others do not.

The members are: Australia, Bahamas, Bangladesh, Barbados, Botswana, Canada, Cyprus, Fiji, Gambia, Ghana, Grenada, Guyana, India, Jamaica, Kenya, Lesotho, Malawi, Malaysia, Malta, Mauritius, New Zealand, Nigeria, Papua New Guinea, St. Lucia, Seychelles, Sierra Leone, Singapore, Sri Lanka, Swaziland, Tanzania, Tonga, Trinidad and Tobago, Uganda, United Kingdom, Western Samoa and Zambia. Nauru, a special member, participates in activities but not in meetings of government heads.

Communicable Disease Center The former name of the *Center for Disease Control.* See entry under that name.

Communications Satellite Corp. *Comsat* is acceptable on second reference.

Headquarters is in Washington.

Communications Workers of America The shortened form *Communications Workers union* is acceptable in all references.

Headquarters is in Washington

communism, communist Lowercase *communism.* Capitalize *Communist* only when referring to the activities of the Communist Party or to individuals who are members of it: *The Communists won the election. She ran on the Communist ticket.*

See the **political parties and philosophies** entry.

commutation See the **pardon, parole, probation** entry.

company, companies Use *Co.* or *Cos.* when a business uses either word at the end of its proper name: *Ford Motor Co., American Broadcasting Cos.* But: *Aluminum Company of America.*

If *company* or *companies* appears alone in second reference, spell the word out.

The forms for possessives: *Ford Motor Co.'s profits, American Broadcasting Cos.' profits.*

THEATRICAL: Spell out *company* in names of theatrical organizations: *the Martha Graham Dance Company.*

company (military) Capitalize only when part of a name: *Company B.* Do not abbreviate.

company names Consult the company or Standard & Poor's Register of Corporations if in doubt about a formal name. Do not, however, use a comma before *Inc.* or *Ltd.*

See the **organizations and institutions** entry.

compared to, compared with Use *compared to* when the intent is to assert, without the need for elaboration, that two or more items are similar: *She compared her work for women's rights to Susan B. Anthony's campaign for women's suffrage.*

Use *compared with* when juxtaposing two or more items to illustrate similarities and/or differences: *His time was 2:11:10, compared with 2:14 for his closest competitor.*

compatible

complacent, complaisant *Complacent* means self-satisfied.
Complaisant means eager to please.

complement, compliment *Complement* is a noun and verb denoting completeness or the process of supplementing something: *The ship has a complement of 200 sailors and 20 officers. The hat complements her dress.*

Compliment is a noun or verb that denotes praise or the expression of courtesy: *The captain complimented the sailors. She was flattered by the compliments on her outfit.*

complementary, complimentary *The husband and wife have complementary careers.*
She received complimentary tickets to the show.

compose, comprise, constitute *Compose* means to create or put together. It commonly is used in both the active and passive voices: *He composed a song. The United States is composed of 50 states. The zoo is composed of many animals.*

Comprise means to contain, to include all or embrace. It is best used only in the active voice, followed by a direct object: *The United States comprises 50 states. The jury comprises five men and seven women. The zoo comprises many animals.*

Constitute, in the sense of form or make up, may be the best word if neither *compose* nor *comprise* seems to fit: *Fifty states constitute the United States. Five men and seven women constitute the jury. A collection of animals can constitute a zoo.*

Use *include* when what follows is only part of the total: *The price includes breakfast. The zoo includes lions and tigers.*

composition titles Apply the guidelines listed here to book titles, movie titles, opera titles, play titles, poem titles, song titles, television program titles, and the titles of lectures, speeches and works of art.

The guidelines, followed by a block of examples:

—Capitalize the principal words, including prepositions and conjunctions of four or more letters.

—Capitalize an article — *the, a, an* — or word of fewer than four letters if it is the first or last word in a title.

—Put quotation marks around the names of all such works except the Bible and books that are primarily catalogs of reference material. In addition to catalogs, this category includes almanacs, directories, dictionaries, encyclopedias, gazetteers, handbooks and similar publications.

—Translate a foreign title into English unless a work is known to the American public by its foreign name.

EXAMPLES: *"The Star-Spangled Banner," "The Rise and Fall of the Third Reich," "Gone With the Wind," "Of Mice and Men," "For Whom the Bell Tolls," "Time After Time,"* the NBC-TV *"Today"* program, the *"CBS Evening News," "The Mary Tyler Moore Show."* See **television program names** for further guidelines and examples.

Reference works: *Jane's All the World's Aircraft; Encyclopaedia Britannica; Webster's New World Dictionary of the American Language, Second Edition.*

Foreign works: *Rousseau's "War,"* not *Rousseau's "La Guerre."* But: *Leonardo da Vinci's "Mona Lisa." Mozart's "The Marriage of Figaro"* and *"The Magic Flute."* But: *"Die*

Walkuere" and *"Gotterdammerung"* from Wagner's *"The Ring of the Nibelungen."*

compound adjectives See the **hyphen** entry.

Comptometer A trademark for a brand of adding machine.

comptroller, controller *Comptroller* generally is the accurate word for government financial officers.

The U.S. comptroller of the currency is an appointed official in the Treasury Department who is responsible for the chartering, supervising and liquidation of banks organized under the federal government's National Bank Act.

Controller generally is the proper word for financial officers of businesses and for other positions such as aircraft controller.

Capitalize *comptroller* and *controller* when used as the formal titles for financial officers. Use lowercase for *aircraft controller* and similar occupational applications of the word.

See **titles.**

conclave A private or secret meeting. In the Roman Catholic Church it describes the private meeting of cardinals to elect a pope.

concrete See **cement.**

Confederate States of America The formal name for the states that seceded during the Civil War. The shortened form *the Confederacy* is acceptable in all references.

confess, confessed In some contexts the words may be erroneous. See **admit.**

confirmation See **sacraments.**

conglomerate A corporation that has diversified its operations, usually by acquiring enterprises in widely varied industries.

Congo In datelines, give the name of the city followed by *Congo:*
BRAZZAVILLE, Congo (AP) —
In stories, *the Congo* or *Congo* as the construction of a sentence dictates.

Congo River Not *the Zaire River.* But when appropriate, stories may mention that Zaire, the nation on one of its banks, calls the river *the Zaire.*

Congregationalist churches The word *Congregational* still is used by some individual congregations. The principal national body that used the term dropped it in 1961 when the Evangelical and Reformed Church merged with the Congregational Christian Churches to form the United Church of Christ. It has some 1.8 million members.

The word *church* is correctly applied only to an individual local church. Each such church is responsible for the doctrine, ministry and ritual of its congregation.

The local churches also appoint delegates to associations. Their functions include recognizing local churches, promoting cooperation among the churches, and the licensing, ordination, installation and dismissal of ministers.

Conferences, generally organized along state lines, recognize associations and specialize in missionary and educational work.

A general synod, made up of delegates elected by associations and conferences, is designed primarily to discuss questions of concern to all the churches and to handle communications with other denominations.

A small body of churches that did not enter the United Church of Christ is known as the National Association of Congregational Churches. Churches in the association have more than 100,000 members.

BELIEFS: Jesus is regarded as man's savior, but no subscription to a set creed is required for membership. Emphasis is placed on the value of having persons band together for common worship and to help each other lead religious lives.

CLERGY: Members of the clergy are known as *ministers. Pastor* applies if a minister leads a congregation.

On first reference, use *the Rev.* before the name of a man or woman. On second reference, use only the last name of a man; use *Miss, Mrs.* or *Ms.* before the last name of a woman depending on her preference.

See **religious titles.**

congress Capitalize *U.S. Congress* and *Congress* when referring to the U.S. Senate and House of Representatives. Although *Congress* sometimes is used as a substitute for the House, it properly is reserved for reference to both the Senate and House.

Capitalize *Congress* also if referring to a foreign body that uses the term, or its equivalent in a foreign language, as part of its formal name: *the Argentine Congress, the Congress.* See **foreign legislative bodies.**

Lowercase when used as a synonym for *convention* or in second reference to an organization that uses the word as part of its formal name: *the Congress of Racial Equality, the congress.*

congressional Lowercase unless part of a proper name: *congressional salaries, the Congressional Quarterly, the Congressional Record.*

Congressional Directory Use this as the reference source for questions about the federal government that are not covered in this stylebook.

congressional districts Use figures and capitalize *district* when joined with a figure: *the 1st Congressional District, the 1st District.*

Lowercase *district* whenever it stands alone.

Congressional Record A daily publication of the proceedings of Congress including a complete stenographic report of all remarks and debates.

congressman, congresswoman Use only in references to members of the U.S. House of Representatives.

See **legislative titles.**

Congress of Racial Equality *CORE* is acceptable on second reference. Headquarters is in New York.

Connecticut Abbrev.: *Conn.* See **state names.**

connote, denote *Connote* means to suggest or imply something beyond the explicit meaning: *To some persons, the word marriage connotes too much restriction.*

Denote means to be explicit about the meaning: *The word demolish denotes destruction.*

Conrail This acronym is acceptable in all references to *Consolidated Rail Corp.* (The corporation originally used *ConRail*, but later changed to *Conrail*.)

A private, for-profit corporation, Conrail was set up by Congress in 1976 to reorganize and consolidate six bankrupt Northeast railroads — the Penn Central, the Erie Lackawanna, Reading, Central of New Jersey, Lehigh Valley, and Lehigh & Hudson River.

The legislation provided for a $2 billion federal loan to the corporation and set a phased schedule of repayments. A total of 25 million shares of common stock were created, but the shares were not made available for public trading. Instead, the shares were issued in the names of voting trustees chosen to represent the individuals designated as the ultimate recipients after the settlement of litigation over the value of the property that Conrail took over.

Do not confuse *Conrail* with *Amtrak* (see separate entry). However, the legislation that set up Conrail also provided for Amtrak to gradually acquire from Conrail some of the property that had been owned by the bankrupt railroads.

Headquarters is in Philadelphia.

consensus

conservative See the **political parties and philosophies** entry.

Conservative Judaism See **Jewish congregations**.

constable Capitalize when used as a formal title before a name.
See **titles**.

constitute See the **compose, comprise, constitute** entry.

constitution Capitalize references to the U.S. Constitution, with or without the *U.S.* modifier: *The president said he supports the Constitution.*
When referring to constitutions of other nations or of states, capitalize only with the name of a nation or a state: *the French Constitution, the Massachusetts Constitution, the nation's constitution, the state constitution, the constitution.*
Lowercase in other uses: *the organization's constitution.*
Lowercase *constitutional* in all uses.

consul, consul general, consuls general Capitalize when used as a formal title before a name.
See **titles**.

consulate A *consulate* is the residence of a consul in a foreign city. It handles the commercial affairs and personal needs of citizens of the appointing country.
Capitalize with the name of a nation; lowercase without it: *the French Consulate, the U.S. Consulate, the consulate.*
See **embassy** for the distinction between a consulate and an embassy.

consumer price index A measurement of changes in the retail prices of a constant marketbasket of goods and services. It is computed by comparing the cost of the marketbasket at a fixed time with its cost at subsequent or prior intervals.
Capitalize when referring to the U.S. index, issued monthly by the Bureau of Labor Statistics, an agency of the Labor Department.
The *U.S. Consumer Price Index* should not be referred to as a *cost-of-living index*, because it does not include the impact of income taxes and Social Security taxes on the cost of living, nor does it reflect changes in buying patterns that result from inflation. It is, however, the basis for computing cost-of-living raises in many union contracts.
The preferred form for second reference is *the index.* Confine *CPI* to quoted material.

Consumer Product Safety Commission

Contac A trademark for a brand of decongestant.

contagious

contemptible

continent The seven continents, in order of their land size: Asia, Africa, North America, South America, Europe, Antarctica and Australia.
Capitalize *the Continent* and *Continental* only when used as synonyms for *Europe* or *European.* Lowercase in other uses such as: *the continent of Europe, the European continent, the African and Asian continents.*
Capitalize *Dark Continent* when used as a synonym for *Africa.*

Continental Airlines Use this spelling of *airlines,* which Continental has adopted for its public identity. Only its incorporation papers still read *air lines.*
Headquarters is in Los Angeles.

Continental Divide The ridge along the Rocky Mountains that separates rivers flowing east from those that flow west.

continental shelf, continental slope Lowercase. The *shelf* is the part of a continent that is submerged in relatively shallow sea at gradually increasing depths, generally up to about 600 feet below sea level.

The *continental slope* begins at the point where the descent to the ocean bottom becomes very steep.

continual, continuous *Continual* means a steady repetition, over and over again: *The merger has been the source of continual litigation.*

Continuous means uninterrupted, steady, unbroken: *All she saw ahead of her was a continuous stretch of desert.*

contractions Contractions reflect informal speech and writing. Webster's New World Dictionary includes many entries for contractions: *aren't* for *are not*, for example.

Avoid excessive use of contractions. Contractions listed in the dictionary are acceptable, however, in informal contexts or circumstances where they reflect the way a phrase commonly appears in speech or writing.

See **Americanisms; colloquialisms; quotations in the news;** and **word selection.**

contrasted to, contrasted with Use *contrasted to* when the intent is to assert, without the need for elaboration, that two items have opposite characteristics: *He contrasted the appearance of the house today to its ramshackle look last year.*

Use *contrasted with* when juxtaposing two or more items to illustrate similarities and/or differences: *He contrasted the Republican platform with the Democratic platform.*

MEMORY AID: See the **compared to, compared with** entry. The same principle applies here.

control, controlled, controlling

controller See the **comptroller, controller** entry.

controversial An overused word; avoid it. See **non-controversial.**

convention Capitalize as part of the name for a specific national or state political convention: *the Democratic National Convention, the Republican State Convention.*

Lowercase in other uses: *the national convention, the state convention, the convention, the annual convention of the American Medical Association.*

convertible bond See **loan terminology.**

convict (v.) Follow with the preposition *of*, not *for*: *He was convicted of murder.*

convince, persuade You may be *convinced that* something or *of* something. You must be persuaded *to do* something.

Right: *The robbers persuaded him to open the vault.*

Wrong: *The robbers convinced him to open the vault.*

Right: *The robbers convinced him that it was the right thing to do.*

Wrong: *The robbers persuaded him that it was the right thing to do.*

cookie, cookies

cooperate, cooperative But *co-op* as a short form of *cooperative*, to distinguish it from *coop*, a cage for animals.

Cooperative for American Relief Everywhere See **CARE.**

coordinate, coordination

cop Often a derogatory term for *police officer*. Confine it to quoted matter.

copter Acceptable shortening of *helicopter*. But use it only as a noun or adjective. It is not a verb.

copy editor Seldom a formal title. See **titles.**

copyright (n., v. and adj.) *The disclosure was made in a copyright story.*

Use *copyrighted* only as the past tense of the verb: *He copyrighted the article.*

co-respondent In a divorce suit.

Corn Belt The region in the north central Midwest where much corn and corn-fed livestock are raised. It extends from western Ohio to eastern Nebraska and northeastern Kansas.

Corp. See **corporation**.

corporal See **military titles**.

corporate names See **company names**.

corporation An entity that is treated as a person in the eyes of the law. It is able to own property, incur debts, sue and be sued.

Abbreviate *corporation* as *Corp.* when a company or government agency uses the word at the end of its name: *Gulf Oil Corp., the Federal Deposit Insurance Corp.*

Spell out *corporation* when it occurs elsewhere in a name: *the Corporation for Public Broadcasting.*

Spell out and lowercase *corporation* whenever it stands alone.

The form for possessives: *Gulf Oil Corp.'s profits.*

corps Capitalize when used with a word or a figure to form a proper name: *the Marine Corps, the Signal Corps, the 9th Corps.*

Capitalize when standing alone only if it is a shortened reference to *U.S. Marine Corps.*

The possessive form is *corps'* for both singular and plural: *one corps' location, two corps' assignments.*

corral, corralled, corralling

correctional facility, correctional institution See the **prison, jail** entry.

Corsica Use instead of *France* in datelines on stories from communities on this island.

Cortes The Spanish parliament. See **foreign legislative bodies.**

cosmonaut The applicable occupational term for Soviet astronauts. Always lowercase.

See **titles.**

cost of living The amount of money needed to pay taxes and to buy the goods and services deemed necessary to make up a given standard of living, taking into account changes that may occur in tastes and buying patterns.

The term often is treated incorrectly as a synonym for the *U.S. Consumer Price Index,* which does not take taxes into account and measures only price changes, keeping the quantities constant over time.

Hyphenate when used as an compound modifier: *The cost of living went up, but he did not receive a cost-of-living raise.*

See the **consumer price index** and **inflation** entries.

cost-plus

Cotton Belt The region in the South and Southeastern sections of the United States where much cotton is grown.

council, councilor, councilman, councilwoman A deliberative body and those who are members of it.

See the **counsel** entry and **legislative titles.**

Council of Economic Advisers A group of advisers who help the U.S. president prepare his annual economic report to Congress and recommend economic measures to him throughout the year.

counsel, counseled, counseling, counselor, counselor at law *To counsel* is to advise. A *counselor* is one who advises.

A *counselor at law* (no hyphens for consistency with *attorney at law*) is a lawyer. See **lawyer**.

count, countess See **nobility**.

counter- The rules in **prefixes** apply, but in general, no hyphen. Some examples:

counteract	counterproposal
countercharge	counterspy
counterfoil	

countryside

county Capitalize when an integral part of a proper name: *Dade County, Nassau County, Suffolk County.*

Capitalize the full names of county governmental units: *the Dade County Commission, the Nassau County Board of Supervisors, the Nassau County Department of Social Services, the Suffolk County Legislature.*

Retain capitalization for the name of a county body if the proper noun is not needed in the context; lowercase the word *county* if it is used to distinguish an agency from state or federal counterparts: *the Board of Supervisors, the county Board of Supervisors; the Department of Social Services, the county Department of Social Services.* Lowercase *the board, the department,* etc. whenever they stand alone.

Capitalize *county* if it is an integral part of a specific body's name even without the proper noun: *the County Commission, the County Legislature.* Lowercase *the commission, the legislature,* etc. when not preceded by the word *county.*

Capitalize as part of a formal title before a name: *County Manager John Smith.* Lowercase when it is not part of the formal title: *county Health Commissioner Frank Jones.*

Avoid *county of* phrases where possible, but when necessary, always lowercase: *the county of Westchester.*

Lowercase plural combinations: *Westchester and Rockland counties.*

Apply the same rules to similar terms such as *parish.*

See **governmental bodies.**

county court In some states, it is not a court but the administrative body of a county. In most cases, the "court" is presided over by a "county judge," who is not a judge in the traditional sense but the chief administrative officer of the county.

The terms should be explained if they are not clear in the context.

Capitalize all references to a specific *county court*, and capitalize *county judge* when used as a formal title before a name. Do not use *judge* alone before a name except in direct quotations.

Examples:

SEVIERVILLE, Tenn. (AP) — A reluctant County Court approved a school budget today that calls for a 10 percent tax increase for property owners.

The county had been given an ultimatum by the state: Approve the budget or shut down the schools.

The chief administrative officer, County Judge Ray Reagan, said . . .

coup d'etat The word *coup* usually is sufficient.

couple When used in the sense of two persons, the word takes plural verbs and pronouns: *The couple were married Saturday and left Sunday on their honeymoon. They will return in two weeks.*

In the sense of a single unit, use a singular verb: *Each couple was asked to give $10.*

couple of The *of* is necessary. Never use *a couple tomatoes* or a similar phrase.

The phrase takes a plural verb in constructions such as: *A couple of tomatoes were stolen.*

coupon See **loan terminology** for its meaning in a financial sense.

course numbers Use Arabic numerals and capitalize the subject when used with a numeral: *History 6, Philosophy 209.*

court decisions Use figures and a hyphen: *The Supreme Court ruled 5-4, a*

5-4 decision. The word *to* is not needed, but use hyphens if it appears in quoted matter: *"the court ruled 5-to-4, the 5-to-4 decision."*

court districts See **court names**.

courtesy titles In general, do not use the courtesy titles *Miss, Mr., Mrs.* or *Ms.* on first reference. Instead, use the first and last names of the person: *Betty Ford, Jimmy Carter.*

Do not use *Mr.* in any reference unless it is combined with *Mrs.*: *Mr. and Mrs. John Smith, Mr. and Mrs. Smith.*

On sports wires, do not use courtesy titles in any reference unless needed to distinguish among persons of the same last name.

On news wires, use courtesy titles for women on second reference, following the woman's preference. Some guidelines:

MARRIED WOMEN: The preferred form on first reference is to identify a woman by her own first name and her husband's last name: *Susan Smith.* Use *Mrs.* on first reference only if a woman requests that her husband's first name be used or her own first name cannot be determined: *Mrs. John Smith.*

On second reference, use *Mrs.* unless a woman initially identified by her own first name prefers *Ms.*: *Carla Hills, Mrs. Hills.*

If a married woman is known by her maiden last name, precede it by *Miss* on second reference unless she prefers *Ms.*: *Jane Fonda, Miss Fonda.*

UNMARRIED WOMEN: For women who have never been married, use *Miss* or *Ms.* on second reference according to the woman's preference.

For divorced women and widows, the normal practice is to use *Mrs.* on second reference. Use *Miss* if the woman returns to the use of her maiden name. Use *Ms.* if she prefers it.

MARITAL STATUS: If a woman prefers *Ms.*, do not include her marital status in a story unless it is clearly pertinent.

See **nobility** and **religious titles**.

courthouse Capitalize with the name of a jurisdiction: *the Cook County Courthouse, the U.S. Courthouse.* Lowercase in other uses: *the county courthouse, the courthouse, the federal courthouse.*

Court House (two words) is used in the proper names of some communities: *Appomattox Court House, Va.*

court-martial, court-martialed, courts-martial

court names Capitalize the full proper names of courts at all levels.

Retain capitalization if *U.S.* or a state name is dropped: *the U.S. Supreme Court, the Supreme Court; the Massachusetts Superior Court, the state Superior Court, the Superior Court, Superior Court.*

For courts identified by a numeral: *2nd District Court, 8th U.S. Circuit Court of Appeals.*

For additional details on federal courts, see **judicial branch** and separate listings under **U.S.** and the court name.

See **judge** for guidelines on titles before the names of judges.

Court of St. James's Note the *'s.* The formal name for the royal court of the British sovereign. Derived from St. James's Palace, the former scene of royal receptions.

courtroom

cover up (v.) **cover-up** (n. and adj.) *He tried to cover up the scandal. He was prosecuted for the cover-up.*

crack up (v.) **crack-up** (n. and adj.)

crawfish Not *crayfish.* An exception to Webster's New World based on the dominant spelling in Louisiana, where it is a popular delicacy.

criminal cases See the **civil cases, criminal cases** entry.

Crisco A trademark for a brand of vegetable shortening.

crisis, crises

crisscross

criterion, criteria

cross country   No hyphen, an exception to Webster's New World based on the practices of U.S. and international governing bodies for the sport.

Scoring for this track event is in minutes, seconds and tenths of a second. Extend to hundredths if available.

Use a basic summary, Example:

National AAU Championship
Cross Country
1, Frank Shorter, Miami, 5:25.67. 2, Tom Coster, Los Angeles, 5:30.72. 3, Etc.

Adapt the basic summary to paragraph form under a dateline for a field of more than 10 competitors. See the **auto racing** and **bowling** entries for examples.

See also the **track and field** entry.

cross-examine, cross-examination

cross-eye (n.) **cross-eyed** (adj.)

cross fire

crossover (n. and adj.)

cross section (n.) **cross-section** (v.)

Cub Scouts   See **Boy Scouts**.

cuckoo clock

cup   Equal to eight fluid ounces. The approximate metric equivalents are 240 milliliters or .24 of a liter.

To convert to liters, multiply by .24 (14 cups x .24 = 3.36 liters, or 3,360 milliliters).

See **liter**.

cupful, cupfuls   Not *cupsful.*

curate   See **religious titles**.

cure-all

Curia   See **Roman Catholic Church**.

currency depreciation, currency devaluation   A nation's money *depreciates* when its value falls in relation to the currency of other nations or in relation to its own prior value.

A nation's money *is devalued* when its government deliberately reduces its value in relation to the currency of other nations.

When a nation devalues its currency, the goods it imports tend to become more expensive. Its exports tend to become less expensive in other nations and thus more competitive.

curtain raiser

customs   Capitalize *U.S. Customs Service*, or simply *the Customs Service*.

Lowercase elsewhere: *a customs official, a customs ruling, he went through customs.*

cut back (v.) **cutback** (n. and adj.) *He cut back spending. The cutback will require frugality.*

cut off (v.) **cutoff** (n. and adj.) *He cut off his son's allowance. The cutoff date for applications is Monday.*

cycling   Use the basic summary format.

cyclone   See **weather terms**.

Cyclone   A trademark for a brand of chain-link fence.

cynic, skeptic   A *skeptic* is a doubter.

A *cynic* is a disbeliever.

czar   Not *tsar*. It was a formal title only for the ruler of Russia and some other Slavic nations.

Lowercase in all other uses.

Dacron A trademark for a brand of polyester fiber.

dalai lama The traditional high priest of Lamaism, a form of Buddhism practiced in Tibet and Mongolia. *Dalai lama* is a title rather than a name, but it is all that is used when referring to the man. Capitalize *Dalai Lama* in references to the holder of the title, in keeping with the principles outlined in the **nobility** entry.

Dallas The city in Texas stands alone in datelines.

Dalles, The A city in Oregon.

dam Capitalize when part of a proper name: *Hoover Dam.*

damage, damages *Damage* is destruction: *Authorities said damage from the storm would total more than $1 billion.*
Damages are awarded by a court as compensation for injury, loss, etc.: *The woman received $25,000 in damages.*

dame See **nobility**.

damn it Use instead of *dammit*, but like other profanity it should be avoided unless there is a compelling reason.
See the **obscenities, profanities, vulgarities** entry.

dangling modifiers Avoid modifiers that do not refer clearly and logically to some word in the sentence.

Dangling: *Taking our seats, the game started.* (*Taking* does not refer to the subject, *game,* nor to any other word in the sentence.)
Correct: *Taking our seats, we watched the opening of the game.* (*Taking* refers to *we*, the subject of the sentence.)

Danish pastry

Dardanelles, the Not *the Dardanelles Strait.*

Dark Ages The period beginning with the sack of Rome and ending with the early Renaissance (A.D. 476 to about 1450). The term is derived from the idea that this period in Europe was characterized by intellectual stagnation, widespread ignorance and poverty.

Dark Continent Africa.

dark horse

dash Follow these guidelines:
ABRUPT CHANGE: Use dashes to denote an abrupt change in thought in a sentence or an emphatic pause: *We will fly to Paris in June — if I get a raise. Smith offered a plan — it was unprecedented — to raise revenues.*
SERIES WITHIN A PHRASE: When a phrase that otherwise would be set off by commas contains a series of words that must be separated by commas, use dashes to set off the full phrase: *He*

listed the qualities — intelligence, charm, beauty, independence — that he liked in women.

ATTRIBUTION: Use a dash before an author's or composer's name at the end of a quotation: *"Who steals my purse steals trash." — Shakespeare.*

IN DATELINES:
NEW YORK (AP) — The city is broke.

IN LISTS: Dashes should be used to introduce individual sections of a list. Capitalize the first word following the dash. Use periods, not semicolons, at the end of each section. Example:
Jones gave the following reasons:
—He never ordered the package.
—If he did, it didn't come.
—If it did, he sent it back.

WITH SPACES: Put a space on both sides of a dash in all uses except the start of a paragraph and sports agate summaries.

LOCATION ON KEYBOARDS: On most manual typewriters, the dash must be indicated by striking the hyphen key twice. On most video display terminals, however, there is a separate key that should be used to provide the unique dash symbol with one keystroke.

data A plural noun, it normally takes plural verbs and pronouns.
See the **collective nouns** entry, however, for an example of when *data* may take singular verbs and pronouns.

date line Two words for the imaginary line that separates one day from another.
See the **international date line** entry.

datelines Datelines on stories should contain a city name, entirely in capital letters, followed in most cases by the name of the state, country or territory where the city is located.

DOMESTIC DATELINES: A list of domestic cities that stand alone in datelines follows. The norms that influenced the selection were the population of the city, the population of its metropolitan region, the frequency of the city's appearance in the news, the uniqueness of its name, and experience that has shown the name to be almost synonymous with the state or nation where it is located.

No state with the following:

ATLANTA	MILWAUKEE
BALTIMORE	MINNEAPOLIS
BOSTON	NEW ORLEANS
CHICAGO	NEW YORK
CINCINNATI	OKLAHOMA CITY
CLEVELAND	PHILADELPHIA
DALLAS	PITTSBURGH
DENVER	ST. LOUIS
DETROIT	SALT LAKE CITY
HONOLULU	SAN DIEGO
HOUSTON	SAN FRANCISCO
INDIANAPOLIS	SEATTLE
LOS ANGELES	WASHINGTON
MIAMI	

Also *HOLLYWOOD* when used instead of *LOS ANGELES* on stories about films and the film industry.
Stories from all other U.S. cities should have both the city and the state name in the dateline, including *KANSAS CITY, Mo.,* and *KANSAS CITY, Kan.*
Spell out *Alaska, Hawaii, Idaho, Iowa, Maine, Ohio, Texas* and *Utah.* Abbreviate others as listed in this book under the full name of each state.
Use *Hawaii* on all cities outside Honolulu. Specify the island in the text if needed.
Follow the same practice for communities on islands within the boundaries of other states: *EDGARTOWN, Mass.,* for example, not *EDGARTOWN, Martha's Vineyard.*

REGIONAL CIRCUITS: On state wires, additional cities in a state or region may stand alone if requested by the newspapers served.
When this is done, provide a list to all offices in the region, to all newspapers affected and to New York headquarters.

U.S. POSSESSIONS: Apply the guidelines listed below in the ISLAND NATIONS AND TERRITORIES section and the OVERSEAS TERRITORIES section.

FOREIGN CITIES: These foreign locations stand alone in datelines:

BERLIN	MONTREAL
GIBRALTAR	MOSCOW
GUATEMALA CITY	OTTAWA
HAVANA	PARIS
HONG KONG	PEKING
JERUSALEM	QUEBEC
KUWAIT	ROME
LONDON	SAN MARINO
LUXEMBOURG	SINGAPORE
MACAO	TOKYO
MEXICO CITY	TORONTO
MONACO	VATICAN CITY

In addition, use *UNITED NATIONS* alone, without a *N.Y.* designation, in stories from U.N. headquarters.

CANADIAN DATELINES: Datelines on stories from Canadian cities other than Montreal, Ottawa, Quebec and Toronto should contain the name of the city in capital letters followed by the name of the province. Do not abbreviate any province or territory name.

SOVIET DATELINES: Datelines on stories from Soviet cities other than Moscow should contain the name of the city in capital letters followed by *U.S.S.R.*

OTHER FOREIGN NATIONS: Stories from other foreign cities that do not stand alone in datelines should contain the name of the country or territory (see the next section) spelled out.

SPELLING AND CHOICE OF NAMES: In most cases, the name of the nation in a dateline is the conventionally accepted short form of its official name: *Argentina*, for example, rather than *Republic of Argentina.* (If in doubt, look for an entry in this book. If none is found, follow Webster's New World Dictionary.)

Note these special cases:

—Instead of *United Kingdom,* use *England, Northern Ireland, Scotland* or *Wales.*

—For divided nations, use the commonly accepted names based on geographic distinctions: *East Germany, West Germany, North Korea, South Korea.*

—Use an article only with *El Salvador.* For all others, use just a country name — *Gambia, Netherlands, Philippines,* etc.

—Use *U.S.S.R.* throughout the *Union of Soviet Socialist Republics.* Identify specific republics, such as *Byelorussian Soviet Socialist Republic* or the *Ukrainian Soviet Socialist Republic,* in the text if necessary.

See **geographic names** for guidelines on spelling the names of foreign cities and nations not listed here or in separate entries.

ISLAND NATIONS AND TERRITORIES: When reporting from nations and territories that are made up primarily of islands but commonly are linked under one name, use the city name and the general name in the dateline. Identify an individual island, if needed, in the text.

Examples:

British Virgin Islands	Netherlands Antilles
Indonesia	Philippines

OVERSEAS TERRITORIES: Some overseas territories, colonies and other areas that are not independent nations commonly have accepted separate identities based on their geographic character or special status under treaties. In these cases, use the commonly accepted territory name after a city name in a dateline.

Examples:

Bermuda	Guam
Canal Zone	Martinique
Corsica	Puerto Rico
Faeroe Islands	Sardinia
Greenland	Sicily
Grenada	Sikkim
Guadeloupe	Tibet

WITHIN STORIES: In citing other cities within the body of a story:

—No further identification is necessary if a city is in the same state as the datelined city in U.S. stories or if it is in the same nation in stories from abroad. Make an exception if confusion would result.

—Follow the city name with further identification in most cases where it is not in the same state or nation as the dateline city. The additional identification may be omitted, however, if no confusion would result — there is no need, for example, to refer to *Boston, Mass.,* in a story datelined *NEW YORK.*

—Provide a state or nation identification for the city if the story is undated. However, cities that stand alone in datelines may be used alone in undated stories if no confusion would result.

dateline selection A dateline should tell the reader that the AP obtained the basic information for the story in the datelined city.

Do not, for example, use a Washington dateline on a story written primarily from information that a newspaper reported under a Washington dateline. Use the home city of the newspaper instead.

Use a foreign dateline only if the basic information in a story was obtained by a full- or part-time correspondent physically present in the dateline community.

If a radio broadcast monitored in another city was the source of information, use the dateline of the city where the monitoring took place and mention the fact in the story.

When a story has been assembled from sources in widely separated areas, use no dateline.

When a datelined story contains supplementary information obtained in another city, make that point clear in the context. Do not put parentheses around such material, however, unless the correspondent in the datelined community was cut off from incoming communications. Note the following examples:

—Material from another area was available in the datelined city:

LONDON (AP) — Prime Minister Wilson submitted his resignation today.

In Washington, a State Department spokesman said the change in government leadership would have no effect on negotiations involving the Common Market.

—Material from another area was not available to the correspondent in the dateline city because communications from the outside world were cut off:

PHNOM PENH, Cambodia (AP) — Khmer Rouge troops pushed into Phnom Penh today, barely hours after the United States ran down the Stars and Stripes and abandoned Cambodia to the Communists.

(In Washington, the State Department said Americans evacuated in a mass airlift had arrived safely aboard aircraft carriers and at bases in Thailand.)

dates Always use Arabic figures, without *st, nd, rd* or *th*. See **months** for examples and punctuation guidelines.

daughter-in-law, daughters-in-law

Daughters of the American Revolution *DAR* is acceptable on second reference.

Headquarters is in Washington.

daylight-saving time Not *savings*. Note the hyphen.

When linking the term with the name of a time zone, use only the word *daylight: Eastern Daylight Time, Pacific Daylight Time*, etc.

Lowercase *daylight-saving time* in all uses and *daylight time* whenever it stands alone.

A federal law, administered by the Transportation Department, specifies that daylight time applies from 2 a.m. on the last Sunday of April until 2 a.m. on the last Sunday of October in areas that do not specifically exempt themselves.

See **time zones**.

daylong

days of the week Capitalize them. Do not abbreviate, except when needed in a tabular format: *Sun, Mon, Tue, Wed, Thu, Fri, Sat* (three letters, without periods, to facilitate tabular composition).

See **time element**.

daytime

day to day, day-to-day Hyphenate when used as a compound modifier: *They have extended the contract on a day-to-day basis.*

D-day June 6, 1944, the day the Allies invaded Europe in World War II.

DDT Preferred in all references for the insecticide *dichlorodiphenyltrichloroethane.*

de- See **foreign particles.**

deacon See the entry for the individual's denomination.

dead center

dead end (n.) **dead-end** (adj.) *She reached a dead end. He has a dead-end job.*

Dead Sea Scrolls

deaf-mute This term may be used, but the preferred form is to say that an individual cannot hear or speak. A *mute* person may be deaf or may be able to hear.
Do not use *deaf and dumb.*

dean Capitalize when used as a formal title before a name: *Dean John Jones, Deans John Jones and Susan Smith.*
Lowercase in other uses: *John Jones, dean of the college; the dean.*

dean's list Lowercase in all uses: *He is on the dean's list. She is a dean's list student.*

deathbed (n. and adj.)

debenture See **loan terminology.**

decades Use Arabic figures to indicate decades of history. Use an apostrophe to indicate numerals that are left out; show plural by adding the letter *s*: *the 1890s, the '90s, the Gay '90s, the 1920s, the mid-1930s.*
See the **historical periods and events** entry.

decathlon Summaries include time or distance performance, points earned in that event and the cumulative total of points earned in previous events.

Contestants are listed in the order of their overall point totals. First name and hometown (or nation) are included only on the first and last events on the first day of competition; on the last day, first names are included only in the first event and in the summary denoting final placings.

Use the basic summary format. Include all entrants in summaries of each of the 10 events.

An example for individual events:

> **Decathlon**
> **(Group A)**
> 100-meter dash—1, Fred Dixon, Los Angeles, 10.8 seconds, 854 points. 2, Bruce Jenner, San Jose State, 11:09, 783. 3, Etc.
> Long jump—1, Dixon, 24-7 (7.34m), 889, 1,743. 2, Jenner, 23-6¼ (7.17m), 855, 1,638. 3, Etc.
>
> Decathlon final—1, Bruce Jenner, San Jose State, 8,524 points. 2, Fred Dixon, Los Angeles, 8,277. 3, Etc.

December See **months.**

deci- A prefix denoting one-tenth of a unit. Move a decimal point one place to the left in converting to the basic unit: 15.5 decigrams = 1.55 grams.

decimal units Use a period and numerals to indicate decimal amounts. Decimalization should not exceed two places in textual material unless there are special circumstances.
See **fractions.**

Declaration of Independence Lowercase *the declaration* whenever it stands alone.

decorations See the **awards and decorations** entry.

Deepfreeze A trademark for a brand of home freezer.
If something is being postponed indefinitely, use two words: *The project is in the deep freeze.*

deep-sea (adj.)

Deep South Capitalize both words when referring to the region that consists of Alabama, Georgia, Louisiana, Mississippi and South Carolina.

deep water (n.) **deep-water** (adj.) *The creature swam in deep water. The ship needs a deep-water port.*

default See **loan terminology**.

defendant

defense Do not use it as a verb.

defense attorney Always lowercase, never abbreviate.
See **attorney** and **titles**.

defense spending *Military spending* usually is the more precise term.

definitely Overused as a vague intensifier. Avoid it.

degree-day See **weather terms**.

degrees See **academic degrees**.

deity Lowercase. See **gods** and **religious references**.

dek- (before a vowel), **deka-** (before a consonant) A prefix denoting 10 units of a measure. Move a decimal point one place to the right to convert to the basic unit: 15.6 dekameters = 156 meters.

Delaware Abbrev.: *Del.* It has a land area of 2,057 square miles. Only Rhode Island is smaller in area, 1,049 square miles.
See **state names**.

delegate The formal title for members of the lower houses of some legislatures. Do not abbreviate. Capitalize only before their names. See **legislative titles**.
Always lowercase in other uses: *convention delegate Richard Henry Lee.*

Delmarva Peninsula The peninsula between Chesapeake Bay and the Atlantic Ocean. It consists of parts of the states of Delaware, Maryland and Virginia.

Delta Air Lines Headquarters is in Atlanta.

demagogue, demagoguery Not *demagog.*

democrat, democratic, Democratic Party See the **political parties and philosophies** entry.

Democratic Governors' Conference Note the apostrophe.

Democratic National Committee On second reference: *the national committee, the committee.*
Similarly: *Democratic State Committee, Democratic County Committee, Democratic City Committee, the state committee, the county committee, the city committee, the committee.*

demolish, destroy Both mean to do away with something completely. Something cannot be *partially demolished* or *destroyed.* It is redundant to say *totally demolished* or *totally destroyed.*

denote See the **connote, denote** entry.

Denver The city in Colorado stands alone in datelines.

depart Follow it with a preposition: *He will depart from LaGuardia. She will depart at 11:30 a.m.*
Do not drop the preposition as some airline dispatchers do.

Department of Agriculture; Department of Commerce; Department of Defense; Department of Energy (*DOE* acceptable on second reference); **Department of Health, Education and Welfare** (*HEW* acceptable on second reference); **Department of Housing and Urban**

Development (*HUD* acceptable on second reference); **Department of Justice; Department of Labor; Department of State; Department of Transportation** (*DOT* acceptable on second reference); **Department of the Treasury.**

The *of* may be dropped and the title flopped while capitalization is retained: *the State Department.*

Lowercase *department* in plural uses, but capitalize the proper name element: *the departments of Labor and Justice.*

A shorthand reference to the proper name element also is capitalized: *Kissinger said, "State and Justice must resolve their differences."* But: *Henry Kissinger, the secretary of state.*

Lowercase *the department* whenever it stands alone.

Do not abbreviate *department* in any usage.

See **academic departments.**

dependent (n. and adj.) Not *dependant.*

depreciation The reduction in the value of capital goods due to wear and tear or obsolescence.

Estimated depreciation may be deducted from income each year as one of the costs of doing business.

depression Capitalize *Depression* and *the Great Depression* when referring to the worldwide economic hard times generally regarded as having begun with the stock market collapse of Oct. 28-29, 1929.

Lowercase in other uses: *the depression of the 1970s.*

depths See **dimensions.**

deputy Capitalize as a formal title before a name. See **titles.**

derogatory terms Do not use derogatory terms such as *krauts* (for Germans) or *niggers* (for Negroes) except in direct quotes, and then only when their use is an integral, essential part of the story.

See the **obscenities, profanities, vulgarities** entry and **word selection.**

-designate Hyphenate: *chairman-designate.* Capitalize only the first word if used as a formal title before a name.

See **titles.**

destroy See the **demolish, destroy** entry.

detective Do not abbreviate. Capitalize before a name only if it is a formal rank: *police Detective Frank Serpico, private detective Richard Diamond.*

See **titles.**

detente

detention center See the **prison, jail** entry.

Detroit The city in Michigan stands alone in datelines.

devaluation See the **currency depreciation, currency devaluation** entry.

devil But capitalize *Satan.*

Dexedrine A trademark for a brand of appetite suppressant. It also may be called *dextroamphetamine sulfate.*

dialect The form of language peculiar to a region or a group, usually in matters of pronunciation or syntax. Dialect should be avoided, even in quoted matter, unless it is clearly pertinent to a story.

There are some words and phrases in everyone's vocabulary that are typical of a particular region or group. Quoting dialect, unless used carefully, implies substandard or illiterate usage.

When there is a compelling reason to use dialect, words or phrases are spelled phonetically, and apostrophes show missing letters and sounds: *"Din't ya yoosta live at Toidy-Toid Street and Sekun' Amya? Across from da moom pitchers?"*

See **Americanisms; colloquialisms; quotes in the news;** and **word selection.**

dialogue (n.)

diarrhea

Dictaphone A trademark for a brand of dictation recorder.

dictionaries For spelling, style and usage questions not covered in this stylebook, consult Webster's New World Dictionary of the American Language, Second College Edition, published by William Collins-World Publishing Co. Inc. of New York and Cleveland.

Use the first spelling listed in Webster's New World unless a specific exception is listed in this book. (The principal exception is the requirement that a hyphen be used in most words that begin with *anti-* or *non-.*)

If Webster's New World provides different spellings in separate entries (*tee shirt* and *T-shirt,* for example), use the spelling that is followed by a full definition (*T-shirt*).

If Webster's New World provides definitions under two different spellings for the same sense of a word, either use is acceptable. For example: *although* or *though.*

If there is no listing in either this book or Webster's New World, the backup dictionary, with more listings, is Webster's Third New International Dictionary, published by G. & C. Merriam Co. of Springfield, Mass.

Webster's New World is also the first reference for geographic names not covered in this stylebook. See **geographic names.**

die-hard (n. and adj.)

Diet The Japanese parliament. See **foreign legislative bodies.**

dietitian Not *dietician.*

different Takes the preposition *from,* not *than.*

differ from, differ with *To differ from* means to be unlike.
To differ with means to disagree.

dilemma It means more than a problem. It implies a choice between two unattractive alternatives.

dimensions Use figures and spell out *inches, feet, yards,* etc., to indicate depth, height, length and width. Hyphenate adjectival forms before nouns.

EXAMPLES: *He is 5 feet 6 inches tall, the 5-foot-6-inch man, the 5-foot-6 man, the 5-foot man, the basketball team signed a 7-footer.*
The car is 17 feet long, 6 feet wide and 5 feet high. The rug is 9 feet by 12 feet, the 9-by-12 rug.
The storm left 5 inches of snow.

Use an apostrophe to indicate feet and quote marks to indicate inches (*5'6"*) only in very technical contexts.

Diners Club No apostrophe, in keeping with the practice the company has adopted for its public identity. Only its incorporation papers still read *Diners' Club.*

Headquarters is in New York.

diocese Capitalize as part of a proper name: *the Diocese of Rochester, the Rochester Diocese, the diocese.*

See **Episcopal Church** and **Roman Catholic Church.**

directions and regions In general, lowercase *north, south, northeast, northern,* etc. when they indicate compass direction; capitalize these words when they designate regions.

Some examples:

COMPASS DIRECTION: *He drove west. The cold front is moving east.*

REGIONS: *A storm system that developed in the Midwest is spreading eastward. It will bring showers to the East Coast by morning and to the entire Northeast by late in the day. Warm temperatures will prevail throughout the Western states.*
The North was victorious. The South will rise again. Settlers from the East

went west in search of new lives. The customs of the East are different from those of the West. The Northeast depends on the Midwest for its food supply.

She has a Southern accent. He is a Northerner. Nations of the Orient are opening doors to Western businessmen. The candidate developed a Southern strategy. She is a Northern liberal.

The storm developed in the South Pacific. Leaders of Western Europe met leaders of Eastern Europe to talk about supplies of oil from Southeast Asia.

WITH NAMES OF NATIONS: Lowercase unless they are part of a proper name or are used to designate a politically divided nation: northern France, eastern Canada, the western United States.

But: Northern Ireland, East Germany, South Korea.

WITH STATES AND CITIES: The preferred form is to lowercase compass points when they describe a section of a state or city: western Texas, southern Atlanta.

But capitalize compass points:
—When part of a proper name: North Dakota, West Virginia.
—When used in denoting widely known sections: Southern California, the South Side of Chicago, the Lower East Side of New York. If in doubt, use lowercase.

IN FORMING PROPER NAMES: When combining with another common noun to form the name for a region or location: the North Woods, the South Pole, the Far East, the Middle East, the West Coast (the entire region, not the coastline itself — see **coast**), the Eastern Shore (see separate entry), the Western Hemisphere.

director The formal title for the individuals who head the Federal Bureau of Investigation and the Central Intelligence Agency. Capitalize when used immediately before their names or those of others for whom director is a formal title: FBI Director J. Edgar Hoover.

Most uses of director, however, involve an occupational description not capitalized in any use: company director Joseph Warren.

See **titles**.

dis- The rules in **prefixes** apply, but in general, no hyphen. Some examples:

dismember disservice
dissemble dissuade

disc jockey DJ is acceptable on second reference in a column or other special context. Use announcer in other contexts.

discreet, discrete Discreet means prudent, circumspect: "I'm afraid I was not very discreet," she wrote.

Discrete means detached, separate: There are four discrete sounds from a quadraphonic system.

discus The disk thrown in track and field events.

diseases Do not capitalize arthritis, emphysema, leukemia, malaria, migraine, pneumonia, etc.

When a disease is known by the name of a person identified with it, capitalize only the individual's name: Bright's disease, Parkinson's disease, etc.

disinterested, uninterested Disinterested means impartial, which is usually the better word to convey the thought.

Uninterested means that someone lacks interest.

dispel, dispelled, dispelling

disposable personal income The income that a person retains after deductions for income taxes, Social Security taxes, property taxes and for other payments such as fines and penalties to various levels of government.

Disposall A trademark for a type of mechanical garbage disposer.

dissociate Not disassociate.

distances Use figures for *10* and above, spell out *one* through *nine: He walked four miles.*

Distant Early Warning line *DEW line* is acceptable on second reference for this series of radar stations near the 70th parallel in North America.

district Always spell it out. Use a figure and capitalize *district* when forming a proper name: *the 2nd District.*

district attorney Do not abbreviate. Capitalize when used as a formal title before a name: *District Attorney Hamilton Burger.*
Use *DA* (no periods) only in quoted matter.
See **titles**.

district court See **court names** and **U.S. District Court.**

District of Columbia Abbreviate as *D.C.* when the context requires that it be used in conjunction with *Washington.* Spell out when used alone.
The district, rather than *D.C.*, should be used in subsequent references.

ditto marks They can be made with quotation marks, but their use in newspapers, even in tabular material, is confusing. Don't use them.

dive, dived, diving Not *dove* for the past tense.

divided nations Use *East Germany, South Korea*, etc. See **datelines** and entries under the names of these nations.

dividend In a financial sense, the word describes the payment per share that a corporation distributes to its stockholders as their return on the money they have invested in its stock.
See **profit terminology.**

diving Use a basic summary.
See **skating, figure** for the style on compulsory dives.

division See the **organizations and institutions** entry; **military units**; and **political divisions.**

divorcee The fact that a woman has been divorced should be mentioned only if a similar story about a man would mention his marital status.
When the woman's marital status is relevant, it seldom belongs in the lead. Avoid stories that begin: *A 35-year-old divorcee . . .*
The preferred form is to say in the body of the story that a woman is divorced.

Dixie cup A trademark for a paper drinking cup.

doctor Use *Dr.* in first reference as a formal title before the name of an individual who holds a doctor of medicine degree: *Dr. Jonas Salk.*
The form *Dr.*, or *Drs.* in a plural construction, applies to all first-reference uses before a name, including direct quotations.
If appropriate in the context, *Dr.* also may be used on first reference before the names of individuals who hold other types of doctoral degrees. However, because the public frequently identifies *Dr.* only with physicians, care should be taken to assure that the individual's specialty is stated in first or second reference. The only exception would be a story in which the context left no doubt that the person was a dentist, psychologist, chemist, historian, etc.
In some instances it also is necessary to specify that an individual identified as *Dr.* is a physician. One frequent case is a story reporting on joint research by physicians, biologists, etc.
Do not use *Dr.* before the names of individuals who hold only honorary doctorates.
Do not continue the use of *Dr.* in subsequent references.
See **academic degrees; courtesy titles**; and **religious titles.**

dogs See **animals.**

dollars Always lowercase. Use figures and the *$* sign in all except casual references or amounts without a figure: *The book cost $4. Dad, please give me a dollar. Dollars are flowing overseas.*

For specified amounts, the word takes a singular verb: *He said $500,000 is what they want.*

For amounts of more than $1 million, use the *$* and numerals up to two decimal places. Do not link the numerals and the word by a hyphen: *He is worth $4.35 million. He is worth exactly $4,351,242. He proposed a $300 billion budget.*

The form for amounts less than $1 million: *$4, $25, $500, $1,000, $650,000.*

See **cents**.

domino, dominoes

door to door, door-to-door Hyphenate when used as a compound modifier: *He is a door-to-door salesman.*

But: *He went from door to door.*

double-faced

doughnut Not *donut.*

Dow Jones & Co. The company publishes the Wall Street Journal and Barron's National Business and Financial Weekly. It also operates the Dow Jones News Service.

For stock market watchers, it provides the Dow Jones industrial average, the Dow Jones transportation average, the Dow Jones utility average, and the Dow Jones composite average.

Headquarters is in New York.

down- The rules in **prefixes** apply, but in general, no hyphen. Some examples:

downgrade	downtown

-down Follow Webster's New World. Some examples, all nouns and/or adjectives:

breakdown	rundown
countdown	sit-down

All are two words when used as verbs.

Down East Use only in reference to Maine.

downstate Lowercase unless part of a proper name: *downstate Illinois.* But: *the Downstate Medical Center.*

Down Under Australia, New Zealand and environs.

Dr. See **doctor**.

draft beer Not *draught beer.*

drama See **composition titles**.

Dramamine A trademark for a brand of motion sickness remedy.

Drambuie A trademark for a brand of Scottish liqueur.

dressing room

Dripolator A trademark for brand of drip coffeemaker.

drive See **addresses**.

drive-in (n.)

drop out (v.) **dropout** (n.)

drought

drowned, was drowned If a person suffocates in water or other fluid, the proper statement is that the individual *drowned.* To say that someone *was drowned* implies that another person caused the death by holding the victim's head under the water.

Dr Pepper A trademark (no period after *Dr*) for a brand of soft drink.

drugs Because the word *drugs* has come to be used as a synonym for narcotics in recent years, *medicine* is frequently the better word to specify that an individual is taking medication.

drunk, drunken *Drunk* is the spelling of the adjective used after a form of the verb *to be: He was drunk.*

Drunken is the spelling of the adjective used before nouns: *a drunken driver, drunken driving.*

drunkenness

duel A contest between two persons. Three persons cannot duel.

duffel Not *duffle.*

duke, duchess See **nobility.**

Dunkirk Use this spelling rather than *Dunkerque,* in keeping with widespread practice.

du Pont, E.I. Note the spelling of the name of U.S. industrialist born in France. Use *du Pont* on second reference.

The company named after him is *E.I. du Pont de Nemours & Co.* of Wilmington, Del. Capitalize the shortened form *Du Pont* in keeping with company practice. The shortened form is acceptable in all references.

See **foreign particles.**

dust storm See **weather terms.**

Dutch oven, Dutch treat, Dutch uncle

dyed-in-the-wool (adj.)

dyeing, dying *Dyeing* refers to changing colors.

Dying refers to death.

each Takes a singular verb.

each other, one another Two persons look at *each other*.

More than two look at *one another*.

Either phrase may be used when the number is indefinite: *We help each other. We help one another.*

earl, countess See **nobility.**

earmark

earnings per share See **profit terminology.**

earth Generally lowercase; capitalize when used as the proper name of the planet. *She is down to earth. How does that pattern apply to Mars, Jupiter, Earth, the sun and the moon? The astronauts returned to Earth. He hopes to move heaven and earth.*

See **planets.**

earthquakes Hundreds of earthquakes occur each year. Most are so small they cannot be felt.

First reports on major earthquakes often come from the National Earthquake Information Service operated by the U.S. Geological Survey in Golden, Colo., or the Uppsala Seismological Institute in Uppsala, Sweden.

There are two important scales in measuring earthquakes, the Richter scale and the Mercalli scale.

The difference between them is what they measure. The Richter scale, the more common, provides information on the magnitude — the inherent strength — of a quake. The Mercalli scale describes the intensity of a quake — the degree to which it is felt in a given area.

Dr. Charles F. Richter, whose work in the 1930s led to the scale that bears his name, illustrates the difference by comparing a quake to a radio signal: The magnitude of the signal is the same no matter where you are. Its intensity varies depending on your distance from the transmitter.

RICHTER SCALE: The Richter scale is a gauge of the energy released by an earthquake, as measured by the ground motion recorded on a seismograph.

Every increase of one number, say from magnitude 5.5 to magnitude 6.5, means that the ground motion is 10 times greater. Some experts say the actual amount of energy released may be 30 times greater.

Theoretically, there is no upper limit to the scale, although it often erroneously is reported to be 10. Readings of 8.9, the highest on record, were computed from seismographic records of a quake off the coast of Ecuador in 1906 and from a quake off the coast of Japan in 1933.

A quake of magnitude 2 is the smallest normally felt by humans.

The relationship between a Richter reading and the potential for damage in populated areas is as follows:

—A quake of magnitude 3.5 can cause slight damage.

—Magnitude 4: The quake can cause moderate damage.

—Magnitude 5: The quake can cause considerable damage.

—Magnitude 6: The quake can cause severe damage.

—Magnitude 7: A major earthquake, capable of widespread, heavy damage.

—Magnitude 8: A "great" earthquake, capable of tremendous damage.

Early in 1977, a group of scientists suggested a new way to compute Richter readings. Officials of the National Earthquake Information Service and similar bodies said they would study the proposal. The method of providing Richter readings would not change, they said, at least until agreement on a new format could be reached through an international conference or similar forum.

MERCALLI SCALE: The Mercalli scale gauges the intensity of an earthquake as felt in a specific location.

The scale runs from 1 to 12: A 1 reading is "not felt except by very few, favorably situated." A 12 reading is "damage total, lines of sight disturbed, objects thrown into the air."

NOTABLE QUAKES: Earthquakes noted for both their magnitude and the amount of damage they caused include:

—Shensi province of China, January 1556: Killed 830,000 people, the largest number of fatalities on record from an earthquake.

—Tokyo and Yokohama, Japan, September 1923: Highest Richter reading later computed as 8.3. The quake and subsequent fires destroyed most of both cities, killing an estimated 200,000 people. Until the China quake of 1976, this was the highest fatality toll in the 20th century.

—San Francisco, April 1906: Highest Richter reading later computed as 8.3. The quake and subsequent fire were blamed for an estimated 700 deaths.

—Alaska, March 1964: Highest Richter reading 8.5. Killed 114 people.

—Guatemala, February 1976: Highest Richter reading 7.5. Authorities reported more than 23,000 deaths.

—Hopeh province of northern China, July 28, 1976: Highest Richter reading 8.3. A government document later said 655,237 people were killed and 779,000 injured. The fatality total was second only to the toll in the Shensi quake of 1556.

OTHER TERMS: The word *temblor* (not *tremblor*) is a synonym for *earthquake*.

The word *epicenter* means the center of an earthquake.

east, eastern See the **directions and regions** entry.

Easter In the computation used by the Latin Rite of the Roman Catholic Church and by Protestant churches, it falls on the first Sunday after the first full moon that occurs on or after March 21. If the full moon falls on a Sunday, Easter is the next Sunday.

Easter may fall, therefore, between March 22 and April 25 inclusive.

Eastern Airlines Use this spelling of *airlines,* which Eastern has adopted for its public identity. Only its incorporation papers still read *air lines.*

Headquarters is in Miami.

Eastern Hemisphere The half of the earth made up primarily of Africa, Asia, Australia and Europe.

Eastern Orthodox churches The term applies to a group of churches that have roots in the earliest days of Christianity and do not recognize papal authority over their activities.

Churches in this tradition were part of the undivided Christendom that existed until the Great Schism of 1054. At that time, many of the churches in the western half of the old Roman Empire accorded the bishop of Rome supremacy over other bishops. The result was a split between eastern and western churches.

The autonomous churches that constitute Eastern Orthodoxy are organized along mostly national lines. They recognize the patriarch of Constantinople (modern-day Istanbul) as their leader. He convenes councils, but his authority is otherwise that of a "first among equals."

Eastern Orthodox churches today count about 200 million members. They include the Greek Orthodox Church, the Romanian Orthodox Church and the Russian Orthodox Church.

In the United States, organizational lines are based on the national backgrounds of various ethnic groups. The largest is the Greek Orthodox Archdiocese of North and South America, with about 2 million members. Next is the Orthodox Church in America, with about 1 million members, including people of Bulgarian, Romanian, Russian and Syrian descent.

BELIEFS: The term *orthodox* (literally "right believing") derives from the adherence of these churches to the teachings of only the seven ecumenical councils held before the Great Schism. The schism was caused, in part, by a Rome-approved change in wording that the Council of Nicea had used in defining the doctrine of the Holy Spirit.

Aside from the question of papal supremacy, beliefs are generally the same as those described in the Roman Catholic Church entry.

Liturgies reflect cultural heritages. The principal worship service is called the Divine Liturgy.

The churches have their own disciplines on matters such as married clergy — a married man may be ordained, but a priest may not marry after ordination.

CLERGY: Some of these churches call the archbishop who leads them a *metropolitan*, others use the term *patriarch*. He normally heads the principal archdiocese within a nation. Working with him are other archbishops, bishops, priests and deacons.

Archbishops and bishops frequently follow a monastic tradition in which they are known only by a first name. When no last name is used, repeat the title before the sole name in subsequent references.

Some forms: *Metropolitan Ireney, archbishop of New York and metropolitan of America and Canada.* On second reference: *Metropolitan Ireney. Archbishop* may be replaced by *the Most Rev.* on first reference. *Bishop* may be replaced by *the Rt. Rev.* on first reference.

Use *the Rev.* before the name of a priest on first reference; *Deacon* before the name of a deacon on first reference. Use only last names, customarily available for priests and deacons, in subsequent references.

See **religious titles**.

Eastern Rite churches The term applies to a group of Roman Catholic churches that are organized along ethnic lines traceable to the churches established during the earliest days of Christianity.

These churches accept the authority of the pope, but they have considerable autonomy in ritual and questions of discipline such as married clergy — a married man may be ordained, but marriage is not permitted after ordination.

Worldwide membership totals more than 10 million.

Among the churches of the Eastern Rite are the Antiochean-Maronite, Armenian Catholic, Byzantine-Byelorussian, Byzantine-Melkite, Byzantine-Romanian, Byzantine-Russian, Byzantine-Ruthenian, Byzantine-Ukrainian and Chaldean Catholic.

See **Roman Catholic Church**.

Eastern Shore A region on the east side of Chesapeake Bay, including parts of Maryland and Virginia.

Eastern Shore is not a synonym for *East Coast*.

Eastern Standard Time (EST), Eastern Daylight Time (EDT) See **time zones**.

East Germany Use both words, not *Germany* alone, after cities and towns in the German Democratic Republic.

See **Berlin** and **West Germany**.

easygoing

ecology The study of the relationship between organisms and their surroundings. It is not synonymous with *environment.*
Right: *The laboratory is studying the ecology of man and the desert.*
Wrong: *Even so simple an undertaking as maintaining a lawn affects ecology.* (Use *environment* instead.)

editor Capitalize *editor* before a name only when it is an official corporate or organizational title. Do not capitalize as a job description.
See **titles.**

editorial, news In references to a newspaper, reserve *news* for the news department, its employees and news articles. Reserve *editorial* for the department that prepares the editorial page, its employees and articles that appear on the editorial page.

editor in chief No hyphens. Capitalize when used as a formal title before a name: *Editor in Chief Horace Greeley.*
See **titles.**

effect See the **affect, effect** entry.

Eglin Air Force Base, Fla. Not *Elgin.*

either Use it to mean *one or the other,* not *both.*
Right: *She said to use either door.*
Wrong: *There were lions on either side of the door.*
Right: *There were lions on each side of the door. There were lions on both sides of the door.*

either . . . or, neither . . . nor The nouns that follow these words do not constitute a compound subject; they are alternate subjects and require a verb that agrees with the nearer subject:
Neither they nor he is going. Neither he nor they are going.

El Al Israel Airlines An *El Al airliner* is acceptable in any reference.
Headquarters is in Tel Aviv.

elder For its use in religious contexts, see the entry for an individual's denomination.

elderly Use this word carefully and sparingly. It is not appropriate in describing anyone under 65 and should not be used casually in referring to anyone beyond that age.
It is appropriate in generic phrases that do not refer to specific individuals: *concern for the elderly, a home for the elderly,* etc.
If the intent is to show that an individual's faculties have deteriorated, cite a graphic example: *His memory fades. She walks with a cane.*
Apply the same principle to terms such as *senior citizen.*

-elect Always hyphenate and lowercase: *President-elect Carter.*

Election Day The first Tuesday after the first Monday in November.

election returns Use figures, with commas every three digits starting at the right and counting left. Use the word *to* (not a hyphen) in separating different totals listed together: *Jimmy Carter defeated Gerald Ford 40,827,292 to 39,146,157 in 1976* (this is the actual final figure).
Use the word *votes* if there is any possibility that the figures could be confused with a ratio: *Nixon defeated McGovern 16 votes to 3 votes in Dixville Notch.*
Do not attempt to create adjectival forms such as *the 40,827,292-39,146,157 vote.*
See **vote tabulations.**

Electoral College But *electoral vote(s).*

electrocardiogram *EKG* is acceptable on second reference.

ellipsis (...) In general, treat an ellipsis as a three-letter word, constructed with three periods and two spaces, as shown here.

Use an ellipsis to indicate the deletion of one or more words in condensing quotes, texts and documents. Be especially careful to avoid deletions that would distort the meaning.

Brief examples of how to use ellipses are provided after guidelines are given. More extensive examples, drawn from the speech in which President Nixon announced his resignation, are in the sections below marked CONDENSATION EXAMPLE and QUOTATIONS.

SPACING REQUIREMENTS: In some computer editing systems the *thin space*, represented here by the || symbol, must be used between the periods of the ellipsis to prevent them from being placed on two different lines when they are sent through a computer that handles hyphenation and justification.

Leave one regular space — never a thin — on both sides of an ellipsis: *I*.||.||. *tried to do what was best.*

PUNCTUATION GUIDELINES: If the words that precede an ellipsis constitute a gramatically complete sentence, either in the original or in the condensation, place a period at the end of the last word before the ellipsis. Follow it with a regular space and an ellipsis: *I no longer have a strong enough political base....*

When the grammatical sense calls for a question mark, exclamation point, comma or colon, the sequence is word, punctuation mark, regular space, ellipsis: *Will you come?...*

When material is deleted at the end of one paragraph and at the beginning of the one that follows, place an ellipsis in both locations.

CONDENSATION EXAMPLE: Here is an example of how the spacing and punctuation guidelines would be applied in condensing President Nixon's resignation announcement:

Good evening....
In all the decisions I have made in my

public life, I have always tried to do what was best for the nation....
... however, it has become evident to me that I no longer have a strong enough political base in the Congress.
... As long as there was a base, I felt strongly that it was necessary to see the constitutional process through to its conclusion, that to do otherwise would be ... a dangerously destabilizing precedent for the future.

QUOTATIONS: In writing a story, do not use ellipses at the beginning and end of direct quotes:
"It has become evident to me that I no longer have a strong enough political base," Nixon said.
Not: *"... it has become evident to me that I no longer have a strong enough political base ...," Nixon said.*

HESITATION: An ellipsis also may be used to indicate a pause or hesitation in speech, or a thought that the speaker or writer does not complete. Substitute a dash for this purpose, however, if the context uses ellipses to indicate that words actually spoken or written have been deleted.

SPECIAL EFFECTS: Ellipses also may be used to separate individual items within a paragraph of show business gossip or similar material. Use periods after items that are complete sentences.

El Salvador The use of the article in the name of this nation helps to distinguish it from its capital, *San Salvador*.

Use *Salvadoran(s)* in references to citizens of the nation.

embargo See the **boycott, embargo** entry.

embargo times See **release times**.

embarrass, embarrassing, embarrassed, embarrassment

embassy An *embassy* is the official residence of an ambassador in a foreign country and the office that handles the political relations of one nation with another.

A *consulate*, the residence of a consul in a foreign city, handles the commercial affairs and personal needs of citizens of the appointing country.

Capitalize with the name of a nation; lowercase without it: *the French Embassy, the U.S. Embassy, the embassy.*

emcee, emceed, emceeing A colloquial verb and noun best avoided. A phrase such as *He was the master of ceremonies* is preferred.

emeritus This word often is added to formal titles to denote that individuals who have retired retain their rank or title.

When used, place *emeritus* after the formal title, in keeping with the general practice of academic institutions: *Professor Emeritus Samuel Eliot Morison, Dean Emeritus Cortney C. Brown, Publisher Emeritus Barnard L. Colby.*

Or: *Samuel Eliot Morison, professor emeritus of history; Cortney C. Brown, dean emeritus of the faculty of business; Barnard L. Colby, publisher emeritus.*

emigrate, immigrate One who leaves a country *emigrates* from it.

One who comes into a country *immigrates*.

The same principle holds for *emigrant* and *immigrant*.

Emmy, Emmys The annual awards by the National Academy of Television Arts and Sciences.

Empirin A trademark for a brand of aspirin compound.

employee Not *employe*.

empty-handed

enact See the **adopt, approve, enact, pass** entry.

encyclopedia But follow the spelling of formal names: *Encyclopaedia Britannica.*

Energy Research and Development Administration It no longer exists. Its functions were transferred in 1977 to the Department of Energy.

enforce But *reinforce*.

engine, motor An *engine* develops its own power, usually through internal combustion or the pressure of air, steam or water passing over vanes attached to a wheel: *an airplane engine, an automobile engine, a jet engine, a missile engine, a steam engine, a turbine engine.*

A *motor* receives power from an outside source: *an electric motor, a hydraulic motor.*

England *London* stands alone in datelines. Use *England* after the names of other English communities in datelines.

See **datelines** and **United Kingdom**.

English muffin, English sparrow, English setter

Enovid A trademark for a brand of birth control pill. It also may be called *norethynodrel with mestranol.*

enquire, enquiry The preferred words are *inquire, inquiry.*

enroll, enrolled, enrolling

en route Always two words.

ensign See **military titles**.

ensure, insure Use *ensure* to mean guarantee: *Steps were taken to ensure accuracy.*

Use *insure* for references to insurance: *The policy insures his life.*

entitled Use it to mean a right to do or have something. Do not use it to mean *titled*.

Right: *She was entitled to the promotion.*

Right: *The book was titled "Gone With the Wind."*

enumerations See examples in the **dash** and **periods** entries.

envelop Other verb forms: *enveloping, enveloped.* But: *envelope* (n.)

environment See **ecology.**

Environmental Protection Agency *EPA* is acceptable on second reference.

envoy Not a formal title. Lowercase. See **titles.**

epicenter The center of an earthquake. See **earthquakes.**

epidemiology

Episcopal, Episcopalian *Episcopal* is the adjective form; use *Episcopalian* only as a noun referring to a member of the Episcopal Church: *She is an Episcopalian.* But: *She is an Episcopal priest.*

Capitalize *Episcopal* when referring to the Episcopal Church. Use lowercase when the reference is simply to a body governed by bishops.

Episcopal Church Acceptable in all references for the *Protestant Episcopal Church*, the U.S. national church that is a member of the Anglican Communion.

The church is governed nationally by two bodies — the permanent Executive Council and the General Convention, which meets every three years.

After the council, the principal organizational units are, in descending order of size, provinces, dioceses or missionary districts, local parishes and local missions.

The National Council is composed of bishops, priests, laymen and laywomen. One bishop is designated the leader and holds the formal title of presiding bishop. The council is responsible for furthering the missionary, educational and social work of the church.

The General Convention has final authority in matters of policy and doctrine. All acts must pass both of its houses — the House of Bishops and the House of Deputies. The latter is composed of an equal number of clergy and lay delegates from each diocese.

A province is composed of several dioceses. Each has a provincial synod made up of a house of bishops and a house of deputies. The synod's primary duty is to coordinate the work of the church in its area.

Within a diocese, a bishop is the principal official. He is helped by the Diocesan Convention, which consists of all the clergy in the diocese and lay representatives from each parish. The convention adopts a budget, elects a bishop in the case of a vacancy, and elects delegates to the General Convention and the Provincial Synod.

The parish or local church is governed by a vestry, composed of the pastor and lay members elected by the congregation.

BELIEFS: See **Anglican Communion.**

CLERGY: The clergy consists of bishops, priests, deacons and brothers. A priest who heads a parish is described as a *rector* rather than a *pastor.* The term *minister* seldom is used.

For first reference to bishops, use *Bishop* before the individual's name: *Bishop John M. Allin.* An acceptable alternative in referring to U.S. bishops is *the Rt. Rev.* The designation *the Most Rev.* is used before the names of the archbishops of Canterbury and York.

For first references to men, use *the Rev.* before the name of a priest, *Deacon* before the name of a deacon, *Brother* before the name of a brother. On second reference, use only the last name.

For first references to women, use *the Rev.* before the name of a priest, *Deacon* before the name of a deacon. On second reference, use *Miss, Mrs.* or *Ms.* before the woman's last name, depending on her preference.

See **Anglican Communion** and **religious titles.**

epoch See the **historical periods and events** entry.

equal An adjective without comparative forms.

When people speak of a *more equal* distribution of wealth, what is meant is *more equitable*.

equal, equaled, equaling

Equal Employment Opportunity Commission *EEOC* is acceptable on second reference.

equally as Do not use the words together; one is sufficient.

Omit the *equally* shown here in parentheses: *She was (equally) as pretty as Marilyn.*

Omit the *as* shown here in parentheses: *She and Marilyn were equally (as) pretty.*

Equal Rights Amendment *ERA* is acceptable on second reference.

Ratification requires approval by three-fourths (38) of the 50 states within seven years of March 22, 1972, the date Congress submitted it to the states.

The text:

Section 1. Equality of rights under the law shall not be denied or abridged by the United States or by any state on account of sex.

Section 2. The Congress shall have the power to enforce, by appropriate legislation, the provisions of this article.

Section 3. This amendment shall take effect two years after the date of ratification.

equal time, fairness doctrine *Equal time* applies to the Federal Communications Commission regulation that requires a radio or television station to provide a candidate for political office with air time equal to any time

that an opponent receives beyond the coverage of news events.

If a station broadcasts material that takes a stand on a controverial issue, the FCC's *fairness doctrine* may require it to give advocates of a different position an opportunity to respond.

equator Always lowercase.

equitable See **equal.**

equity When used in a financial sense, *equity* means the value of property beyond the amount that is owed on it.

A *stockholder's equity* in a corporation is the value of the shares he holds.

A *homeowner's equity* is the difference between the value of the house and the amount of the unpaid mortgage.

ERA Acceptable in all references to baseball's *earned run average.*

Acceptable on second reference for *Equal Rights Amendment.*

eras See the **historical periods and events** entry.

escalator Formerly a trademark, now a generic term.

escalator clause A clause in a contract providing for increases or decreases in wages, prices, etc., based on fluctuations in the cost of living, production, expenses, etc.

escapee The preferred words are *escaped convict* or *fugitive.*

Eskimo, Eskimos

espresso The coffee is *espresso*, not *expresso.*

essential clauses, non-essential clauses These terms are used in this book instead of *restrictive clause* and *non-restrictive clause* to convey the distinction between the two in a more easily remembered manner.

Both types of clauses provide additional information about a word or phrase in the sentence.

The difference between them is that the essential clause cannot be eliminated without changing the meaning of the sentence — it so "restricts" the meaning of the word or phrase that its absence would lead to a substantially different interpretation of what the author meant.

The non-essential clause, however, can be eliminated without altering the basic meaning of the sentence — it does not "restrict" the meaning so significantly that its absence would radically alter the author's thought.

PUNCTUATION: An essential clause must not be set off from the rest of a sentence by commas. A non-essential clause must be set off by commas.

The presence or absence of commas provides the reader with critical information about the writer's intended meaning. Note the following examples:

—*Reporters who do not read the stylebook should not criticize their editors.* (The writer is saying that only one class of reporters, those who do not read the stylebook, should not criticize their editors. If the *who . . . stylebook* phrase were deleted, the meaning of the sentence would be changed substantially.)

—*Reporters, who do not read the stylebook, should not criticize their editors.* (The writer is saying that all reporters should not criticize their editors. If the *who . . . stylebook* phrase were deleted, this meaning would not be changed.)

USE OF WHO, THAT, WHICH: When an essential or non-essential clause refers to a human being or an animal with a name, it should be introduced by *who* or *whom.* (See the **who, whom** entry.) Do not use commas if the clause is essential to the meaning; use them if it is not.

That is the preferred pronoun to introduce essential clauses that refer to an inanimate object or an animal without a name. *Which* is the only acceptable pronoun to introduce a non-essential clause

that refers to an inanimate object or an animal without a name.

The pronoun *which* occasionally may be substituted for *that* in the introduction of an essential clause that refers to an inanimate object or an animal without a name. In general, this use of *which* should appear only when *that* is used as a conjunction to introduce another clause in the same sentence: *He said Monday that the part of the army which suffered severe casualties needs reinforcement.*

See **that (conjunction)** for guidelines on the use of *that* as a conjunction.

essential phrases, non-essential phrases These terms are used in this book instead of *restrictive phrase* and *non-restrictive phrase* to convey the distinction between the two in a more easily remembered manner.

The underlying concept is the one that also applies to clauses:

An essential phrase is a word or group of words critical to the reader's understanding of what the author had in mind.

A non-essential phrase provides more information about something. Although the information may be helpful to the reader's comprehension, the reader would not be misled if the information were not there.

PUNCTUATION: Do not set an essential phrase off from the rest of a sentence by commas:

We saw the award-winning movie "One Flew Over the Cuckoo's Nest." (No comma, because many movies have won awards, and without the name of the movie the reader would not know which movie was meant.)

They ate dinner with their daughter Julie. (Because they have more than one daughter, the inclusion of Julie's name is critical if the reader is to know which daughter is meant.)

Set off non-essential phrases by commas:

We saw the 1976 winner in the Academy Award competition for best movie, "One Flew Over the Cuckoo's Nest."

(Only one movie won the award. The name is informative, but even without the name no other movie could be meant.)

They ate dinner with their daughter Julie and her husband, David. (Julie has only one husband. If the phrase read *and her husband David,* it would suggest that she had more than one husband.)

The company chairman, Henry Ford II, spoke. (In the context, only one person could be meant.)

Indian corn, or maize, was harvested. (*Maize* provides the reader with the name of the corn, but its absence would not change the meaning of the sentence.)

DESCRIPTIVE WORDS: Do not confuse punctuation rules for non-essential clauses with the correct punctuation when a non-essential word is used as a descriptive adjective. The distinguishing clue often is the lack of an article or pronoun:

Right: *Julie and husband David went shopping. Julie and her husband, David, went shopping.*

Right: *Company Chairman Henry Ford II made the announcement. The company chairman, Henry Ford II, made the announcement.*

Eurasian Of European and Asian descent.

Eurodollar A U.S. dollar on deposit in a European bank, including foreign branches of U.S. banks.

European Economic Community *Common Market* is acceptable in all references. See **Common Market** for a listing of members.

EEC is acceptable on second reference if the full name has appeared earlier in the story.

evangelical See **religious movements**.

Evangelical Friends Alliance See **Quakers**.

evangelism See **religious movements**.

evangelist Capitalize only in references to the men credited with writing the Gospels: *The four Evangelists were Matthew, Mark, Luke and John.*

In lowercase, it means a preacher who makes a profession of seeking conversions.

eve Capitalize when used after the name of a holiday: *New Year's Eve, Christmas Eve.* But: *the eve of Christmas.*

even-steven Not *even-stephen.*

every day (adv.) **everyday** (adj.) *He goes to work every day. She wears everyday shoes.*

every one, everyone Two words when it means each individual item: *Every one of the clues was worthless.*

One word when used as a pronoun meaning all persons: *Everyone wants his life to be happy.* (Note that *everyone* takes singular verbs and pronouns.)

ex- Use no hyphen for words that use *ex-* in the sense of *out of:*

excommunicate   expropriate

Hyphenate when using *ex-* in the sense of *former:*

ex-convict   ex-president

Do not capitalize *ex-* when attached to a formal title before a name: *ex-President Nixon.* The prefix modifies the entire term: *ex-New York Gov. Nelson Rockefeller;* not *New York ex Gov.*

Usually *former* is better.

exaggerate

Excedrin A trademark for a brand of aspirin compound.

except See the **accept, except** entry.

exclamation point (!) Follow these guidelines:

EMPHATIC EXPRESSIONS: Use the mark to express a high degree of surprise, incredulity or other strong emotion.

AVOID OVERUSE: Use a comma after mild interjections. End mildly exclamatory sentences with a period.

PLACEMENT WITH QUOTES: Place the mark inside quotation marks when it is part of the quoted material: *"How wonderful!" he exclaimed. "Never!" she shouted.*
Place the mark outside quotation marks when it is not part of the quoted material: *I hated reading Spenser's "Faerie Queene"!*

MISCELLANEOUS: Do not use a comma or a period after the exclamation mark:
Wrong: *"Halt!," the corporal cried.*
Right: *"Halt!" the corporal cried.*

execute *To execute* a person is to kill him in compliance with a military order or judicial decision.
See the **assassin, killer, murderer** entry and the **homicide, murder, manslaughter** entry.

executive branch Always lowercase.

executive director Capitalize before a name only if it is a formal corporate or organizational title.
See **titles.**

Executive Mansion Capitalize only in references to the *White House.*

Executive Protective Service It is now the *Secret Service Uniformed Division.*
See **Secret Service.**

executor Use for both men and women.
Not a formal title. Always lowercase.
See **titles.**

exorcise, exorcism Not *exorcize.*

expel, expelled, expelling

Explorers See **Boy Scouts.**

Export-Import Bank of the United States *Export-Import Bank* is acceptable in all references; *Ex-Im Bank* is acceptable on second.
Headquarters is in Washington.

extol, extolled, extolling

extra- Do not use a hyphen when *extra-* means *outside of* unless the prefix is followed by a word beginning with *a* or a capitalized word:

extralegal   extraterrestrial
extramarital   extraterritorial
But:
extra-alimentary   extra-Britannic
Follow *extra-* with a hyphen when it is part of a compound modifier describing a condition beyond the usual size, extent or degree:

extra-base hit   extra-large book
extra-dry drink   extra-mild taste

extraordinary loss, extraordinary income See **profit terminology.**

extrasensory perception *ESP* is acceptable on second reference.

extreme unction See **sacraments.**

Exxon Corp. Formerly Standard Oil Co. (New Jersey).
Headquarters is in New York.

eye, eyed, eyeing

eyestrain

eye to eye, eye-to-eye Hyphenate when used as a compound modifier: *an eye-to-eye confrontation.*

eyewitness

facade

face to face When a story says two persons met for discussions, talks or debate, it is unnecessary to say they met *face to face.*

fact-finding (adj.)

fade out (v.) **fade-out** (n.)

Faeroe Islands Use in datelines after a community name in stories from this group of Danish islands in the northern Atlantic Ocean between Iceland and the Shetland Islands.

Fahrenheit The temperature scale commonly used in the United States.

The scale is named for Gabriel Daniel Fahrenheit, a German physicist who designed it. In it, the freezing point of water is 32 degrees and the boiling point is 212 degrees.

To convert to Celsius, subtract 32 from the Fahrenheit figure, multiply by 5 and divide by 9 (77 − 32 = 45, times 5 = 225, divided by 9 = 25 degrees Celsius).

In cases that require mention of the scale, use these forms: *86 degrees Fahrenheit* or *86 F* (note the space and no period after the *F*) if degrees and Fahrenheit are clear from the context.

See **Celsius** and **Kelvin.**

For guidelines on when Celsius temperatures should be used, see the **metric system** entry.

TEMPERATURE CONVERSIONS

Following is a temperature conversion table. Celsius temperatures have been rounded to the nearest whole number.

F	C	F	C	F	C
− 26	− 32	19	− 7	64	18
− 24	− 31	21	− 6	66	19
− 22	− 30	23	− 5	68	20
− 20	− 29	25	− 4	70	21
− 18	− 28	27	− 3	72	22
− 17	− 27	28	− 2	73	23
− 15	− 26	30	− 1	75	24
− 13	− 25	32	0	77	25
− 11	− 24	34	1	79	26
− 9	− 23	36	2	81	27
− 8	− 22	37	3	82	28
− 6	− 21	39	4	84	29
− 4	− 20	41	5	86	30
− 2	− 19	43	6	88	31
0	− 18	45	7	90	32
1	− 17	46	8	91	33
3	− 16	48	9	93	34
5	− 15	50	10	95	35
7	− 14	52	11	97	36
9	− 13	54	12	99	37
10	− 12	55	13	100	38
12	− 11	57	14	102	39
14	− 10	59	15	104	40
16	− 9	61	16	106	41
18	− 8	63	17	108	42

fairness doctrine See the **equal time, fairness doctrine** entry.

fall See **seasons**.

fallout (n.)

false titles Always lowercase them. See **titles**.

family names Capitalize words denoting family relationships only when they precede the name of a person or when they stand unmodified as a substitute for a person's name: *I wrote to Grandfather Smith. I wrote Mother a letter. I wrote my mother a letter.*

Fannie Mae See **Federal National Mortgage Association.**

Fanny May A trademark for a brand of candy.

Far East The easternmost portions of the continent of Asia: China, Japan, North and South Korea, Taiwan, Hong Kong and the eastern portions of the Soviet Union.
Confine *Far East* to this restricted sense, as defined in the Columbia Lippincott Gazetteer. Use the *Far East and Southeast Asia* when referring to a wider portion of eastern Asia.
See the **Asian subcontinent** and **Southeast Asia** entries.

far-flung (adj.)

far-off (adj.)

far-ranging (adj.)

farsighted When used in a medical sense, it means that a person can see objects at a distance but has difficulty seeing material at close range.

farther, further *Farther* refers to physical distance: *He walked farther into the woods.*
Further refers to an extension of time or degree: *She will look further into the mystery.*

Far West For the U.S. region, generally west of the Rocky Mountains.

fascism, fascist See the **political parties and philosophies** entry.

father Use *the Rev.* in first reference before the names of Episcopal, Orthodox and Roman Catholic priests. Use *Father* before a name only in direct quotations.
See **religious titles.**

father-in-law, fathers-in-law

Father's Day The third Sunday in June.

Father Time

faze, phase *Faze* means to embarrass or disturb: *The snub did not faze her.*
Phase denotes an aspect or stage: *They will phase in a new system.*

FBI Acceptable in all references for *Federal Bureau of Investigation.*

feather bedding, featherbedding *Feather bedding* is a mattress stuffed with feathers.
Featherbedding is the practice of requiring an employer to hire more workers than needed to handle a job.

features They are not exempt from normal style rules. See **special contexts** for guidelines on some limited exceptions.

February See **months**.

federal Use a capital letter for the architectural style and for corporate or governmental bodies that use the word as part of their formal names: *Federal Express, the Federal Trade Commission.* (See separate entries for governmental agencies.)
Lowercase when used as an adjective to distinguish something from state, county, city, town or private entities:

federal assistance, federal court, the federal government, a federal judge.

Also: *federal District Court* (but *U.S. District Court* is preferred) and *federal Judge John Sirica* (but *U.S. District Judge John Sirica* is preferred).

Federal Aviation Administration
FAA is acceptable on second reference.

Federal Bureau of Investigation
FBI is acceptable in all references. To avoid alphabet soup, however, use *the bureau* in some references.

Federal Communications Commission
FCC is acceptable on second reference.

federal court
Always lowercase. The preferred form for first reference is to use the proper name of the court. See entries under **U.S.** and the court name.

Do not create non-existent entities such as *Manhattan Federal Court.* Instead, use *a federal court in Manhattan.*
See **judicial branch.**

Federal Crop Insurance Corp.
Do not abbreviate.

Federal Deposit Insurance Corp.
FDIC is acceptable on second reference.

Federal Energy Regulatory Commission
This agency replaced the Federal Power Commission in 1977. It regulates interstate natural gas and electricity transactions.

FERC is acceptable on second reference, but *the agency* or *the commission* is preferred.

Federal Farm Credit Board
Do not abbreviate.

Federal Highway Administration
Reserve the *FHA* abbreviation for the *Federal Housing Administration.*

Federal Home Loan Bank Board
Do not abbreviate.

Federal Housing Administration
FHA is acceptable on second reference.

federal legal holidays
See the **holidays and holy days** entry.

Federal Maritime Commission
Do not abbreviate.

Federal Mediation and Conciliation Service
Do not abbreviate. Use *the service* on second reference.

Federal National Mortgage Association
Fannie Mae is acceptable on second reference, but it should be identified as the nickname for the agency if the story is not being written primarily for business-oriented readers.

The association's bonds are known as *Fannie Maes.*

Federal Power Commission
It no longer exists. See **Federal Energy Regulatory Commission.**

Federal Register
This publication, issued every workday, is the legal medium for recording and communicating the rules and regulations established by the executive branch of the federal government.

Individuals or corporations cannot be held legally responsible for compliance with a regulation unless it has been published in the Register.

In addition, executive agencies are required to publish in advance some types of proposed regulations.

Federal Reserve System, Federal Reserve Board
On second reference, use *the Federal Reserve, the Reserve, the Fed, the system* or *the board.*

Also: *the Federal Reserve Bank of New York (Boston,* etc.), *the bank.*

Federal Trade Commission
FTC is acceptable on second reference.

felony, misdemeanor
A *felony* is a serious crime. A *misdemeanor* is a minor offense against the law.

A fuller definition of what constitutes a felony or misdemeanor depends on the governmental jurisdiction involved.

At the federal level, a *misdemeanor* is a crime that carries a potential penalty of no more than a year in jail. A *felony* is a crime that carries a potential penalty of more than a year in prison. Often, however, a statute gives a judge options such as imposing a fine or probation in addition to or instead of a jail or prison sentence.

A **felon** is a person who has been convicted of a felony, regardless of whether the individual actually spends time in confinement or is given probation or a fine instead.

See the **prison, jail** entry.

fencing Identify epee, foil and saber classes as: *men's individual foil, women's team foil,* etc.

Use a match summary for early rounds of major events, for lesser dual meets and for tournaments.

Use a basic summary for final results of major championships.

For major events, where competitors meet in a round-robin and are divided into pools, use this form:

Epee, first round (four qualify for semifinals) Pool 1—Joe Smith, Springfield, Mass., 4 1. Enrique Lopez, Chile, 3-2. Etc.

Ferris wheel

ferryboat

fertility rate As calculated by the federal government, it is the number of live births per 1,000 females age 15 through 44 years.

fewer, less In general, use *fewer* for individual items, *less* for bulk or quantity.

Wrong: *The trend is toward more machines and less people.* (*People* in this sense refers to individuals.)

Wrong: *She was fewer than 60 years old.* (*Years* in this sense refers to a period of time, not individual years.)

Right: *Fewer than 10 applicants called.* (Individuals.)

Right: *I had less than $50 in my pocket.* (An amount.) But: *I had fewer than 50 $1 bills in my pocket.* (Individual items.)

fiance (man) **fiancee** (woman)

Fiberglas Note the single *s.* A trademark for fiberglass or glass fiber.

field house

figuratively, literally *Figuratively* means in an analogous sense, but not in the exact sense: *He bled them white.*

Literally means in an exact sense; do not use it to mean figuratively.

Wrong: *He literally bled them white.* (Unless the blood was drained from their bodies.)

figure The symbol for a number: *the figure 5.*

See **numerals**.

figure skating See **skating, figure** for guidelines on the summary form.

filibuster *To filibuster* is to make long speeches to obstruct the passage of legislation.

A legislator who uses such methods also is a *filibuster,* not a *filibusterer.*

Filipinos The people of the Philippines.

film ratings See **movie ratings**.

financial editor Capitalize only as a formal title before a name.

See **titles**.

fiord Not *fjord.*

firearms See **weapons**.

fire department See the **governmental bodies** entry for the basic rules on capitalization.

See **titles** and **military titles** for guidelines on titles.

firefighter, fireman The preferred term to describe a person who fights fires is *firefighter*.

One meaning of *fireman* is a person who tends fires in a furnace. *Fireman* is also an acceptable synonym for *firefighter*.

firm A business partnership is correctly referred to as a *firm*: *He joined a law firm.*

Do not use *firm* in references to an incorporated business entity. Use *the company* or *the corporation* instead.

first degree, first-degree Hyphenate when used as a compound modifier: *It was murder in the first degree. He was convicted of first-degree murder.*

first family Always lowercase.

first lady Not a formal title. Do not capitalize, even when used before the name of a chief of state's wife.

See **titles.**

first quarter, first-quarter Hyphenate when used as a compound modifier: *He scored in the first quarter. The team took the lead on his first-quarter goal.*

fiscal, monetary *Fiscal* applies to budgetary matters.

Monetary applies to money supply.

fiscal year The 12-month period that a corporation or governmental body uses for bookkeeping purposes.

The federal government's fiscal year starts three months ahead of the calendar year — fiscal 1978, for example, runs from Oct. 1, 1977, to Sept. 30, 1978.

fitful It means restless, not a condition of being fit.

flack, flak *Flack* is slang for *press agent*.

Flak is a type of anti-aircraft fire, hence figuratively a barrage of criticism.

flagpole, flagship

flail, flay *To flail* is to swing the arms widely.

To flay is, literally, to strip off the skin by whipping. Figuratively, *to flay* means to tongue-lash a person.

flair, flare *Flair* is conspicuous talent.

Flare is a verb meaning to blaze with sudden, bright light or to burst out in anger. It is also a noun meaning a flame.

flak See the **flack, flak** entry.

flare up (v.) **flare-up** (n.) See the **flair, flare** entry.

flash flood See **weather terms.**

flaunt, flout *To flaunt* is to make an ostentatious or defiant display: *She flaunted her beauty.*

To flout is to show contempt for: *He flouts the law.*

flautist The preferred word is *flutist*.

fleet Use figures and capitalize *fleet* when forming a proper name: *the 6th Fleet.*

Lowercase *fleet* whenever it stands alone.

flier, flyer *Flier* is the preferred term for an aviator or a handbill.

Flyer is the proper name of some trains and buses: *the Western Flyer.*

flimflam, flimflammed

flip-flop

floods, flood stage See **weather terms.**

floodwaters

floor leader Treat it as a job description, lowercased, rather than a formal title: *Republican floor leader John Smith.*

Do not use when a formal title such as *majority leader, minority leader* or *whip* would be the accurate description.

See the **legislative titles** and **titles** entries.

Florida Abbrev.: *Fla.* See **state names**.

Florida Keys A chain of small islands extending southwest from the southern tip of mainland Florida.

Cities, or the islands themselves, are followed by *Fla.* in datelines:

KEY WEST, Fla. (AP)—

flounder, founder A *flounder* is a fish; *to flounder* is to move clumsily or jerkily, to flop about: *The fish floundered on land.*

To founder is to bog down, become disabled or sink: *The ship floundered in the heavy seas for hours, then foundered.*

flout See the **flaunt, flout** entry.

flowers See **plants**.

fluid ounce Equal to 1.8 cubic inches, two tablespoons or six teaspoons. The metric equivalent is approximately 30 milliliters.

To convert to milliliters, multiply by 30 (3 ounces × 30 = 90 milliliters).

See **liter**.

fluorescent

flush To become red in the face. See **livid**.

flutist The preferred term, rather than *flautist.*

flyer See the **flier, flyer** entry.

FM Acceptable in all references for the *frequency modulation* system of radio transmission.

f.o.b. Acceptable on first reference for *free on board.* The concept should be explained, however, in contexts not addressed to business-oriented audiences: The seller agrees to put an item on a truck, ship, etc. at no charge, but the transportation costs must be paid by the buyer.

-fold No hyphen:

twofold   fourfold

folk singer, folk song

following The word usually is a noun, verb or adjective: *He has a large following. He is following his conscience. The following statement was made.*

Although Webster's New World records its use as a preposition, the preferred word is *after: He spoke after dinner.* Not: *He spoke following dinner.*

follow up (v.) **follow-up** (n. and adj.)

food Most food names are lowercase: *apples, cheese, peanut butter.*

Capitalize brand names and trademarks: *Roquefort cheese, Tabasco sauce, Smithfield ham.*

Most proper nouns or adjectives are capitalized when they occur in a food name: *Boston brown bread, Russian dressing, Swiss cheese, Waldorf salad.*

Lowercase is used, however, when the food does not depend on the proper noun or adjective for its meaning: *french fries, graham crackers, manhattan cocktail.*

If a question arises, check the separate entries in this book. If there is no entry, follow Webster's New World. Use lowercase if the dictionary lists it as an acceptable form for the sense in which the word is used.

The same principles apply to foreign names for foods: *mousse de saumon* (salmon mousse), *pomme de terre* (literally, "apple of the earth"—for potatoes), *salade Russe* (Russian salad).

Food and Agriculture Organization Not *Agricultural. FAO* is acceptable on second reference to this U.N. agency.

Food and Drug Administration
FDA is acceptable on second reference.

foot The basic unit of length in the measuring system that has been used in the United States. Its origin was a calculation that this was the length of the average human foot.

The metric equivalent is exactly 30.48 centimeters, which may be rounded to 30 centimeters for most comparisons.

For most conversions to centimeters, it is adequate to multiply by 30 (5 feet × 30 = 150 centimeters). For more exact figures, multiply by 30.48 (5 feet × 30.48 = 152.4 centimeters).

To convert to meters, multiply by .3 (5 feet × .3 = 1.5 meters).

See **centimeter; meter;** and **dimensions.**

football The spellings of some frequently used words and phrases:

ball carrier	lineman
ballclub	line of scrimmage
blitz (n., v.)	out of bounds (adv.)
end line	out-of-bounds (adj.)
end zone	pitchout (n.)
fair catch	place kick
field goal	place-kicker
fourth-and-one (adj.)	play off (v.)
fullback	playoff (n., adj.)
goal line	quarterback
goal-line stand	runback (n.)
halfback	running back
halftime	split end
handoff	tailback
kick off (v.)	tight end
kickoff (adj.)	touchback
left guard	touchdown
linebacker	wide receiver

NUMBERS: Use figures for yardage: *The 5-yard line, the 10-yard line, a 5-yard pass play, he plunged in from the 2, he ran 6 yards, a 7-yard gain.* But: *a fourth-and-two play.*

Some other uses of numbers: *The final score was 21-14. The team won its fourth game in 10 starts. The team record is 4-5-1.*

LEAGUE: In general, spell out *National Football League* on first reference. A phrase such as *the NFL's National Conference* may be used on first reference, however, to avoid a cumbersome lead.

For subdivisions: *the Eastern Division of the American Conference, the Central Division of the National Conference, the American Conference East.* On second reference: *the AFC West, the division, the conference,* etc.

STATISTICS: All football games, whether using the one- or two-point conversion, use the same summary style.

The visiting team always is listed first.

Field goals are measured from the point where the ball was kicked — not the line of scrimmage. The goal posts are 10 yards behind the goal lines. Include that distance.

Abbreviate team names to four letters or less on the scoring and statistical lines as illustrated.

The passing line shows, in order: completions-attempts-had intercepted.

A sample agate package:

```
Stanford              16  7  3  2—28
Army                   8  6 15  6—35
  Army—John 6 run (Chambers run)
  Stan—Temple 2 run (Central pass from
Temple)
  Stan—Powers 26 run (Powers run)
  Army—Tennyson 11 run (kick failed)
  Stan—Lutz 22 pass from Chambers
(Chambers kick)
  Stan—FG Lutz 23
  Army—Tennyson 34 pass interception
(Jones kick)
  Army—Brandt 22 punt return (Jones
pass from Tennyson)
  Stan—Safety Doakes tackled in end
zone
  Army—Hallmark 16 pass from Tenny-
son (run failed)
  A—26,571
```

	Stan	Army
First downs	5	7
Rushes-yards	51-172	47-238
Passing yards	90	112
Return yards	50	52
Passes	7-18-2	13-19-2
Punts	5-47	5-39
Fumbles-lost	3-0	2-1
Penalties-yards	3-25	4-30

INDIVIDUAL LEADERS

Rushing—Stanford, Foreman 10-55, Newman 9-44, Etc. Army, Halden 10-77, Etc.

Passing—Stanford, Chambers 11-20-2-150, Lee 1-3-0-49. Army, Tennyson 6-9-1-50.

Receiving—Stanford, Lutz 2-26, Temple 3-25, Ardmore 1-12, Etc. Army, Etc.

The rushing and receiving paragraphs for individual leaders show attempts and yardage gained. The passing paragraph shows completions, attempts, number of attempts intercepted, and total yards gained.

STANDINGS: The form for **professional standings**:

	W	L	T	Pct.	PF	PA
American Conference						
East						
Baltimore	10	4	0	.714	395	269
New England	9	5	0	.643	387	275
Etc.						

The form for **college conference standings**:

	Conference					All Games				
	W	L	T	Pts.	OP	W	L	T	Pts.	OP
UCLA	6	1	0	215	123	8	2	1	326	233
Etc.										

In college conference standings, limit team names to nine letters or fewer. Abbreviate as necessary.

forbear, forebear To *forbear* is to avoid or shun.
A *forebear* is an ancestor.

forbid, forbade, forbidding

forcible rape A redundancy that usually should be avoided. It may be used, however, in stories dealing with both rape and statutory rape, which does not necessarily involve the use of force.

Ford Motor Co. Use *Ford*, not *FMC*, on second reference.
Headquarters is in Dearborn, Mich.

fore- The rules in **prefixes** apply, but in general, no hyphen. Some examples:
forebrain	foregoing
forefather	foretooth

There are three nautical exceptions, based on long-standing practice:
fore-topgallant	fore-topsail
fore-topmast	

forecast Use *forecast* also for the past tense, not *forecasted*.
See **weather terms**.

forego, forgo To *forego* means to go before, as in *foregone conclusion*.
To *forgo* means to abstain from.

foreign governmental bodies Capitalize the names of specific foreign governmental agenices and departments, either with the name of the nation or without it if clear in the context: *the French Foreign Ministry, the Foreign Ministry*.
Lowercase *the ministry* or a similar term when standing alone.

foreign legislative bodies In general, capitalize the proper name of a specific legislative body abroad, whether using the name in a foreign language or an English equivalent.
The most frequent names in use are *congress, national assembly* and *parliament*.

GENERIC USES: Lowercase *parliament* or a similar term only when used generically to describe a body for which the foreign name is being given: *the Diet, Japan's parliament.* But capitalize *parliament* or similar term when used independently of the foreign name:
TOKYO (AP) — Demonstrators gathered outside the Japanese Parliament today.
Parliament is the appropriate generic descriptive for the Diet, the Cortes in Spain, the Knesset in Israel and the Supreme Soviet in the Soviet Union.

PLURALS: Lowercase *parliament* and similar terms in plural constructions: *the parliaments of England and France, the English and French parliaments*.

INDIVIDUAL HOUSES: The principle applies also to individual houses of a nation's legislature, just as *Senate* and *House* are capitalized in the United States:
ROME (AP) — New leaders have taken control in the Chamber of Deputies.

PARLIAMENTS: Nations in which *parliament* is the name include:

Australia, Canada, Denmark, Finland, France, India, Iran, Ireland, Italy, New Zealand, Norway, Poland and the United Kingdom.

NATIONAL ASSEMBLIES: Nations in which *national assembly* is the name include: Bulgaria, Czechoslovakia, Egypt, Hungary, Nepal, Pakistan, Portugal, Tunisia, Uganda, Zaire and Zambia.

Lowercase *assembly* when used as a shortened reference to *national assembly*.

In many countries, *national assembly* is the name of a unicameral legislative body. In some, such as France, it is the name for the lower house of a legislative body known by some other name such as *parliament*.

foreign money Generally, amounts of foreign money mentioned in news stories should be converted to dollars. If it is necessary to mention the foreign amount, provide the dollar equivalent in parentheses.

The basic monetary units of nations are listed in Webster's New World Dictionary among the M's under "Monetary Units of All Nations." Do not use the exchange rates listed in the dictionary. Instead, use, as appropriate, the official exchange rates, which change from day to day on the world's markets.

foreign names For foreign place names, use the primary spelling in Webster's New World Dictionary. If it has no entry, follow the Columbia Lippincott Gazetteer of the World.

For personal names, follow the individual's preference for an English spelling if it can be determined. Otherwise:

—Use the nearest phonetic equivalent in English if one exists: *Alexander Solzhenitsyn*, for example, rather than *Aleksandr*, the spelling that would result from a transliteration of the Russian letters into the English alphabet.

—If a name has no close phonetic equivalent in English, express it with an English spelling that approximates the sound in the original language: *Anwar Sadat*.

For additional guidelines, see **Arabic names; Chinese names; Russian names;** and **Spanish and Portuguese names**.

When a question arises, the news services will announce a common policy.

foreign particles Lowercase particles such as *de, la,* and *von* when part of a given name: *Charles de Gaulle, Baron Manfred von Richthofen.*

Capitalize the particles only when the last name starts a sentence: *De Gaulle spoke to von Richthofen.*

foreign words Some foreign words and abbreviations have been accepted universally into the English language: *bon voyage; versus, vs.; et cetera, etc.* They may be used without explanation if they are clear in the context.

Many foreign words and their abbreviations are not understood universally, although they may be used in special applications such as medical or legal terminology. Such words are marked in Webster's New World by a double dagger (‡). If such a word or phrase is needed in a story, place it in quotation marks and provide an explanation: *"ad astra per aspera,"* a Latin phrase meaning *"to the stars through difficulty."*

foreman, forewoman Seldom a formal title.
See **titles**.

formal titles See **titles**.

former Always lowercase. But retain capitalization for a formal title used immediately before a name: *former President Nixon.*

Formica A trademark for a brand of laminated plastic.

Formosa See **Taiwan**.

Formosa Strait Not *the Straits of Taiwan.*

formula, formulas Use figures in writing formulas, as illustrated in the entries on metric units.

forsake, forsook, forsaken

fort Do not abbreviate, for cities or for military installations.
In datelines for cities:
FORT LAUDERDALE, Fla. (AP) —
In datelines for military installations:
FORT BRAGG, N.C. (AP) —

fortnight The expression *two weeks* is preferred.

fortuneteller, fortunetelling

forty, forty-niner *'49er* also is acceptable.

forward Not *forwards*.

foul, fowl *Foul* means offensive, out of line.
A *fowl* is a bird, especially the larger domestic birds used as food: chickens, ducks, turkeys.

founder See the **flounder, founder** entry.

four-flush (stud poker)

Four-H Club *4-H Club* is preferred. Members are *4-H'ers.*

four-star general

Fourth Estate Capitalize when used as a collective name for journalism and journalists.
The description is attributed to Edmund Burke, who is reported to have called the reporters' gallery in Parliament a "Fourth Estate."
The three estates of early English society were the Lords Spiritual (the clergy), the Lords Temporal (the nobility) and the Commons (the bourgeoisie).

Fourth of July, July Fourth Also: *Independence Day.* The federal legal holiday is observed on Friday if July 4 falls on a Saturday, on Monday if it falls on a Sunday.

fractions Spell out amounts less than *1* in stories, using hyphens between the words: *two-thirds, four-fifths, seven-sixteenths,* etc.
Use figures for precise amounts larger than *1*, converting to decimals whenever practical.
Fractions are preferred, however, in stories about stocks. See **stock market prices**.
When using fractional characters, remember that most newspaper type fonts can set only ¹⁄₈, ¹⁄₄, ³⁄₈, ¹⁄₂, ⁵⁄₈, ³⁄₄ and ⁷⁄₈ as one unit; use *1¹⁄₂, 2⁵⁄₈,* etc. with no space between the figure and the fraction. Other fractions require a hyphen and individual figures, with a space between the whole number and the fraction: *1 3-16, 2 1-3, 5 9-10.*
In tabular material, use figures exclusively, converting to decimals if the amounts involve extensive use of fractions that cannot be expressed as a single character.
See **percentages**.

fragment, fragmentary *Fragment* describes a piece or pieces broken from the whole: *She sang a fragment of the song.*
Fragmentary describes disconnected and incomplete parts: *Early returns were fragmentary.*

frame up (v.) **frame-up** (n.)

frankfurters They first were called *hot dogs* in 1906 when a cartoonist, T.A. "Tad" Dorgan, showed a dachshund inside an elongated bun.

fraternal organizations and service clubs Capitalize the proper names: *American Legion, Lions Club, Independent Order of Odd Fellows, Rotary Club.*
Capitalize also words describing membership: *He is a Legionnaire, a Lion, an Odd Fellow, an Optimist and a Rotarian.* See **American Legion** for the rationale on *Legionnaire.*
Capitalize the formal titles of officeholders when used before a name. See **titles**.

free-for-all (n. and adj.)

free-lance (v. and adj.) The noun: *free-lancer.*

free on board See **f.o.b.**

freewheeling

Free World An imprecise description. Use only in quoted matter.

freeze-dry, freeze-dried, freeze-drying

freezing drizzle, freezing rain See **weather terms.**

French Canadian, French Canadians Without a hyphen. An exception to the normal practice in describing a dual ethnic heritage.

French Foreign Legion Retain capitalization if shortened to *the Foreign Legion.*
Lowercase *the legion* and *legionnaries.* Unlike the situation with the American Legion, the French Foreign Legion is a group of active soldiers.

french fries See **capitalization** and **food.**

frequency modulation *FM* is acceptable in all references.

Friday See **days of the week.**

Friends General Conference, Friends United Meeting See **Quakers.**

Frigidaire A trademark for a brand of refrigerator.

Frisbee A trademark for a plastic disk thrown as a toy.

Frontier Airlines Headquarters is in Denver.

front line (n.) **front-line** (adj.)

front page (n.) **front-page** (adj.)

front-runner

frost See **weather terms.**

fruits See **food.**

fulfill, fulfilled, fulfilling

full- Hyphenate when used to form compound modifiers:
full-dress	full-page
full-fledged	full-scale
full-length	
See the listings that follow and Webster's New World Dictionary for the spelling of other combinations.

full faith and credit bond See **loan terminology.**

full house (poker)

full time, full-time Hyphenate when used as a compound modifier: *He works full time. She has a full-time job.*

fulsome It means disgustingly excessive. Do not use it to mean lavish, profuse.

fundamentalist See **religious movements.**

fund raising, fund-raising, fund-raiser *Fund raising is difficult. They planned a fund-raising campaign. A fund-raiser was hired.*

funnel cloud See **weather terms.**

furlough

further See the **farther, further** entry.

fuselage

fusillade

F.W. Woolworth Co. *Woolworth's* is acceptable in all references. Headquarters is in New York.

G The *general audience* rating. See **movie ratings**.

gage, gauge A *gage* is a security or a pledge.

A *gauge* is a device to measure something.

Gauge is also a term used to designate the size of shotguns. See **weapons**.

gaiety

gale See **weather terms**.

gallon Equal to 128 fluid ounces. The metric equivalent is approximately 3.8 liters.

To convert to liters, multiply by 3.8 (3 gallons x 3.8 = 11.4 liters).

See **imperial gallon; liter;** and **metric system**.

Gallup Poll Prepared by The American Institute of Public Opinion, Princeton, N.J.

game plan

gamut, gantlet, gauntlet A *gamut* is a scale of notes or any complete range or extent.

A *gantlet* is a flogging ordeal, literally or figuratively.

A *gauntlet* is a glove. *To throw down the gauntlet* means to issue a challenge. *To take up the gauntlet* means to accept a challenge.

gamy, gamier, gamiest

garnish, garnishee *Garnish* means to adorn or decorate.

As a verb, *garnishee* (*garnisheed, garnisheeing*) means to attach a debtor's property or wages to satisfy a debt. As a noun, it identifies the individual whose property was attached.

gauge See the **gage, gauge** entry.

gay Do not use as a noun meaning a homosexual unless it appears in the formal name of an organization or in quoted matter.

In a story about homosexuals, *gay* may be used as an adjective meaning homosexual.

general, general of the air force, general of the army See **military titles**.

General Accounting Office This federal agency, the investigative arm of Congress, may be referred to as the *GAO* in second reference.

general assembly See **legislature** for its treatment as the name of a state's legislative body.

Capitalize when it is the formal name for the ruling or consultative body of an organization: *the General Assembly of the World Council of Churches.*

General Assembly (U.N.) *General Assembly* may be used on first reference in a story under a United Nations dateline.

Use *U.N. General Assembly* in other first references, *the General Assembly* or *the assembly* in subsequent references.

general court Part of the official proper name for the legislatures in Massachusetts and New Hampshire. Capitalize specific references with or without the state name: *the Massachusetts General Court, the General Court.*

In keeping with accepted practice, however, *Legislature* may be used instead and treated as the proper name. See **legislature**.

Lowercase *legislature* in a generic use such as: *The General Court is the legislature in Massachusetts.*

General Electric Co. *GE* is acceptable on second reference.

Headquarters is in Fairfield, Conn.

general manager Capitalize only as a formal title before a name.
See **titles**.

General Motors Corp. *GM* is acceptable on second reference.

The company makes a distinction between its corporate headquarters, in New York, and its main office, in Detroit, where the president and chairman of the board are based.

general obligation bond See **loan terminology**.

General Services Administration *GSA* is acceptable on second reference.

genie Not *jinni*, the spelling under which Webster's New World gives the definition.

gentile Generally, any person not a Jew; often, specifically a Christian. But to Mormons it is anyone not a Mormon.

gentleman Do not use as a synonym for *man.* See **lady**.

geographic names The basic guidelines:

DOMESTIC: The authority for spelling place names in the 50 U.S. states and territories is the U.S. Postal Service Directory of Post Offices, with two exceptions:

—Do not use the postal abbreviations for state names. For acceptable abbreviations, see entries in this book under each state's name. See **state names** for rules on when the abbreviations may be used.

—Abbreviate *saint* as *St.* (But abbreviate *Sault Sainte Marie* as *Sault Ste. Marie.*)

FOREIGN: The first source for the spelling of all foreign place names is Webster's New World Dictionary as follows:

—Use the first-listed spelling if an entry gives more than one.

—If the dictionary provides different spellings in separate entries, use the spelling that is followed by a full description of the location. There are four exceptions:

1. Use *West Germany, East Germany,* etc., for divided nations. See the **datelines** entry.

2. Use *Cameroon,* not *Cameroons* or *Cameroun.*

3. Use *Maldives,* not *Maldive Islands.*

4. Use *Sri Lanka,* not *Ceylon.*

The latter three exceptions have been made to conform with the practices of the United Nations and the U.S. Board of Geographic Names. (See the NEW NAMES paragraph below.)

If the dictionary does not have an entry, use the first-listed spelling in the Columbia Lippincott Gazetteer of the World, published by Columbia University Press, New York, by arrangement with J.B. Lippincott Co.

NEW NAMES: Follow the styles adopted by the United Nations and the U.S. Board of Geographic Names on new cities, new independent nations and nations that change their names. If the two do not agree, the news services will announce a common policy.

DATELINES: See the **datelines** entry.

CAPITALIZATION: Capitalize common nouns when they form an integral part of a proper name, but lowercase them when they stand alone: *Pennsylvania Avenue, the avenue*; *the Philippine Islands, the islands*; *the Mississippi River, the river.*

Lowercase common nouns that are not part of a specific proper name: *the Pacific islands, the Swiss mountains, Chekiang province.*

For additional guidelines, see **addresses**; **capitalization**; the **directions and regions** entry; and **island.**

Georgia Abbrev.: *Ga.* See **state names.**

German measles Also known as *rubella.*

Germany Use *East Germany* in datelines after the names of communities in the German Democratic Republic.

Use *West Germany* after the names of communities in the Federal Republic of Germany.

Berlin stands alone in datelines. See the **Berlin** entry.

getaway (n.)

get-together (n.)

ghetto, ghettos Do not use indiscriminately as a synonym for the sections of cities inhabited by minorities or the poor. *Ghetto* has a connotation that government decree has forced people to live in a certain area.

In most cases, *section, district, slum, area* or *quarter* is the more accurate word. Sometimes a place name alone has connotations that make it best: *Harlem, Watts.*

GI, GIs *Soldier* is preferred unless the story contains the term in quoted matter or involves a subject such as the *GI Bill of Rights.*

gibe, jibe *To gibe* means to taunt or sneer: *They gibed him about his mistakes.*

Jibe means to shift direction or, colloquially, to agree: *They jibed their ship across the wind. Their stories didn't jibe.*

Gibraltar, Strait of The British colony on the peninsula that juts into the strait, *Gibraltar,* stands alone in datelines.

giga- A prefix denoting 1 billion units of a measure. Move a decimal point nine places to the right, adding zeros if necessary, to convert to the basic unit: 5.5 gigatons = 5,500,000,000 tons.

girl Applicable until 18th birthday is reached. Use *woman* or *young woman* afterward.

girlfriend, boyfriend

Girl Scouts The full name of the national organization is the *Girl Scouts of the United States of America.* Headquarters is in New York.

Girls aged 6 through 8 are called *Brownies.* Girls 9 through 17 are *Girl Scouts.*

See **Boy Scouts** for programs run by a separate organization.

gizmo Not *gismo.*

glamour One of the few *our* endings still used in American writing. But the adjective is *glamorous.*

globe-trotter, globe-trotting But the proper name of the basketball team is the *Harlem Globetrotters.*

GMT For *Greenwich Mean Time.* See **time zones.**

gobbledygook

go-between (n.)

godchild, goddaughter Also: *god-father, godliness, godmother, godsend, godson, godspeed.* Always lowercase.

gods and goddesses Capitalize *God* in references to the deity of all monotheistic religions. Capitalize all noun references to the deity: *God the Father, Holy Ghost, Holy Spirit,* etc. Lowercase personal pronouns: *he, him, thee, thou.*

Lowercase *gods* and *goddesses* in references to the deities of polytheistic religions.

Lowercase *god, gods* and *goddesses* in references to false gods: *He made money his god.*

See **religious references.**

go-go

golf Some frequently used terms and some definitions:

Americas Cup No possessive.

birdie, birdies One stroke under par.

bogey, bogeys One stroke over par. The past tense is *bogeyed.*

eagle Two strokes under par.

fairway

Masters Tournament No possessive. Use *the Masters* on second reference.

tee, tee off

U.S. Open Championship Use *the U.S. Open* or *the Open* on second reference.

NUMBERS: Some sample uses of numbers:

Use figures for handicaps: *He has a 3 handicap; a 3-handicap golfer; a handicap of 3 strokes; a 3-stroke handicap.*

Use figures for par listings: *He had a par 5 to finish 2-up for the round; a par-4 hole; a 7-under-par 64, the par-3 seventh hole.*

Use figures for club ratings: *a No. 5 iron, a 5-iron, a 7-iron shot, a 4-wood.*

Miscellaneous: *the first hole, the ninth hole, the 10th hole, the back nine, the final 18, the third round. He won 3 and 2.*

ASSOCIATIONS: In general, spell out *Professional Golfers' Association* (note the apostrophe) on first reference. A phrase such as *PGA tournament* may be used on first reference, however, to avoid a cumbersome lead.

The same principle applies to the *Ladies Professional Golf Association* (no apostrophe, in keeping with *LPGA* practice).

SUMMARIES-Stroke (Medal) Play: List scores in ascending order. Use a dash before the final figure, hyphens between others.

Example:

```
First round:
Jack Nicklaus                35-35—70
Johnny Miller                36-35—71
Etc.
  Second round:
Jack Nicklaus                70-70—140
Johnny Miller                71-70—141
Etc.
```

Final round, professional tournaments, including prize money:

```
Jack Nicklaus, $30,000       70-70-70-68—278
Johnny Miller, $17,500       71-70-70-69—280
Etc.
```

Use hometowns, if ordered, only on national championship amateur tournaments. Use home countries, if ordered, only on major international events such as the British Open. If used, the hometown or country is placed on a second line, indented one space:

```
Arnold Palmer                70-69-68-70—277
  United States
Tony Jacklin                 71-70-70-70—281
  England
```

The form for cards:

```
Par out                      444 343 544-35
Watson out                   454 333 435-34
Nicklaus out                 434 243 544-33
Par in                   434 443 454-35—70
Watson in                434 342 443-31—65
Nicklaus in              433 443 453-33—66
```

SUMMARIES-Match Play: In the first example that follows, the *and 1* means that the 18th hole was skipped because Nicklaus had a 2-hole lead after 17. In the second, the match went 18 holes. In the third, a 19th hole was played because the golfers were tied after 18.

> Jack Nicklaus def. Lee Trevino, 2 and 1.
> Sam Snead def. Ben Hogan, 2-up.
> Arnold Palmer def. Johnny Miller, 1-up (19).

good, well *Good* is an adjective that means something is as it should be or is better than average.

When used as an adjective, *well* means suitable, proper, healthy. When used as an adverb, *well* means in a satisfactory manner or skillfully.

Good should not be used as an adverb. It does not lose its status as an adjective in a sentence such as *I feel good.* Such a statement is the idiomatic equivalent of *I am in good health.* An alternative, *I feel well,* could be interpreted as meaning that your sense of touch was good.

See the **bad, badly** entry and **well**.

goodbye Not *goodby.*

Good Conduct Medal

Good Friday The Friday before Easter.

good will (n.) **goodwill** (adj.)

GOP See **Grand Old Party**.

Gospel(s), gospel Capitalize when referring to any or all of the first four books of the New Testament: *the Gospel of St. John, the Gospels.*

Lowercase in other references: *She is a famous gospel singer.*

gourmand, gourmet A *gourmand* is a person who likes good food and tends to eat to excess; a glutton.

A *gourmet* is a person who likes fine food and is an excellent judge of food and drink.

government Always lowercase, never abbreviate: *the federal government, the state government, the U.S. government.*

government, junta, regime A *government* is an established system of political administration: *the U.S. government.*

A *junta* is a group or council that often rules after a coup: *A military junta controls the nation.* A junta becomes a government after it establishes a system of political administration.

The word *regime* is a synonym for *political system: a democratic regime, an authoritarian regime.* Do not use *regime* to mean government or junta. For example, use *the Franco government* in referring to the government of Spain under Francisco Franco, not *Franco regime.* But: *The Franco government was an authoritarian regime.*

An *administration* consists of officials who make up the executive branch of a government: *the Carter administration.*

governmental bodies Follow these guidelines:

FULL NAME: Capitalize the full proper names of governmental agencies, departments, and offices: *the U.S. Department of State, the Georgia Department of Human Resources, the Boston City Council, the Chicago Fire Department.*

WITHOUT JURISDICTION: Retain capitalization in referring to a specific body if the dateline or context makes the name of the nation, state, county, city, etc. unnecessary: *the Department of State* (in a story from Washington), *the Department of Human Resources* or *the state Department of Human Resources* (in a story from Georgia), *the City Council* (in a story from Boston), *the Fire Department* or *the city Fire Department* (in a story from Chicago).

Lowercase further condensations of the name: *the department, the council,* etc.

For additional guidance see **assembly; city council; committee; congress; federal; legislature; house of representatives; senate; Supreme Court of the United States;** and **supreme courts of the states**.

FLIP-FLOPPED NAMES: Retain capital letters for the name of a governmental body if its formal name is flopped to delete the word *of*: *the State Department, the Human Resources Department.*

GENERIC EQUIVALENTS: If a generic term has become the equivalent of a proper name in popular use, treat it as a proper name: *Walpole State Prison,* for example, even though the proper name is the *Massachusetts Correctional Institution-Walpole.*

For additional examples, see **legislature**; **police department**; and the **prison, jail** entry.

PLURALS, NON-SPECIFIC REFERENCES: All words that are capitalized when part of a proper name should be lowercased when they are used in the plural or do not refer to a specific, existing body. Some examples:
All states except Nebraska have a state senate. The town does not have a fire department. The bill requires city councils to provide matching funds. The president will address the lower houses of the New York and New Jersey legislatures.

FOREIGN BODIES: The same principles apply. See **foreign governmental bodies** and **foreign legislative bodies**.

governor Capitalize and abbreviate as *Gov.* or *Govs.* when used as a formal title before one or more names in regular text. Capitalize and spell out when used as a formal title before one or more names in direct quotations.

Lowercase and spell out in all other uses.

See the next entry and **titles**.

governor general, governors general The formal title for the British sovereign's representatives in Canada and elsewhere.

Do not abbreviate in any use.

grade, grader Hyphenate both the noun forms (*first-grader, second-grader, 10th-grader,* etc.) and the adjectival forms (*a fourth-grade pupil, a 12th-grade pupil*)

graduate (v.) *Graduate* is correctly used in the active voice: *She graduated from the university.* It is correct, but unnecessary, to use the passive voice: *He was graduated from the university.*

Do not, however, drop *from*: *John Adams graduated from Harvard.* Not: *John Adams graduated Harvard.*

graham, graham crackers The crackers are made from a finely ground whole-wheat flour named for Sylvester Graham, a U.S. dietary reformer.

grain The smallest unit in the system of weights that has been used in the United States. It originally was defined as the weight of o1.e grain of wheat.

It takes 437.5 grains to make an ounce.

See **ounce (weight)** and **pound**.

gram The basic unit of weight in the metric system. It is the weight of one cubic centimeter of water at 4 degrees Celsius.

A gram is roughly equivalent to the weight of a paper clip, or approximately one-twenty-eighth of an ounce.

To convert to ounces, multiply by .035 (86 grams x .035 = 3 ounces).

See **metric system**.

grammar

granddad, granddaughter Also: *grandfather, grandmother, grandson.*

grand jury Always lowercase: *a Los Angeles County grand jury, the grand jury.*

This style has been adopted because, unlike the case with *city council* and similar governmental units, a jurisdiction frequently has more than one grand jury in session.

Grand Old Party *GOP* is acceptable as a second-reference synonym for *Republican Party* without first spelling out *Grand Old Party.*

grant-in-aid, grants-in-aid

gray Not *grey*. But: *greyhound*.

great- Hyphenate *great-grandfather, great-great-grandmother*, etc.
Use *great grandfather* only if the intended meaning is that the grandfather was a great man.

Great Atlantic & Pacific Tea Co. Inc. *A&P* is acceptable in all references. Headquarters is in Montvale, N.J.

Great Britain It consists of England, Scotland and Wales, but not Northern Ireland.
Britain is acceptable in all references. See **United Kingdom**.

Great Depression See **Depression**.

greater Capitalize when used to define a community and its surrounding region: *Greater Boston*.

Great Lakes The five, from the largest to the smallest: Lake Superior, Lake Huron, Lake Michigan, Lake Erie, Lake Ontario.

Great Plains Capitalize *Great Plains* or *the Plains* when referring to the U.S. prairie lands that extend from North Dakota to Texas and from the Missouri River to the Rocky Mountains.
Use *northern Plains, southwestern Plains*, etc., when referring to a portion of the region.

Greek Orthodox Archdiocese of North and South America See **Eastern Orthodox churches**.

Greek Orthodox Church See **Eastern Orthodox churches**.

Green Revolution The substantial increase in agricultural yields that resulted from the development of new varieties of grains.

Greenwich Mean Time (GMT) See **time zones** and **meridians**.

gringo See the **nationalities and races** entry.

grisly, grizzly *Grisly* is horrifying, repugnant.
Grizzly means grayish or is a short form for *grizzly bear*.

grits Ground hominy. The word normally takes plural verbs and pronouns: *Grits are to country ham what Yorkshire pudding is to roast beef.*

gross national product The total value at retail prices of all the goods and services produced by a nation's economy in a given time period.
As calculated quarterly by the Department of Commerce, the gross national product of the United States is considered the broadest available measure of the nation's economic activity.
Lowercase in all uses.

gross profit, gross revenue See **profit terminology**.

Groundhog Day Feb. 2.

groundskeeper

groundswell

group Takes singular verbs and pronouns: *The group is reviewing its position.*

grown-up (n. and adj.)

Grumman Corp. Headquarters is in Bethpage, N.Y.

G-string

Guadalupe (Mexico)

Guadeloupe (West Indies)

Guam Use in datelines after the name of a community. See **datelines**.

guarantee Preferred to *guaranty*, except in proper names.

guard Usually a job description, not a formal title. See **titles**.

guardsman See **National Guard** and **Coast Guardsman**.

Guatemala City Stands alone in datelines.

gubernatorial

guerrilla Unorthodox soldiers and their tactics.

guest Do not use as a verb except in quoted matter. (An exception to a use recorded by Webster's New World.)

Guild, The See **Newspaper Guild, The**.

Gulf & Western Industries Inc. Headquarters is in New York.

Gulf Coast Capitalize when referring to the region of the United States lying along the Gulf of Mexico.
See **coast**.

Gulf of Iran Use the long-established name, *Persian Gulf,* unless directly quoting the government of Iran.
When *Gulf of Iran* is used, explain in the text that this body of water off the southern coast of Iran is more commonly known as *the Persian Gulf.*

Gulf Oil Corp. Headquarters is in Pittsburgh.

Gulf Stream But the racetrack is *Gulfstream Park.*

gunbattle, gunboat, gunfight, gunfire, gunpoint, gunpowder

gung-ho A colloquialism to be used sparingly.

guns See **weapons**.

guru

gymnastics Scoring is by points. Identify events by name: *sidehorse, horizontal bars,* etc.
Use a basic summary. Example:

> Sidehorse—1, John Leaper, Penn State, 8.8 points. 2, Jo Jumper, Ohio State, 7.9. 3, Etc.

gypsy, gypsies Capitalize references to the wandering Caucasoid people found throughout the world.
Lowercase when used generically to mean one who is constantly on the move: *I plan to become a gypsy. She hailed a gypsy cab.*

gypsy moth

habeas corpus A writ or form of petition filed to seek the prompt release of someone in custody. It places the burden of proof on those detaining the person to justify it.

When *habeas corpus* is used in a story, define it.

Hades But lowercase *hell.*

Hague, The In datelines:
THE HAGUE, Netherlands (AP) —
In text: *The Hague.*

half It is not necessary to use the preposition *of: half the time* is correct, but *half of the time* is not wrong.

half- Follow Webster's New World Dictionary. Hyphenate if not listed there.

Some frequently used words without a hyphen:

halfback	halftone
halfhearted	halftrack

Also: *halftime,* an exception to the dictionary in keeping with widespread practice in sports copy.

Some frequently used combinations that are two words without a hyphen:

half brother	half size
half dollar	half sole (n.)
half note	half tide

Some frequently used combinations that include a hyphen:

half-baked	half-life
half-blood	half-moon
half-cocked	half-sole (v.)
half-hour	half-truth

half-mast, half-staff On ships and at naval stations ashore, flags are flown at *half-mast.*

Elsewhere ashore, flags are flown at *half-staff.*

hallelujah

Halley's comet After Edmund Halley, an English astronomer who predicted the comet's appearance once every 75 years, last seen in 1910.

Halloween

halo, halos

handball Games are won by the first player to score 21 points, unless it is necessary to continue until one player has a two-point spread. Most matches go to the first winner of two games.

Use a match summary. Example:

Bob Richards, Yale, def. Paul Johnson, Dartmouth, 21-18, 21-19.
Tom Brennan, Massachusetts, def. Bill Stevens, Michigan, 21-19, 17-21, 22-20.

handicaps Use figures, hyphenating adjectival forms before a noun: *He has a 3 handicap, he is a 3-handicap golfer, a handicap of 3 strokes, a 3-stroke handicap.*

handmade

hand-picked

hands off, hands-off Hyphenate when used as a compound modifier: *He kept his hands off the matter. He follows a hands-off policy.*

hand to hand, hand-to-hand, hand to mouth, hand-to-mouth Hyphenate when used as compound modifiers: *The cup was passed from hand to hand. They live a hand-to-mouth existence.*

hang, hanged, hung One *hangs* a picture, a criminal or oneself.

For past tense or the passive, use *hanged* when referring to executions or suicides, *hung* for other actions.

hangar, hanger A *hangar* is a building.

A *hanger* is used for clothes.

hangover

hanky-panky

Hanukkah The Jewish Feast of Lights, an eight-day commemoration of the re-dedication of the Temple by the Macabees after their victory over the Syrians.

Usually occurs in December but sometimes falls in late November.

harass, harassment

harebrained

harelip

Harris Survey Prepared by Louis Harris & Associates of New York.

Havana The city in Cuba stands alone in datelines.

Hawaii Do not abbreviate. Residents are *Hawaiians.*

The state comprises 132 islands about 2,400 miles southwest of San Francisco. Collectively, they are the *Hawaiian Islands.*

Eight islands — Hawaii, Kahoolawe, Kauai, Lanai, Maui, Molokai, Niihau and Oahu — account for all but three square miles of the 6,450 in the state.

The largest island in land area is Hawaii. Honolulu and Pearl Harbor are on Oahu, where more than 80 per cent of the state's residents live.

Honolulu stands alone in datelines. Use *Hawaii* after all other cities in datelines, specifying the island in the text, if needed.

See **datelines** and **state names**.

Hawaiian Airlines Headquarters is in Honolulu.

H-bomb Use *hydrogen bomb* unless a direct quotation is involved.

he, him, his, thee, thou Personal pronouns referring to the deity are lowercase.

See **deity**.

headlong

head-on (adj., adv.)

headquarters May take a singular or a plural verb.

Do not use *headquarter* as a verb.

hearing examiner See **administrative law judge**.

hearsay

heaven

heavenly bodies Capitalize the proper names of planets, stars, constellations, etc.: *Mars, Arcturus, the Big Dipper, Aries.* See **earth**.

For comets, capitalize only the proper noun element of the name: *Halley's comet.*

Lowercase *sun* and *moon,* but if their Greek names are used, capitalize them: *Helios* and *Luna.*

Lowercase nouns and adjectives derived from the proper names of planets and other heavenly bodies: *jovian, lunar, martian, solar, venusian.*

hect- (before a vowel), **hecto-** (before a consonant) A prefix denoting 100 units of a measure. Move a decimal point two places to the right, adding zeros if necessary, to convert to the basic unit: 5.5 hectometers = 550 meters.

hectare A unit of surface measure in the metric system equal to 100 ares or 10,000 square meters.

A hectare is equal to 2.47 acres, 107,639.1 square feet or 11,959.9 square yards.

To convert to acres, multiply by 2.47 (5 hectares x 2.47 = 12.35 acres).

See **acre** and **metric system**.

heights See **dimensions**.

heliport

hell But capitalize *Hades*.

helter-skelter

hemisphere Capitalize *Northern Hemisphere, Western Hemisphere*, etc.

Lowercase *hemisphere* in other uses: *the Eastern and Western hemispheres, the hemisphere*.

hemorrhage

hemorrhoid

her Do not use this pronoun in reference to nations or ships, except in quoted matter.

Use *it* instead.

here The word is frequently redundant, particularly in the lead of a date-lined story. Use it only if there is some specific need to stress that the event being reported took place in the community.

If the location must be stressed in the body of a story, repeat the name of the datelined community, both for the reader's convenience and to avoid problems if the story is topped with a different dateline.

Her Majesty Capitalize when it appears in quotations or is appropriate before a name as the long form of a formal title.

For other purposes, use the woman's name or *the queen*.

See **nobility**.

heroin The narcotic, originally a trademark.

hertz This term, the same in singular or plural, has been adopted as the international unit of frequency equal to one cycle per second.

In contexts where it would not be understood by most readers, it should be followed by a parenthetical explanation: *15,400 hertz (cycles per second)*.

Do not abbreviate.

hideaway

hi-fi

highway designations Use these forms, as appropriate in the context, for highways identified by number: *U.S. Highway 1, U.S. Route 1, U.S. 1, Route 1, Illinois 34, Illinois Route 34, state Route 34, Route 34, Interstate Highway 495, Interstate 495*. On second reference only for *Interstate: I-495*.

When a letter is appended to a number, capitalize it but do not use a hyphen: *Route 1A*.

See **addresses**.

highway patrol Capitalize if used in the formal name of a police agency: *the Kansas Highway Patrol, the Highway Patrol*. Lowercase *highway patrolman* in all uses.

See **state police**.

hike People take *hikes* through the woods, but they *increase* prices.

Hiroshima On Aug. 6, 1945, this Japanese city and military base were the targets of the first atomic bomb dropped as a weapon. The explosion had the force of 20,000 tons (20 kilotons) of TNT. It destroyed more than four square miles and killed or injured 160,000 people.

his, her Do not presume maleness in constructing a sentence, but use the pronoun *his* when an indefinite antecedent may be male or female: *A reporter attempts to protect his sources.* (Not *his or her* sources, but note the use of the word *reporter* rather than *newsman.*)

Frequently, however, the best choice is a slight revision of the sentence: *Reporters attempt to protect their sources.*

His Majesty Capitalize when it appears in quotations or is appropriate before a name as the long form of a formal title.

For other purposes, use the man's name or *the king.*

See **nobility.**

Hispaniola The island shared by the Dominican Republic and Haiti.

See **Western Hemisphere.**

historic, historical A *historic* event is an important occurrence, one that stands out in history.

Any occurrence in the past is a *historical* event.

historical periods and events Capitalize the names of widely recognized epochs in anthropology, archaeology, geology and history: *the Bronze Age, the Dark Ages, the Middle Ages, the Pliocene Epoch.*

Capitalize also widely recognized popular names for periods and events: *the Atomic Age, the Boston Tea Party, the Civil War, the Exodus* (of the Israelites from Egypt), *the Great Depression, Prohibition.*

Lowercase *century: the 18th century.*

Capitalize only the proper nouns or adjectives in general descriptions of a period: *ancient Greece, classical Rome, the Victorian era, the fall of Rome.*

For additional guidance, see separate entries in this book for many epochs,

events and historical periods. If this book has no entry, follow the capitalization in Webster's New World Dictionary, using lowercase if the dictionary lists it as an acceptable form for the sense in which the word is used.

history Avoid the redundant *past history.*

hit and run (v.) **hit-and-run** (n. and adj.) *The coach told him to hit and run. He scored on a hit-and-run. She was struck by a hit-and-run driver.*

hitchhike, hitchhiker

hockey The spellings of some frequently used words:

blue line	play off (v.)
crease	playoff (n., adj.)
face off (v.)	power play
faceoff (n., adj.)	power-play goal
goalie	red line
goal line	short-handed
goal post	slap shot
goaltender	two-on-one break
penalty box	

The term *hat trick* applies when a player has scored three goals in a game. Use it sparingly, however.

LEAGUES: In general, spell out *National Hockey League* on first reference. A phrase such as *NHL playoffs* may be used on first reference, however, to avoid a cumbersome lead.

The same applies to *WHA* for *World Hockey Association.*

For NHL subdivisions: *the Patrick Division of the Campbell Conference, the division, the conference,* etc.

SUMMARIES: The visiting team always is listed first in the score by periods.

Note that each goal is numbered according to its sequence in the game.

The figure after the name of a scoring player shows his total goals for the season. Provide this only for NHL and WHA games.

Names in parentheses are players credited with an assist on a goal.

The final figure in the listing of each goal is the number of minutes elapsed in the period when the goal was scored.

Do not use the designation *minor* after a penalty unless part of a major-minor combination.

```
Philadelphia              0  0  1—1
NY Islanders              3  0  2—5
  First period—1, New York, Trottier 28
(D. Potvin, J. Potvin), 3:39. 2, New York,
St. Laurent 8 (Howatt, Nystrom), 6:40. 3,
New York, Howatt 21, 9:15. Penalty—
Clarke, Phi, 2:32.
  Second period—None. Penalties—None.
  Third period—4, New York, D. Potvin
30 (Parise, Westfall), 2:10. 5, New York,
Trottier 29 (Gillies), 2:55. 6, Philadelphia,
Barber 46 (Bladon, Clarke), 5:33. Penal-
ties—Watson, Phi, major-minor (miscon-
duct), 1:09; Parise, NY, major, 4:15; Bla-
don, Phi, 10:25; Phi, bench (served by
King), 13:10.
  Shots on goal—Philadelphia 10-10-17-37.
New York 16-12-5-33.
  Goalies—Philadelphia, Stephenson. New
York, Resch. A—14,865.
```

STANDINGS: The form:

	W	L	T	Pts.	GF	GA
Campbell Conference						
Patrick Division						
Philadelphia	47	10	14	108	314	184
NY Islanders	45	17	9	99	310	192
Etc.						

hocus-pocus

hodgepodge

Hodgkin's disease After Dr. Thomas Hodgkin, the English physician who first described the disease of the lymph nodes.

ho-hum

holding company A company whose principal assets are the securities it owns in companies that actually provide goods or services.

The usual reason for forming a holding company is to enable one corporation and its directors to control several companies by holding a majority of their stock.

hold up (v.) **holdup** (n. and adj.)

holidays and holy days Capitalize them: *New Year's Eve, New Year's Day, Groundhog Day, Easter, Hanukkah,* etc.

The legal holidays in federal law are New Year's, Washington's Birthday, Memorial Day, Independence Day, Labor Day, Columbus Day, Veterans Day, Thanksgiving and Christmas. See individual entries for the official dates and when they are observed if they fall on a weekend.

The designation of a day as a federal legal holiday means that federal employees receive the day off or are paid overtime if they must work. Other requirements that may apply to holidays generally are left to the states. Many follow the federal lead in designating holidays, but they are not required to do so.

Hollywood Stands alone in datelines when used instead of *Los Angeles* on stories about films and the film industry.

Holocaine A trademark for a type of local anesthetic.

Holy Communion See **sacraments**.

Holy Father The preferred form is to use *the pope* or *the pontiff,* or to give the individual's name.

Use *Holy Father* in direct quotations or special contexts where a particular literary effect is desired.

Holy Orders See **sacraments**.

Holy See The headquarters of the Roman Catholic Church in Vatican City.

Holy Spirit Now preferred over *Holy Ghost* in most usage.

Holy Week The week before Easter.

homemade

hometown See **comma** for guidelines on how to list a hometown after an individual's name.

homicide, murder, manslaughter

Homicide is a legal term for slaying or killing.

Murder is malicious, premeditated homicide. Some states arbitrarily define certain homicides as murder if the killing occurs in the course of armed robbery, rape, etc.

Manslaughter is homicide without malice or premeditation.

A person should not be described as a *murderer* until convicted of the charge.

Unless authorities say premeditation was obvious, do not say that a victim *was murdered* until someone has been convicted of murder in court. Instead, say that a victim *was killed* or *slain.*

See **execute** and the **assassin, killer, murderer** entry.

Hong Kong Stands alone in datelines.

honky A term of abuse directed toward whites by blacks. Use it only in quoted matter.

See the **nationalities and races** entry.

Honolulu The city in Hawaii stands alone in datelines. It is on the island of Oahu.

See **Hawaii.**

honorary degrees All references to honorary degrees should specify that the degree was honorary.

Do not use *Dr.* before the name of an individual whose only doctorate is honorary.

honorary titles See **nobility.**

hoof-and-mouth disease

hooky Not *hookey.*

hopefully It means in a hopeful manner. Do not use it to mean it is hoped, let us hope or we hope.

Right: *It is hoped that we will complete our work in June.*

Right: *We hope that we will complete our work in June.*

Wrong as a way to express the thought in the previous two sentences: *Hopefully, we will complete our work in June.*

horsepower

horse races Capitalize their formal names: *Kentucky Derby, Preakness, Belmont Stakes*, etc.

horse racing Some frequently used terms and their definitions:

colt A male horse from 2 to 5 years old.

horse A male horse 5 years or older.

gelding A castrated male horse.

filly A female horse 2 to 5 years old.

mare A female horse 5 years or older.

stallion A male horse used for breeding.

broodmare A female horse used for breeding.

furlong One-eighth of a mile. Race distances are given in furlongs up through seven furlongs, after that in miles, as in *one-mile, 1 1-16 miles.*

entry Two or more horses owned by same owner running as a single betting interest. In some states two or more horses trained by same person but having different owners also are coupled in betting.

mutuel field Two or more horses, long shots, that have different owners and trainers. They are coupled as a single betting interest to give the field not more than 12 wagering interests. There cannot be more than 12 betting interests in a race. The bettor wins if either horse finishes in the money.

half-mile pole The pole on a race track that marks one-half mile from the finish. All distances are measured from the finish line, meaning that when a horse reaches the quarter pole, he is one-quarter mile from the finish.

bug boy An apprentice jockey, so called because of the asterisk beside the individual's name in a program. It means that the jockey's mount gets a five-pound weight allowance.

horses' names Capitalize. See **animals**.

host Do not use it as a verb. (Exception to a usage recorded in Webster's New World.)

hotel Capitalize as part of the proper name for a specific hotel: *the Waldorf-Astoria Hotel.*

Lowercase when standing alone or used in an indefinite reference to one hotel in a chain: *The city has a Sheraton hotel.*

Hotel and Restaurant Employees and Bartenders International Union The shortened forms *Hotel and Restaurant Employees union* and *Bartenders union* are acceptable in all references.

Headquarters is in Cincinnati.

hot line The circuit linking the United States and the Soviet Union. Lowercase.

household, housing unit In the sense used by the Census Bureau, a *household* is made up of all persons who occupy a house, room, group of rooms or an apartment that constitutes a housing unit. A household may contain more than one family or may be used by one person.

A *housing unit*, as defined by the bureau, is a group of rooms or a single room occupied by persons who do not live and eat with any other persons in the structure. It must have either direct access from the outside or through a common hall, or have a kitchen or cooking equipment for the exclusive use of the occupants.

House of Commons, House of Lords The two houses of the British Parliament.

On second reference: *Commons* or *the Commons, Lords* or *the Lords.*

house of delegates See the next entry.

house of representatives Capitalize when referring to a specific governmental body: *the U.S. House of Representatives, the Massachusetts House of Representatives.*

Capitalize shortened references that delete the words *of Representatives: the U.S. House, the Massachusetts House.*

Retain capitalization if *U.S.* or the name of a state is dropped but the reference is to a specific body:

BOSTON (AP) — The House has adjourned for the year.

Lowercase plural uses: *the Massachusetts and Rhode Island houses.*

Apply the same principles to similar legislative bodies such as *the Virginia House of Delegates.*

See the **organizations and institutions** entry for guidelines on how to handle the term when it is used by a nongovernmental body.

housing unit See the **household, housing unit** entry.

Houston The city in Texas stands alone in datelines.

Hovercraft A trademark for a vehicle that travels on a cushion of air.

howitzer See **weapons**.

Hughes Airwest Headquarters is in San Mateo, Calif.

human, human being *Human* is preferred, but either is acceptable.

hurly-burly

hurricanes Capitalize *hurricane* when it is part of the name that weather forecasters assign to a storm: *Hurricane Hazel.*

But use *it* and *its* — not *she, her* or *hers* — in pronoun references.

And do not use the presence of a woman's name as an excuse to attribute sexist images of women's behavior to a storm. Avoid, for example such sentences as: *The fickle Hazel teased the Louisiana coast.*

See **weather terms**.

husband, widower Use *husband*, not *widower*, in referring to the spouse of a woman who dies.

hush-hush

Hyannis Port, Mass.

hydro- The rules in **prefixes** apply, but in general, no hyphen. Some examples:

hydroelectric   hydrophobia

hyper- The rules in **prefixes** apply, but in general, no hyphen. Some examples:

hyperactive   hypercritical

hyphen Hyphens are joiners. Use them to avoid ambiguity or to form a single idea from two or more words.
Some guidelines:

AVOID AMBIGUITY: Use a hyphen whenever ambiguity would result if it were omitted: *The president will speak to small-business men.* (*Businessmen* normally is one word. But *The president will speak to small businessmen* is unclear.)
Others: *He recovered his health. He re-covered the leaky roof.*

COMPOUND MODIFIERS: When a compound modifier — two or more words that express a single concept — precedes a noun, use hyphens to link all the words in the compound except the adverb *very* and all adverbs that end in *ly*: *a first-quarter touchdown, a bluish-green dress, a full-time job, a well-known man, a better-qualified woman, a know-it-all attitude, a very good time, an easily remembered rule.*
Many combinations that are hyphenated before a noun are not hyphenated when they occur after a noun: *The team scored in the first quarter. The dress, a bluish green, was attractive on her. She works full time. His attitude suggested that he knew it all.*
But when a modifier that would be hyphenated before a noun occurs instead after a form of the verb *to be*, the hyphen usually must be retained to avoid confusion: *The man is well-known. The woman is quick-witted. The children are soft-spoken. The play is second-rate.*

The principle of using a hyphen to avoid confusion explains why no hyphen is required with *very* and *ly* words. Readers can expect them to modify the word that follows. But if a combination such as *little-known man* were not hyphenated, the reader could logically be expecting *little* to be followed by a noun, as in *little man.* Instead, the reader encountering *little known* would have to back up mentally and make the compound connection on his own.

TWO-THOUGHT COMPOUNDS: *serio-comic, socio-economic.*

COMPOUND PROPER NOUNS AND ADJECTIVES: Use a hyphen to designate dual heritage: *Italian-American, Mexican-American.*
No hyphen, however, for *French Canadian* or *Latin American.*

PREFIXES AND SUFFIXES: See the **prefixes** and **suffixes** entries, and separate entries for the most frequently used prefixes and suffixes.

AVOID DUPLICATED VOWELS, TRIPLED CONSONANTS: Examples: *anti-intellectual, pre-empt, shell-like.*

WITH NUMERALS: Use a hyphen to separate figures in odds, ratios, scores, some fractions and some vote tabulations. See examples in entries under these headings.
When large numbers must be spelled out, use a hyphen to connect a word ending in *y* to another word: *twenty-one, fifty-five,* etc.

SUSPENSIVE HYPHENATION: The form: *He received a 10- to 20-year sentence in prison.*

I

Iberia Air Lines of Spain An *Iberia airliner* is acceptable in any reference.
Headquarters is in Madrid.

ICBM, ICBMs Acceptable on first reference for *intercontinental ballistic missile(s)*, but the term should be defined in the body of a story.
Avoid the redundant *ICBM missiles*.

ice age Lowercase, because it denotes not a single period but any of a series of cold periods marked by glaciation alternating with periods of relative warmth.
Capitalize the proper nouns in the names of individual ice ages, such as *the Wisconsin ice age*.
Together, the ice ages, which began about 600,000 years ago, make up glacial epochs. During the first, called the *Pleistocene*, glaciers covered much of North America and northwestern Europe.
The present epoch, the *Helocene* or *Recent*, began about 12,000 years ago, with glaciers restricted to Antarctica and Greenland.

Icelandic Airlines Headquarters is in Reykjavik, Iceland.

ice storm See **weather terms**.

IC4A See **Intercollegiate Association of Amateur Athletes of America**.

Idaho Do not abbreviate. See **state names**.

illegal Use *illegal* only to mean a violation of the law. Be especially careful in labor-management disputes, where one side often calls an action by the other side *illegal*. Usually it is a charge that a contract or rule, not a law, has been violated.

Illinois Abbrev.: *Ill.* See **state names**.

illusion See the **allusion, illusion** entry.

imam Lowercase when describing the leader of a prayer in a Moslem mosque. Capitalize before a name when used as the formal title for a Moslem leader or ruler.
See **religious titles**.

immigrate See the **emigrate, immigrate** entry.

impassable, impassible, impassive *Impassable* means that passage is impossible: *The bridge was impassable.*
Impassible and *impassive* describe lack of sensitivity to pain or suffering. Webster's New World notes, however, that *impassible* suggests an inability to be affected, while *impassive* implies only that no reaction was noticeable: *She was impassive throughout the ordeal.*

impel, impelled, impelling

imperial gallon The standard British gallon, equal to 277.42 cubic inches or about 1.2 U.S. gallons.

The metric equivalent is approximately 4.5 liters.
See **liter**.

imperial quart One-fourth of an imperial gallon.

implausible

imply, infer Writers or speakers *imply* in the words they use.
A listener or reader *infers* something from the words.

impostor Not *imposter*.

impromptu It means without preparation or advance thought.

in, into *In* indicates location: *He was in the room.*
Into indicates motion: *She walked into the room.*

"in" When employed to indicate that something is in vogue, use quotation marks only if followed by a noun: *It was the "in" thing to do. Raccoon coats are in again.*

in- No hyphen when it means not:

inaccurate	insufferable

Often solid in other cases:

inbound	infighting
indoor	inpatient (n., adj.)
infield	

A few combinations take a hyphen, however:

in-depth	in-house
in-group	in-law

Follow Webster's New World when in doubt.

-in Precede with a hyphen:

break-in	walk-in
cave-in	write-in

inasmuch as

Inauguration Day Capitalize only when referring to the total collection of events that include the inauguration of a U.S. president; lowercase in other uses: *Inauguration Day is Jan. 20. The inauguration day for the change has not been set.*

Inc. See **incorporated**.

inch Equal to one-twelfth of a foot.
The metric equivalent is exactly 2.54 centimeters.
To convert to centimeters, multiply by 2.54 (6 inches x 2.54 = 15.24 centimeters).
See **centimeter**; **foot**; and **dimensions**.

inches per second A rating used for the speed of tape recorders.
The abbreviation *ips* (no periods) is acceptable on first reference in specialized contexts such as a records column; otherwise do not use *ips* until second reference.

include Use *include* to introduce a series when the items that follow are only part of the total: *The price includes breakfast. The zoo includes lions and tigers.*
Use *comprise* when the full list of individual elements is given: *The zoo comprises 100 types of animals, including lions and tigers.*
See the **compose, comprise, constitute** entry.

income See **profit terminology**.

incorporated Abbreviate and capitalize as *Inc.* when used as part of a corporate name. It usually is not needed, but when it is used, do not set off with commas: *J.C. Penney Co. Inc. announced...*
See **company names**.

incorporator Do not capitalize when used before a name.
See **titles**.

incredible, incredulous *Incredible* means unbelievable.
Incredulous means skeptical.

incur, incurred, incurring

Independence Day *July Fourth* or *Fourth of July* also are acceptable.

The federal legal holiday is observed on Friday if July 4 falls on a Saturday, on Monday if it falls on a Sunday.

index, indexes

Index of Leading Economic Indicators A composite of 12 economic measurements that was developed to help forecast likely shifts in the U.S. economy as a whole.

It is compiled by the Commerce Department.

Indiana Abbrev.: *Ind.* See **state names.**

Indianapolis The city in Indiana stands alone in datelines.

Indian Ocean See **oceans.**

Indians In news stories about American Indians, such words as *wampum, warpath, powwow, tepee, brave, squaw,* etc., can be disparaging and offensive. Avoid them.

Indict Use *indict* only in connection with the legal process of bringing charges against an individual or corporation.

To avoid any suggestion that someone is being judged before a trial, do not use phrases such as *indicted for killing* or *indicted for bribery.* Instead, use *indicted on a charge of killing, indicted on a bribery charge.*

For guidelines on related words, see the entries under **accuse; allege;** and **arrest.**

indiscreet, indiscrete *Indiscreet* means lacking prudence. Its noun form is *indiscretion.*

Indiscrete means not separated into distinct parts. Its noun form is *indiscreteness.*

indiscriminate, indiscriminately

indispensable

Indo- Usually hyphenated and capitalized:

Indo-Aryan   Indo-Hitite
Indo-German   Indo-Iranian
But: *Indochina.*

Indochina Formerly French Indochina, now divided into Cambodia, Laos and Vietnam.

Indochinese Peninsula Located here are the nations of Burma, Cambodia, Laos, Thailand and Vietnam.

Indonesia Use after the name of a community in datelines on stories from this nation.

Specify an individual island, if needed, in the text.

indoor (adj.) **indoors** (adv.) *He plays indoor tennis. He went indoors.*

infant Applicable to children through 12 months old.

infantile paralysis The preferred term is *polio.*

inflation A sustained increase in prices. The result is a decrease in the purchasing power of money.

There are two basic types of inflation:

—*Cost-push inflation* occurs when rising costs are the chief reason for the increased prices.

—*Demand-pull inflation* occurs when the amount of money available exceeds the amount of goods and services available for sale.

infra- The rules in **prefixes** apply, but in general, no hyphen. Some examples:

infrared   infrastructure

initials Use periods and no space when an individual uses initials instead of a first name: *H.L. Mencken.*

This format has been adopted to assure that in typesetting the initials are set on the same line.

Do not give a name with a single initial (*J. Jones*) unless it is the individual's preference or a first name cannot be learned.

See **middle initials**.

injuries They are *suffered* or *sustained*, not *received*.

in-law

Inner Light See **Quakers**.

innocent Use *innocent*, rather than *not guilty*, in describing a defendant's plea or a jury's verdict, to guard against the word *not* being dropped inadvertently.

innocuous

innuendo

inoculate

inquire, inquiry Not *enquire, enquiry*.

insignia Singular and plural.

insofar as

in spite of *Despite* means the same thing and is shorter.

intelligence quotient *IQ* is acceptable in all references.

inter- The rules in **prefixes** apply, but in general, no hyphen. Some examples:

inter-American   interstate
interracial

Intercollegiate Association of Amateur Athletes of America In general, spell out on first reference.

A phrase such as *IC4A tournament* may be used on first reference, however, to avoid a cumbersome lead. If this is done, provide the full name later in the story.

intercontinental ballistic missile See **ICBM, ICBMs**.

Internal Revenue Service *IRS* is acceptable on second reference.

Capitalize also *Internal Revenue*, but lowercase *the revenue service*.

International Association of Machinists and Aerospace Workers The shortened form *Machinists union* is acceptable in all references.

Headquarters is in Washington.

International Bank for Reconstruction and Development *World Bank* is acceptable in all references.

Headquarters is in Washington.

International Brotherhood of Electrical Workers Use the full name on first reference to avoid confusion with the United Electrical, Radio and Machine Workers of America.

IBEW is acceptable on second reference.

Headquarters is in Washington.

International Brotherhood of Painters and Allied Trades of the United States and Canada The shortened form *Painters union* is acceptable in all references.

Headquarters is in Washington.

International Brotherhood of Teamsters, Chauffeurs, Warehousemen and Helpers of America The shortened form *Teamsters union* is acceptable in all references.

Capitalize *Teamsters* and *the Teamsters* in references to the union or its members.

Lowercase *teamster* when no specific reference to the union is intended.

Headquarters is in Washington.

International Business Machines Corp. *IBM* is acceptable on second reference.

Headquarters is in Armonk, N.Y.

International Court of Justice
The principal judicial organ of the United Nations, established at The Hague in 1945.

The court is not open to individuals. It has jurisdiction over all matters specifically provided for either in the U.N. charter or in treaties and conventions in force. It also has jurisdiction over cases referred to it by U.N. members and by non-members such as Switzerland that subscribe to the court statute.

The court serves as the successor to the Permanent Court of International Justice of the League of Nations, which also was known as the World Court.

On second reference use *international court* or *world court* in lowercase. Do not abbreviate.

International Criminal Police Organization *Interpol* is acceptable in all references.

Headquarters is in Paris.

international date line The imaginary line drawn north and south through the Pacific Ocean, largely along the 180th meridian.

By international agreement, when it is 12:01 a.m. Sunday just west of the line, it is 12:01 a.m. Saturday just east of it.

See **time zones**.

International Labor Organization *ILO* is acceptable on second reference.

Headquarters is in Geneva, Switzerland.

International Ladies' Garment Workers Union The shortened forms *Ladies' Garment Workers* and *Ladies' Garment Workers union* are acceptable in all references.

ILGWU is acceptable on second reference if the full name has been used.

Lowercase *garment workers* when no specific reference to the union is intended.

Headquarters is in New York.

International Longshoremen's and Warehousemen's Union *ILWU* is acceptable on second reference.

Headquarters is in San Francisco.

International Longshoremen's Association *ILA* is acceptable on second reference.

Headquarters is in New York.

International Monetary Fund *IMF* is acceptable on second reference.

Headquarters is in Washington.

International Telecommunications Satellite Organization *Intelsat* is acceptable on first reference, but the body of the story should identify it as the shortened form of the full name.

(The original name was International Telecommunications Satellite Consortium.)

Headquarters is in Washington.

International Telephone and Telegraph Corp. Note the *and*, not an ampersand. *ITT* is acceptable on second reference.

Headquarters is in New York.

International Union, United Automobile, Aerospace and Agricultural Implement Workers of America
This is the full, formal name for the union known more commonly as the *United Auto Workers*.

See the entry that begins **United Automobile**.

Interpol Acceptable in all references for *International Criminal Police Organization.*

Interstate Commerce Commission *ICC* is acceptable on second reference.

intra- The rules in **prefixes** apply, but in general, no hyphen. Some examples:

intramural   intrastate

IOU, IOUs

Iowa Do not abbreviate. See **state names**.

ips See **inches per second**.

IQ Acceptable in all references for *intelligence quotient.*

Iran The nation formerly called Persia. It is not an Arab country.
The people are *Iranians,* not *Persians* or *Irani.*
For the language, use *Persian,* the word widely accepted outside Iran. Inside Iran, the language is called *Farsi.*

Iraq The Arab nation coinciding roughly with ancient Mesopotamia.
Its people are *Iraqis.* The dialect of Arabic is *Iraqi.*

Ireland Acceptable in most references to the independent nation known formally as the Irish Republic.
Use *Irish Republic* when a distinction must be made between this nation and *Northern Ireland,* a part of the United Kingdom.

Irish coffee Brewed coffee containing Irish whiskey, topped with cream or whipped cream.

Irish International Airlines The preferred name is *Aer Lingus.*
Headquarters is in Dublin, Ireland.

Irish Republican Army A group that fights to wrest Northern Ireland from British rule and unite it with the Irish Republic.
IRA is acceptable on second reference.

Iron Curtain Use it only in quoted matter.

irregardless *Regardless* is correct.

Islam The Moslem religion. Its deity is Allah. Mohammed is its founder and prophet.
The adjective is *Islamic.*
See **Moslem**.

island Capitalize *island* or *islands* as part of a proper name: *Prince Edward Island, the Hawaiian Islands.*
Lowercase *island* and *islands* when they stand alone or when the reference is to the islands in a given area: *the Pacific islands.*
Lowercase all *island of* constructions: *the island of Nantucket.*

U.S. DATELINES: For communities on islands within the boundaries of the United States, use the community name and the state name:
EDGARTOWN, Mass. (AP) —
Honolulu stands alone, however.

DATELINES ABROAD: If an island has an identity of its own (*Bermuda, Prince Edward Island, Puerto Rico, Sardinia, Taiwan,* etc.) use the community name and the island name:
HAMILTON, Bermuda (AP) —
Havana, Hong Kong, Macao and *Singapore* stand alone, however.
If the island is part of a chain, use the community name and the name of the chain:
MANILA, Philippines (AP) —
Identify the name of the island in the text if relevant: *Manila is on the island of Luzon.*
For additional guidelines, see **datelines**.

it Use this pronoun, rather than *she,* in references to nations and ships.

it's, its *It's* is a contraction for *it is* or *it has: It's up to you. It's been a long time.*
Its is the possessive form of the neuter pronoun: *The company lost its assets.*

IUD Acceptable on second reference for *intrauterine device.*

Ivy League Brown University, Columbia University, Cornell University, Dartmouth College, Harvard University, Princeton University, the University of Pennsylvania and Yale University.

jail Not interchangeable with *prison.* See the **prison, jail** entry.

Jamaica rum Not *Jamaican rum.*

Jane's All the World's Aircraft, Jane's Fighting Ships The reference sources for questions about aircraft and military ships not covered in this book.

The reference for non-military ships is Lloyd's Register of Shipping.

January See **months.**

Japan Air Lines *JAL* is acceptable on second reference.

Headquarters is in Tokyo.

Japan Current A warm current flowing from the Philippine Sea east of Taiwan and northeast past Japan.

jargon The special vocabulary and idioms of a particular class or occupational group.

In general, avoid jargon. When it is appropriate in a special context, include an explanation of any words likely to be unfamiliar to most readers.

See **dialect** and **word selection.**

Jaycees The proper name for the former Junior Chamber of Commerce. The United States Jaycees, the parent domestic organization, is affiliated with the worldwide body, the Jaycees International.

U.S. headquarters is in Tulsa, Okla.

See the **fraternal organizations and service clubs** entry.

J.C. Penney Co. Inc. Headquarters is in New York.

jeep, Jeep Lowercase the military vehicle.

Capitalize if referring to the rugged, four-wheel drive civilian vehicle so trademarked.

Jehovah's Witnesses The denomination was founded in Pittsburgh in 1872 by Charles Taze Russell, a former Congregationalist layman.

Witnesses do most of their work through three legal corporations: the Watch Tower and Tract Society of Pennsylvania, the Watchtower Bible and Tract Society of New York Inc., and, in England, the International Bible Students Association. The principal officers of the corporations elect a director, who becomes the international head of the Jehovah's Witnesses.

U.S. membership is listed at more than 500,000.

BELIEFS: Witnesses believe that they adhere to the oldest religion on earth, the worship of Almighty God revealed in the Bible as Jehovah.

They regard civil authority as necessary and obey it "as long as its laws do not contradict God's law." Witnesses refuse to bear arms, salute the flag or participate in secular government.

They refuse blood transfusions as being against the Bible, citing the section of Leviticus that reads: "Whatsoever man . . . eats any manner of blood, I will cut him off from among his people."

CLERGY: Witnesses consider themselves a society of ministers. A public ceremony of water immersion sets an individual apart as a minister of Jehovah.

There are no formal titles, but there are four levels of ministry: *publishers* (part-time workers expected to devote 60 hours a month to distributing literature), *general pioneers* and *special pioneers* (terms for part-time workers who devote more than 60 hours a month to activities) and *pioneers* (full-time workers).

Jell-O A trademark for a brand of gelatin dessert.

Jerusalem Stands alone in datelines.

Jesus The central figure of Christianity, he also may be called *Jesus Christ.*

Personal pronouns referring to *him* are lowercase.

jet, jetliner, jet plane See **aircraft terms.**

Jew Use for men and women. Do not use *Jewess.*

Jewish congregations A Jewish congregation is autonomous. No synods, assemblies or hierarchies control the activities of an individual synagogue.

In the United States, there are three major expressions of Judaism:

1. Orthodox Judaism. Most of its congregations are represented nationally by the Union of Orthodox Jewish Congregations of America. Most of its rabbis are members of the Rabbinical Council of America.

2. Reform Judaism. Its national representatives are the Union of American Hebrew Congregations and the Central Conference of American Rabbis.

3. Conservative Judaism. Its national representatives are the United Synagogue of America and the Rabbinical Assembly.

These six groups make up the New York-based Synagogue Council of America. It is the vehicle for consultation among the three expressions and coordinates joint activities.

The council estimates that its members represent about 3 million synagogue-affiliated American Jews, divided about equally among the three major groupings. The council also estimates that 1 million American Jews, most of them Orthodox, are members of congregations not represented by council members.

BELIEFS: Jews generally believe that a divine kingdom will be established on earth, opening a messianic era that will be marked by peace and bliss. They also believe that they have a mandate from God to work toward this kingdom.

The key to beliefs is the Torah, or Law of Moses, which consists of the first five books of the Bible. Jewish Scripture also includes the other books of the Old Testament. Additional elements of Jewish belief are contained in the Talmud, a detailed interpretation of the written and oral law of the faith.

Orthodox Jews expect the coming of the Messiah, who is to be a descendant of King David. They are strict adherents of the biblical dietary laws, ritual forms and traditional holy days.

Reform Jews believe in the coming of a messianic age, but not a personal Messiah. They regard dietary laws and ritual forms as concessions to the customs of ancient times that may be adapted to the modern needs.

Conservative Jews take a middle position, generally adhering to traditional customs of diet and ritual but stressing that faith is not static and should adapt to the needs of contemporary culture.

CLERGY: The only formal titles in use are *rabbi,* for the spiritual leader of a congregation, and *cantor,* for the individual who leads the congregation in song. Capitalize these titles before an individual's full name on first reference. On second reference, use only the last name of a man; use *Miss, Mrs.* or *Ms.* before the last name of a woman depending on her preference.

See **religious titles** and **Zionism.**

Jewish holy days See separate listings for Hanukkah, Passover, Purim, Rosh Hashana, Shavuot, Sukkot and Yom Kippur.

The High Holy Days are Rosh Hashana and Yom Kippur.

jibe See the **gibe, jibe** entry.

job descriptions Always lowercase. See **titles.**

John F. Kennedy Space Center Located in Cape Canaveral, Fla., it is the National Aeronautics and Space Administration's principal launch site for manned spacecraft.

Kennedy Space Center is acceptable in all references.

For datelines on launch stories:

CAPE CANAVERAL, Fla. (AP) —

See **Lyndon B. Johnson Space Center.**

Johns Hopkins University No apostrophes.

Joint Chiefs of Staff Also: *the Joint Chiefs.* But lowercase *the chiefs* or *the chiefs of staff.*

Jr. See the **junior, senior** entry.

judge Capitalize before a name when it is the formal title for an individual who presides in a court of law. Do not continue to use the title in second reference.

Do not use *court* as part of the title unless confusion would result without it:

—No *court* in the title: *U.S. District Judge John Sirica, District Judge John Sirica, federal Judge John Sirica, Judge John Sirica, U.S. Circuit Judge Homer Thornberry, appellate Judge John Blair.*

—*Court* needed in the title: *Juvenile Court Judge John Jones, Criminal Court Judge John Jones, Superior Court Judge Robert Harrison, state Supreme Court Judge William Cushing.*

When the formal title *chief judge* is relevant, put the court name after the judge's name: *Chief Judge John Sirica of the U.S. District Court in Washington, D.C.; Chief Judge Clement F. Haynsworth Jr. of the 4th U.S. Circuit Court of Appeals.*

Do not pile up long court names before the name of a judge. Make it *Judge John Smith of Allegheny County Common Pleas Court.* Not: *Allegheny County Common Pleas Court Judge John Smith.*

Lowercase *judge* as an occupational designation in phrases such as *beauty contest judge Bert Parks.*

See **administrative law judge; court names; judicial branch;** and **justice.**

judge advocate The plural: *judge advocates.* Also: *judge advocate general, judge advocates general.*

Capitalize as a formal title before a name.

See **titles.**

judgment Not *judgement.*

judicial branch Always lowercase.

The federal court system that exists today as the outgrowth of Article 3 of the Constitution is composed of the Supreme Court of the United States, the U.S. Court of Appeals, U.S. District Courts, the U.S. Court of Claims, the U.S. Court of Customs and Patent Appeals, and the U.S. Customs Court. There are also four district judges for U.S. territories.

The U.S. Tax Court and the U.S. Court of Military Appeals are not part of the judicial branch as such.

For more detail on all federal courts, see separate entries under the names listed here.

Judicial Conference of the United States This rule-making body for the courts of the judicial branch meets twice a year. Its 25 members are the chief justice, the chief judges of the 11 circuit courts, one district judge from each of the circuits, and the chief judges of the U.S. Court of Claims and the U.S. Court of Customs and Patent Appeals.

Day-to-day functions are handled by the Administrative Office of U.S. Courts.

judo Use the basic summary format by weight divisions for major tournaments; the match summary for dual and lesser meets.

jukebox

July See **months**.

jumbo jet Any very large jet plane, including the Boeing 747, the DC-10, the L-1011 and the C-5A.

June See **months**.

junior, senior Abbreviate as *Jr.* and *Sr.* only with full names of persons or animals. Do not precede by a comma: *Joseph P. Kennedy Jr.*

The notation *II* or *2nd* may be used if it is the individual's preference. Note, however, that *II* and *2nd* are not necessarily the equivalent of *junior* — they often are used by a grandson or nephew.

If necessary to distinguish between father and son in second reference, use the *elder Smith* or the *younger Smith*.

See **names**.

Junior Chamber of Commerce It no longer exists. See **Jaycees**.

junta See the **government, junta, regime** entry.

jury The word takes singular verbs and pronouns: *The jury has been sequestered until it reaches a verdict.*

Do not use awkward phrases such as *seven-man, five-woman jury*. Make it: *a jury of seven men and five women*.

Do not capitalize: *a U.S. District Court jury, a federal jury, a Massachusetts Superior Court jury, a Los Angeles County grand jury*.

See **grand jury**.

justice Capitalize before a name when it is the formal title. It is the formal title for members of the U.S. Supreme Court and for jurists on some state courts. In such cases, do not use *judge* in first or subsequent references.

See **judge**; **Supreme Court of the United States**; and **titles**.

justice of the peace Capitalize as a formal title before a name. Do not abbreviate.

See **titles**.

juvenile delinquent Juveniles may be declared delinquents in many states for antisocial behavior or for breaking the law. In some states, laws prohibit publishing or broadcasting the names of juvenile delinquents.

Follow the local practice unless there is a compelling reason to the contrary. Consult with the General Desk if you believe such an exception is warranted.

Kansas Abbrev.: *Kan.* See **state names**.

Kansas City Use *KANSAS CITY, Kan.*, or *KANSAS CITY, Mo.*, in datelines to avoid confusion between the two.

karat See the **carat, caret, karat** entry.

Kelvin scale A scale of temperature based on, but different from, the Celsius scale. It is used primarily in science to record very high and very low temperatures. The Kelvin scale starts at zero and indicates the total absence of heat (absolute zero).

Zero on the Kelvin scale is equal to minus 273.15 degrees Celsius and minus 460 degrees Fahrenheit.

The freezing point of water is 273.16 degrees Kelvin. The boiling point of water is 373.16 degrees Kelvin.

See **Celsius** and **Fahrenheit**.

Kennedy Space Center See **John F. Kennedy Space Center**.

Kentucky Abbrev.: *Ky.* Legally a commonwealth, not a state.

See **state** and **state names**.

Kentucky Derby *The Derby* on second reference. An exception to normal second-reference practice.

See **capitalization**.

kerosene Formerly a trademark, now a generic term.

ketchup Not *catchup* or *catsup*.

keynote address Also: *keynote speech*.

Keystone Kops

KGB Acceptable on first reference, but the story should contain a phrase identifying it as the Soviet secret police and intelligence agency.

The initials stand for the Russian words meaning *Committee for State Security*.

kibbutz An Israeli collective settlement.

The plural is *kibbutzim*.

kidnap, kidnapped, kidnapping, kidnapper

kids Use *children* unless you are talking about goats, or the use of *kids* as an informal synonym for *children* is appropriate in the context.

killer See the **assassin, killer, murderer** entry.

kilo- A prefix denoting 1,000 units of a measure. Move a decimal point three places to the right, adding zeros if necessary, to convert to the basic unit: 10.5 kilograms = 10,500 grams.

kilocycles The new term is *kilohertz*.

kilogram The metric term for 1,000 grams.

A kilogram is equal to approximately 2.2 pounds or 35 ounces.

To convert to pounds, multiply by 2.2 (9 kilograms × 2.2 = 19.8 pounds).

See **gram**; **metric system**; and **pound**.

kilohertz Equals 1,000 hertz (1,000 cycles per second), replacing *kilocycles* as the correct term in applications such as broadcast frequencies.

The official abbreviation *kHz* is acceptable on second reference if clear in the context.

kilometer The metric term for 1,000 meters.

A kilometer is equal to approximately 3,281 feet, or five-eighths (0.62) of a mile.

To convert to miles, multiply by 0.62 (5 kilometers × 0.62 = 3.1 miles).

See **meter**; **metric system**; and **miles**.

kiloton, kilotonnage A unit used to measure the power of nuclear explosions. One kiloton has the explosive force of 1,000 tons of TNT.

The atomic bomb dropped Aug. 6, 1945, on Hiroshima, Japan, in the first use of the bomb as a weapon had an explosive force of 20 kilotons.

A *megaton* has the force of a million tons of TNT. A *gigaton* has the force of a billion tons of TNT.

kilowatt-hour The amount of electrical energy consumed when 1,000 watts are used for one hour.

The abbreviation *kwh* is acceptable on second reference.

kindergarten

king Capitalize only when used before the name of royalty: *King George VI.* Continue in subsequent references that use the king's given name: *King George,* not *George.*

Lowercase *king* when it stands alone.

Capitalize in plural uses before names: *Kings George and Edward.*

Lowercase in phrases such as *chess king Bobby Fischer.*

See **nobility** and **titles**.

Klan in America See **Ku Klux Klan**.

Kleenex A trademark for a brand of facial tissue.

KLM Royal Dutch Airlines A *KLM airliner* is acceptable in any reference.

Headquarters is in Amsterdam, Netherlands.

Knesset The Israeli parliament. See **foreign legislative bodies**.

knickknack

knight See **nobility**.

Knights of Columbus *K. of C.* or *the Knights* may be used on second reference.

See the **fraternal organizations and service clubs** entry.

knot A knot is one nautical mile (6,076.10 feet) per hour. It is redundant to say *knots per hour.*

A knot is computed as the length of one minute of a meridian. To convert knots into approximate statute miles per hour, multiply knots by 1.15.

Always use figures: *Winds were at 7 to 9 knots; a 10-knot wind.*

know-how

Kodak A trademark for cameras and other photographic products made by Eastman Kodak Co. of Rochester, N.Y.

Koran The sacred book of Moslems, who believe that it contains the words of Allah dictated to the Prophet Mohammed through the Angel Gabriel.

Korean War But lowercase *Korean conflict.*

kosher Always lowercase.

kowtow

Kriss Kringle Not *Kris.*

kudos It means credit or praise for an achievement.
The word takes plural verbs: *Kudos go to John Jones.*

Ku Klux Klan There are 42 separate organizations known as the *Klan in America.*
Some of them do not use the full name *Ku Klux Klan,* but each may be called that, and the *KKK* initials may be used for any of them on second reference.
The two largest Klan organizations are the National Knights of the Ku Klux Klan, based at Stone Mountain, Ga., and the United Klans of America, based at Tuscaloosa, Ala.
An Imperial Board, composed of leaders from the various groups, meets occasionally to coordinate activities.
Capitalize formal titles before a name: *Imperial Wizard James R. Venable, Grand Dragon Dale Reusch.* Members are *Klansmen.*

Kuomintang The Chinese Nationalist political party. Do not follow with the word *party. Tang* means party.

Kuril Islands Use in datelines after a community name in stories from these islands. Name an individual island, if needed, in the text.
Explain in the text that the islands are claimed by Japan but have been occupied by the Soviet Union since 1945.

Kuwait Stands alone in datelines.

la See **foreign particles.**

Labor Day The first Monday in September.

Laborers' International Union of North America The shortened form *Laborers' union* is acceptable in all references.
Headquarters is in Washington.

Labor Party Not *labour,* even if British.

Labrador The mainland portion of the Canadian province of Newfoundland.
Use *Newfoundland* in datelines after the name of a community. Specify in the text that it is in Labrador.

lacrosse Scoring is in goals, worth one point each.
The playing field is 110 yards long. The goals are 80 yards apart, with 15 yards of playing area behind each goal.
A match consists of four 15-minute periods. Overtimes of varying lengths may be played to break a tie.
Adapt the summary format in **hockey.**

Ladies' Home Journal

Ladies Professional Golf Association No apostrophe after *Ladies.* In general, spell out on first reference.
A phrase such as *LPGA tournament* may be used on first reference to avoid a cumbersome lead. If this is done, provide the full name later in the story.

lady Do not use as a synonym for *woman. Lady* may be used when it is a courtesy title or when a specific reference to fine manners is appropriate without patronizing overtones.
See **nobility.**

Laetrile A trademark for a substance derived from the chemical amygdalin, found naturally in the pits of apricots and peaches and in bitter almonds. It is believed by some to be an effective cancer treatment. The U.S. Food and Drug Administration has said that the substance has not been proved safe and effective as an anti-cancer agent and has banned interstate transportation. Marketed in some areas under the names *Bee-Seventeen* or *Aprikern.*

lager (beer)

lake Capitalize as part of a proper name: *Lake Erie, Canandaigua Lake, the Finger Lakes.*
Lowercase in plural uses: *lakes Erie and Ontario; Canandaigua and Seneca lakes.*

lamebrain

lame duck (n.) **lame-duck** (adj.)

Land-Rover With a hyphen. A trademark for a brand of all-terrain vehicle.

languages Capitalize the proper names of languages and dialects: *Aramaic, Cajun, English, Gullah, Persian, Serbo-Croatian, Yiddish.*

lanolin Formerly a trademark, now a generic term.

larceny See the **burglary, larceny, robbery, theft** entry.

last Avoid the use of *last* as a synonym for *latest* if it might imply finality. *The last time it rained, I forgot my umbrella,* is acceptable. But: *The last announcement was made at noon today* may leave the reader wondering whether the announcement was the final announcement, or whether others are to follow.

The word *last* is not necessary to convey the notion of most recent when the name of a month or day is used:

Preferred: *It happened Wednesday. It happened in April.* Correct, but redundant: *It happened last Wednesday.*

But: *It happened last week. It happened last month.*

Lastex A trademark for a type of elastic yarn.

Last Supper

late Do not use it to describe someone's actions while alive.

Wrong: *Only the late senator opposed this bill.* (He was not dead at that time.)

latex A resin-based substance used in making elastic materials and paints.

Latin America See **Western Hemisphere**.

Latin Rite See **Roman Catholic Church**.

latitude and longitude *Latitude,* the distance north or south of the equator, is designated by parallels. *Longitude,* the distance east or west of Greenwich, England, is designated by meridians.

Use these forms to express degrees of latitude and longitude: *New York City lies at 40 degrees 45 minutes north latitude and 74 degrees 0 minutes west longitude; New York City lies south of the 41st parallel north and along the 74th meridian west.*

Latter Day Saints, Latter-day Saints See **Church of Jesus Christ of Latter-day Saints**.

Laundromat A trademark for a coin-operated laundry.

Law Enforcement Assistance Administration *LEAA* is acceptable on second reference.

laws Capitalize legislative acts but not bills: *the Taft-Hartley Act, the Kennedy bill.*

lawsuit

lawyer A generic term for all members of the bar.

An *attorney* is someone legally appointed or empowered to act for another, usually, but not always, a lawyer. An *attorney at law* is a lawyer.

A *barrister* is an English lawyer who is specially trained and appears exclusively as a trial lawyer in higher courts. He is retained by a solicitor, not directly by the client. There is no equivalent term in the United States.

Counselor, when used in a legal sense, means a person who conducts a case in court, usually, but not always, a lawyer. A *counselor at law* is a lawyer. *Counsel* frequently is used collectively for a group of counselors.

A *solicitor* in England is a lawyer who performs legal services for the public. A solicitor appears in lower courts but does not have the right to appear in higher courts, which are reserved to barristers.

A *solicitor* in the United States is a lawyer employed by a governmental body. Solicitor is generally a job description, but in some agencies it is a formal title.

Solicitor general is the formal title for a chief law officer (where there is no attorney general) or for the chief assistant to the law officer (when there is an attorney general). Capitalize when used before a name.

Do not use *lawyer* as a formal title.

See the **attorney, lawyer** entry and **titles**.

lay, lie The action word is **lay**. It takes a direct object. *Laid* is the form for its past tense and its past participle. Its present participle is *laying*.

Lie indicates a state of reclining along a horizontal plane. It does not take a direct object. Its past tense is *lay*. Its past participle is *lain*. Its present participle is *lying*.

When **lie** means to make an untrue statement, the verb forms are *lie, lied, lying*.

Some examples:

PRESENT OR FUTURE TENSES:
Right: *I will lay the book on the table. The prosecutor tried to lay the blame on him.*
Wrong: *He lays on the beach all day. I will lay down.*
Right: *He lies on the beach all day. I will lie down.*

IN THE PAST TENSE:
I laid the book on the table. The prosecutor has laid the blame on him.
He lay on the beach all day. He has lain on the beach all day. I lay down. I have lain down.

WITH THE PRESENT PARTICIPLE:
I am laying the book on the table. The prosecutor is laying the blame on him.
He is lying on the beach. I am lying down.

Leaning Tower of Pisa

leatherneck Lowercase this nickname for a member of the U.S. Marine Corps. It is derived from the leather lining that was formerly part of the collar on the Marine uniform.

lectern, podium, pulpit, rostrum A speaker stands *behind a lectern, on a podium* or *rostrum,* or *in the pulpit.*

lecturer A formal title in the Christian Science Church. An occupational description in other uses.

lectures Capitalize and use quotation marks for their formal titles, as described in **composition titles**.

left hand (n.) **left-handed** (adj.) **left-hander** (n.)

leftist, ultra-leftist In general, avoid these terms in favor of a more precise description of an individual's political philosophy.

As popularly used today, particularly abroad, *leftist* often applies to someone who is merely liberal or believes in a form of democratic socialism.

Ultra-leftist suggests an individual who subscribes to a communist view or one holding that liberal or socialist change cannot come within the present form of goverment.

See **radical** and the **rightist, ultra-rightist** entry.

left wing (n.) But: *left-wing* (adj.), *left-winger* (n.).

legal holiday See the **holidays and holy days** entry.

legerdemain

legion, legionnaire See **American Legion** and **French Foreign Legion**.

legislative titles

FIRST REFERENCE FORM: Use *Rep., Reps., Sen.* and *Sens.* as formal titles before one or more names in regular text. Spell out and capitalize these titles before one or more names in a direct quotation. Spell out and lowercase *representative* and *senator* in other uses.

Spell out other legislative titles in all uses. Capitalize formal titles such as *assemblyman, assemblywoman, city* councilor, *delegate*, etc., when they are used before a name. Lowercase in other uses.

Add *U.S.* or *state* before a title only if necessary to avoid confusion: *U.S. Sen. Herman Talmadge spoke with state Sen. Hugh Carter.*

FIRST REFERENCE PRACTICE: The use of a title such as *Rep.* or *Sen.* in first reference is normal in most stories. It is not mandatory, however, provided an individual's title is given later in the story.

Deletion of the title on first reference is frequently appropriate, for example, when an individual has become well known: *Barry Goldwater endorsed President Ford today. The Arizona senator said he believes the president deserves another term.*

SECOND REFERENCE: Do not use legislative titles before a name on second reference unless they are part of a direct quotation.

CONGRESSMAN, CONGRESSWOMAN: *Rep.* and *U.S. Rep.* are the preferred first-reference forms when a formal title is used before the name of a U.S. House member. The words *congressman* or *congresswoman*, in lowercase, may be used in subsequent references that do not use an individual's name, just as *senator* is used in references to members of the Senate.

Congressman and *congresswoman* should appear as capitalized formal titles before a name only in direct quotation.

ORGANIZATIONAL TITLES: Capitalize titles for formal, organizational offices within a legislative body when they are used before a name: *Speaker Thomas P. O'Neill, Majority Leader Robert C. Byrd, Minority Leader John J. Rhodes, Democratic Whip James C. Wright, Chairman John J. Sparkman of the Senate Foreign Relations Committee, President Pro Tem John C. Stennis.*

See **party affiliation** and **titles**.

legislature Capitalize when preceded by the name of a state: *the Kansas Legislature.*

Retain capitalization when the state name is dropped but the reference is specifically to that state's legislature:

TOPEKA, Kan. (AP) — Both houses of the Legislature adjourned today.

Capitalize *legislature* in subsequent specific references and in such constructions as: *the 100th Legislature, the state Legislature.*

Although the word *legislature* is not part of the formal, proper name for the lawmaking bodies in many states, it commonly is used that way and should be treated as such in any story that does not use the formal name.

If a given context or local practice calls for the use of a formal name such as *Missouri General Assembly,* retain the capital letters if the name of the state can be dropped, but lowercase the word *assembly* if it stands alone. Lowercase *legislature* if a story uses it in a subsequent reference to a body identified as a general assembly.

Lowercase *legislature* when used generically: *No legislature has approved the amendment.*

Use *legislature* in lowercase for all plural references: *The Arkansas and Colorado legislatures are considering the amendment.*

In 49 states the separate bodies are a *senate* and a *house* or *assembly.* The *Nebraska Legislature* is a unicameral body.

See **assembly; governmental bodies; general assembly; house of representatives;** and **senate**.

Lent The period from Ash Wednesday through Holy Saturday, the day before Easter. The 40-day Lenten period for penance, suggested by Christ's 40 days in the desert, does not include the six Sundays between Ash Wednesday and Easter.

See **Easter** for the method of computing when Easter occurs.

lesbian, lesbianism Lowercase in references to homosexual women, except in names of organizations.

less See the **fewer, less** entry.

-less No hyphen before this suffix:
childless   waterless
tailless

let up (v.) **letup** (n. and adj.)

Levi's A trademark for a brand of jeans.

liabilities When used in a financial sense, the word means all the claims against a corporation.
They include accounts payable, wages and salaries due but not paid, dividends declared payable, taxes payable, and fixed or long-term obligations such as bonds, debentures and bank loans.
See **assets**.

liaison

liberal, liberalism See the **political parties and philosophies** entry.

lie See the **lay, lie** entry.

lie in state Only persons who are entitled to a state funeral may formally lie in state. In the United States, this occurs in the rotunda in the Capitol.
Those entitled to a state funeral are a president, a former president, a president-elect or any other person designated by the president.
Members of Congress may lie in state, and a number have done so. The decision is either house's to make, although the formal process normally begins with a request from the president.
Those entitled to an official funeral, but not to lie in state, are the vice president, the chief justice, Cabinet members and other government officials when designated by the president.

lieutenant See **military titles**.

lieutenant governor Capitalize and abbreviate as *Lt. Gov.* or *Lt. Govs.* when used as a formal title before one or more names in regular text. Capitalize and spell out when used as a formal title before one or more names in direct quotations.
Lowercase and spell out in all other uses.
See **titles**.

Life Saver, Life Savers Trademarks for a brand of roll candy.

life-size

lifestyle This form, an exception to Webster's New World, has been adopted in keeping with the spelling used by many newspapers.

lifetime

light, lighted, lighting Do not use *lit* as the past tense form.

lightning The electrical discharge.

light-year The distance that light travels in one year at the rate of 186,282 miles per second. It works out to about 5.88 trillion miles (5,878,612,800,000 miles).

likable Not *likeable*.

like, as Use *like* as a preposition to compare nouns and pronouns. It requires an object: *Jim blocks like a pro.*
The conjunction *as* is the correct word to introduce clauses: *Jim blocks the linebacker as he should.*

like- Follow with a hyphen when used as a prefix meaning similar to:
like-minded   like-natured
No hyphen in words that have meanings of their own:
likelihood   likewise
likeness

-like Do not precede this suffix by a hyphen unless the letter *l* would be tripled:

bill-like   lifelike
businesslike   shell-like

limited Abbreviate and capitalize as *Ltd.* when used as part of a formal corporate name. Do not set off from the name with commas.

limousine

linage, lineage *Linage* is the number of lines.
Lineage is ancestry or descent.

Lincoln's Birthday Capitalize *birthday* in references to the holiday.
Lincoln was born Feb. 12. His birthday is not a federal legal holiday.

line numbers Use figures and lowercase the word *line* in naming individual lines of a text: *line 1, line 9.* But: *the first line, the 10th line.*

linoleum Formerly a trademark, now a generic term.

Linotype A trademark for a brand of typesetting machine that casts an entire line of type in one bar or slug.

lion's share The term comes from an Aesop fable in which the lion took all the spoils of a joint hunt.
Use it to mean the whole of something, or the best and biggest portion.
Do not use it to mean majority.

liquidation When used in a financial sense, the word means the process of converting stock or other assets into cash.
When a company is liquidated, the cash obtained is first used to pay debts and obligations to holders of bonds and preferred stock. Whatever cash remains is distributed on a per-share basis to the holders of common stock.

liquidity The ease with which assets can be converted to cash without loss in value.

liter The basic unit of volume in the metric system. It is defined as the volume occupied by one kilogram of distilled water at 4 degrees Celsius. It works out to a total of 1,000 cubic centimeters (one cubic decimeter).
It takes 1,000 milliliters to make a liter.
A liter is equal to approximately 34 fluid ounces or 1.06 liquid quarts. A liter equals .91 of a dry quart. The metric system makes no distinction between dry volume and liquid volume.
To convert to liquid quarts, multiply by 1.06 (4 liters × 1.06 = 4.24 liquid quarts).
To convert to dry quarts, multiply by .91 (4 liters × .91 = 3.64 dry quarts).
To convert to liquid gallons, multiply by .26 (8 liters × .26 = 2.08 gallons).
See **gallon; kilogram; metric system; quart (dry);** and **quart (fluid).**

literally See the **figuratively, literally** entry.

literature See **composition titles.**

livable Not *liveable.*

livid It is not a synonym for *fiery, bright, crimson, red* or *flaming.* If a person turns livid with rage, his face becomes ashen or pale. It can mean *blue, bluish gray, gray, dull white, dull purple* or *grayish black.*

Lloyds Bank International Ltd. A prominent bank with headquarters in London.

Lloyd's of London A prominent insurance company with headquarters in London.

Lloyd's Register of Shipping The reference source for questions about non-military ships not covered in this book.

It is published by Lloyd's Register of Shipping Trust Corp. Ltd. in London.

loan terminology Note the meanings of these terms in describing loans by governments and corporations:

bond A certificate issued by a corporation or government stating the amount of a loan, the interest to be paid, the time for repayment and the collateral pledged if payment cannot be made. Repayment generally is not due for a long period, usually seven years or more.

collateral Stock or other property that a borrower is obligated to turn over to a lender if unable to repay a loan.

commercial paper A document describing the details of a short-term loan between corporations.

convertible bond A bond carrying the stipulation that it may be exchanged for a specific amount of stock in the company that issued it.

coupon A slip of paper attached to a bond that the bondholder clips at specified times and returns to the issuer for payment of the interest due.

default A person, corporation or government is in default if it fails to meet the terms for repayment.

debenture A certificate stating the amount of a loan, the interest to be paid and the time for repayment, but not providing collateral. It is backed only by the corporation's reputation and promise to pay.

full faith and credit bond An alternate term for a *general obligation bond*, often used to contrast such a bond with a *moral obligation bond*.

general obligation bond A bond that has had the formal approval of either the voters or their legislature. The government's promise to repay the principal and pay the interest is constitutionally guaranteed on the strength of its ability to tax the population.

maturity The date on which a bond, debenture or note must be repaid.

moral obligation bond A government bond that has not had the formal approval of either the voters or their legislature. It is backed only by the government's "moral obligation" to repay the principal and interest on time.

municipal bond A general obligation bond issued by a state, county, city, town, village, possession or territory, or a bond issued by an agency or authority set up by one of these governmental units. In general, interest paid on municipal bonds is exempt from federal income taxes. It also usually is exempt from state and local income taxes if held by someone living within the state of issue.

note A certificate issued by a corporation or government stating the amount of a loan, the interest to be paid and the collateral pledged in the event payment cannot be made. The date for repayment is generally more than a year after issue but not more than seven or eight years later. The shorter interval for repayment is the principal difference between a note and a bond.

revenue bond A bond backed only by the revenue of the airport, turnpike or other facility that was built with the money it raised.

Treasury borrowing A **Treasury bill** is a certificate representing a loan to the federal government that matures in three, six or 12 months. A **Treasury note** may mature in one to 10 years. A **Treasury bond** matures in seven years or more.

local Avoid the irrelevant use of the word.
Irrelevant: *The injured were taken to a local hospital.*
Better: *The injured were taken to a hospital.*

local of a union Always use a figure and capitalize *local* when giving the name of a union subdivision: *Local 222 of The Newspaper Guild.*

Lowercase *local* standing alone or in plural uses: *The local will vote Tuesday. He spoke to locals 2, 4 and 10.*

Lockheed Aircraft Corp. Headquarters is in Burbank, Calif.

lodges See the **fraternal organizations and service clubs** entry.

London The city in England stands alone in datelines.

long distance, long-distance Always a hyphen in reference to telephone calls: *We keep in touch by long-distance. He called long-distance. She took the long-distance call.*

In other uses, hyphenate only when used as a compound modifier: *She traveled a long distance. She made a long-distance trip.*

longitude See the **latitude and longitude** entry.

longshoreman Capitalize *longshoreman* only if the intended meaning is that the individual is a member of the International Longshoremen's and Warehousemen's Union or the International Longshoremen's Association.

long term, long-term Hyphenate when used as a compound modifier: *We will win in the long term. He has a long-term assignment.*

long time, longtime *They have known each other a long time. They are longtime partners.*

long ton Also known as a *British ton.* Equal to 2,240 pounds. See **ton.**

Lord's Supper See **sacraments.**

Los Angeles The city in California stands alone in datelines.

Confine *LA* to quoted matter.

LOT Polish Airlines Headquarters is in Warsaw, Poland.

Louisiana Abbrev.: *La.* See **state names.**

Low Countries Belgium, Luxembourg and Netherlands.

lowercase One word (n., v., adj.) when referring to the absence of capital letters. An exception to Webster's New World, in keeping with printers' practice.

LSD Acceptable in all references for *lysergic acid diethylamide.*

Ltd. See **limited.**

Lt. Gov. See **lieutenant governor.**

Lucite A trademark for acrylic plastic.

Lufthansa German Airlines A *Lufthansa airliner* is acceptable in any reference.

Headquarters is in Cologne, West Germany.

Lutheran churches The basic unit of government in Lutheran practice is the congregation. It normally is administered by a council, headed either by the senior pastor or a lay person elected from the membership of the council. The council customarily consists of congregation's clergy and elected lay persons.

National church bodies are made up of congregations and governed by conventions. Congregations are grouped into territorial districts or synods whose functions vary. The term *synod* also is used in the names of some national bodies.

The Lutheran Church in America is the largest of three major Lutheran bodies in the United States. Of the three, it takes the least rigid or literalistic stand on doctrine and Bible interpretation. Formed in 1962 from a merger of four bodies with Danish, Finnish, German and Swedish backgrounds, it has almost 3 million members.

The Lutheran Church-Missouri Synod, with about 2.7 million members, is regarded as the most conservative of the three bodies. A split has developed within the synod over the question of Bible interpretation and synod leadership. Its background is predominantly German.

The American Lutheran Church, with some 2.4 million members, generally is regarded as middle of the road in doctrinal emphasis. It was formed in 1960 through a merger of four bodies with Danish, German and Norwegian backgrounds.

All three bodies are members of the New York-based Lutheran Council in the U.S.A., which coordinates various joint activities.

BELIEFS: Lutheran teachings go back to Martin Luther, a 16th century Roman Catholic priest whose objections to elements of Roman Catholic practice began the movement known as the Protestant Reformation.

Lutherans believe in the Trinity and emphasize both the divinity and humanity of Christ. There are two sacraments, baptism and the Lord's Supper.

In recent years, the question of Bible interpretation has divided Lutherans into "moderate" and "conservative" camps. Conservatives argue for a literal interpretation of passages others consider symbolic. Moderates argue that some truths in the Bible are expressed in allegories.

CLERGY: Members of the clergy are known as *ministers. Pastor* applies if a minister leads a congregation.

On first reference, use *the Rev.* before the name of a man or woman. On second reference, use only the last name of a man; use *Miss, Mrs.* or *Ms.* before the last name of a woman depending on her preference.

In the American Lutheran Church, the president and district presidents are often referred to as bishops. Use *Bishop* before such an individual's name on first reference.

See **religious titles**.

OTHER OFFICIALS: Lay members of a church council frequently are designated *elders, deacons* or *trustees.* The preferred form for identifying them is a construction that requires commas to set their names off from these titles. Capitalize *elder, deacon* or *trustee* when used before a name on first reference. On second reference, use only the last name of a man; use *Miss, Mrs.* or *Ms.* before the last name of a woman depending on her preference.

Luxembourg Stands alone in datelines.

·ly Do not use a hyphen between adverbs ending in *-ly* and adjectives they modify: *an easily remembered rule, a badly damaged island, a fully informed woman.*

See the compound modifiers section of the **hyphen** entry.

Lyndon B. Johnson Space Center Formerly the Manned Spacecraft Center. Located in Houston, it is the National Aeronautics and Space Administration's principal control and training center for manned spaceflight.

Johnson Space Center is acceptable in all references.

In datelines:

SPACE CENTER, Houston (AP) —

See **John F. Kennedy Space Center**.

Macao Stands alone in datelines.

Mace A trademark, shortened from *Chemical Mace,* for a brand of tear gas that is packaged in an aerosol canister and temporarily stuns its victims.

machine gun (n.) But: *machine-gun* (v. and adj.), *machine-gunner.*
See **weapons**.

Mach number Named for Ernst Mach, an Austrian physicist, the figure represents the ratio of the speed of an object to the speed of sound in the surrounding medium, such as air, through which the object is moving.
A rule of thumb for speed of sound is approximately 750 miles per hour at sea level and approximately 660 miles per hour at 30,000 feet above sea level.
A body traveling at *Mach 1* would be traveling at the speed of sound. *Mach 2* would equal twice the speed of sound.

Mafia, Mafiosi The secret society of criminals and its members. Do not use as a synonym for *organized crime* or the *underworld.*

magazine names Capitalize the name but do not place it in quotes. Lowercase *magazine* unless it is part of the publication's formal title: *Harper's Magazine, Newsweek magazine, Time magazine.*
Check the masthead if in doubt.

magistrate Capitalize when used as a formal title before a name. See **titles**.

Magna Charta The charter the English barons forced King John of England to grant at Runnymede in June 1215. It guaranteed certain civil and political liberties.

Mailgram A trademark for a telegram sent to a post office near the recipient's address and delivered to the address by letter carrier.

mailman *Letter carrier* is preferable because many women hold this job.

Maine Do not abbreviate. See **state names**.

mainland China See **China**.

major See **military titles**.

Majorca Use instead of *Spain* in datelines on stories from communities on this island.

majority, plurality *Majority* means more than half of an amount.
Plurality means more than the next highest number.

COMPUTING MAJORITY: To describe how large a majority is, take the figure that is more than half and subtract everything else from it: If 100,000 votes were cast in an election and one candidate received 60,000 while opponents received 40,000, the winner would have a *majority* of 20,000 votes.

COMPUTING PLURALITY: To describe how large a plurality is, take the highest number and subtract from it the next highest number: If, in the election example above, the second-place finisher had 25,000 votes, the winner's *plurality* would be 35,000 votes.

Suppose, however, that no candidate in this example had a majority. If the first-place finisher had 40,000 votes and the second-place finisher had 30,000, for example, the leader's *plurality* would be 10,000 votes.

USAGE: When *majority* and *plurality* are used alone, they take singular verbs and pronouns: *The majority has made its decision.*

If a plural word follows an *of* construction, the decision on whether to use a singular or plural verb depends on the sense of the sentence: *A majority of two votes is not adequate to control the committee. The majority of the houses on the block were destroyed.*

majority leader Capitalize when used as a formal title before a name: *Majority Leader Robert C. Byrd.* Lowercase elsewhere.
See **legislative titles** and **titles**.

make up (v.)   **makeup** (n. and adj.)

malarkey Not *malarky.*

Maldives Use this official name with a community name in a dateline. The body of the story should note that the nation frequently is called *the Maldive Islands.*

man, mankind Either may be used when both men and women are involved and no other term is convenient. In these cases, do not use duplicate phrases such as *a man or a woman* or *mankind and womankind.*
Frequently the best choice is a substitute such as *humanity, a person* or *an individual.*
See **women**.

manageable

manager Capitalize when used as a formal title before a name: *Manager Casey Stengel, General Manager Dick O'Connell.*
Do not capitalize in job descriptions such as *equipment manager John Smith.*
See **titles**.

managing editor Capitalize when used as a formal title before a name.
See **titles**.

Manitoba A province of central Canada. Do not abbreviate.
See **datelines**.

manslaughter See the **homicide, murder, manslaughter** entry.

mantel, mantle A *mantel* is a shelf. A *mantle* is a cloak.

Maoism (Maoist) The communist philosophy and policies of Mao Tse-tung. See the **political parties and philosophies** entry.

marathon Use the formats illustrated in the **cross country** and **track and field** entries.

March See **months**.

Mardi Gras Literally "fat Tuesday," the term describes a day of merrymaking on the Tuesday before Ash Wednesday.
In New Orleans and many Roman Catholic countries, the Tuesday celebration is preceded by a week or more of parades and parties.

marijuana Not *marihuana.*

Marines Capitalize when referring to U.S. forces: *the U.S. Marines, the Marines, the Marine Corps, Marine regulations.* Do not use the abbreviation *USMC.*

Capitalize *Marine* when referring to an individual in a Marine Corps unit: *He is a Marine.*

Maritime Provinces The Canadian provinces of Nova Scotia, New Brunswick and Prince Edward Island.

marketbasket, marketplace

marquess, marchioness See **nobility.**

marshal, marshaled, marshaling, Marshall *Marshal* is the spelling for both the verb and the noun: *Marilyn will marshal her forces. Erwin Rommel was a field marshal.*
Marshall is used in proper names: *George C. Marshall, John Marshall, the Marshall Islands.*

Marshall Islands Named for John Marshall, a British explorer.
In datelines, give the name of a city and *Marshall Islands*. List the name of an individual island in the text.

Marxism (Marxist) The system of thought developed by Karl Marx and Friedrich Engels. See the **political parties and philosophies** entry.

Maryland Abbrev.: *Md.* See **state names.**

Mason-Dixon Line The boundary line between Pennsylvania and Maryland, generally regarded as separating the North from the South.

Masonite A trademark for a brand of hardboard.

Mass It is *celebrated, said* or *sung.* Always capitalize when referring to the ceremony, but lowercase any preceding adjectives: *high Mass, low Mass, requiem Mass.*
In Eastern Orthodox churches the correct term is *Divine Liturgy.*
See **Roman Catholic Church.**

Massachusetts Abbrev.: *Mass.* Legally a commonwealth, not a state.
See **state** and **state names.**

master of arts, master of science A *master's degree* or a *master's* is acceptable in any reference.
See **academic degrees** for guidelines on when the abbreviations *M.A.* and *M.S.* are acceptable.

match summary This format for summarizing sports events applies to one vs. one contests such as tennis, match play golf, etc.
Give a competitor's name, followed either by a home town or by a college or club affiliation. For competitors from outside the United States, a country name alone is sufficient in summaries sent for domestic use.
Example:

> Jimmy Connors, Belleville, Ill., def.
> Manuel Orantes, Spain, 2-6, 6-3, 6-2, 6-1.

matrimony See **sacraments.**

maturity In a financial sense, the date on which a bond, debenture or note must be repaid.
See **loan terminology.**

May See **months.**

May Day, mayday *May Day* is May 1, often observed as a festive or political holiday.
Mayday is the international distress signal, from the French *m'aidez,* a reflexive verb meaning "help me."

mayors' conference See **U.S. Conference of Mayors.**

MC For *master of ceremonies,* but only in quoted matter. See **emcee.**

McDonnell Douglas Corp. Headquarters is in St. Louis.

M.D. A word such as *physician* or *surgeon* is preferred.
See **doctor** and **academic titles.**

meager

mean See the **average, mean, median, norm** entry.

Medal of Freedom It is now the *Presidential Medal of Freedom.* See entry under that name.

Medal of Honor The nation's highest military honor, given by Congress for risk of life in combat beyond the call of duty.

There is no *Congressional Medal of Honor.*

media In the sense of mass communication, such as magazines, newspapers, the news services, radio and television, the word is plural: *The news media are resisting attempts to limit their freedom.*

median See the **average, mean, median, norm** entry.

mediate See the **arbitrate, mediate** entry.

Medicaid A federal-state program that helps pay for health care for the needy, aged, blind and disabled, and for low-income families with children.

A state determines eligibility and which health services are covered. The federal government reimburses a percentage of the state's expenditures.

Medicare The federal health care insurance program for people aged 65 and over, and for the disabled. Eligibility is based mainly on eligibility for Social Security.

Medicare helps pay charges for hospitalization, for stays in skilled nursing facilities, for physician's charges and for some associated health costs. There are limitations on the length of stay and type of care.

In Canada, *Medicare* refers to the nation's national health insurance program.

medicine See the **drugs, medicine** entry.

medieval

mega- A prefix denoting 1 million units of a measure. Move a decimal point six places to the right, adding zeros if necessary, to convert to the basic unit: 5.5 megatons = 5,500,000 tons.

melee

Melkite Church See **Eastern Rite churches.**

memento, mementos

memo, memos

memorandum, memorandums

Memorial Day Formerly May 30. The federal legal holiday is the last Monday in May.

menage a trois

menswear Not *men's wear.*

Mercalli scale See **earthquakes.**

Mercurochrome A trademark for a brand of antiseptic for wounds.

meridians Use numerals and lowercase to identify the imaginary locater lines that ring the globe from north to south through the poles. They are measured in units of 0 to 180 degrees east and west of the *prime meridian,* which runs through Greenwich, England.

Examples: *33rd meridian* (if location east or west of Greenwich is obvious), *1st meridian west, 100th meridian.*

See the **latitude and longitude** entry.

merry-go-round

messiah Capitalize in religious uses. Lowercase when used generically to mean a liberator.

meter The basic unit of length in the metric system. It is defined as being equal to 1,650,763.73 wavelengths of the orange-red radiation of an isotope of krypton.

It is equal to approximately 39.37 inches, which may be rounded off to 39.5 inches in most comparisons.

It takes 100 centimeters to make a meter.

It takes 1,000 meters to make a kilometer.

To convert to inches, multiply by 39.37 (5 meters $\times$ 39.37 = 196.85 inches).

To convert to yards, multiply by 1.1 (5 meters $\times$ 1.1 = 5.5 yards).

See **inches; metric system**; and **yards**.

Methodist churches The term *Methodist* originated as a nickname applied to a group of 18th century Oxford University students known for their methodical application to Scripture study and prayer.

The principal Methodist body in the United States is the United Methodist Church, which also has some member conferences outside the United States. It was formed in 1968 by the merger of the Methodist Church and the Evangelical United Brethren Church. It has about 10 million members.

The government of the United Methodist Church follows a stratified pattern from the General Conference through several intermediate conferences down to the local congregation.

The General Conference, which meets every four years, has final authority in all matters. Its members, half lay and half clergy, are elected by the annual conferences.

Jurisdictional conferences covering major sections of the nation are composed of ministers and lay delegates. Their principal function is to elect bishops.

Annual conferences, generally organized along state lines, elect delegates to higher conferences and make official appointments within their areas.

A Methodist bishop presides over a "church area," which may embrace one or more annual conferences. Bishops have extensive administrative powers, including the authority to place, transfer and remove local church pastors, usually in consultation with district superintendents.

Districts in each conference are responsible for promotion of mission work, support of colleges, hospitals and publications, and examination of candidates for the ministry.

Members of a congregation form a charge conference. It elects officers to a board that assists the pastor.

Methodism in the United States also includes three major black denominations: the African Methodist Episcopal Church, the African Methodist Episcopal Zion Church and the Christian Methodist Episcopal Church.

BELIEFS: Methodist teachings emphasize that the Holy Scriptures contain all the knowledge necessary for salvation. Tradition is not acknowledged as a valid source of revelation, although the writings of John Wesley, a leader of the Oxford University group, are regarded as sound interpretations of the Scriptures.

Methodists believe in the Trinity and the humanity and divinity of Christ. There are two sacraments, baptism and the Lord's Supper.

CLERGY: Ordained individuals are known as *bishops* and *ministers*. *Pastor* applies if a minister leads a congregation.

For first references to bishops, use the word: *Bishop W. Kenneth Goodson of Richmond, Va.* The designations *the Most Rev.* or *the Rt. Rev.* do not apply.

For first reference to ministers, use *the Rev.* before the name of a man or woman. On second reference, use only the last name of a man; use *Miss, Mrs.* or *Ms.* before the last name of a woman depending on her preference.

See **religious titles**.

metric system In general, metric terms should be included in a story when they are relevant.

There are no hard-and-fast rules on when they are relevant, but the following two guidelines have been developed to cover questions likely to arise as metric measurements gain increased acceptance in the United States:

—Use metric terms when they are the primary form in which the source of a story has provided statistics. Follow the metric units with equivalents in the terms more widely known in the United States. Normally, the equivalent should be in parentheses after the metric figure. A general statement such as, *A kilometer equals about five-eighths of a mile*, would be acceptable, however, to avoid repeated use of parenthetical equivalents in a story that used kilometers many times.

—Provide metric equivalents for traditional forms if a metric unit has become widely known. As speedometers with kilometer markings become more prevalent, for example, a story about speed limits might list miles per hour and provide kilometers per hour in parentheses.

CONVERSION FORMULAS: A conversion table for frequently used metric terms is printed on this page.

In addition, separate entries for *gram, meter, liter, Celsius* and other frequently used metric units define them and give examples of how to convert them to

METRIC CONVERSION CHART

INTO METRIC

If You Know	Multiply By	To Get
LENGTH		
inches	2.54	centimeters
feet	30	centimeters
yards	0.91	meters
miles	1.6	kilometers
AREA		
sq. inches	6.5	sq. centimeters
sq. feet	0.09	sq. meters
sq. yards	0.8	sq. meters
sq. miles	2.6	sq. kilometers
acres	0.4	hectares
MASS (Weight)		
ounces	28	grams
pounds	0.45	kilograms
short ton	0.9	metric ton
VOLUME		
teaspoons	5	milliliters
tablespoons	15	milliliters
fluid ounces	30	milliliters
cups	0.24	liters
pints	0.47	liters
quarts	0.95	liters
gallons	3.8	liters
cubic feet	0.03	cubic meters
cubic yards	0.76	cubic meters
TEMPERATURE		
Fahrenheit	Subtract 32 then multiply by 5/9ths	Celsius

OUT OF METRIC

If You Know	Multiply By	To Get
LENGTH		
millimeters	0.04	inches
centimeters	0.4	inches
meters	3.3	feet
kilometers	0.62	miles
AREA		
sq. centimeters	0.16	sq. inches
sq. meters	1.2	sq. yards
sq. kilometers	0.4	sq. miles
hectares	2.47	acres
MASS (Weight)		
grams	0.035	ounces
kilograms	2.2	pounds
metric tons	1.1	short tons
VOLUME		
milliliters	0.03	fluid ounces
liters	2.1	pints
liters	1.06	quarts
liters	0.26	gallons
cubic meters	35	cubic feet
cubic meters	1.3	cubic yards
TEMPERATURE		
Celsius	Multiply by 9/5ths, then add 32	Fahrenheit

equivalents in the terminology that has been used in the United States.

Similarly, entries for *pound, inch, quart, Fahrenheit,* etc., contain examples of how to convert these terms to metric forms.

To avoid the need for long strings of figures, prefixes are added to the metric units to denote fractional elements or large multiples. The prefixes are: *pico-* (one-trillionth), *nano-* (one-billionth), *micro-* (one-millionth), *milli-* (one-thousandth), *centi-* (one hundredth), *deci-* (one-tenth), *deka-* (10 units), *hecto-* (100 units), *kilo-* (1,000 units), *mega-* (1 million units), *giga-* (1 billion units), *tera-* (1 trillion units). Entries for each prefix show how to convert a unit preceded by the prefix to the basic unit.

ABBREVIATIONS: The abbreviation *mm* for *millimeter* is acceptable in references to film widths (*8mm film*) and weapons (*a 105mm cannon*).

Do not otherwise use metric abbreviations in news copy.

The principal abbreviations, for reference in the event they are used by a source, are: *g* (gram), *kg* (kilogram), *t* (metric ton), *m* (meter), *cm* (centimeter), *km* (kilometer), *mm* (millimeter), *L* (liter, capital *L* to avoid confusion with the figure *1*) and *mL* (milliliter).

metric ton Equal to approximately 2,204.62 pounds. See **ton.**

Metro-Goldwyn-Mayer Inc. *MGM* is acceptable in all references.

Headquarters is in Culver City, Calif.

metropolitan See **Eastern Orthodox churches.**

Mexico City The city in Mexico stands alone in datelines.

Miami The city in Florida stands alone in datelines.

Michigan Abbrev.: *Mich.* See **state names.**

micro- A prefix denoting one-millionth of a unit. Move a decimal point six places to the left in converting to the basic unit: 2,999,888.5 microseconds = 2.9998885 seconds.

mid- No hyphen unless a capitalized word follows:

mid-America	midsemester
mid-Atlantic	midterm

But use a hyphen when *mid-* precedes a figure: *mid-30s.*

Middle Ages A.D. 476 to A.D. 1450.

Middle Atlantic States As defined by the U.S. Census Bureau, they are New Jersey, New York and Pennsylvania.

Less formal references often consider Delaware part of the group.

See **Northeast region.**

middle class, middle-class *He is a member of the middle class. She has middle-class values.*

Middle East As defined by the Columbia Lippincott Gazetteer, the term applies to southwest Asia west of Pakistan (Afghanistan, Iran, Iraq, Israel, Kuwait, Jordan, Lebanon, Oman, Qatar, Saudi Arabia, South Yemen, Syria, Turkey, United Arab Emirates and Yemen), northeastern Africa (Egypt and Sudan), and the island of Cyprus.

Popular usage once distinguished between the *Near East* (the westerly nations in the listing) and the *Middle East* (the easterly nations), but the gazetteer advises that the two terms now overlap, with current practice favoring *Middle East* for both areas.

Use *Middle East* unless *Near East* is used by a source in a story.

Mideast is also acceptable, but *Middle East* is preferred.

middle initials In general, use them. They are an integral part of a person's name.

Particular care should be taken to include middle initials in stories where they help identify a specific individual. Examples include casualty lists and stories naming the accused in a crime.

A middle initial may be dropped if a person does not use one or is publicly known without it: *Mickey Mantle* (not *Mickey C.*), *the Rev. Billy Graham* (not *Billy F.*).

See **names**.

middleman

midnight Do not put a *12* in front of it. It is part of the day that is ending, not the one that is beginning.

midshipman See **military academies**.

midwest, midwestern See the **directions and regions** entry.

MiG The *i* in this designation for a type of Soviet fighter is lowercased because it is the Russian word for *and*. The initials are from the last names of the designers, Arten Mikovan and Mikhail Gurevich.

The forms: *MiG-19, MiG-21s*.

See **aircraft names**.

mile Also called a *statute mile*, it equals 5,280 feet.

The metric equivalent is approximately 1.6 kilometers.

To convert to kilometers, multiply by 1.6 (5 miles × 1.6 = 8 kilometers).

See **foot**; **kilometer**; **knot**; and **nautical mile**.

Use figures for amounts under 10 in dimensions, formulas and speeds: *The farm measures 5 miles by 4 miles. The car slowed to 7 miles per hour. The new model gets 4 miles more per gallon.*

Spell out below 10 in distances: *He drove four miles.*

miles per gallon The abbreviation *mpg* is acceptable on second reference.

miles per hour The abbreviation *mph* (no periods) is acceptable in all references.

military academies Capitalize *U.S. Air Force Academy, U.S. Coast Guard Academy, U.S. Military Academy, U.S. Naval Academy*. Retain capitalization if the *U.S.* is dropped: *the Air Force Academy*, etc.

Lowercase *academy* whenever it stands alone.

Cadet is the proper title on first reference for men and women enrolled at the Army and Air Force academies. *Midshipman* is the proper title for men and women enrolled at the Navy and Coast Guard academies.

Use the appropriate title on first reference. On second reference to a man, use his last name; on second reference to a woman, use *Miss* or *Ms.* before her last name depending on her preference.

military titles Capitalize a military rank when used as a formal title before an individual's name.

See the lists that follow to determine whether the title should be spelled out or abbreviated in regular text. Spell out any title used before a name in a direct quotation.

On first reference, use the appropriate title before the full name of a member of the military.

In subsequent references, do not continue using the title before a name. Use only the last name of a man. Use *Miss, Mrs.* or *Ms.* before the last name of a woman depending on her preference.

Spell out and lowercase a title when it is substituted for a name: *Gen. John J. Pershing arrived today. An aide said the general would review the troops.*

In some cases, it may be necessary to explain the significance of a title: *Army Sgt. Maj. John Jones described the attack. Jones, who holds the Army's highest rank for enlisted men, said it was unprovoked.*

In addition to the ranks listed on the next page, each service has ratings such as *machinist, radarman, torpedoman*, etc., that are job descriptions. Do not use any of these designations as a title on first reference. If one is used before a name in a subsequent reference, do not capitalize or abbreviate it.

ABBREVIATIONS: The abbreviations, with the highest ranks listed first:

MILITARY TITLES

Rank	Usage before a name

ARMY
Commissioned Officers

general	Gen.
lieutenant general	Lt. Gen.
major general	Maj. Gen.
brigadier general	Brig. Gen.
colonel	Col.
lieutenant colonel	Lt. Col.
major	Maj.
captain	Capt.
first lieutenant	1st Lt.
second lieutenant	2nd Lt.

Warrant Officers

chief warrant officer	Chief Warrant Officer
warrant officer	Warrant Officer

Enlisted Personnel

sergeant major of the Army	Army Sgt. Maj.
command sergeant major	Command Sgt. Maj.
staff sergeant major	Staff Sgt. Maj.
first sergeant	1st Sgt.
master sergeant	Master Sgt.
platoon sergeant	Platoon Sgt.
sergeant first class	Sgt. 1st Class
specialist seven	Spec. 7
staff sergeant	Staff Sgt.
specialist six	Spec. 6
sergeant	Sgt.
specialist five	Spec. 5
corporal	Cpl.
specialist four	Spec. 4
private first class	Pfc.
private 2	Pvt. 2
private 1	Pvt. 1

NAVY, COAST GUARD
Commissioned Officers

admiral	Adm.
vice admiral	Vice Adm.
rear admiral	Rear Adm.
commodore	Commodore
captain	Capt.
commander	Cmdr.
lieutenant commander	Lt. Cmdr.
lieutenant	Lt.
lieutenant junior grade	Lt. j.g.
ensign	Ensign

Warrant Officers

commissioned warrant officer	Commissioned Warrant Officer
warrant officer	Warrant Officer

Enlisted Personnel

master chief petty officer	Master Chief Petty Officer
senior chief petty officer	Senior Chief Petty Officer
chief petty officer	Chief Petty Officer
petty officer first class	Petty Officer 1st Class
petty officer second class	Petty Officer 2nd Class
petty officer third class	Petty Officer 3rd Class
seaman	Seaman
seaman apprentice	Seaman Apprentice
seaman recruit	Seaman Recruit

MARINE CORPS

Ranks and abbreviations for commissioned officers are the same as those in the Army. Warrant officer ratings follow the same system used in the Navy. There are no specialist ratings.

Others

sergeant major	Sgt. Maj.
master gunnery sergeant	Master Gunnery Sgt.
master sergeant	Master Sgt.
first sergeant	1st Sgt.
gunnery sergeant	Gunnery Sgt.
staff sergeant	Staff Sgt.
sergeant	Sgt.
corporal	Cpl.
lance corporal	Lance Cpl.
private first class	Pfc.
private	Pvt.

AIR FORCE

Ranks and abbreviations for commissioned officers are the same as those in the Army.

Enlisted Designations

chief master sergeant	Chief Master Sgt.
senior master sergeant	Senior Master Sgt.
master sergeant	Master Sgt.
technical sergeant	Tech. Sgt.
staff sergeant	Staff Sgt.
sergeant	Sgt.
airman first class	Airman 1st Class
airman	Airman
airman basic	Airman

PLURALS: Add *s* to the principal element in the title: *Majs. John Jones and Robert Smith; Maj. Gens. John Jones and Robert Smith; Specs. 4 John Jones and Robert Smith.*

RETIRED OFFICERS: A military rank may be used in first reference before the name of an officer who has retired if it is relevant to a story. Do not, however, use the military abbreviation *Ret.*

Instead, use *retired* just as *former* would be used before the title of a civilian: *They invited retired Army Gen. John Smith.*

FIREFIGHTERS, POLICE OFFICERS: Use the abbreviations listed here when a military-style title is used before the name of a firefighter or police officer outside a direct quotation. Add *police* or *fire* before the title if needed for clarity: *police Sgt. William Smith, fire Capt. David Jones.*

Spell out titles such as *detective* that are not used in the armed forces.

military units Use Arabic figures and capitalize the key words when linked with the figures: *1st Infantry Division* (or *the 1st Division*), *5th Battalion, 395th Field Artillery, 7th Fleet.*

But: *the division, the battalion, the artillery, the fleet.*

milli- A prefix denoting one-thousandth of a unit. Move a decimal point three places to the left in converting to the basic unit: 1,567.5 millimeters = 1.5675 meters.

milligram One-thousandth of a gram.

Equal to approximately twenty-eight-thousandth of an ounce.

To convert to ounces, multiply by 0.000035 (140 milligrams × 0.000035 = 0.0049 ounces).

See **metric system**.

milliliter One-thousandth of a liter.

Equal to approximately one-fifth of a teaspoon.

Thirty milliliters equal one fluid ounce.

To convert to teaspoons, multiply by .2 (5 milliliters × .2 = 1 teaspoon).

See **liter** and **metric system**.

millimeter One-thousandth of a meter.

It takes 10 millimeters to make a centimeter.

A millimeter is roughly equal to the thickness of a paper clip.

To convert to inches, multiply by .04 (5 millimeters × .04 = .2 of an inch).

May be abbreviated as *mm* (no space) when used with a numeral in first or subsequent references to film or weapons: *35mm film, 105mm artillery piece.*

See **meter**; **metric system**; and **inch**.

millions, billions Use figures with *million* or *billion* in all except casual uses: *I'd like to make a billion dollars.* But: *The nation has 1 million citizens. I need $7 billion.*

Do not go beyond two decimals: *7.51 million persons, $2.56 billion, 7,542,500 persons, $2,565,750,000.* Decimals are preferred where practical: *1.5 million.* Not: *1½ million.*

Do not mix *millions* and *billions* in the same figure: *2.6 billion.* Not: *2 billion 600 million.*

Do not drop the word *million* or *billion* in the first figure of a range: *He is worth from $2 million to $4 million.* Not: *$2 to $4 million,* unless you really mean *$2.*

Note that a hyphen is not used to join the figures and the word *million* or *billion*, even in this type of phrase: *The president submitted a $300 billion budget.*

milquetoast Not *milk toast* when referring to a shrinking, apologetic person. Derived from Caspar Milquetoast, a character in a comic strip by Harold T. Webster.

Milwaukee The city in Wisconsin stands alone in datelines.

mimeograph Formerly a trademark, now a generic term.

mini- The rules in **prefixes** apply, but in general, no hyphen. Some examples:

minibus   miniskirt
miniseries

minister It is not a formal title. Do not use it before the name of a member of the clergy.
See **religious titles** and the entry for an individual's denomination.

ministry See **foreign governmental bodies**.

Minneapolis The city in Minnesota stands alone in datelines.

Minnesota Abbrev.: *Minn.* See **state names**.

minority leader Treat the same as *majority leader*. See that entry and **legislative titles**.

minuscule Not *miniscule*.

minus sign Use a hyphen, not a dash, but use the word *minus* if there is any danger of confusion.
Use a word, not a minus sign, to indicate temperatures below zero: *minus 10* or *5 below zero*.

MIRV, MIRVs Acceptable on first reference for *multiple independently targetable re-entry vehicle(s)*.
Explain in the text that a MIRV is an intercontinental ballistic missile with several warheads, each of which can be directed to a different target.

misdemeanor See the **felony, misdemeanor** entry.

mishap A minor misfortune. People are not killed in mishaps.

Miss See **courtesy titles**.

missile names Use Arabic figures and capitalize the proper name but not the word *missile*: *Titan 2 missile*.
See **ABM**; **ICBM**; **MIRV**; and **SAM**.

Mississippi Abbrev.: *Miss.* See **state names**.

Missouri Abbrev.: *Mo.* See **state names**.

mix up (v.) **mix-up** (n. and adj.)

Mobil Corp. Headquarters is in New York.
Mobil Oil Corp. is a subsidiary.

mock-up (n.)

model numbers See **serial numbers**.

Mohammed The spelling for the founder of the Moslem religion.

Monaco After the Vatican, the world's smallest state.
The *Monaco* section stands alone in datelines. The other two sections, *La Condamine* and *Monte Carlo*, are followed by *Monaco*:
MONTE CARLO, Monaco (AP) —

Monday See **days of the week**.

Monday morning quarterback One who second guesses.

M-1, M-14 See **weapons**.

monetary See the **fiscal, monetary** entry.

monetary units See **cents**; **dollars**; and **pounds**.

moneymaker

monsignor See **Roman Catholic Church**.

Montana Abbrev.: *Mont.* See **state names**.

Montessori method After Maria Montessori, a system of training young children. It emphasizes training of the senses and guidance to encourage self-education.

monthlong

months Capitalize the names of months in all uses. When a month is used with a specific date, abbreviate only *Jan., Feb., Aug. Sept., Oct., Nov.* and *Dec.* Spell out when using alone, or with a year alone.

When a phrase lists only a month and a year, do not separate the year with commas. When a phrase refers to a month, day and year, set off the year with commas.

EXAMPLES: *January 1972 was a cold month. Jan. 2 was the coldest day of the month. His birthday is May 15. Feb. 14, 1976, was the target date.*

In tabular material, use these three-letter forms without a period: *Jan, Feb, Mar, Apr, May, Jun, Jul, Aug, Sep, Oct, Nov, Dec.*

See **dates** and **years**.

Montreal The city in Canada stands alone in datelines.

monuments Capitalize the popular names of monuments and similar public attractions: *Lincoln Memorial, Statue of Liberty, Washington Monument, Leaning Tower of Pisa,* etc.

moon Lowercase. See **heavenly bodies**.

mop up (v.)   **mop-up** (n. and adj.)

moral obligation bond See **loan terminology**.

more than See **over**.

Mormon Church Acceptable in all references for *Church of Jesus Christ of Latter-day Saints*, but always include the full name in a story dealing primarily with church activites.

See the entry under the formal name.

Moscow The city in the Soviet Union stands alone in datelines.

Moslem(s) The preferred term to describe adherents of Islam.

In the names of certain U.S. organizations, such as the *Black Muslims,* and in references to their members, *Muslims* may be used.

mosquito, mosquitoes

mother-in-law, mothers-in-law

Mother Nature

Mother's Day The second Sunday in May.

motor See the **engine, motor** entry.

motorboat racing Scoring may be posted in miles per hour, points or laps, depending on the competition.

In general, use the basic summary format. For some major events, adapt the basic summary to paragraph form under a dateline. See the **auto racing** entry for an example.

motorcycle racing Follow the formats shown under **auto racing**.

mount Spell out in all uses, including the names of communities and of mountains: *Mount Clemens, Mich.; Mount Everest.*

mountains Capitalize as part of a proper name: *Appalachian Mountains, Ozark Mountains, Rocky Mountains.*

Or simply: *the Appalachians, the Ozarks, the Rockies.*

Mountain Standard Time (MST), Mountain Daylight Time (MDT) See **time zones**.

Mountain States As defined by the U.S. Census Bureau, the eight are Arizona, Colorado, Idaho, Montana, Nevada, New Mexico, Utah and Wyoming.

movie ratings The rankings used by the Motion Picture Association of America Inc. are:

G For *general audiences.* All ages admitted.

PG For *parental guidance.* Some material may not be suitable for children less than 13 years old.

R For *restricted.* Persons under 17 must be accompanied by a parent or adult guardian.

X For *no one under 17 admitted.* (The age limit may be different in some areas.)

When the ratings are used in news stories or reviews, use these forms as appropriate: *the movie has an X rating, an X-rated movie, the movie is X-rated.*

movie titles See **composition titles.**

mph Acceptable in all references for *miles per hour* or *miles an hour.*

Mr., Mrs. The plural of *Mr.* is *Messrs.*; the plural of *Mrs.* is *Mmes.*

These abbreviated spellings apply in all uses, including direct quotations.

See **courtesy titles** for guidelines on when to use *Mr.* and *Mrs.*

Ms. This is the spelling and punctuation for all uses of the courtesy title, including direct quotations.

There is no plural. If several women who prefer *Ms.* must be listed in a series, repeat *Ms.* before each name.

See **courtesy titles** for guidelines on when to use *Ms.*

multi- The rules in **prefixes** apply, but in general, no hyphen. Some examples:

multicolored	multimillion
multilateral	multimillionaire

Multigraph A trademark for a brand of dictating machine.

Multilith A trademark for a brand of duplicating machine.

municipal bond See **loan terminology.**

murder See the **homicide, murder, manslaughter** entry.

murderer See the **assassin, killer, murderer** entry.

Murphy's law The law is: If something can go wrong, it will.

music The basic guidelines for capitalizing and using quotation marks on the titles of musical works are listed in **composition titles.**

Capitalize, but do not use quotation marks, on descriptive titles for orchestral works: *Bach's Suite No. 1 for Orchestra*; *Beethoven's Serenade for Flute, Violin and Viola.* If the instrumentation is not part of the title but is added for explanatory purposes, the names of the instruments are lowercased: *Mozart's Sinfonia Concertante in E flat major* (the common title) *for violin and viola.* If in doubt, lowercase the names of the instruments.

Use quotation marks for non-musical terms in a title: *Beethoven's "Eroica" Symphony.* If the work has a special full title, all of it is quoted: *"Symphonie Fantastique," "Rhapsody in Blue."*

In subsequent references, lowercase *symphony, concerto,* etc.

musket See **weapons.**

Muslims See **Moslem(s).**

Mutual Broadcasting System Inc. *Mutual Radio* is acceptable in all references. Use *Mutual,* not *MBS,* in subsequent references.

Muzak A trademark for a type of recorded background music.

n. See **nouns**.

naive

names In general, people are entitled to be known however they want to be known, as long as their identities are clear.

When an individual elects to change the name by which he has been known, such as Cassius Clay's transition to Muhammad Ali, provide both names in stories until the new name is known by the public. After that, use only the new name unless there is a specific reason for including the earlier identification.

See the **junior, senior** entry and the entries under **middle initials; nicknames;** and **sex changes.**

nano- A prefix denoting one-billionth of a unit. Move a decimal point nine places to the left in converting to the basic unit: 2,999,888,777.5 nanoseconds = 2.9998887775 seconds.

naphtha See the **oil** entry.

narrow-minded

national See the **citizen, resident, subject, national, native** entry.

National Aeronautics and Space Administration *NASA* is acceptable on second reference.

If *the space agency* is used in first reference to avoid a cumbersome lead, mention the full name later.

National Airlines Headquarters is in Miami.

national anthem Lowercase. But: *"The Star-Spangled Banner."*

national assembly See **foreign legislative bodies.**

National Association for Stock Car Auto Racing In general, spell out on first reference.

A phrase such as *NASCAR competition* is acceptable on first reference, however, to avoid a cumbersome lead. If this is done, provide the full name later in the story.

National Association for the Advancement of Colored People *NAACP* is acceptable on first reference to avoid a cumbersome lead, but provide the full name in the body of the story.

Headquarters is in New York.

National Association of Letter Carriers The shortened form *Letter Carriers union* is acceptable in all references.

Headquarters is in Washington.

National Association of Securities Dealers *NASD* is acceptable on second reference.

The association operates the *National Association of Securities Dealers Automated Quotations* system — *NASDAQ* on second reference.

Headquarters is in Washington.

National Baptist Convention of America See **Baptist churches.**

National Baptist Convention U.S.A. Inc. See **Baptist churches.**

National Broadcasting Co. See **NBC.**

national chairman Capitalize when used before the name of the individual who heads a political party: *Democratic National Chairman Kenneth M. Curtis.*

National Collegiate Athletic Association In general, spell out on first reference.

A phrase such as *NCAA Division 2 playoffs* may be used on first reference, however, to avoid a cumbersome lead.

National Conference of Catholic Bishops See **Roman Catholic Church.**

National Council of the Churches of Christ in the U.S.A. This interdenominational, cooperative body includes most major Protestant and Eastern Orthodox denominations in the United States.

The shortened form *National Council of Churches* is acceptable in all references.

Headquarters is in New York.

See **World Council of Churches.**

National Education Association *NEA* is acceptable on second reference.

Headquarters is in Washington.

National Governors' Conference Note the apostrophe. Represents the governors of the 50 states and four territories.

Its office is in Washington.

national guard Capitalize when referring to U.S. or state-level forces: *the National Guard, the Guard, the Iowa National Guard, Iowa's National Guard, National Guard troops.*

Use lowercase for the forces of other nations.

National Guardsman Note spelling. Capitalize as a proper noun when referring to an individual in a federal or state National Guard unit: *He is a National Guardsman.*

Lowercase *guardsman* when it stands alone.

See **military titles.**

National Hurricane Center See **weather terms.**

National Institutes of Health This agency within the Department of Health, Education and Welfare is the principal biomedical research arm of the federal government.

It consists of the National Library of Medicine, 11 separate institutes and various divisions that provide centralized support services for the individual institutes.

The 11 institutes are: National Cancer Institute; National Eye Institute; National Heart, Lung, and Blood Institute; National Institute of Allergy and Infectious Diseases; National Institute of Arthritis, Metabolism, and Digestive Diseases; National Institute of Child Health and Human Development; National Institute of Dental Research; National Institute of Environmental Health Sciences; National Institute of General Medical Sciences; National Institute of Neurological and Communicative Disorders and Stroke; National Institute on Aging.

nationalist Lowercase when referring to a partisan of a country. Capitalize only when referring to alignment with a political party for which this is the proper name.

See the **political parties and philosophies** entry.

Nationalist China See **China.**

nationalities and races Capitalize the proper names of nationalities, peoples, races, tribes, etc: *Arab, Arabic, African, Afro-American, American, Caucasian, Cherokee, Chinese* (both singular and plural), *Eskimo* (plural

Eskimos), *French Canadian, Gypsy* (Gypsies), *Japanese* (singular and plural), *Jew, Jewish, Latin, Negro* (Negroes), *Nordic, Oriental, Sioux, Swede,* etc.

Lowercase *black* (noun or adjective), *white, red, mulatto,* etc. See **colored**.

See **race** for guidelines on when racial identification is pertinent in a story.

Lowercase derogatory terms such as *honky* and *nigger*. Use them only in direct quotes when essential to the story.

National Labor Relations Board

NLRB is acceptable on second reference.

National League of Cities Its

members are the governments of cities and towns and state municipal leagues.

It is separate from the U.S. Conference of Mayors, whose membership is limited to mayors of cities with 30,000 or more residents. The organizations often engage in joint projects, however.

The office is in Washington.

National Organization for Women

Not *of. NOW* is acceptable on second reference.

Headquarters is in Washington.

National Rifle Association *NRA* is

acceptable on second reference.

Headquarters is in Washington.

National Weather Service No

longer the U.S. Weather Bureau. *The weather service* or *weather bureau* (lowercase) may be used in any reference.

See **weather terms.**

nationwide

native See the **citizen, resident, subject, national, native** entry.

NATO Acceptable in all references for the *North Atlantic Treaty Organization*, but use it sparingly. A phrase such as *the alliance* is less burdensome to the reader.

Naugahyde A trademark for a brand of simulated leather.

nautical mile It equals 6,076.11549 feet, or 1,852 meters. To convert to approximate statute miles (5,280 feet), multiply the number of nautical miles by 1.15.

See **knot.**

naval, navel *Naval* pertains to a navy.

A *navel* is a bellybutton.

A *navel orange* is a seedless orange, so named because it has a small depression, like a navel, at its apex.

naval station Capitalize only as part of a proper name: *Norfolk Naval Station.*

navy Capitalize when referring to U.S. forces: *the U.S. Navy, the Navy, Navy policy.* Do not use the abbreviation *USN.*

Lowercase when referring to the naval forces of other nations: *the British navy.*

This approach has been adopted for consistency, because many foreign nations do not use *navy* as the proper name.

See **military academies** and **military titles.**

Nazi, Nazism After the National Socialist German Workers' Party, the fascist political party founded in 1919 and abolished in 1945. Under Adolf Hitler, it seized control of Germany in 1933.

See the **political parties and philosophies** entry.

NBC Acceptable in all references for the *National Broadcasting Co.,* a subsidiary of RCA Corp.

Divisions are NBC News, NBC Radio and NBC-TV.

NCR Corp. Formerly National Cash Register Co.

Headquarters is in Dayton, Ohio.

Near East There is no longer a substantial distinction between this term and *Middle East*.

See the **Middle East** entry.

nearsighted When used in a medical sense, it means an individual can see well at close range but has difficulty seeing objects at a distance.

Nebraska Abbrev.: *Neb.* See **state names**.

Negro, Negroes Use *black* or *Negro*, as appropriate in the context, for both men and women. Do not use *Negress*.

See the **nationalities and races** entry and **race**.

neither . . . nor See the **either . . . or, neither . . . nor** entry.

Netherlands In datelines, give the name of the community followed by *Netherlands:*

AMSTERDAM, Netherlands (AP) —

In stories: *the Netherlands* or *Netherlands* as the construction of a sentence dictates.

Netherlands Antilles In datelines, give the name of the community followed by *Netherlands Antilles*. Do not abbreviate.

Identify an individual island, if needed, in the text.

net income, net profit See **profit terminology**.

Nevada Abbrev.: *Nev.* See **state names**.

New Brunswick One of the three Maritime Provinces of Canada. Do not abbreviate.

See **datelines**.

New England Connecticut, Maine, Massachusetts, New Hampshire, Rhode Island and Vermont.

Newfoundland This Canadian province comprises the island of Newfoundland and the mainland section known as Labrador. Do not abbreviate.

In datelines, use *Newfoundland* after the names of all cities and towns. Specify in the text whether the community is on the island or in Labrador.

See **datelines**.

New Hampshire Abbrev.: *N.H.* See **state names**.

New Jersey Abbrev.: *N.J.* See **state names**.

New Mexico Abbrev.: *N.M.* See **state names**

New Orleans The city in Louisiana stands alone in datelines.

New South The era that began in the South in the 1960s with a thriving economy and the election of officials who advocated the abolition of racial segregation.

Old South applies to the South before the Civil War.

Newspaper Guild, The Formerly the American Newspaper Guild, it is a union for newspaper and news service employees, generally those in the news and business departments.

On second reference: *the Guild.*

Headquarters is in Washington.

newspaper names Capitalize *the* in a newspaper's name if that is the way the publication prefers to be known.

Lowercase *the* before newspaper names if a story mentions several papers, some of which use *the* as part of the name and some of which do not.

Where location is needed but is not part of the official name, use parentheses: *The Huntsville (Ala.) Times.*

Consult the International Year Book published by Editor & Publisher to determine whether a two-name combination is hyphenated.

newsstand

New Testament See **Bible**.

New World The Western Hemisphere.

New Year's, New Year's Day, New Year's Eve But: *What will the new year bring?*
The federal legal holiday is observed on Friday if Jan. 1 falls on a Saturday, on Monday if it falls on a Sunday.

New York Abbrev.: *N.Y.* Use *New York state* when a distinction must be made between state and city. See **state names**.

New York City Use *NEW YORK* in datelines, not the name of an individual community or borough such as *Flushing* or *Queens*.
Identify the borough in the body of the story if pertinent.

New York Stock Exchange *NYSE* is acceptable on second reference as an adjective. Use *the stock exchange* or *the exchange* for other second references.
Capitalize the nickname *Big Board* when used.

nicknames A nickname should be used in place of a person's given name in news stories only when it is the way the individual prefers to be known: *Jimmy Carter.*
When a nickname is inserted into the identification of an individual, use quotation marks: *Sen. Henry M. "Scoop" Jackson.* Also: *Jackson is known as "Scoop."*
In sports stories and sports columns, commonly used nicknames may be substituted for a first name without the use of quotation marks: *Woody Hayes, Bear Bryant, Catfish Hunter, Bubba Smith,* etc. But in sports stories where the given name is used, and in all news stories: *Paul "Bear" Bryant.*
Capitalize without quotation marks such terms as *Sunshine State, the Old Dominion, Motown, the Magic City, Old Hickory, Old Glory, Galloping Ghost.*
See **names**.

nightclub

nighttime

nitpicking

nitty-gritty

No. Use as the abbreviation for *number* in conjunction with a figure to indicate position or rank: *No. 1 man, No. 3 choice.*
Do not use in street addresses, with this exception: *No. 10 Downing St.,* the residence of Britain's prime minister.
Do not use in the names of schools: *Public School 19.*

Nobel Prize, Nobel Prizes The five established under terms of the will of Alfred Nobel are: Nobel Peace Prize, Nobel Prize in chemistry, Nobel Prize in literature, Nobel Prize in physics, Nobel Prize in physiology or medicine. (Note the capitalization styles.)
The Nobel Memorial Prize in Economic Science is not a Nobel Prize in the same sense. The Central Bank of Sweden established it in 1968 as a memorial to Alfred Nobel. References to this prize should include the word *Memorial* to help make this distinction. Explain the status of the prize in the story when appropriate.
Capitalize *prize* in references that do not mention the category: *He is a Nobel Prize winner. She is a Nobel Prize-winning scientist.*
Lowercase *prize* when not linked with the word *Nobel: The peace prize was awarded Monday.*

nobility References to members of the nobility in nations that have a system of rank present special problems because nobles frequently are known by their titles rather than their given or family names. Their titles, in effect, become their names.
The guidelines here relate to Britain's nobility. Adapt them as appropriate to members of the nobility in other nations.

Orders of rank among British nobility begin with the royal family. The term *royalty* is reserved for the families of living and deceased sovereigns.

Next, in descending order, are dukes, marquesses, earls, viscounts and barons. Many hold inherited titles; others have been raised to the nobility by the sovereign for their lifetimes. Occasionally the sovereign raises an individual to the nobility and makes the title inheritable by the person's heirs, but the practice is increasingly rare.

Sovereigns also confer honorary titles, which do not make an individual a member of the nobility. The principal designations, in descending order, are baronet and knight.

In general, the guidelines in **courtesy titles** and **titles** apply. However, honorary titles and titles of nobility are capitalized when they serve as an alternate name.

Some guidelines and examples:

ROYALTY: Capitalize *king, queen, prince* and *princess* when they are used directly before one or more names; lowercase when they stand alone:

Queen Elizabeth II, Queen Elizabeth, the queen of England, the queen. Kings George and Edward. Queen Mother Elizabeth, the queen mother.

When a longer form of the sovereign's title is appropriate in the context or is being quoted: *Her Majesty Queen Elizabeth.*

Use *Prince* or *Princess* before the names of a sovereign's children: *Princess Anne, the princess.*

The male heir to the throne normally is designated *Prince of Wales*, and the title becomes, in common usage, an alternate name. Capitalize when used: *The queen invested her eldest son as Prince of Wales. Prince Charles is now the Prince of Wales. The prince is a bachelor. Charles, Prince of Wales, was married today.*

DUKE: The full title — *Duke of Wellington*, for example — is an alternate name, capitalized in all uses. Lowercase *duke* when it stands alone.

The designation *Arthur, Duke of Wellington*, is appropriate in some cases, but never *Duke Arthur* or *Lord Arthur*.

The wife of a duke is a duchess: *the Duchess of Wellington, the duchess*, but never *Duchess Diana* or *Lady Diana*.

A duke normally also has a lesser title. It is commonly used for his eldest son if he has one. Use the courtesy titles *Lord* or *Lady* before the names of a duke's children.

Some examples:

Lady Jane Wellesley, only daughter of the eighth Duke of Wellington, has been linked romantically with Prince Charles, heir to the British throne. The eldest of Lady Jane's four brothers is Arthur Charles, the Marquess Douro. The Wellingtons, whose family name is Wellesley, are not of royal blood. However, they rank among the nation's most famous aristocrats thanks to the first duke, the victor at Waterloo.

MARQUESS, EARL, VISCOUNT, BARON: The full titles serve as alternate names and should be capitalized. Frequently, however, the holder of such a title is identified as a lord: *The Marquess of Bath*, for example, more commonly is known as *Lord Bath*.

Use *Lady* before the name of a woman married to a man who holds one of these titles. The wife of a marquess is a marchioness, the wife of an earl is a countess (earl is the British equivalent of count), the wife of a viscount is a viscountess, the wife of a baron is a baroness.

Use *Lord* or *Lady* before the names of the children of a marquess.

Use *Lady* before the name of an earl's daughter.

The Honorable often appears before the names of sons of earls, viscounts and barons who do not have titles. Their names should stand alone in news stories, however.

The Honorable also appears frequently before the names of unmarried daughters of viscounts and barons. In news stories, however, use a full name on first reference, a last name preceded by *Miss* on second.

Some examples:

Queen Elizabeth gave her sister's husband, Antony Armstrong-Jones, the title Earl of Snowdon. Their son, David, is the Viscount Linley. They also have a daughter, Lady Sarah Armstrong-Jones. Lord Snowdon, a photographer, was known as Antony Armstrong-Jones before he received his title.

BARONET, KNIGHT: Use *Sir* before a name if appropriate in the context; otherwise follow routine practice for names: *Sir Harold Wilson* on first reference, *Sir Harold* (not *Sir Wilson*) on second. Or: *Prime Minister Harold Wilson* on first reference, *Wilson* on second.

Do not use both an honorary title and a title of authority such as *prime minister* before a name.

Use *Lady* before the name of the wife of a baronet or knight.

For a woman who has received an honor in her own right, use *Dame* before her name if it is the way she is known or it is appropriate in the context: *Dame Margot Fonteyn* on first reference, *Dame Margot* on second.

nobody, no one

noisome, noisy *Noisome* means offensive, noxious.
Noisy means clamorous.

nolo contendere The literal meaning is, "I do not wish to contend." Terms such as *no contest* or *no-contest plea* are acceptable in all references.

When a defendant in a criminal case enters this plea, it means that he is not admitting guilt but is stating that he will offer no defense. The person is then subject to being judged guilty and punished as if he had pleaded guilty or had been convicted. The principal difference is that the defendant retains the option of denying the same charge in another legal proceeding.

no man's land

non- Hyphenate all except the following words, which have specific meanings of their own:

nonchalance   nonsense
nonchalant   nonsensical
nondescript

non-aligned nations A political rather than economic or geographic term. Although non-aligned nations do not belong to Western or Eastern military alliances or blocs, they profess not to be neutral, like Switzerland, but activist alternatives.

Do not confuse *non-aligned* with *Third World*, although many Third World nations belong to the non-aligned group. For example, Yugoslavia is a non-aligned nation because it does not belong to the Warsaw Pact, but it is not a Third World nation.

See the **Third World** entry.

non-controversial All issues are controversial. A *non-controversial issue* is impossible. A *controversial issue* is redundant.

none It usually means no single one. When used in this sense, it always takes singular verbs and pronouns: *None of the seats was in its right place.*

Use a plural verb only if the sense is no two or no amount: *None of the consultants agree on the same approach. None of the taxes have been paid.*

non-restrictive clauses See the **essential clauses, non-essential clauses** entry.

noon Do not put a *12* in front of it.

no one

norm See the **average, mean, median, norm** entry.

north, northern, northeast, northwest See the **directions and regions** entry.

North America See **Western Hemisphere.**

Proofreader's Marks

⊙ Period.

, Comma.

= Hyphen.

: Colon.

; Semicolon.

✓ Apostrophe.

❝/❞ Quotations.

▣ Indent one em; doubled for two ems, and so on.

⊥/m One em dash; change figure for longer dash.

⌡ Push down lead or space.

⌒ Close up.

✓ Less space.

∧ Caret—something to be inserted.

⊋ Turn—letter, line or matter.

Insert space.

tr. Transpose—letters, lines or matter.

ↄ◌ Character to go around letters, words, phrases, sentences or paragraphs to indicate that they are to be transposed, always to be accompanied by the mark "tr," on the margin of the proof.

stet. Let it stand—this when something has been inadvertently crossed out; dots placed under the matter will usually suffice, but the term "stet" will better avoid misunderstanding.

ℐ Delete—take out.

X Broken letter or bad type.

¶ Paragraph; with "no" preceding it when no paragraph is intended.

w.f. Wrong font—letter or character belonging to another face.

✓✓✓ Equalize spacing.

cap Capitalize word or words—in copy indicated by three under-strokes.

sm.c Small capitals—indicated by two under-strokes.

l.c. Lower-case—reduce from a capital to a small letter.

✳/✓/✓ Superior characters—for footnotes, in horse racing tables, etc.

$\widehat{1}\,\widehat{2}$ Inferior figures—used in chemical formulas, mathematical problems, etc.

ital. Italic type—indicated in copy by underscoring the word or words to be italicized.

rom. Roman—from italic or full-face.

⊐or⊏ Set out to margin indicated.

⊓or⊔ Move up or down.

( ) Parentheses.

[ ] Brackets.

spell Spell out, if figures.

○ A circle around figures in copy means spell out; if around a word, set in figures.

(Most of these marks are also applicable to manuscript)

Pica - 8 LINES - 2 COPY INCHES

Elite - 7 lines - 2 col. INCHES

North Atlantic Treaty Organization *NATO* is acceptable in all references, but use it sparingly.

North Carolina Abbrev.: *N.C.* See **state names.**

North Central Airlines Headquarters is in Minneapolis.

North Central region As defined by the U.S. Census Bureau, the 12-state region is broken into eastern and western divisions.

The five *East North Central* states are Indiana, Illinois, Michigan, Ohio and Wisconsin.

The seven *West North Central* states are Iowa, Kansas, Minnesota, Missouri, Nebraska, North Dakota and South Dakota.

See **Northeast region; South;** and **West** for the bureau's other regional breakdowns.

North Dakota Abbrev.: *N.D.* See **state names.**

Northeast region As defined by the U.S. Census Bureau, the nine-state region is broken into two divisions — the *New England* states and the *Middle Atlantic* states.

Connecticut, Maine, Massachusetts, New Hampshire, Rhode Island and Vermont are the *New England* states.

New Jersey, New York and Pennsylvania are classified as the *Middle Atlantic* states.

See **North Central region; South;** and **West** for the bureau's other regional breakdowns.

Northern Ireland Use *Northern Ireland* after the names of all communities in datelines.

See **datelines** and **United Kingdom.**

North Slope The portion of Alaska north of Brooks Range, a string of mountains extending across the northern part of the state.

Northwest Orient Airlines *Northwest Airlines* is acceptable in all references.

Headquarters is in St. Paul, Minn.

Northwest Territories A territorial section of Canada. Do not abbreviate. Use in datelines after the names of all cities and towns in the territory.

If necessary, specify in the text whether the community is in one of the three territorial subdivisions: Franklin, Keewatin and Mackenzie.

See **Canada.**

nouns The abbreviation *n.* is used in this book to identify the spelling of the noun forms of words frequently misspelled.

Nova Scotia One of the three Maritime Provinces of Canada. Do not abbreviate.

See **datelines.**

November See **months.**

Novocain A trademark for a drug used as a local anesthetic. It also may be called *procain.*

nowadays Not *nowdays.*

Nuclear Regulatory Commission This commission has taken over the regulatory functions previously performed by the Atomic Energy Commission.

NRC is acceptable on second reference, but *the agency* or *the commission* is preferred.

numerals A numeral is a figure, letter, word or group of words expressing a number.

Roman numerals use the letters *I, V, X, L, C, D* and *M.* Use Roman numerals for wars and to show personal sequence for animals and people: *World War II, Native Dancer II, King George VI, Pope John XXIII.* See **Roman numerals.**

Arabic numerals use the figures *1, 2, 3, 4, 5, 6, 7, 8, 9* and *0.* Use Arabic forms unless Roman numerals are specifically required. See **Arabic numerals.**

The figures *1, 2, 10, 101,* etc. and the corresponding words — *one, two, ten, one hundred one,* etc. — are called **cardinal numbers.** The term **ordinal number** applies to *1st, 2nd, 10th, 101st, first, second, tenth, one hundred first,* etc.

Follow these guidelines in using numerals:

LARGE NUMBERS: When large numbers must be spelled out, use a hyphen to connect a word ending in *y* to another word; do not use commas between other separate words that are part of one number: *twenty; thirty; twenty-one; thirty-one; one hundred forty-three; one thousand one hundred fifty-five; one million two hundred seventy-six thousand five hundred eighty-seven.*

SENTENCE START: Spell out a numeral at the beginning of a sentence. If necessary, recast the sentence. There is one exception — a numeral that identifies a calendar year.

Wrong: *993 freshman entered the college last year.*

Right: *Last year 993 freshmen entered the college.*

Right: *1976 was a very good year.*

CASUAL USES: Spell out casual expressions:

A thousand times no! Thanks a million. He walked a quarter of a mile.

PROPER NAMES: Use words or numerals according to an organization's practice: *20th Century-Fox, Twentieth Century Fund, Big Ten.*

FRACTIONS: See the **fractions** entry.

DECIMALS: See the **decimal units** entry.

FIGURES OR WORDS? For ordinals:

—Spell out *first* through *ninth* when they indicate sequence in time or location — *first base, the First Amendment, he was first in line.* Starting with *10th,* use figures.

—Use *1st, 2nd, 3rd, 4th,* etc. when the sequence has been assigned in forming names. The principal examples are geo-

graphic, military and political designations such as *1st Ward, 7th Fleet* and *1st Sgt.* See examples in the separate entries listed below.

For cardinal numbers, consult the following separate entries:

act numbers	heights
addresses	highway designations
ages	latitude and longitude
aircraft names	mile
amendments to	model numbers
the Constitution	monetary units
betting odds	No.
century	page numbers
channel	parallels
chapters	percentages
congressional districts	political divisions
course numbers	proportions
court decisions	ratios
court names	recipes
dates	room numbers
decades	route numbers
decimal units	scene numbers
dimensions	scores
distances	serial numbers
district	sizes
earthquakes	spacecraft
election returns	designations
fleet	speeds
formula	telephone numbers
fractions	temperatures
handicaps	years

OTHER USES: For uses not covered by these listings: Spell out whole numbers below 10, use figures for *10* and above. Typical examples: *The woman has three sons and two daughters. He has a fleet of 10 station wagons and two buses.*

IN A SERIES: Apply the appropriate guidelines: They had 10 dogs, six cats and 97 hamsters. *They had four four-room houses, 10 three-room houses and 12 10-room houses.*

nuns See **sister.**

Nuremberg Use this spelling for the city in West Germany, instead of *Nuernberg,* in keeping with widespread practice.

nylon Not a trademark.

oasis, oases

obscenities, profanities, vulgarities Do not use them in stories unless they are part of direct quotations and there is a compelling reason for them.

When a profanity, obscenity or vulgarity is used, flag the story at the top:
↑Editors: Language in 4th graf may be offensive to some readers. ←

Then confine the offending language, in quotation marks, to a separate paragraph that can be deleted easily by editors who do not want it.

In reporting profanity that normally would use the words *damn* or *god,* lowercase *god* and use the following forms: *damn, damn it, goddamn it.* Do not, however, change the offending words to euphemisms. Do not, for example, change *damn it* to *darn it.*

If a full quote that contains profanity, obscenity or vulgarity cannot be dropped but there is no compelling reason for the offensive language, replace letters of an offensive word with a hyphen. The word *damn,* for example, would become *d---* or *----.*

When the subject matter of a story may be considered offensive, but the story does not contain quoted profanity, obscenities or vulgarities, flag the story at the top:
↑Editors: The contents may be offensive to some readers. ←

For guidelines on racial or ethnic slurs, see the **nationalities and races** entry.

Occident, Occidental Capitalize when referring to Europe, the Western Hemisphere or an inhabitant of these regions.

Occidental Petroleum Corp. Headquarters is in Los Angeles.

Occupational Safety and Health Administration *OSHA* is acceptable on second reference.

occupational titles They are always lowercase. See **titles.**

occur, occurred, occurring Also: *occurrence.*

oceangoing

oceans The five, from the largest to the smallest: Pacific Ocean, Atlantic Ocean, Indian Ocean, Antarctic Ocean, Arctic Ocean.

Lowercase *ocean* standing alone or in plural uses: *the ocean, the Atlantic and Pacific oceans.*

October See **months.**

odd- Follow with a hyphen:
odd-looking   odd-numbered

odds See **betting odds.**

oddsmaker

off-, -off Follow Webster's New World Dictionary. Hyphenate if not listed there.

Some commonly used combinations with a hyphen:

off-color
off-peak
off-season

off-white
send-off
stop-off

Some combinations without a hyphen:

blastoff
cutoff
offhand
offset
offshore

offside
offstage
playoff
standoff
takeoff

off-Broadway, off-off-Broadway See the **Broadway, off-Broadway, off-off-Broadway** entry.

office Capitalize *office* when it is part of an agency's formal name: *Office of Management and Budget.*

Lowercase all other uses, including phrases such as: *the office of the attorney general, the U.S. attorney's office.*

See **Oval Office.**

officeholder

off of The *of* is unnecessary: *He fell off the bed.* Not: *He fell off of the bed.*

Ohio Do not abbreviate. See **state names.**

oil In shipping, oil and oil products normally are measured by the ton. For news stories, convert these tonnage figures to gallons.

There are 42 gallons to each barrel of oil. The number of barrels per ton varies, depending on the type of oil product.

To convert tonnage to gallons:

—Determine the type of oil.

—Consult the table below to find out how many barrels per ton for that type of oil.

—Multiply the number of tons by the number of barrels per ton. The result is the number of barrels in the shipment.

—Multiply the number of barrels by 42. The result is the number of gallons.

EXAMPLE: A tanker spills 20,000 metric tons of foreign crude petroleum. The table shows 6.998 barrels of foreign crude petroleum per metric ton. Multiply 6.998 x 20,000 = 139,960 barrels. Multiply 139,960 x 42 = 5,878,320 gallons.

TABLE: The table below is based on figures supplied by the American Petroleum Institute:

OIL EQUIVALENCY TABLE

Type of Product	Barrels Per Short Ton (2,000 lbs.)	Barrels Per Metric Ton (2,204.6 lbs)	Barrels Per Long Ton (2,240 lbs.)
crude oil, foreign	6.349	6.998	7.111
crude oil, domestic	6.770	7.463	7.582
gasoline and naptha	7.721	8.511	8.648
kerosene	7.053	7.775	7.900
distillate fuel oil	6.580	7.253	7.369
residual fuel oil	6.041	6.660	6.766
lubricating oil	6.349	6.998	7.111
lubricating grease	6.665	7.346	7.464
wax	7.134	7.864	7.990
asphalt	5.540	6.106	6.205
coke	4.990	5.500	5.589
road oil	5.900	6.503	6.608
jelly and petrolatum	6.665	7.346	7.464
liquefied pet. gas	10.526	11.603	11.789
Gilsonite	5.515	6.080	6.177

Oil, Chemical and Atomic Workers International Union The shortened forms *Oil Workers union, Chemical Workers union* and *Atomic Workers union* are acceptable in all references.

Headquarters is in Denver.

OK, OK'd, OK'ing, OKs Do not use *okay.*

Oklahoma Abbrev.: *Okla.* See **state names**.

Oklahoma City Stands alone in datelines.

Old City of Jerusalem The walled part of the city.

Old South The South before the Civil War. See **New South**.

Old Testament See **Bible**.

old-time, old-timer, old times

Old West The American West as it was being settled in the 19th century.

Old World The Eastern Hemisphere: Asia, Europe, Africa. The term also may be an allusion to European culture and customs.

Olympic Airways Headquarters is in Athens, Greece.

olympics Capitalize all references to the international athletic contests held every four years: *the Olympics, the Winter Olympics, the Olympic Games, the Games, an Olympic-sized pool.*

An Olympic-sized pool is 50 meters long by 25 meters wide.

Lowercase other uses: *a beer-drinking olympics.*

on Do not use *on* before a date or day of the week when its absence would not lead to confusion: *The meeting will be held Monday. He will be inaugurated Jan. 20.*

Use *on* to avoid an awkward juxtaposition of a date and a proper name: *John met Mary on Monday. He told Carter on Thursday that the bill was doomed.*

Use *on* also to avoid any suggestion that a date is the object of a transitive verb: *The House killed on Tuesday a bid to raise taxes. The Senate postponed on Wednesday its consideration of a bill to reduce import duties.*

one- Hyphenate when used in writing fractions:

one-half   one-third

Use phrases such as *a half* or *a third* if precision is not intended.

See **fractions**.

one another See the **each other, one another** entry.

one man, one vote The adjective form: *one-man, one-vote. He supports the principle of one man, one vote. The one-man, one-vote rule.*

one-sided

one time, one-time *He did it one time. He is a one-time winner. She is a one-time friend.*

Ontario This Canadian province is the nation's first in total population and second to Quebec in area. Do not abbreviate.

See **datelines**.

operas See **composition titles**.

opinion polls See the **polls and surveys** entry.

opossum The only North American marsupial. No apostrophe is needed to indicate missing letters in a phrase such as *playing possum.*

option In a financial sense, the word means an agreement that allows a person or a corporation to buy or sell something, such as shares of stock, within a stipulated time and for a certain price.

A *put option* gives the holder the right to sell blocks of 100 shares of stock within a specified time at an agreed-upon price.

A *call option* gives the holder the right to buy blocks of 100 shares of stock within a specified time at an agreed-upon price.

oral, verbal, written Use *oral* to refer to spoken words: *He gave an oral promise.*

Use *written* to refer to words committed to paper: *We had a written agreement.*

Use *verbal* to compare words with some other form of communication: *His tears revealed the sentiments that his poor verbal skills could not express.*

ordinal numbers See **numerals**.

Oregon Abbrev.: *Ore.* See **state names**.

Oreo A trademark for a brand of chocolate sandwich cookies held together by a white filling.

The use of the word by blacks indicates belief that another black is "black outside but white inside."

Organization of American States *OAS* is acceptable on second reference. Headquarters is in Washington.

Organization of Petroleum Exporting Countries Use the full name for most first references. *OPEC* may be used on first reference in business-oriented copy, but the body of the story should identify it as the shortened form of the name.

The 13 OPEC members, as of 1977: Algeria, Ecuador, Gabon, Indonesia, Iran, Iraq, Kuwait, Libya, Nigeria, Qatar, Saudi Arabia, United Arab Emirates, Venezuela.

Headquarters is in Vienna, Austria.

organizations and institutions Capitalize the full names of organizations and institutions: *the American Medical Association; First Presbyterian Church; General Motors Corp.; Harvard University, Harvard University Medical School; the Procrastinators Club; the Society of Professional Journalists, Sigma Delta Chi.*

Retain capitalization if *Co., Corp.* or a similar word is deleted from the full proper name: *General Motors.* See **company; corporation**; and **incorporated**.

SUBSIDIARIES: Capitalize the names of major subdivisions: *the Pontiac Motor Division of General Motors.*

INTERNAL ELEMENTS: Use lowercase for internal elements of an organization when they have names that are widely used generic terms: *the board of directors of General Motors, the board of trustees of Columbia University, the history department of Harvard University, the sports department of the Daily Citizen-Leader.*

Capitalize internal elements of an organization when they have names that are not widely used generic terms: *the General Assembly of the World Council of Churches, the House of Delegates of the American Medical Association, the House of Bishops and House of Deputies of the Episcopal Church.*

FLIP-FLOPPED NAMES: Retain capital letters when commonly accepted practice flops a name to delete the word *of: College of the Holy Cross, Holy Cross College; Harvard School of Dental Medicine, Harvard Dental School.*

Do not, however, flop formal names that are known to the public with the word *of: Massachusetts Institute of Technology,* for example, not *Massachusetts Technology Institute.*

ABBREVIATIONS AND ACRONYMS: Some organizations and institutions are widely recognized by their abbreviations: *ALCOA, GOP, NAACP, NATO.* For guidelines on when such abbreviations may be used, see the individual listings and the entries under **abbreviations and acronymns** and **second reference**.

Orient, Oriental Capitalize when referring to the Far East nations of Asia and nearby islands or to an inhabitant of these regions.

Also: *Oriental rug, Oriental cuisine.*

Orlon A trademark for a form of acrylic fiber similar to nylon.

orthodox Capitalize when referring to membership in or the activities of an Eastern Orthodox church. See **Eastern Orthodox churches.**

Capitalize also in phrases such as *Orthodox Judaism* or *Orthodox Jew.* See **Jewish congregations.**

Do not describe a member of an Eastern Orthodox church as a *Protestant.* Use a phrase such as *Orthodox Christian* instead.

Lowercase *orthodox* in non-religious uses: *an orthodox procedure.*

Orthodox Church in America See **Eastern Orthodox churches.**

Oscar, Oscars See **Academy Awards.**

oscillating theory See **big-bang theory.**

Ottawa The capital of Canada stands alone in datelines.

Ouija A trademark for a board used in spiritual seances.

ounce (dry) Units of dry volume are not customarily carried to this level.

See **pint (dry).**

ounce (liquid) See **fluid ounce.**

ounce (weight) It is defined as 437.5 grains.

The metric equivalent is approximately 28 grams.

To convert to grams, multiply by 28 (5 ounces x 28 = 140 grams).

See **grain** and **gram.**

out- Follow Webster's New World. Hyphenate if not listed there.

Some frequently used words:

outargue	outpost
outbox	output
outdated	outscore
outfield	outstrip
outfox	outtalk
outpatient (n., adj.)	

-out Follow Webster's New World. Hyphenate nouns and adjectives not listed there.

Some frequently used words (all nouns):

cop-out	hide-out
fade-out	pullout
fallout	walkout
flameout	washout

Two words for verbs:

fade out	walk out
hide out	wash out
pull out	

Outer Banks The sandy islands along the North Carolina coast.

out of bounds But as a modifier: *out-of-bounds. The ball went out of bounds. He took an out-of-bounds pass.*

out of court, out-of-court *They settled out of court. He accepted an out-of-court settlement.*

Oval Office The White House office of the president.

over It is not interchangeable with *more than.*

Over refers to spatial relationships: *The plane flew over the city.*

More than is used with figures: *More than 40,000 fans were in the stadium.*

over- Follow Webster's New World. A hyphen seldom is used. Some frequently used words:

overbuy	overrate
overexert	override

See the **overall** entry.

-over Follow Webster's New World Dictionary. Hyphenate if not listed there.

Some frequently used words (all are nouns, some also are used as adjectives):

carry-over	stopover
holdover	walkover
takeover	

Use two words when any of these occurs as a verb.

See **suffixes.**

overall A single word in adjectival and adverbial use: *Overall, the Democrats succeeded. Overall policy.*

The word for the garment is *overalls.*

Overseas National Airways Headquarters is in New York.

owner Not a formal title. Always lowercase: *Atlanta Braves owner Ted Turner.*

Oyez Not *oyes.* The cry of court and public officials to command silence.

Ozark Air Lines Headquarters is in St. Louis.

Ozark Mountains Or simply: *the Ozarks.*

Pablum A trademark for a soft, bland food.

In lowercase, *pablum* means any oversimplified or bland writing or idea.

pacemaker Formerly a trademark, now a generic term for a device that electronically helps a person's heart maintain a steady beat.

Pacific Ocean See **oceans**.

Pacific Standard Time (PST), Pacific Daylight Time (PDT) See **time zones**.

Pacific 10 Conference Arizona, Arizona State, California, Oregon, Oregon State, Southern Cal, Stanford, University of California at Los Angeles (UCLA), Washington, Washington State.

Pac-10 is acceptable on second reference.

paddy wagon

page numbers Use figures and capitalize *page* when used with a figure. When a letter is appended to the figure, capitalize it but do not use a hyphen: *Page 1, Page 10, Page 20A*.

One exception: *It's a Page One story*.

paintings See **composition titles**.

palate, palette, pallet *Palate* is the roof of the mouth.

A *palette* is an artist's paint board.

A *pallet* is a bed.

Palestine Liberation Organization Not *Palestinian*. *PLO* is acceptable on second reference.

pan- No hyphen when combined with a common noun:

panchromatic   pantheism.

Most combinations with *pan-* are proper nouns, however, and both *pan-* and the proper name it is combined with are capitalized:

Pan-African   Pan-Asiatic
Pan-American

Panama Canal Zone In datelines, give the name of a city or town followed by *Canal Zone:*

BALBOA, Canal Zone (AP) —

Do not use the abbreviation *C.Z.*

In text: *the Canal Zone, the canal, the zone*.

Panama City Use *PANAMA CITY, Fla.,* or *PANAMA CITY, Panama,* in datelines to avoid confusion between the two.

Pan American World Airways A *Pan Am airliner* is acceptable in any reference.

Headquarters is in New York.

pantsuit Not *pants suit*.

pantyhose

papal nuncio Do not confuse with an *apostolic delegate*. See the **apostolic delegate, papal nuncio** entry.

Pap test (or **smear**) After George Papanicolaou, the U.S. anatomist who developed this test for cervical and uterine cancer.

parallel, paralleled, paralleling

parallels Use figures and lowercase to identify the imaginary locater lines that ring the globe from east to west. They are measured in units of 0 to 90 degrees north or south of the equator.

Examples: *4th parallel north, 89th parallel south,* or, if location north or south of the equator is obvious: *19th parallel.*

See the **latitude and longitude** entry.

pardon, parole, probation The terms often are confused, but each has a specific meaning. Do not use them interchangeably.

A *pardon* forgives and releases a person from further punishment. It is granted by a chief of state or a governor. By itself, it does not expunge a record of conviction, if one exists, and it does not by itself restore civil rights.

A *general pardon*, usually for political offenses, is called *amnesty.*

Parole is the release of a prisoner before the sentence has expired, on condition of good behavior. It is granted by a parole board, part of the executive branch of government, and can be revoked only by the board.

Probation is the suspension of sentence for a person convicted, but not yet imprisoned, on condition of good behavior. It is imposed and revoked only by a judge.

parentheses In general, use parentheses around logos, as shown in the **datelines** entry, but otherwise be sparing with them.

Parentheses are jarring to the reader. Because they do not appear on many news service printers, there is also the danger that material inside them may be misinterpreted.

The temptation to use parentheses is a clue that a sentence is becoming contorted. Try to write it another way. If a sentence must contain incidental material, then commas or two dashes are frequently more effective. Use these alternatives whenever possible.

There are occasions, however, when parentheses are the only effective means of inserting necessary background or reference information. When they are necessary, follow these guidelines:

WITHIN QUOTATIONS: If parenthetical information inserted in a direct quotation is at all sensitive, place an editor's note under a dash at the bottom of a story alerting copy desks to what was inserted.

PUNCTUATION: Place a period outside a closing parenthesis if the material inside is not a sentence *(such as this fragment).*

(An independent parenthetical sentence such as this one takes a period before the closing parenthesis.)

When a phrase placed in parentheses *(this one is an example)* might normally qualify as a complete sentence but is dependent on the surrounding material, do not capitalize the first word or end with a period.

MATERIAL FROM OTHER AREAS: If a story contains information from outside the datelined city, put the material in parentheses only if the correspondent in the datelined community was cut off from incoming communications. See **dateline selection**.

INSERTIONS IN A PROPER NAME: Use parentheses if a state name or similar information is inserted within a proper name: *The Huntsville (Ala.) Times.* But use commas if no proper name is involved: *The Selma, Ala., group saw the governor.*

NEVER USED: Do not use parentheses to denote a political figure's party affiliation and jurisdiction. Instead, set them off with commas, as shown under **party affiliation**.

Do not use *(cq)* or similar notation to indicate that an unusual spelling or term is correct. Include the confirmation in an editor's note under a dash at the bottom of a story.

parent-teacher association *PTA* is acceptable in all references. Capitalize when part of a proper name: *the Franklin School Parent-Teacher Association* or *the Parent-Teacher Association of the Franklin School.*

pari-mutuel

Paris The city in France stands alone in datelines.

parish Capitalize as part of the formal name for a church congregation or a governmental jurisdiction: *St. John's Parish, Jefferson Parish.*

Lowercase standing alone or in plural combinations: *the parish, St. John's and St. Mary's parishes, Jefferson and Plaquemines parishes.*

See **county** for additional guidelines on governmental jurisdictions.

parishioner

Parkinson's disease After James Parkinson, the English physician who described this degenerative disease of later life.

Parkinson's law After C. Northcote Parkinson, the British economist who came to the satirical conclusion that work expands to fill the time allotted to it.

parliament See **foreign legislative bodies.**

parliamentary Lowercase unless part of a proper name.

parole See the **pardon, parole, probation** entry.

partial quotes See **quotation marks.**

particles See **foreign particles.**

part time, part-time Hyphenate when used as a compound modifier: *She works part time. She has a part-time job.*

party See the **political parties and philosophies** entry.

party affiliation Let relevance be the guide in determining whether to include a political figure's party affiliation in a story.

Party affiliation is pointless in some stories, such as an account of a governor accepting a button from a poster child.

It will occur naturally in many political stories.

For stories between these extremes, include party affiliation if readers need it for understanding or are likely to be curious about what it is.

GENERAL FORMS: When party designation is given, use any of these approaches as logical in constructing a story:

—*Democratic Sen. Hubert Humphrey of Minnesota said...*
—*Sen. Hubert Humphrey, D-Minn., said...*
—*Sen. Hubert Humphrey also spoke. The Minnesota Democrat said...*
—*Rep. Morris Udall of Arizona is seeking the Democratic presidential nomination.* Not: *Rep. Morris Udall, D-Ariz., is seeking the Democratic...*

In stories about party meetings, such as a report on the Republican National Convention, no specific reference to party affiliation is necessary unless an individual is not a member of the party in question.

SHORT-FORM PUNCTUATION: Set short forms such as *D-Minn.* off from a name by commas, as illustrated above.

Use the abbreviations listed in the entries for each state. (No abbreviations for *Alaska, Hawaii, Idaho, Iowa, Maine, Ohio, Texas* and *Utah.*)

Use *R-* for Republicans, *D-* for Democrats, and three-letter combinations for other affiliations: *Sen. James Buckley, R-Con-N.Y., spoke with Sen. Harry Byrd, D-Ind-Va.*

FORM FOR U.S. HOUSE MEMBERS: The normal practice for U.S. House members is to identify them by party and state. In contexts where state affiliation is clear and home city is relevant, such as a state election roundup, identify representatives by party and city: *U.S. Reps. Thomas P. O'Neill Jr., D-Cambridge, and Margaret Heckler, R-Wellesley.* If this option is used, be consistent throughout the story.

FORM FOR STATE LEGISLATORS: Short-form listings showing party and home city are appropriate in state wire stories. For trunk wire stories, the normal practice is to say that the individual is a *Republican* or *Democrat.* Use a short-form listing only if the legislator's home city is relevant.
See **legislative titles.**

pass See the **adopt, approve, enact, pass** entry.

passenger lists When providing a list of victims in a disaster, arrange names alphabetically according to last name, include street addresses if available, and use a paragraph for each name:
Jones, Joseph, 260 Town St., Sample, N.Y.
Williams, Susan, 780 Main St., Example, N.J.

passenger mile One passenger carried one mile, or its equivalent, such as two passengers carried one-half mile.

passer-by, passers-by

Passover The week-long Jewish commemoration of the deliverance of the ancient Hebrews from slavery in Egypt. Occurs in March or April.

pasteurize

pastor See **religious titles** and the entry for the individual's denomination.

patriarch Lowercase when describing someone of great age and dignity.
Capitalize as a formal title before a name in some religious uses. See **Eastern Orthodox churches; religious titles;** and **Roman Catholic Church.**

Patriots' Day April 19, a legal holiday in Massachusetts.

patrol, patrolled, patrolling

patrolman, patrolwoman Capitalize before a name only if the word is a formal title. In some cities, the formal title is *police officer.*
See **titles.**

payload

peacekeeping

peacemaker, peacemaking

peace offering

peacetime

peacock It applies only to the male. The female is a *peahen.* Both are *peafowl.*

peck A unit of dry measure equal to eight dry quarts or one-fourth of a bushel.
The metric equivalent is approximately 8.8 liters.
To convert to liters, multiply by 8.8 (5 pecks x 8.8 = 44 liters).
See **liter.**

pedal, peddle When riding a bicycle or similar vehicle, you *pedal* it.
When selling something, you may *peddle* it.

peddler

Peking The city in China stands alone in datelines.

pell-mell

penance See **sacraments.**

peninsula Capitalize as part of a proper name: *the Florida Peninsula, the Upper Peninsula of Michigan.*

penitentiary See the **prison, jail** entry.

Pennsylvania Abbrev.: *Pa.* Legally a commonwealth, not a state. See **state** and **state names.**

Pennsylvania Dutch The individuals are of German descent. The word *Dutch* is a corruption of *Deutsch*, the German word for "German."

penny-wise See **-wise.** Also: *pound-foolish.*

Pentecost The seventh Sunday after Easter.

Pentecostalism See **religious movements.**

people, persons Use *people* when speaking of a large or uncounted number of individuals: *Thousands of people attended the fair. Some rich people pay few taxes. What will people say?* Do not use *persons* in this sense.

Persons usually is used when speaking of a relatively small number of people who can be counted, but *people* also may be used:

Right: *There were 20 persons in the room.*

Right: *There were 20 people in the room.*

People is also a collective noun that takes a plural verb and is used to refer to a single race or nation: *The American people are united.* In this sense, the plural is *peoples: The peoples of Africa speak many languages.*

people's Use this possessive form when the word occurs in the formal name of a nation: *the People's Republic of Albania.*

Use this form also in such phrases as *the people's desire for freedom.*

Pepsi, Pepsi-Cola Trademarks for a brand of cola soft drink.

Pepsico Inc. Formerly the Pepsi-Cola Co.

Headquarters is in Purchase, N.Y.

percent One word. It takes a singular verb when standing alone or when a singular word follows an *of* construction: *The teacher said 60 percent was a failing grade. He said 50 percent of the membership was there.*

It takes a plural verb when a plural word follows an *of* construction: *He said 50 percent of the members were there.*

percentages Use figures: *1 percent, 2.5 percent* (use decimals, not fractions), *10 percent.*

For amounts less than 1 percent, precede the decimal with a zero: *The cost of living rose 0.6 percent.*

Repeat *percent* with each individual figure: *He said 10 percent to 30 percent of the electorate may not vote.*

periods Follow these guidelines:

END OF DECLARATIVE SENTENCE: *The stylebook is finished.*

END OF A MILDLY IMPERATIVE SENTENCE: *Shut the door.*

Use an exclamation point if greater emphasis is desired: *Be careful!*

END OF SOME RHETORICAL QUESTIONS: A period is preferable if a statement is more a suggestion than a question: *Why don't we go.*

END OF AN INDIRECT QUESTION: *He asked what the score was.*

MANY ABBREVIATIONS: For guidelines, see the **abbreviations and acronyms** entry. For the form of a frequently used abbreviation, see the entry under the full name or term.

INITIALS: *John F. Kennedy, T.S. Eliot.* (No space between *T.* and *S.,* to prevent them from being placed on two lines in typesetting.)

Abbreviations using only the initials of a name do not take periods: *JFK, LBJ.*

ELLIPSIS: See **ellipsis.**

ENUMERATIONS: After numbers or letters in enumerating elements of a summary: *1. Wash the car. 2. Clean the basement.* Or: *A. Punctuate properly. B. Write simply.*

PLACEMENT WITH QUOTATION MARKS: Periods always go inside quotation marks. See **quotation marks**.

perk A shortened form of *perquisite*, often used by legislators to describe fringe benefits. In the state of New York, legislators also use the word *lulu* to describe the benefits they receive in lieu of pay.

When either word is used, define it.

permissible

Persian Gulf Use this long-established name unless directly quoting the Iranian government, which calls it the *Gulf of Iran*.

When *Gulf of Iran* is used, explain in the text that this body of water off the southern coast of Iran more commonly is known as the *Persian Gulf.*

personifications Capitalize them: *Grim Reaper, John Barleycorn, Mother Nature, Old Man Winter, Sol,* etc.

persons See the **people, persons** entry.

-persons Do not use coined words such as *chairperson* or *spokesperson* in regular text.

Instead, use *chairman* or *spokesman* if referring to a man or the office in general. Use *chairwoman* or *spokeswoman* if referring to a woman. Or, if applicable, use a neutral word such as *leader* or *representative.*

Use *chairperson* or similar coinage only in direct quotations or when it is the formal description for an office.

persuade See the **convince, persuade** entry.

Peter Principle It is: Each employee is promoted until he reaches his level of incompetence.

From the book by Laurence J. Peter.

petty officer See **military titles**.

PG The *parental guidance* rating. See **movie ratings**.

phase See the **faze, phase** entry.

Ph.D., Ph.D.s The preferred form is to say a person *holds a doctorate* and name the individual's area of specialty.

See **academic degrees** and **doctor**.

phenomenon, phenomena

Philadelphia The city in Pennsylvania stands alone in datelines.

Philippines In datelines, give the name of a city or town followed by *Philippines:*

MANILA, Philippines (AP) —

Specify the name of an individual island, if needed, in the text.

In stories: *the Philippines* or *the Philippine Islands* as the construction of a sentence dictates.

The people are *Filipinos.*

Photostat A trademark for a type of photocopy.

piano, pianos

pica A unit of measure in printing, equal to a fraction less than one-sixth of an inch.

A pica contains 12 points.

picket, pickets, picketed, picket line *Picket* is both the verb and the noun. Do not use *picketer*.

picnic, picnicked, picnicking, picnicker

pico- A prefix denoting one-trillionth of a unit. Move a decimal point 12 places to the left in converting to the basic unit: 2,999,888,777,666.5 picoseconds = 2.9998887776665 seconds.

Piedmont Aviation A *Piedmont airliner* is acceptable in any reference.

Headquarters is in Winston-Salem, N.C.

pigeon

pigeonhole (n. and v.)

Pikes Peak No apostrophe. After Zebulon Montgomery Pike, a U.S. general and explorer. The 14,110-foot peak is in the Rockies of central Colorado.

pile up (v.) **pileup** (n., adj.)

pill Do not capitalize in references to oral contraceptives. Use *birth control pill* on first reference if necessary for clarity.

pilot Not a formal title. Do not capitalize before a name.
See **titles**.

pingpong A synonym for *table tennis*.
The trademark name is *Ping-Pong*.

pint (dry) Equal to 33.6 cubic inches, or one-half of a dry quart.
The metric equivalent is approximately .55 of a liter.
To convert to liters, multiply by .55 (5 dry pints x .55 = 2.75 liters).
See **liter** and **quart (dry)**.

pint (liquid) Equal to 16 fluid ounces, or two cups.
The approximate metric equivalents are 470 milliliters or .47 of a liter.
To convert to liters, multiply by .47 (4 pints x .47 = 1.88 liters).
See **liter**.

pipeline

pistol A pistol can be either an automatic or a revolver, but *automatic* and *revolver* are not synonymous. A revolver has a revolving cylinder that holds the cartridges; an automatic does not.
See **weapons**.

Pittsburgh The city in Pennsylvania stands alone in datelines.

The spelling is *Pittsburg* (no *h*) for communities in California, Illinois, Kansas, New Hampshire, Oklahoma and Texas.

plains See **Great Plains**.

planets Capitalize the proper names of planets: *Jupiter, Mars, Mercury, Neptune, Pluto, Saturn, Uranus, Venus.*
Capitalize *earth* when used as the proper name of our planet: *The astronauts returned to Earth.*
Lowercase nouns and adjectives derived from the proper names of planets and other heavenly bodies: *martian, jovian, lunar, solar, venusian.*
See **earth** and **heavenly bodies**.

planning Avoid the redundant *future planning*.

plants In general, lowercase the names of plants, but capitalize proper nouns or adjectives that occur in a name.
Some examples: *tree, fir, white fir, Douglas fir; Dutch elm, Scotch pine; clover, white clover, white Dutch clover.*
If a botanical name is used, capitalize the first word; lowercase others: *pine tree (Pinus), red cedera (Juniperus virginiana), blue azalea (Callicarpa americana), Kentucky coffee tree (Gynnocladus dioica).*

Plastic Wood A trademark for a brand of wood-filler compound.

platform tennis See **tennis**.

play off (v.) **playoff, playoffs** (n. and adj.) The noun and adjective forms are exceptions to Webster's New World Dictionary, in keeping with widespread practice in the sports world.

play titles See **composition titles**.

plead, pleaded, pleading Do not use the colloquial past tense form, *pled.*

Plexiglas Note the single *s*. A trademark for a synthetic glass, generically called *plexiglass*.

plow Not *plough*.

plurality See the **majority, plurality** entry.

plurals Follow these guidelines in forming and using plural words:

MOST WORDS: Add *s: boys, girls, ships, villages.*

WORDS ENDING IN CH, S, SH, SS, X and Z: Add *es: churches, lenses, parishes, glasses, boxes, buzzes.* (*Monarchs* is an exception.)

WORDS ENDING IN IS: Change *is* to *es: oases, parentheses, theses.*

WORDS ENDING IN Y: If *y* is preceded by a consonant or *qu*, change *y* to *i* and add *es: armies, cities, navies, soliloquies.* (See PROPER NAMES below for an exception.)
Otherwise add *s: donkeys, monkeys.*

WORDS ENDING IN O: If *o* is preceded by a consonant, most plurals require *es: buffaloes, dominoes, echoes, heroes, potatoes.* But there are exceptions: *pianos.* See individual entries in this book for many of these exceptions.

WORDS ENDING IN F: Change *f* to *v* and add *es: leaves, selves.*

LATIN ENDINGS: Latin-root words ending in *us* change *us* to *i: alumnus alumni.*
Most ending in *a* change to *ae: alumna, alumnae (formula, formulas* is an exception).
Those ending in *on* change to *a: phenomenon, phenomena.*
Most ending in *um* add *s: memorandums, referendums, stadiums.* Among those that still use the Latin ending: *addenda, curricula, media.*
Use the plural that Webster's New World lists as most common for a particular sense of a word.

FORM CHANGE: *man, men; child, children; foot, feet; mouse, mice;* etc.

Caution: When *s* is used with any of these words it indicates possession and must be preceded by an apostrophe: *men's, children's,* etc.

WORDS THE SAME IN SINGULAR AND PLURAL: *corps, chassis, deer, moose, sheep,* etc.
The sense in a particular sentence is conveyed by the use of a singular or plural verb.

WORDS PLURAL IN FORM, SINGULAR IN MEANING: Some take singular verbs: *measles, mumps, news.*
Others take plural verbs: *grits, scissors.*

COMPOUND WORDS: Those written solid add *s* at the end: *cupfuls, handfuls, tablespoonfuls.*
For those that involve separate words or words linked by a hyphen, make the most significant word plural:
—Significant word first: *adjutants general, aides-de-camp, attorneys general, courts-martial, daughters-in-law, passers-by, postmasters general, presidents-elect, secretaries general, sergeants major.*
—Significant word in the middle: *assistant attorneys general, deputy chiefs of staff.*
—Significant word last: *assistant attorneys, assistant corporation counsels, deputy sheriffs, lieutenant colonels, major generals.*

WORDS AS WORDS: Do not use *'s: His speech had too many ifs, ands and buts.* (Exception to Webster's New World.)

PROPER NAMES: Most ending in *es* or *z* add *es: Charleses, Joneses, Gonzalezes.*
Most ending in *y* add *s* even if preceded by a consonant: *the Duffys, the Kennedys, the two Germanys, the two Kansas Citys.* Exceptions include *Alleghenies* and *Rockies.*
For others, add *s: the Carters, the McCoys, the Mondales.*

FIGURES: Add *s: The custom began in the 1920s. The airline has two 727s. Temperatures will be in the low 20s. There were five size 7s.* (No apostrophes, an exception to Webster's New World guideline under "apostrophe.")

SINGLE LETTERS: Use *'s: Mind your p's and q's. He learned the three R's and brought home a report card with four A's and two B's. The Oakland A's won the pennant.*

MULTIPLE LETTERS: Add *s: She knows her ABCs. I gave him five IOUs. Four VIPs were there.*

PROBLEMS, DOUBTS: Separate entries in this book give plurals for troublesome words and guidance on whether certain words should be used with singular or plural verbs and pronouns. See also **collective nouns** and **possessives.**

For questions not covered by this book, use the plural that Webster's New World lists as most common for a particular sense of a word.

Note also the guidelines that the dictionary provides under its "plural" entry.

p.m., a.m. Lowercase, with periods. Avoid the redundant *10 p.m. tonight.*

pocket veto Occurs only when Congress has adjourned. If Congress is in session, a bill that remains on the president's desk for 10 days becomes law without his signature. If Congress adjourns, however, a bill that fails to get his signature within 10 days is vetoed.

Many states have similar procedures, but the precise requirements vary.

podium See the **lectern, podium, pulpit, rostrum** entry.

poetic license It is valid for poetry, not news or feature stories.
See **colloquialisms** and **special contexts.**

poetry See **composition titles** for guidelines on the names of poems.

Capitalize the first word in a line of poetry unless the author deliberately has used lowercase for a special effect. Do not, however, capitalize the first word on indented lines that must be created simply because the writer's line is too long for the available printing width.

poinsettia Note the *ia.*

point Do not abbreviate. Capitalize as part of a proper name: *Point Pleasant.*

point (printing) As a unit of measure in printing, a point equals a fraction less than a seventy-second of an inch. A pica contains 12 points.
See **pica.**

point-blank

Polaroid A trademark for Polaroid Land instant-picture cameras and for transparent material containing embedded crystals capable of polarizing light.

police department In communities where this is the formal name, capitalize *police department* with or without the name of the community: *the Los Angeles Police Department, the Police Department.*

If a police agency has some other formal name such as *Division of Police,* use that name if it is the way the department is known to the public. If the story uses *police department* as a generic term for such an agency, put *police department* in lowercase.

If a police agency with an unusual formal name is known to the public as a *police department,* treat *police department* as the name, capitalizing it with or without the name of the community. Use the formal name only if there is a special reason in the story.

If the proper name cannot be determined for some reason, such as the need to write about a police agency from a distance, treat *police department* as the proper name, capitalizing it with or without the name of the community.

Lowercase *police department* in plural uses: *the Los Angeles and San Francisco police departments.*

Lowercase *the department* whenever it stands alone.

police titles See **military titles** and **titles.**

policy-maker (n.) **policy-making** (n. and adj.)

polio The preferred term for *poliomyelitis* and *infantile paralysis.*

Politburo Acceptable in all references for the *Political Bureau of the Communist Party.* It is the chief policymaking body in the Soviet Union and other Communist nations.

political divisions Use Arabic figures and capitalize the accompanying word when used with the figure: *1st Ward, 10th Ward, 3rd Precinct, 22nd Precinct, the ward, the precinct.*

political parties and philosophies Capitalize both the name of the party and the word *party* if it is customarily used as part of the organization's proper name: *the Democratic Party, the Republican Party.*

Capitalize *Communist, Conservative, Democrat, Liberal, Republican, Socialist,* etc., when they refer to the activities of a specific party or to individuals who are members of it. Lowercase these words when they refer to political philosophy (see examples below).

Lowercase the name of a philosophy in noun and adjective forms unless it is the derivative of a proper name: *communism, communist; fascism, fascist.* But: *Marxism, Marxist; Nazism, Nazi.*

EXAMPLES: *John Adams was a Federalist, but a man who subscribed to his philosophy today would be described as a federalist. The liberal Republican senator and his Conservative Party colleague said they believe that democracy and communism are incompatible. The Communist said he is basically a socialist who has reservations about Marxism.*

See **convention** and **party affiliation.**

politicking

politics Usually it takes a plural verb: *My politics are my own business.*

As a study or science, it takes a singular verb: *Politics is a demanding profession.*

polls and surveys In stories about a canvass of public opinion, consider the following points. They are based on questions the National Council on Public Polls has suggested that editors ask before using a poll.

1. Who paid for the poll?
2. When was the poll taken? (Most pollsters concede that rapid, last-minute changes in voter sentiment can take place.)
3. How were the interviews obtained? (Some pollsters think people are less candid on the telephone than in person.)
4. How were the questions worded? (They can be "loaded" to achieve a desired result. Even the sequence of questions should be considered.)
5. Who was interviewed? How were they chosen — from a census list, a voter registration list, a telephone book? How were the selections made from this base — at random or by using some other procedure?
6. How many people were in the group to be contacted? How many responded? What is the margin of error in projecting the results to a larger group? (The larger the number of responses, the smaller the margin for error.)
7. If responses from a group smaller than the total sample are cited, how large was the smaller group and what is the margin of error in projecting the results? (A nationwide poll of 1,500 people, for example, might show one set of figures on overall attitudes toward abortion, while also reporting on the attitude of Catholics toward abortion. If the attitude of Catholics is cited, how many Catholics were interviewed?)

If a story on the poll is used, provide some indication of the methods the pollster employed.

pom-pom, pompon *Pom-pom* is sometimes used to describe a rapid-firing automatic weapon. Define the word if it must be used.

A *pompon* is a large ball of crepe paper or fluffed cloth, often waved by cheerleaders or used atop a hat. It is also a flower that appears on some varieties of chrysanthemums.

pontiff Not a formal title. Always lowercase.

pooh-pooh

pope Capitalize when used as a formal title before a name; lowercase in all other uses: *Pope Paul spoke to the crowd. At the close of his address, the pope gave his blessing.*

See **Roman Catholic Church** and **titles.**

Popsicle A trademark for a brand of flavored ice on a stick.

popular names See **capitalization.**

pore, pour The verb *pore* means to gaze intently or steadily: *She pored over her books.*

The verb *pour* means to flow in a continuous stream: *It poured rain. He poured the coffee.*

Portuguese names See the **Spanish and Portuguese names** entry.

possessives Follow these guidelines:

PLURAL NOUNS NOT ENDING IN S: Add *'s: the alumni's contributions, women's rights.*

PLURAL NOUNS ENDING IN S: Add only an apostrophe: *the churches' needs, the girls' toys, the horses' food, the ships' wake, states' rights, the VIPs' entrance.*

NOUNS PLURAL IN FORM, SINGULAR IN MEANING: Add only an apostrophe: *mathematics' rules, measles' effects.* (But see INANIMATE OBJECTS below.)

Apply the same principle when a plural word occurs in the formal name of a singular entity: *General Motors' profits, the United States' wealth.*

NOUNS THE SAME IN SINGULAR AND PLURAL: Treat them the same as plurals, even if the meaning is singular: *one corps' location, the two deer's tracks, the lone moose's antlers.*

SINGULAR NOUNS NOT ENDING IN S: Add *'s: the church's needs, the girl's toys, the horse's food, the ship's route, the VIP's seat.*

Some style guides say that singular nouns ending in *s* sounds such as *ce, x,* and *z* may take either the apostrophe alone or *'s.* See SPECIAL EXPRESSIONS below, but otherwise, for consistency and ease in remembering a rule, always use *'s* if the word does not end in the letter *s: Butz's policies, the fox's den, the justice's verdict, Marx's theories, the prince's life, Xerox's profits.*

SINGULAR COMMON NOUNS ENDING IN S: Add *'s* unless the next word begins with *s: the hostess's invitation, the hostess' seat; the witness's answer, the witness' story.*

SINGULAR PROPER NAMES ENDING IN S: Use only an apostrophe: *Achilles' heel, Agnes' book, Ceres' rites, Descartes' theories, Dickens' novels, Euripides' dramas, Hercules' labors, Jesus' life, Jules' seat, Kansas' schools, Moses' law, Socrates' life, Tennessee Williams' plays, Xerxes' armies.*

SPECIAL EXPRESSIONS: The following exceptions to the general rule for words not ending in *s* apply to words that end in an *s* sound and are followed by a word that begins with *s: for appearance' sake, for conscience' sake, for goodness' sake.* Use *'s* otherwise: *the appearance's cost, my conscience's voice.*

PRONOUNS: Personal, interrogative and relative pronouns have separate forms for the possessive. None involve an apostrophe: *mine, ours, your, yours, his, hers, its, theirs, whose.*

Caution: If you are using an apostrophe with a pronoun, always double-check to be sure that the meaning calls for a contraction: *you're, it's, there's, who's.*

Follow the rules listed above in forming the possessives of other pronouns: *another's idea, others' plans, someone's guess.*

COMPOUND WORDS: Applying the rules above, add an apostrophe or *'s* to the word closest to the object possessed:

the major general's decision, the major generals' decisions, the attorney general's request, the attorneys general's request. See the **plurals** entry for guidelines on forming the plurals of these words.

Also: anyone else's attitude, John Adams Jr.'s father, Benjamin Franklin of Pennsylvania's motion. Whenever practical, however, recast the phrase to avoid ambiguity: the motion by Benjamin Franklin of Pennsylvania.

JOINT POSSESSION, INDIVIDUAL POSSESSION: Use a possessive form after only the last word if ownership is joint: Fred and Sylvia's apartment, Fred and Sylvia's stocks.

Use a possessive form after both words if the objects are individually owned: Fred's and Sylvia's books.

DESCRIPTIVE PHRASES: Do not add an apostrophe to a word ending in s when it is used primarily in a descriptive sense: citizens band radio, a Cincinnati Reds infielder, a teachers college, a Teamsters request, a writers guide.

Memory Aid: The apostrophe usually is not used if for or by rather than of would be appropriate in the longer form: a radio band for citizens, a college for teachers, a guide for writers, a request by the Teamsters.

An 's is required, however, when a term involves a plural word that does not end in s: a children's hospital, a people's republic, the Young Men's Christian Association.

DESCRIPTIVE NAMES: Some governmental, corporate and institutional organizations with a descriptive word in their names use an apostrophe; some do not. Follow the user's practice: Actors Equity, Diners Club, the Ladies' Home Journal, the National Governors' Conference, the Veterans Administration. See separate entries for these and similar names frequently in the news.

QUASI POSSESSIVES: Follow the rules above in composing the possessive form of words that occur in such phrases as a day's pay, two weeks' vacation, three days' work, your money's worth.

Frequently, however, a hyphenated form is clearer: a two-week vacation, a three-day job.

DOUBLE POSSESSIVE: Two conditions must apply for a double possessive — a phrase such as a friend of John's — to occur: 1. The word after of must refer to an animate object, and 2. The word before of must involve only a portion of the animate object's possessions.

Otherwise, do not use the possessive form on the word after of: The friends of John Adams mourned his death. (All the friends were involved.) He is a friend of the college. (Not college's, because college is inanimate).

Memory Aid: This construction occurs most often, and quite naturally, with the possessive forms of personal pronouns: He is a friend of mine.

INANIMATE OBJECTS: There is no blanket rule against creating a possessive form for an inanimate object, particularly if the object is treated in a personified sense. See some of the earlier examples, and note these: death's call, the wind's murmur.

In general, however, avoid excessive personalization of inanimate objects, and give preference to an of construction when it fits the makeup of the sentence. For example, the earlier references to mathematics' rules and measles' effects would better be phrased: the rules of mathematics, the effects of measles.

post- Follow Webster's New World. Hyphenate if not listed there.

Some words without a hyphen:

postdate	postnuptial
postdoctoral	postoperaive
postelection	postscript
postgraduate	postwar

Some words that use a hyphen:

post-bellum	post-mortem

post office It may be used but it is no longer capitalized because the agency is now the U.S. Postal Service.

Use lowercase in referring to an individual office: I went to the post office.

potato, potatoes

pothole

pound (monetary) The English pound sign is not used. Convert the figures to dollars in most cases. Use a figure and spell out *pounds* if the actual figure is relevant.

pound (weight) Equal to 16 ounces. The metric equivalent is approximately 454 grams, or .45 kilograms.
To convert to kilograms, multiply the number of pounds by .45 (20 pounds x .45 = 9 kilograms).
See **gram** and **kilogram**.

pour See the **pore, pour** entry.

poverty level An income level judged inadequate to provide a family or individual with the essentials of life. The figure for the United States is adjusted regularly to reflect changes in the Consumer Price Index.

practitioner See **Church of Christ, Scientist.**

pre- The rules in **prefixes** apply. The following examples of exceptions to first-listed spellings in Webster's New World are based on the general rule that a hyphen is used if a prefix ends in a vowel and the word that follows begins with the same vowel:

pre-election	pre-establish
pre-eminent	pre-exist
pre-empt	

Otherwise, follow Webster's New World, hyphenating if not listed there. Some examples:

prearrange	prehistoric
precondition	preignition
precook	prejudge
predate	premarital
predecease	prenatal
predispose	pretax
preflight	pretest
preheat	prewar

Some hyphenated coinages, not listed in the dictionary:

pre-convention	pre-dawn

preacher A job description, not a formal religious title. Do not capitalize. See **titles** and **religious titles**.

precincts See **political divisions**.

predominant, predominantly Use these primary spellings listed in Webster's New World for the adjectival and adverbial forms. Do not use the alternates it records, *predominate* and *predominately.*
The verb form, however, is *predominate.*

preferred stock See the **common stock, preferred stock** entry.

prefixes See separate listings for commonly used prefixes.
Three rules are constant, although they yield some exceptions to first-listed spellings in Webster's New World Dictionary:
—Except for *cooperate* and *coordinate,* use a hyphen if the prefix ends in a vowel and the word that follows begins with the same vowel.
—Use a hyphen if the word that follows is capitalized.
—Use a hyphen to join doubled prefixes: *sub-subparagraph.*

premier, prime minister These two titles often are used interchangeably in translating to English the title of an individual who is the first minister in a national government that has a council of ministers.
Prime minister is the correct title throughout the Commonwealth, formerly the British Commonwealth. See **Commonwealth** for a list of members.
Prime minister is the best or traditional translation from most other languages. For consistency, use it throughout the rest of the world with these exceptions:
—Use *premier* for France and its former colonies.
—Use *premier* for the Communist nations of Eastern Europe and Asia.
—Use *chancellor* in Austria and West Germany.

—Follow the practice of a nation if there is a specific preference that varies from this general practice.

Premier is also the correct title for the individuals who lead the provincial governments in Canada and Australia. See **titles**.

premiere A first performance.

Presbyterian churches There are four levels of authority in Presbyterian practice — individual congregations, presbyteries, synods and a general assembly.

Congregations are led by a pastor, who provides guidance in spiritual matters, and by a session, composed of ruling elders chosen by the congregation to represent the members in matters of government and discipline.

A presbytery is composed of all the ministers and an equal number of ruling elders, including at least one from each congregation, in a given district. Although the next two levels are technically higher, the presbytery has the authority to rule on many types of material and spiritual questions.

Presbyteries unite to form a synod, whose members are elected by the presbyteries. A synod generally meets once a year to decide matters such as the creation of new presbyteries and to pass judgment on appeals and complaints that do not affect the doctrine or constitution of the church.

A general assembly, composed of delegations of pastors and ruling elders from each presbytery, meets yearly to decide issues of doctrine and discipline within a Presbyterian body. It also may create new synods, divide old ones and correspond with general assemblies of other Presbyterian bodies.

The assembly also chooses the stated clerk and the moderator for a denomination. The stated clerk, the chief administrative officer, normally serves for an extended period. The moderator, the presiding officer, serves for a year.

The largest Presbyterian body in the United States is the United Presbyterian Church in the United States of America. It has some 2.7 million members throughout the nation, although membership is concentrated in the North.

The Presbyterian Church in the United States, with slightly less than 1 million members, is the principal Southern body.

BELIEFS: The characteristic teachings rely heavily on the writings of John Calvin, a 16th century French lawyer turned theologian who emphasized the "sovereignty of God." He taught that church government is a purely human organization, quasi-democratic in nature. Christ, rather than any human individual, is the only real head of the church.

Presbyterians believe in the Trinity and the humanity and divinity of Christ. Baptism, which may be administered to children, and the Lord's Supper are the only sacraments.

The basic doctrinal standard is the Westminster Confession of Faith, a document drawn up by an assembly of leaders who met from 1643 to 1648 in England.

CLERGY: All Presbyterian clergymen may be described as *ministers*. *Pastor* applies if a minister leads a congregation.

On first reference, use *the Rev.* before the name of a man or woman. On second reference, use only the last name of a man; use *Miss, Mrs.* or *Ms.* before the last name of a woman depending on her preference.

See **religious titles**.

OTHER OFFICIALS: The preferred form for elected officials such as *elders* and *deacons* is to put the title after the name, with no religious title before the name. Capitalize *stated clerk, moderator, elder* and *deacon* when used before a name.

presently Use it to mean *in a little while* or *shortly,* but not to mean *now.*

presidency Always lowercase.

president Capitalize *president* only as a formal title before one or more names: *President Carter, Presidents Ford and Carter.*

Lowercase in all other uses: *The president said today. He is running for president. Lincoln was president during the Civil War.*

See **titles.**

FIRST NAMES: In most cases, the first name of a current or former U.S. president is not necessary on first reference. Use first names when necessary to avoid confusion: *President Andrew Johnson, President Lyndon Johnson.* First names also may be used for literary effect, or in feature or personality contexts.

For presidents of other nations and of organizations and institutions, capitalize *president* as a formal title before a full name: *President Josip Broz Tito of Yugoslavia* (not: *President Tito* on first reference), *President John Smith of Acme Corp.*

On second reference, use only the last name of a man. Use *Miss, Mrs.* or *Ms.* before the last name of a woman, depending on her preference.

presidential Lowercase unless part of a proper name.

Presidential Medal of Freedom This is the nation's highest civilian honor. It is given by the president, on the recommendation of the Distinguished Civilian Service Board, for "exceptionally meritorious contribution to the security of the United States or other significant public or private endeavors."

Until 1963 it was known as the Medal of Freedom.

presiding officer Always lowercase.

press conference *News conference* is preferred.

press secretary Seldom a formal title. For consistency, always use lowercase, even when used before an individual's name.

(The formal title for the person who serves a U.S. president in this capacity is *assistant to the president for press relations.*)

See **titles.**

pretense, pretext A *pretext* is something that is put forward to conceal a truth: *He was discharged for tardiness, but the reason given was only a pretext for general incompetence.*

A *pretense* is a false show, a more overt act intended to conceal personal feelings: *My profuse compliments were all pretense.*

price-earnings ratio The price of a share of stock divided by earnings per share for a 12-month period. Ratios in AP stock tables reflect earnings for the most recent 12 months.

For example, a stock selling for $60 per share and earning $6 per share would be selling at a price-earnings ratio of 10-to-1.

See **profit terminology.**

priest A vocational description, not a formal title. Do not capitalize.

See **religious titles** and the entries for the **Roman Catholic Church** and **Episcopal Church.**

prima-facie (adj.)

primary Do not capitalize: *the New Hampshire primary, the Democratic primary, the primary.*

primary day Use lowercase for any of the days set aside for balloting in a primary.

prime meridian See **meridians.**

prime minister See the **premier, prime minister** entry.

prime rate The interest rate that commercial banks charge on loans to their borrowers with the best credit ratings.

Fluctuations in the prime rate seldom have an immediate impact on consumer loan rates. Over the long term, however, consistent increases (or decreases) in the prime rate can lead to increases (or decreases) in the interest rates for mortgages and all types of personal loans.

prince, princess Capitalize when used as a royal title before a name; lowercase when used alone: *Prince Charles, the prince.*
See **nobility**.

Prince Edward Island One of the three Maritime Provinces of Canada. Do not abbreviate.
See **datelines**.

principal, principle *Principal* is a noun and adjective meaning someone or something first in rank, authority, importance or degree: *She is the school principal. He was the principal player in the trade. Money is the principal problem.*
Principle is a noun that means a fundamental truth, law, doctrine or motivating force: *They fought for the principle of self-determination.*

prior to *Before* is less stilted for most uses. *Prior to* is appropriate, however, when a notion of requirement is involved: *The fee must be paid prior to the examination.*

prison, jail Do not use the two words interchangeably.

DEFINITIONS: **Prison** is a generic term that may be applied to the maximum security institutions often known as *penitentiaries* and to the medium security facilities often called *correctional institutions* or *reformatories*. All such facilities confine persons serving sentences for felonies.

A **jail** is a facility normally used to confine persons serving sentences for misdemeanors, persons awaiting trial or sentencing on either felony or misdemeanor charges, and persons confined for civil matters such as failure to pay alimony and other types of contempt of court.

See the **felony, misdemeanor** entry.

The guidelines for capitalization:

PRISONS: Many states have given elaborate formal names to their prisons. They should be capitalized when used, but commonly accepted substitutes should also be capitalized as if they were proper names. For example, use either *Massachusetts Correctional Institution-Walpole* or *Walpole State Prison* for the maximum security institution in Massachusetts.

Do not, however, construct a substitute when the formal name is commonly accepted: It is *the Colorado State Penitentiary,* for example, not *Colorado State Prison.*

On second reference, any of the following may be used, all in lowercase: *the state prison, the prison, the state penitentiary, the penitentiary.*

Use lowercase for all plural constructions: *the Colorado and Kansas state penitentiaries.*

JAILS: Capitalize *jail* when linked with the name of the jurisdiction: *Los Angeles County Jail.* Lowercase *county jail, city jail* and *jail* when they stand alone.

FEDERAL INSTITUTIONS: Maximum security institutions are known as *penitentiaries: the U.S. Penitentiary at Lewisburg* or *Lewisburg Penitentiary* on first reference; *the federal penitentiary* or *the penitentiary* on second reference.

Medium security institutions include the word *federal* as part of their formal names: *the Federal Correctional Institution at Danbury, Conn.* On second reference: *the correctional institution, the federal prison, the prison.*

Most federal facilities used to house persons awaiting trial or serving sentences of a year or less have the proper name *Federal Detention Center.* The term *Metropolian Correctional Center* is being adopted for some new installations. On second reference: *the detention center, the correctional center.*

prisoner of war *POW* is acceptable on second reference.

Hyphenate when used as a compound modifier: *a prisoner-of-war trial.*

private See **military titles.**

privilege, privileged

pro- Use a hyphen when coining words that denote support for something. Some examples:

pro-business	pro-life
pro-labor	pro-war

No hyphen when *pro* is used in other senses: *produce, profile, pronoun,* etc.

probation See the **pardon, parole, probation** entry.

Procter & Gamble Co. *P&G* is acceptable on second reference.

Headquarters is in Cincinnati.

profanity See the **obscenities, profanities, vulgarities** entry.

Professional Golfers' Association Note the apostrophe. In general, spell out on first reference.

A phrase such as *PGA tournament* may be used on first reference, however, to avoid a cumbersome lead. If this is done, provide the full name later in the story.

professor Never abbreviate. Capitalize when used as a formal title before a full name. Do not continue in second reference unless part of a quotation. See **academic titles** and **titles.**

profit-sharing (n. and adj.) The hyphen for the noun is an exception to Webster's New World.

profit-taking (n. and adj.)

profit terminology Note the meanings of the following terms in reporting a company's financial status. Always be careful to specify whether the figures given apply to quarterly or annual results.

The terms, listed in the order in which they might occur in analyzing a company's financial condition:

revenue The amount of money a company took in, including interest earned and receipts from sales, services provided, rents and royalties.

The figure also may include excise taxes and sales taxes collected for the government. If it does, the fact should be noted in any report on revenue.

The terms *gross earnings* and *gross income* are seldom-used synonyms for *revenue.*

sales The money a company received for the goods and services it sold.

In some cases the figure includes receipts from rents and royalties. In others, particularly when rentals and royalties make up a large portion of a company's income, figures for these activities are listed separately.

gross profit The difference between the sales price of an item or service and the expenses directly attributed to it, such as the cost of raw materials, labor and overhead linked to the production effort.

income before taxes Gross profits minus company-wide expenses not directly attributed to specific products or services. These expenses typically include interest costs, advertising and sales costs, and general administrative overhead.

net income, profit, earnings The amount left after taxes have been paid.

A portion may be committed to pay preferred dividends. Some of what remains may be paid in dividends to holders of common stocks. The rest may be invested to obtain interest revenue or spent to acquire new buildings or equipment to increase the company's ability to make future profits.

To avoid confusion, do not use the word *income* alone — always specify whether the figure is *income before taxes* or *net income.*

The terms *profit* and *earnings* commonly are interpreted as meaning the amount left after taxes. The terms *net profit* and *net earnings* are acceptable synonyms.

earnings per share The figure obtained by dividing the number of outstanding shares of common stock into the amount left after dividends have been paid on any preferred stock.

dividend The amount paid per share per year to holders of common stock. Payments generally are made in quarterly installments.

The dividend usually is a portion of the earnings per share. However, if a company shows no profit during a given period, it may be able to use earnings retained from profitable periods to pay its dividend on schedule.

return on investment A percentage figure obtained by dividing the company's assets into its net income.

extraordinary loss, extraordinary income An expense or source of income that does not occur on a regular basis, such as a loss due to a major fire or the revenue from the sale of a subsidiary. Extraordinary items should be identified in any report on the company's financial status to avoid creating the false impression that its overall profit trend has suddenly plunged or soared.

Prohibition Capitalize when referring to the period that began when the 18th Amendment to the Constitution prohibited the manufacture, sale or transportation of alcoholic liquors.

The amendment was declared ratified Jan. 29, 1919, and took effect Jan. 16, 1920. It was repealed by the 21st Amendment, which took effect Dec. 5, 1933, the day it was declared ratified.

propeller

proper nouns See **capitalization**.

prophecy (n.) **prophesy** (v.)

proportions Always use figures: *2 parts powder to 6 parts water.*

proposition Do not abbreviate. Capitalize when used with a figure in describing a ballot question: *He is uncommitted on Proposition 15.*

prosecutor Capitalize before a name when it is the formal title. In most cases, however, the formal title is a term such as *attorney general, state's attorney* or *U.S. attorney*. If so, use the formal title on first reference.

Lowercase *prosecutor* if used before a name on a subsequent reference, generally to help the reader distinguish between prosecutor and defense attorney without having to look back to the start of the story.

See **titles**.

prostate gland Not *prostrate.*

Protestant, Protestantism Capitalize these words when they refer either to denominations formed as a result of the break from the Roman Catholic Church in the 16th century or to the members of these denominations.

Church groups covered by the term include Anglican, Baptist, Congregational, Methodist, Lutheran, Presbyterian and Quaker denominations. See separate entries for each.

Protestant is not generally applied to Christian Scientists, Jehovah's Witnesses or Mormons.

Do not use *Protestant* to describe a member of an Eastern Orthodox church. Use a phrase such as *Orthodox Christian* instead.

See **religious movements**.

Protestant Episcopal Church See **Episcopal Church**.

protester Not *protestor.*

prove, proved, proving Use *proven* only as an adjective: *a proven remedy.*

provinces Names of provinces are set off from community names by commas, just as the names of U.S. states are set off from city names: *They went to Halifax, Nova Scotia, on their vacation.*

Do not capitalize *province: They visited the province of Nova Scotia. The earthquake struck Shensi province.*

See **datelines.**

proviso, provisos

provost marshal The plural: *provost marshals.*

PTA See **parent-teacher association.**

PT boat It stands for *patrol torpedo boat.*

Public Broadcasting Service It is not a network, but an association of public television stations organized to buy and distribute programs selected by a vote of the members.

PBS is acceptable on first reference only within contexts such as a television column. Otherwise, do not use *PBS* until second reference.

public schools Use figures and capitalize *public school* when used with a figure: *Public School 3, Public School 10.*

If a school has a commemorative name: *Benjamin Franklin School.*

publisher Capitalize when used as a formal title before an individual's name: *Publisher Isaiah Thomas of the Massachusetts Spy.*

See **titles.**

Puerto Rico Do not abbreviate. See **datelines.**

Pulitzer Prizes These yearly awards for outstanding work in journalism and the arts were endowed by the late Joseph Pulitzer, publisher of the old New York World, and first given in 1917. They are awarded by the trustees of Columbia University on recommendation of an advisory board.

Awards in the journalism category are for: public service, national reporting, international reporting, general local reporting, special local reporting, editorial writing, editorial cartooning, spot news photography, feature photography, commentary, criticism.

Awards in the arts category are for: biography, drama, fiction, general nonfiction, history, music, poetry.

Capitalize *Pulitzer Prize*, but lowercase the categories: *Pulitzer Prize for public service, Pulitzer Prize for fiction,* etc.

Also: *She is a Pulitzer Prize winner. He is a Pulitzer Prize-winning author.*

pull back (v.) **pullback** (n.)

pull out (v.) **pullout** (n.)

pulpit See the **lectern, podium, pulpit, rostrum** entry.

punctuation Think of it as a courtesy to your readers, designed to help them understand a story.

Inevitably, a mandate of this scope involves gray areas. For this reason, the punctuation entries in this book refer to guidelines rather than rules. Guidelines should not be treated casually, however.

See separate entries under: **colon; comma; dash; ellipsis; exclamation mark; hyphen; parentheses; period; question mark; quotation marks;** and **semicolon.**

pupil, student Use *pupil* for children in kindergarten through eighth grade.

Student or *pupil* is acceptable for grades nine through 12.

Use *student* for college and beyond.

Purim The Jewish Feast of Lots, commemorating Esther's deliverance of the Jews in Persia from a massacre plotted by Haman. Occurs in February or March.

push-button (n., adj.)

push up (v.)   **push-up** (n., adj.)

put out (v.)   **putout** (n.)

pygmy

Pyrex A trademark for a brand of oven glassware.

q-and-a format See **question mark.**

Qantas Airways Headquarters is in Sydney, Australia.

QE2 Acceptable on second reference for the ocean liner *Queen Elizabeth 2.*
(But use a Roman numeral for the monarch: *Queen Elizabeth II.*)

Q-Tips A trademark for a brand of cotton swabs.

Quakers This informal name may be used in all references to members of the *Religious Society of Friends*, but always include the full name in a story dealing primarily with Quaker activities.

The denomination originated with George Fox, an Englishman who objected to Anglican emphasis on ceremony. In the 1640s, he said he heard a voice that opened the way for him to develop a personal relationship with Christ, described as the Inner Light, a term based on the Gospel description of Christ as the "true light."

Brought to court for opposing the established church, Fox tangled with a judge who derided him as a "Quaker" in a reference to his agitation over religious matters.

The basic unit of Quaker organization is the weekly meeting, which corresponds to the congregation in other churches. A monthly meeting receives and records members, extends spiritual care and, if necessary, material aid for members of one or more weekly meetings.

A quarterly meeting consists of representatives from several monthly meetings. Quarterly meetings unite into larger groups called yearly meetings, which are the rough equivalent of conventions, conferences, synods or dioceses in other faiths.

Capitalize references to a specific meeting, such as *the Yearly Meeting of the Philadelphia Society of Friends.* On second reference: *the yearly meeting* or *the meeting.*

Various yearly meetings form larger associations that assemble at intervals of a year or more. The largest is the Friends United Meeting. Its 15 yearly meeting members represent about half the Friends in the world.

Others include the Evangelical Friends Alliance and the Friends General Conference. Members of the conference include some yearly meetings that also are affiliated with the Friends United Meeting.

Overall, Friends count about 120,000 members in the United States and Canada and a total of 200,000 worldwide.

BELIEFS: Fox taught that the Inner Light emancipates a person from adherence to any creed, ecclesiastical authority or ritual forms. Many weekly meetings of worship involve silent meditation, in which any participant may speak when spiritually moved to do so. In others, there is a service of prayer and preaching.

CLERGY: There is no recognized ranking of clergy over lay people. However, meeting officers, called *elders* or *ministers,* are chosen by acclamation for their ability in leadership, but they do not go through an ordination ceremony. Many Quaker ministers, particularly in the Midwest and West, use *the Rev.* before their names and describe themselves as *pastors.*

Capitalize *elder, minister* or *pastor* when used as a formal title before a name. Use *the Rev.* before a name on first reference if it is a minister's practice. On second reference, use only the last name of a man; use *Miss, Mrs.* or *Ms.* before the last name of a woman depending on her preference.

See **religious titles.**

quakes See **earthquakes.**

quart (dry) Equal in volume to 67.2 cubic inches. The metric equivalent is approximately 1.1 liters.

To convert to liters, multiply by 1.1 (5 dry quarts x 1.1 = 5.5 liters).

See **liter.**

quart (liquid) Equal in volume to 57.75 cubic inches. Also equals 32 fluid ounces.

The approximate metric equivalents are 950 milliliters or .95 of a liter.

To convert to liters, multiply by .95 (4 quarts x .95 = 3.8 liters).

See **liter.**

quasar Acceptable in all references for a *quasi-stellar astronomical object,* often a radio source. Most astronomers consider quasars the most distant objects observable in the heavens.

Quebec The city in Canada stands alone in datelines.

Use *Quebec City* in the body of a story if the city must be distinguished from the province.

Do not abbreviate any reference to the province of Quebec, Canada's largest in area and second largest in population.

See **datelines.**

queen Capitalize only when used before the name of royalty: *Queen Elizabeth II.* Continue in second references that use the queen's given name: *Queen Elizabeth.*

Lowercase *queen* when it stands alone.

Capitalize in plural uses: *Queens Elizabeth and Victoria.*

See **nobility** and **titles.**

queen mother The mother of a reigning monarch. See **nobility.**

question mark Follow these guidelines:

END OF A DIRECT QUESTION: *Who started the riot?*
Did he ask who started the riot? (The sentence as a whole is a direct question despite the indirect question at the end.)
You started the riot? (A question in the form of a declarative statement.)

INTERPOLATED QUESTION: *You told me — Did I hear you correctly? — that you started the riot.*

MULTIPLE QUESTIONS: Use a single question mark at the end of the full sentence:
Did you hear him say, "What right have you to ask about the riot?"
Did he plan the riot, employ assistants, and give the signal to begin?
Or, to cause full stops and throw emphasis on each element, break into separate sentences: *Did he plan the riot? Employ assistants? Give the signal to begin?*

CAUTION: Do not use question marks to indicate the end of indirect questions:
He asked who started the riot. To ask why the riot started is unnecessary. I want to know what the cause of the riot was. How foolish it is to ask what caused the riot.

QUESTION AND ANSWER FORMAT: Do not use quotation marks. Paragraph each speaker's words:
Q: Where did you keep it?
A: In a little tin box.

PLACEMENT WITH QUOTATION MARKS: Inside or outside, depending on the meaning:
Who wrote "Gone With the Wind"?
He asked, "How long will it take?"

MISCELLANEOUS: The question mark supersedes the comma that normally is used when supplying attribution for a quotation: *"Who is there?" she asked.*

questionnaire

quick-witted

quotation marks The basic guidelines for open-quote marks (") and close-quote marks ("):

FOR DIRECT QUOTATIONS: To surround the exact words of a speaker or writer when reported in a story:
"I have no intention of staying," he replied.
"I do not object," he said, "to the tenor of the report."
Franklin said, "A penny saved is a penny earned."
A speculator said the practice is "too conservative for inflationary times."

RUNNING QUOTATIONS: If a full paragraph of quoted material is followed by a paragraph that continues the quotation, do not put close-quote marks at the end of the first paragraph. Do, however, put open-quote marks at the start of the second paragraph. Continue in this fashion for any succeeding paragraphs, using close-quote marks only at the end of the quoted material.
If a paragraph does not start with quotation marks but ends with a quotation that is continued in the next paragraph, do not use close-quote marks at the end of the introductory paragraph if the quoted material constitutes a full sentence. Use close-quote marks, however, if the quoted material does not constitute a full sentence. For example:
He said, "I am shocked and horrified by the incident.
"I am so horrified, in fact, that I will ask for the death penalty." But:

He said he was "shocked and horrified by the incident."
"I am so horrified, in fact, that I will ask for the death penalty," he said.

DIALOGUE OR CONVERSATION: Each person's words, no matter how brief, are placed in a separate paragraph, with quotation marks at the beginning and the end of each person's speech:
"Will you go?"
"Yes."
"When?"
"Thursday."

NOT IN Q-and-A: Quotation marks are not required in formats that identify questions and answers by *Q:* and *A:*. See the **question mark** entry for example.

NOT IN TEXTS: Quotation marks are not required in full texts, condensed texts or textual excerpts. See **ellipsis.**

COMPOSITION TITLES: See the **composition titles** entry for guidelines on the use of quotation marks in book titles, movie titles, etc.

NICKNAMES: See the **nicknames** entry.

IRONY: Put quotation marks around a word or words used in an ironical sense:
The "debate" turned into a free-for-all.

UNFAMILIAR TERMS: A word or words being introduced to readers may be placed in quotation marks on first reference:
Broadcast frequencies are measured in "kilohertz."
Do not put subsequent references to *kilohertz* in quotation marks.
See the **foreign words** entry.

AVOID UNNECESSARY FRAGMENTS: Do not use quotation marks to report a few ordinary words that a speaker or writer has used:
Wrong: *The senator said he would "go home to Michigan" if he lost the election.*
Right: *The senator said he would go home to Michigan if he lost the election.*

PARTIAL QUOTES: When a partial quote is used, do not put quotation marks around words that the speaker could not have used.

Suppose the individual said, *"I am horrified at your slovenly manners."*

Wrong: *She said she "was horrified at their slovenly manners."*

Right: *She said she was horrified at their "slovenly manners."*

Better when practical: Use the full quote.

QUOTES WITHIN QUOTES: Alternate between double quotation marks (" or ") and single marks (' or '):

She said, *"I quote from his letter, 'I agree with Kipling that "the female of the species is more deadly than the male," but the phenomenon is not an unchangeable law of nature,' a remark he did not explain."*

Use three marks together if two quoted elements end at the same time: *She said, "He told me, 'I love you.'"*

PLACEMENT WITH OTHER PUNCTUATION: Follow these long-established printers' rules:

—The period and the comma always go within the quotation marks.

—The dash, the semicolon, the question mark and the exclamation point go within the quotation marks when they apply to the quoted matter only. They go outside when they apply to the whole sentence.

See **comma**.

quotations in the news Quotations normally should be corrected to avoid the errors in grammar and word usage that often occur unnoticed when someone is speaking but are embarrassing in print.

Do not routinely use abnormal spellings such as *gonna* in attempts to convey regional dialects or mispronunciations. Such spellings are appropriate, however, when the usage, dialect or mispronunciation is relevant or helps to convey a desired touch in a feature.

FULL vs. PARTIAL QUOTES: In general, avoid fragmentary quotes. If a speaker's words are clear and concise, favor the full quote. If cumbersome language can be paraphrased fairly, use an indirect construction, reserving quotation marks for sensitive or controversial passages that must be identified specifically as coming from the speaker.

CONTEXT: Remember that you can misquote someone by giving a startling remark without its modifying passage or qualifiers. The manner of delivery sometimes is part of the context. Reporting a smile or a deprecatory gesture may be as important as conveying the words themselves.

OFFENSIVE LANGUAGE: See the **obscenities, profanities, vulgarities** entry.

PUNCTUATION: See the **quotation marks** entry.

R

R The *restricted* rating. See **movie ratings.**

rabbi See **Jewish congregations.**

Rabbinical Assembly See **Jewish congregations.**

Rabbinical Council of America See **Jewish congregations.**

raccoon

race Identification by race is pertinent:

—In biographical and announcement stories, particularly when they involve a feat or appointment that has not routinely been associated with members of a particular race.

—When it provides the reader with a substantial insight into conflicting emotions known or likely to be involved in a demonstration or similar event.

—When describing a person sought in a manhunt.

In some stories that involve a conflict, it is equally important to specify that an issue cuts across racial lines. If, for example, a demonstration by supporters of busing to achieve racial balance in schools includes a substantial number of whites, that fact should be noted.

Do not use racially derogatory terms unless they are part of a quotation that is essential to the story.

See the **obscenities, profanities, vulgarities** entry and the **nationalities and races** entry.

rack, wrack The noun *rack* applies to various types of framework; the verb *rack* means to arrange on a rack, to torture, trouble or torment: *He was placed in the rack. She racked her brain.*

The noun *wrack* means ruin or destruction, and generally is confined to the phrase *wrack and ruin.*

The verb *wrack* has substantially the same meaning as the verb *rack*, which is preferred.

racket Not *racquet*, for the light bat used in tennis and badminton.

racquetball Games are won by the first player to score 21 points, unless it is necessary to continue until one player has a two-point spread. Most matches go to the first winner of two games.

Use a match summary. Examples:

John Smith, Rutgers, def. Paul Giroux, Harvard, 21-8, 17-21, 22-20.
Frank Tivnan, Columbia, def. Tim Leland, Princeton, 21-17, 21-19.

radar A lowercase acronym for *radio detection and ranging.*

radical In general, avoid this description in favor of a more precise definition of an individual's political views.

When used, it suggests that an individual believes change must be made by tearing up the roots or foundation of the present order.

Although *radical* often is applied to individuals who hold strong socialist or communist views, it also is applied at times to individuals who believe an existing form of government must be replaced by a more authoritarian or militaristic one.

See the **leftist, ultra-leftist** and **rightist, ultra-rightist** entries.

radio Capitalize and use before a name to indicate an official voice of the government: *Radio Moscow.*

Lowercase and place after the name when indicating only that the information was obtained from broadcasts in a city. *Havana radio,* for example, is the form used in referring to reports that are broadcast on various stations in the Cuban capital.

radio station The call letters alone are frequently adequate, but when this phrase is needed, use lowercase: *radio station WHEC.*

See **call letters.**

railroads Capitalize when part of a name: *the Illinois Central Gulf Railroad.*

Railroad companies vary the spellings of their names, using *Railroad, Rail Road, Railway,* etc. Consult the Official Railway Guide-Freight Service and the Official Railway Guide-Passenger Service for official spellings.

Use *the railroad* for all lines in second references.

Use *railroads* in lowercase for all plurals: *the Penn Central and Santa Fe railroads.*

See **Amtrak** and **Conrail.**

rainstorm See **weather terms.**

raised, reared Only humans may be *reared.*

Any living thing, including humans, may be *raised.*

ranges The form: *$12 million to $14 million.* Not: *$12 to $14 million.*

rank and file (n.) The adjective form: *rank-and-file.*

rarely It means seldom. *Rarely ever* is redundant, but *rarely if ever* often is the appropriate phrase.

ratios Use figures and a hyphen: *the ratio was 2-to-1, a ratio of 2-to-1, a 2-1 ratio.* As illustrated, the word *to* should be omitted when the numbers precede the word *ratio.*

Always use the word *ratio* or a phrase such as *a 2-1 majority* to avoid confusion with actual figures.

ravage, ravish *To ravage* is to wreak great destruction or devastation: *Union troops ravaged Atlanta.*

To ravish is to abduct, rape or carry away with emotion: *Soldiers ravished the women.*

Although both words connote an element of violence, they are not interchangeable. Buildings and towns cannot be *ravished.*

rayon Not a trademark.

RCA Corp. Formerly Radio Corporation of America. *RCA* is acceptable on second reference.

Headquarters is in New York.

re- The rules in **prefixes** apply. The following examples of exceptions to first-listed spellings in Webster's New World are based on the general rule that a hyphen is used if a prefix ends in a vowel and the word that follows begins with the same vowel:

re-elect	re-enlist
re-election	re-enter
re-emerge	re-entry
re-employ	re-equip
re-enact	re-establish
re-engage	re-examine

For many other words, the sense is the governing factor:

recover (regain)	re-cover (cover again)
reform (improve)	re-form (form again)
resign (quit)	re-sign (sign again)

Otherwise, follow Webster's New World. Use a hyphen for words not listed there unless the hyphen would distort the sense.

reader See **Church of Christ, Scientist**.

Realtor The term *real estate agent* is preferred. Use *Realtor* only if there is a reason to indicate that the individual is a member of the National Association of Realtors.
See **service marks**.

reared See the **raised, reared** entry.

rebut, refute *Rebut* means to argue to the contrary: *He rebutted his opponent's statement.*
Refute connotes success in argument and almost always implies an editorial judgment. Instead, use *deny, dispute, rebut* or *respond to.*

recipes Always use figures. See **fractions**.
Do not use abbreviations. Spell out *teaspoon, tablespoon,* etc.
See the **food** entry for guidelines on when to capitalize the names of foods.

reconnaissance

Reconstruction The process of reorganizing the Southern states after the Civil War.

record Avoid the redundant *new record.*

record holder

rector See **religious titles**.

recur, recurred, recurring Not *reoccur.*

Red Capitalize when used as a political, geographic or military term: *the Red army.*

Red China See **China**.

red-haired, redhead, redheaded All are acceptable for a person with red hair.

Redhead also is used colloquially to describe a type of North American diving duck.

red-handed (adj. and adv.)

red-hot

redneck From the characteristic sunburned neck acquired in the fields by farm laborers. It refers to poor, white rural residents of the South and often is a derogatory term.

re-elect, re-election

refer See the **allude, refer** entry.

referable

reference works Capitalize their proper names.
Do not use quotation marks around the names of books that are primarily catalogs of reference material. In addition to catalogs, this category includes almanacs, directories, dictionaries, encyclopedias, gazetteers, handbooks and similar publications.
EXAMPLES: *Congressional Directory, Webster's New World Dictionary, the AP Stylebook.* But: *"The Careful Writer"* and *"Modern American Usage."*
See the bibliography for the principal reference works used in preparing this book.

referendum, referendums

reformatory See the **prison, jail** entry.

Reform Judaism See **Jewish congregations**.

refute See the **rebut, refute** entry.

regime See the **government, junta, regime** entry.

regions See the **directions and regions** entry.

reign, rein The leather strap for a horse is a *rein*, hence figuratively: *seize the reins, give free rein to, put a check rein on.*
Reign is the period a ruler is on the throne: *The king began his reign.*

release times Follow these guidelines:

TIME SET BY SOURCE: If a source provides material on condition that it not be published or broadcast until a specific time, the story should contain a boldface slug to that effect:

↑*Adv 10 a.m. EST, time set by source.*←

MOVEMENT TIME SET BY SOURCE: If a source provides material on condition that it not be moved on any wire read by newspapers or broadcasters until a specific time, the request will be respected. Consult the General Desk if any problems arise.

RELEASE SPECIFIED BY SOURCE: If a source does not specify a particular hour but says material is for release in morning papers, the automatic release time for print and broadcast is 6:30 p.m. Eastern time.
If a source says only that material is for release in afternoon papers, the automatic release time for print and broadcast is 6:30 a.m. Eastern time.
In either case, the story should contain a boldface slug to that effect:

↑*Adv 6:30 p.m. EST.* ←

↑*Adv 6:30 a.m. EST.* ←

ENTERPRISE COPY: Stories sent in advance for a specified cycle and date are released for broadcast use at 6:30 p.m. if the advance was sent for morning papers, 6:30 a.m. if the advance was sent for afternoon papers.

religious affiliations Capitalize the names and the related terms applied to members of the orders: *He is member of the Society of Jesus. He is a Jesuit.*

religious movements The terms that follow have been grouped under a single entry because they are interrelated and frequently cross denominational lines.

evangelical Historically, *evangelical* was used as an adjective describing dedication to conveying the message of Christ. Today it also is used as a noun, referring to a category of doctrinally conservative Christians. They emphasize the need for a definite, adult commitment or conversion to faith in Christ and the duty of all believers to persuade others to a decision accepting Christ.
Evangelicals make up some conservative denominations and are numerous in broader denominations. Evangelicals stress both doctrinal absolutes and vigorous efforts to win others to belief.
The National Association of Evangelicals is an interdenominational, cooperative body of relatively small, conservative Protestant denominations. It has a total of about 2.5 million members and maintains headquarters in Wheaton, Ill.

evangelism The word refers to activity directed outside the church fold to influence others to commit themselves to faith in Christ, to his work of serving others and to infuse his principles into society's conduct.
Styles of evangelism vary from direct preaching appeals at large public meetings to practical deeds of caring in the name of Christ, indirectly conveying the same call to allegiance to him.
The word *evangelism* is derived from the Greek *evangelion*, which means the gospel or good news of Christ's saving action in behalf of humanity.

fundamentalist The word gained usage in an early 20th century fundamentalist-modernist controversy within Protestantism. In recent years, however, *fundamentalist* has to a large extent taken on pejorative connotations except when applied to groups that stress strict, literal interpretations of Scripture and separation from other Christians.

In general, do not use *fundamentalist* unless a group applies the word to itself.

liberal In general, avoid this word as a descriptive classification in religion. It has objectionable implications to many believers.

Acceptable alternate descriptions include *activist, more flexible* and *broadview.*

Moderate is appropriate when used by the contending parties, as is the case in the conflict between the moderate or more flexible wing of the Lutheran Church-Missouri Synod and conservatives, who argue for literal interpretations of biblical passages others consider symbolic.

Do not use the term *Bible-believing* to distinguish one faction from another, because all Christians believe the Bible. The differences are over interpretations.

neo-Pentecostal, charismatic These terms apply to a movement that has developed within mainline Protestant and Roman Catholic denominations since the mid-20th century. It is distinguished by its emotional expressiveness, spontaneity in worship, speaking or praying in "unknown tongues" and healing. Participants often characterize themselves as "spirit-filled" Christians.

Unlike the earlier Pentecostal movement, which led to separate denominations, this movement has swelled within major churches.

Pentecostalism A movement that arose in the early 20th century and separated from historic Protestant denominations. It is distinguished by belief in tangible manifestations of the Holy Spirit, often in demonstrative, emotional ways such as speaking in "unknown tongues" and healing.

Pentecostal denominations include the Assemblies of God, the Pentecostal Holiness Church, the United Pentecostal Church Inc. and the International Church of the Foursquare Gospel founded by Aimee Semple McPherson.

religious references The basic guidelines:

DEITIES: Capitalize the proper names of monotheistic deities: *God, Allah, the Father, the Son, Jesus Christ, the Son of God, the Redeemer, the Holy Spirit,* etc.

Lowercase pronouns referring to the deity: *he, him, his, thee, thou, who, whose, thy,* etc.

Lowercase *gods* in referring to the deities of polytheistic religions.

Capitalize the proper names of pagan and mythological gods and goddesses: *Neptune, Thor, Venus,* etc.

Lowercase such words as *god-awful, goddamn, godlike, godliness, godsend.*

LIFE OF CHRIST: Capitalize the names of major events in the life of Jesus Christ in references that do not use his name: *The doctrines of the Last Supper, the Crucifixion, the Resurrection and the Ascension are central to Christian belief.*

But use lowercase when the words are used with his name: *The ascension of Jesus into heaven took place 40 days after his resurrection from the dead.*

Apply the principle also to events in the life of his mother: *He cited the doctrines of the Immaculate Conception and the Assumption.* But: *She referred to the assumption of Mary into heaven.*

RITES: Capitalize proper names for rites that commemorate the Last Supper or signify a belief in Christ's presence: *the Lord's Supper, Holy Communion, Holy Eucharist.*

Lowercase the names of other sacraments. See the **sacraments** entry.

Capitalize *Benediction* and the *Mass.* But: *a high Mass, a low Mass, a requiem Mass.*

HOLY DAYS: Capitalize the names of holy days. See the **holidays and holy days** entry and separate entries for major Christian and Jewish feasts.

OTHER WORDS: Lowercase *heaven, hell, devil, angel, cherub, an apostle, a priest,* etc.

Capitalize *Hades* and *Satan.*

For additional details, see **Bible**, entries for frequently used religious terms, the entries for major denominations, **religious movements** and **religious titles**.

Religious Society of Friends See Quakers.

religious titles The first reference to a clergyman, clergywoman or nun normally should include a capitalized title or courtesy title before the individual's name.

In many cases, *the Rev.* is the designation that applies before a name on first reference. Use *the Rev. Dr.* only if the individual has an earned doctoral degree (doctor of divinity degrees frequently are honorary) and reference to the degree is relevant.

On second reference to members of the clergy:

—To a man: Use only a last name if he uses a surname: *the Rev. Billy Graham* on first reference, *Graham* on second. If a man is known only by a religious name, repeat the title: *Pope Paul VI* or *Pope Paul* on first reference, *Pope Paul, the pope* (not *Paul*) or *the pontiff* on second; *Metropolitan Ireney* on first reference, *Metropolitan Ireney* or *the metropolitan* on second.

—To a woman: Use *Miss, Mrs.* or *Ms.* before her last name depending on her preference.

Detailed guidance on specific titles and descriptive words such as *priest* and *minister* is provided in the entries for major denominations. In general, however:

CARDINALS, ARCHBISHOPS, BISHOPS: The preferred form for first reference is to use *Cardinal, Archbishop* or *Bishop* before the individual's name: *Cardinal Timothy Manning, archbishop of Los Angeles.* On second reference: *Manning* or *the cardinal.*

Substitute *the Most Rev.* if applicable and appropriate in the context: *He spoke to the Most Rev. Joseph L. Bernardin, archbishop of Cincinnati.* On second reference: *Bernardin* or *the archbishop.*

Entries for individual denominations tell when *the Most. Rev., the Very Rev.,* etc., are applicable.

MINISTERS AND PRIESTS: Use *the Rev.* before a name on first reference.

Substitute *Monsignor* before the name of a Roman Catholic priest who has received this honor.

Do not routinely use *curate, father, pastor* and similar words before an individual's name. If they appear before a name in a quotation, capitalize them.

RABBIS: Use *Rabbi* before a name on first reference. On second reference, use only the last name of a man; use *Miss, Mrs.* or *Ms.* before a woman's last name depending on her preference.

NUNS: Always use *Sister,* or *Mother* if applicable, before a name: *Sister Agnes Rita* in all references if the nun uses only a religious name; *Sister Clare Regina Torpy* on first reference if she uses a surname, *Sister Torpy* on second.

OFFICEHOLDERS: The preferred first-reference form for persons who hold church office but are not ordained clergy in the usual sense is to use a construction that sets the title apart from the name by commas. Capitalize the formal title of an office, however, if it is used directly before an individual's name.

reluctant, reticent *Reluctant* means unwilling to act: *He is reluctant to enter the primary.*

Reticent means unwilling to speak: *The candidate's husband is reticent.*

Reorganized Church of Jesus Christ of Latter Day Saints Not properly described as a *Mormon church.* See the explanation under **Church of Jesus Christ of Latter-day Saints**.

representative, Rep. See **legislative titles** and **party affiliation**.

republic Capitalize *republic* when used as part of a nation's full, formal name: *the Republic of Argentina.*

See **datelines**.

republican, Republican Party *GOP* may be used on second reference.

See the **political parties and philosophies** entry.

Republican Governors' Association Note the apostrophe.

Republican National Committee On second reference: *the national committee, the committee.*

Similarly: *Republican State Committee, Republican County Committee, Republican City Committee, the state committee, the county committee, the city committee, the committee.*

reputation See the **character, reputation** entry.

Reserve Officers' Training Corps The *s'* is military practice. *ROTC* is acceptable in all references.

When the service is specified, use *Army ROTC, Navy ROTC* or *Air Force ROTC,* not *AROTC, NROTC* or *AFROTC.*

resident See the **citizen, resident, subject, national, native** entry.

resistible

restaurateur Not *restauranteur.*

restrictive clauses See the **essential clauses, non-essential clauses** entry.

restrictive phrases See the **essential phrases, non-essential phrases** entry.

Retail Clerks International Association The shortened form *Retail Clerks union* is acceptable in all references.

Headquarters is in Washington.

retail sales The sales of retail stores, including merchandise sold and receipts for repairs and similar services.

A business is considered a *retail store* if it is engaged primarily in selling merchandise for personal, household or farm consumption.

retired See **military titles.**

return on investment See **profit terminology.**

Reuters A private British news agency, named for Baron Paul Julius von Reuter, the founder.

The official name is *Reuters Ltd.* It is referred to as *Reuters.* When it is used as an adjective, the *s* is dropped: *a Reuter correspondent, a Reuter story.*

Rev. When this description is used before an individual's name, precede it with the word *the* because, unlike the case with *Mr.* and *Mrs.,* the abbreviation *Rev.* does not stand for a noun.

If an individual has a secular title such as *Rep.,* use whichever is appropriate to the context.

See **religious titles.**

revenue See **profit terminology.**

revenue bond See **profit terminology.**

Revolution Capitalize when part of a name for a specific historical event: *the American Revolution, the Bolshevik Revolution, the French Revolution.*

The Revolution, capitalized, also may be used as a shorthand reference to the *American Revolution.* Also: *the Revolutionary War.*

Lowercase in other uses: *a revolution, the revolution, the American and French revolutions.*

revolutions per minute The abbreviation *rpm* is acceptable on first reference in specialized contexts such as an auto column. Otherwise do not use it until second reference.

revolver See **pistol** and **weapons.**

Rh factor Also: *Rh negative, Rh positive.*

Rhode Island Abbrev.: *R.I.* Smallest of the 50 states in total land area: 1,049 square miles.
See **state names.**

Richter scale See **earthquakes.**

riffraff

rifle See **weapons.**

rifle, riffle *To rifle* is to plunder or steal.
To riffle is to leaf rapidly through a book or pile of papers.

right hand (n.) **right-handed** (adj.) **right-hander** (n.)

rightist, ultra-rightist In general, avoid these terms in favor of more precise descriptions of an individual's political philosophy.
As popularly used today, particularly abroad, *rightist* often applies to someone who is conservative or opposed to socialism. It also often indicates an individual who supports an authoritarian government that is militantly anti-communist or anti-socialist.
Ultra-rightist suggests an individual who subscribes to rigid interpretations of a conservative doctrine or to forms of fascism that stress authoritarian, often militaristic, views.
See **radical** and the **leftist, ultra-leftist** entry.

right of way, rights of way

right-to-work (adj.) A right-to-work law prohibits a company and a union from signing a contract that would require the affected workers to be union members.
Federal labor laws generally permit such contracts. There is no federal right-to-work law, but Section 14B of the Taft-Hartley Act allows states to pass such laws if they wish. Many states have done so.
The repeal of Section 14B would have the effect of voiding all right-to-work laws. By itself, the repeal would not require workers to be union members, but in states that now have right-to-work laws, the repeal would open the way to contracts requiring union membership.
See **closed shop** for definitions of various agreements that require union membership.

right wing (n.) But: *right-wing* (adj.), *right-winger* (n.).

Ringling Bros. and Barnum & Bailey Circus Note the *and, &.*
Headquarters is in Washington.

Rio Grande Not *Rio Grande River.* (*Rio* means river.)

rip off (v.) **rip-off** (n., adj.)

river Capitalize as part of a proper name: *the Mississippi River.*
Lowercase in other uses: *the river, the Mississippi and Missouri rivers.*

road Do not abbreviate. See **addresses.**

Roaring '20s See **decades.**

robbery See the **burglary, larceny, robbery, theft** entry.

rock 'n' roll

Rocky Mountains Or simply: *the Rockies.*

rodeo Use the basic summary format by classes, listing points.

roll call (n.) **roll-call** (adj.)

Rolls-Royce Note the hyphen in this trademark for a make of automobile.

roly-poly

Roman Catholic Church The church traces its origin to Christ's choice of the apostle Peter to lead his church on earth and his promise that "whatever you bind on earth shall be bound in heaven and whatever you loose on earth shall be loosed in heaven."

The church teaches that its bishops have been established as the legitimate successors of the apostles through generations of ceremonies in which authority was passed down by a laying-on of hands.

Responsibility for teaching the faithful and administering the church rests with the bishops. However, the church holds that the pope has final authority over their actions because he is the bishop of Rome, the office that it teaches was held by Peter at his death.

The shared teaching power — often called *collegiality* — of the bishops is particularly manifest when a pope summons an ecumenical council, a meeting of all bishops to regulate church worship and define new expressions of its teachings. Council actions must be approved by the pope, however, before they can take effect.

Although the pope is empowered to speak infallibly on faith and morals, he does so only in formal pronouncements that specifically state he is speaking from the chair (*ex cathedra*) of St. Peter. This rarely used prerogative was most recently invoked in 1950, when Pope Pius XII declared that Mary was assumed bodily into heaven.

The Curia serves as a form of governmental cabinet. Its members, appointed by the pope, handle both administrative and judicial functions.

The pope also chooses members of the College of Cardinals, who serve as his principal counselors. When a new pope must be chosen, they meet in a conclave to select a new pope by majority vote. In practice, cardinals are bishops, but there is no requirement that a cardinal be a bishop.

In the Latin Rite used by Catholics in the Western world, there are no national "churches" in the sense that applies in other denominations. Bishops in various nations do, however, organize conferences that develop programs to further the needs of the church in their nations. The National Conference of Catholic Bishops is the national organization of Roman Catholic bishops in the United States. Its administrative arm is the United States Catholic Conference, with offices in Washington.

In the Eastern Rite, followed by many Roman Catholics who live in the Middle East or trace their origins to it, there are national churches. They and the archbishops (often called *patriarchs*) who head them have considerable autonomy in ritual and discipline, but they acknowledge the authority of the pope. See the **Eastern rite** entry.

In the United States, the church's principal organizational units are archdioceses and dioceses. They are headed, respectively, by archbishops and bishops, who have final responsibility for many activities within their jurisdictions and report directly to Rome. Although the seat of an archdiocese once served as a meeting place for the bishops of other dioceses within a region, there is little practical difference between the two in the Latin Rite. An archbishop, however, is required to report to Rome if he believes that abuses have occurred in a diocese within his region.

MEMBERSHIP: The church counts more than 600 million members worldwide. In the United States it has more than 48 million members, making it the largest single body of Christians in the nation.

BELIEFS: Roman Catholics believe in the Trinity — that there is one God who exists as three divine persons, the Father, the Son and the Holy Spirit. They believe that the Son became man as Jesus Christ.

Other beliefs include salvation through Christ, and everlasting heaven and hell.

The essential elements of belief are contained in the Bible and in "tradition," the body of teachings passed on both orally and in writing by the apostles and their successors.

The Mass is the central act of worship. Christ is believed to be present in the Holy Eucharist, which is consecrated during Mass.

In addition to the Holy Eucharist, there are six other sacraments — baptism, confirmation, penance (often called the sacrament of reconciliation), matrimony, holy orders, and the sacrament of the sick (formerly extreme unction).

CLERGY: Ranks below the pope are, in descending order, cardinal, archbishop, bishop, monsignor, priest and deacon. In religious orders, some men who are not priests have the title brother.

Capitalize *pope* when used as a title before a name: *Pope Paul VI, Pope Paul.* Lowercase in all other uses. See the **titles** entry.

The first-reference forms for other titles follow. Use only last names on second reference.

Cardinals: *Cardinal Timothy Manning.* The usage *Timothy Cardinal Manning,* a practice traceable to the nobility's custom of identifications such as *William, Duke of Norfolk,* is still used in formal documents but otherwise is considered archaic.

Archbishops: *Archbishop Joseph L. Bernardin,* or *the Most Rev. Joseph L. Bernardin, archbishop of Cincinnati.*

Bishops: *Bishop Bernard J. Flanagan,* or *the Most Rev. Bernard J. Flanagan, bishop of Worcester.*

Monsignors: *Monsignor Joseph E. Vogt.* Do not use the abbreviation *Msgr.* Do not use *the Rt. Rev.* or *the Very Rev.* — this distinction between types of monsignors no longer is made.

Priests: *the Rev. John J. Paret.* When necessary in quotations on second reference: *Father Paret.*

Deacons: *Deacon Mark Smith.*

Brothers: *Brother Thomas Garvey.*

Nuns: See the **sister** entry.

See **religious titles**.

Romania Not *Rumania.*

Romanian Orthodox Church The Romanian Orthodox Church in America is an autonomous archdiocese of the Romanian Orthodox Church. The Romanian Orthodox Episcopate of America is an autonomous archdiocese within the Orthodox Church in America.

See **Eastern Orthodox churches.**

Roman numerals They use letters (*I, X,* etc.) to express numbers.

Use Roman numerals for wars and to establish personal sequence for people and animals: *World War I, Native Dancer II, King George V, Pope John XXIII, John Jones I, John Jones II, John Jones III.* See the **junior, senior** entry.

Use Arabic numerals in all other cases. See **Arabic numerals** and **numerals**.

In Roman numerals, the capital letter *I* equals 1, *V* equals 5, *X* equals 10, *L* equals 50, *C* equals 100, *D* equals 500 and *M* equals 1,000. Do not use *M* to mean million, as some newspapers occasionally do in headlines.

Other numbers are formed from these by adding or subtracting as follows:

—The value of a letter following another of the same or greater value is added: *III* equals 3.

—The value of a letter preceding one of greater value is subtracted: *IV* equals 4.

Rome The city in Italy stands alone in datelines.

room numbers Use figures and capitalize *room* when used with a figure: *Room 2, Room 211.*

rooms Capitalize the names of specially designated rooms: *Blue Room, Lincoln Room, Oval Office, Persian Room.*

Roquefort cheese, Roquefort dressing A trademark for a blue cheese.

rosary It is *recited* or *said,* never *read.* Always lowercase.

Rosh Hashana The Jewish new year. Occurs in September or October.

rostrum See the **lectern, podium, pulpit, rostrum** entry.

ROTC Acceptable in all references for *Reserve Officers' Training Corps.*

When the service is specified, use *Army ROTC, Navy ROTC* or *Air Force ROTC*, not *AROTC, NROTC* or *AFROTC*.

round up (v.) **round-up** (n.)

route numbers Do not abbreviate *route*. See **highway designations**.

rowing Scoring is in minutes, seconds and tenths of a second. Extend to hundredths if available.

Use a basic summary. An example, for a major event where qualifying heats are required:

> Single Sculls Heats (first two in each heat qualify for Monday's quarterfinals, losers go to repechage Friday): Heat 1— 1, Peter Smith, Australia, 4:24.7. 2, Etc. Heat 2—1, John Jones, Canada, 4:26.3. 72, Etc.

Royal Dutch-Shell Group of Companies This holding company, based in London and The Hague, owns substantial portions of the stock in numerous corporations that specialize in petroleum and related products. Most have *Shell* in their names.

Among them is Shell Oil Co., a U.S. corporation, with headquarters in Houston.

royal titles See **nobility**.

R.S.V.P. The abbreviation for the French *repondez s'il vous plait*, it means please reply.

Rt. Rev. See the entry for an individual's denomination.

rubber stamp (n.) **rubber-stamp** (v. and adj.)

rubella Also known as *German measles.*

runner-up, runners-up

running mate

rush hour (n.) **rush-hour** (adj.)

Russia, Soviet Union *Soviet people* and *the Soviets* are acceptable umbrella terms in referring to all the people who live within the 15 republics that make up the *Union of Soviet Socialist Republics,* popularly known as the *Soviet Union.*

The Russian Soviet Federated Socialist Republic is the dominant state, and its leaders effectively control the other 14 republics. For this reason, *Russia, Russian* and *Russians* are acceptable synonyms for *Soviets* and *Soviet Union* when referring to the governmental apparatus. For example: *Russia is considering the U.S. proposal. The United States is negotiating with the Russians.*

Do not, however, use *Russia, Russian* or *Russians* in references to all the people of the Soviet Union. Make it *Soviet hockey team,* for example, not *Russian hockey team,* in a story about a group that includes Soviet citizens of many nationalities.

When relevant, identify the nationalities of the individuals involved. While a first reference might say *Soviet gymnast,* for example, indicate later in the story where the individual comes from in the Soviet Union.

In addition to the *Russians,* national groups within the Soviet Union include *Armenians, Georgians, Latvians, Lithuanians* and *Ukrainians.*

DATELINES: *MOSCOW* stands alone. Follow all other community names with *U.S.S.R.* In the body of a story use *Soviet Union* or the full name, not *U.S.S.R.*

Identify a republic in the text if relevant.

REPUBLICS: The Russian republic includes Moscow and pre-revolutionary Russia. It is the largest in area and population.

The other 14, from the most populous to the least populous, are: the Ukrainian, Byelorussian, Uzbeck, Kazakh, Georgian, Azerbaidzhan, Lithuanian, Moldavian, Latvian, Kirgiz, Tadzhik, Armenian, Estonian and Turkmen Soviet Socialist Republics.

The Ukrainian and Byelorussian republics have their own memberships in the United Nations.

Russian names When a first name in Russian has a close phonetic equivalent in English, use the equivalent in translating the name: *Alexander Solzhenitsyn* rather than *Aleksandr*, the spelling that would result from a transliteration of the Russian letters into the English alphabet.

When a first name has no close phonetic equivalent in English, express it with an English spelling that approximates the sound in Russian: *Nikita*, for example.

For last names, use the English spelling that most closely approximates the pronunciation in Russian.

If an individual has a preference for an English spelling that is different from the one that would result by applying these guidelines, follow the individual's preference.

Women's last names have feminine endings. But use them only if the woman is not married or if she is known under that name (*the ballerina Maya Plissetskaya*). Otherwise, use the masculine form: *Victoria Brezhnev*, not *Brezhneva*.

Russian names never end in *off*, except for common mistransliterations such as *Rachmaninoff*. Instead, the transliterations should end in *ov*: *Romanov*.

Russian Orthodox Church See **Eastern Orthodox churches**.

Russian Revolution Also: *the Bolshevik Revolution*.

Sabbath Capitalize in religious references; lowercase to mean a period of rest.

Sabena Belgian World Airlines A *Sabena airliner* is acceptable in any reference.

Headquarters is in Brussels, Belgium.

saboteur

sacraments Capitalize the proper names used for a sacramental rite that commemorates the life of Jesus Christ or signifies a belief in his presence: *the Lord's Supper, Holy Communion, Holy Eucharist.*

Lowercase the names of other sacraments: *baptism, confirmation, penance* (now often called *the sacrament of reconciliation*), *matrimony, holy orders,* and *the sacrament of anointing the sick* (formerly *extreme unction*).

See entries for the major religious denominations and **religious references.**

sacrilegious

Safeway Stores Inc. Headquarters is in Oakland, Calif.

saint Abbreviate as *St.* in the names of saints, cities and other places: *St. Jude; St. Paul, Minn.; St. John's, Newfoundland; St. Lawrence Seaway.*

But see the entries for **Saint John** and **Sault Ste. Marie.**

Saint John The spelling for the city in New Brunswick.

To distinguish it from *St. John's, Newfoundland.*

salable

sales See **profit terminology**

SALT See **Strategic Arms Limitation Talks.**

Salt Lake City Stands alone in datelines.

salvo, salvos

SAM, SAMs Acceptable on second reference for *surface-to-air missile(s).*

sandbag (n.) The verbs: *sandbagged, sandbagging.* And: *sandbagger.*

San Diego The city in California stands alone in datelines.

sandstorm See **weather terms.**

sandwich

Sanforized A trademark denoting that a fabric has been pre-shrunk according to a particular standard.

A related trademark, **Sanforset,** describes a Sanforized fabric that has been treated to meet standards for smoothness.

San Francisco The city in California stands alone in datelines.

sanitarium, sanitariums

San Marino Use alone in datelines on stories from the Republic of San Marino.

Santa Claus

Sardinia Use instead of *Italy* in datelines on stories from communities on this island.

Saskatchewan A province of Canada north of Montana and North Dakota. Do not abbreviate.
See **datelines**.

Satan But lowercase *devil* and *satanic*.

satellites See **spacecraft designations**.

Saturday See **days of the week**.

Saturday Night Special See **weapons**.

Sault Ste. Marie, Mich., Sault Ste. Marie, Ontario The abbreviation is *Ste.* instead of *St.* because the full name is *Sault Sainte Marie.*

savings and loan associations They are not banks. Use *the association* on second reference.

savior Use this spelling for all senses, rather than the alternate form, *saviour.*

Scandinavian Airlines System *SAS* is acceptable on second reference.
Headquarters is in Stockholm, Sweden.

scene numbers Capitalize *scene* when used with a figure: *Scene 2; Act 2, Scene 4.*
But: *the second scene, the third scene.*

scheme Do not use as a synonym for *a plan* or *a project.*

school Capitalize when part of a proper name: *Public School 3, Madison Elementary School, Doherty Junior High School, Crocker High School.*

scissors Takes plural verbs and pronouns: *The scissors are on the table. Leave them there.*

scores Use figures exclusively, placing a hyphen between the totals of the winning and losing teams: *The Reds defeated the Red Sox 4-3, the Giants scored a 12-6 football victory over the Cardinals, the golfer had a 5 on the first hole but finished with a 2-under-par score.*
Use a comma in this format: *Boston 6, Baltimore 5.*
See individual listings for each sport for further details.

Scot, Scots, Scottish A native of Scotland is a *Scot.* The people are *the Scots,* not *the Scotch.*
Somebody or something is *Scottish.*

scotch barley, scotch broth, scotch salmon, scotch sour

Scotch tape A trademark for a brand of transparent tape.

Scotch whisky A type of whiskey distilled in Scotland from malted barley. The malt is dried over a peat fire.
Capitalize *Scotch* and use the spelling *whisky* only when the two words are used together.
Lowercase *scotch* standing alone: *Give me some scotch.*
Use the spelling *whiskey* for generic references to the beverage, which may be distilled from any of several grains.
The verb **to scotch** means to stamp out, put an end to.

Scotland Use *Scotland* after the names of Scottish communities in datelines.
See **datelines** and **United Kingdom**.

Scripture, Scriptures Capitalize when referring to the religious writings in the Bible.
See **Bible**.

scuba Lowercased acronym for *self-contained underwater breathing apparatus.*

sculptor Use for both men and women.

scurrilous

Seaboard World Airlines Headquarters is in New York.

Sea Islands A chain of islands off the coasts of South Carolina, Georgia and Florida.
Islands within the boundaries of South Carolina include Parris Island, Port Royal Island, and St. Helena Island.
Those within Georgia include Cumberland Island (largest in the chain), St. Simons Island and St. Catherines Island (no apostrophes), and Sea Island.
Amelia Island is within the boundaries of Florida.
Several communities have names taken from the island name — Port Royal is a town on Port Royal Island, Sea Island is a resort on Sea Island, and St. Simons Island is a village on St. Simons Island.
In datelines:
PORT ROYAL, S.C. (AP) —
ST. SIMONS ISLAND, Ga. (AP) —

seaman See **military titles.**

Sears, Roebuck and Co. Headquarters is in Chicago.

seasons Lowercase *spring, summer, fall, winter* and derivatives such as *springtime* unless part of a formal name: *Dartmouth Winter Carnival, Winter Olympics, Summer Olympics.*

Seattle The city in the state of Washington stands alone in datelines.

second guess (n.) The verb form: *second-guess.* Also: *second-guesser.*

second hand (n.) **secondhand** (adj. and adv.) *Secondhand Rose had a watch with a second hand that she bought secondhand.*

second-rate (adj.) All uses: *A second-rate play. The play is second-rate.*

second reference When used in this book, the term applies to all subsequent references to an organization or individual within a story.
Acceptable abbreviations and acronyms for organizations frequently in the news are listed under the organization's full name. A few prominent acronyms acceptable on first reference also are listed alphabetically according to the letters of the acronym.
The listing of an acceptable term for second reference does not mean that it always must be used after the first reference. Often a generic word such as *the agency, the commission* or *the company* is more appropriate and less jarring to the reader. At other times, the full name may need to be repeated for clarity.
For additional guidelines that apply to organizations, see the **abbreviations and acronyms** entry and **capitalization**.
For additional guidelines that apply to individuals, see **courtesy titles** and **titles**.

secretary Capitalize before a name only if it is an official corporate or organizational title. Do not abbreviate.
See **titles**.

secretary-general With a hyphen. Capitalize as a formal title before a name: *Secretary-General Dag Hammarskjold.*
See **titles**.

secretary of state Capitalize as a formal title before a name.
See **titles**.

secretary-treasurer With a hyphen. Capitalize as a formal title before a name.

See **titles**.

Secret Service A federal agency administered by the Treasury Department.

The *Secret Service Uniformed Division*, which protects the president's residence and offices and the embassies in Washington, formerly was known as the Executive Protective Service.

section Capitalize when used with a figure to identify part of a law or bill: *Section 14B of the Taft-Hartley Act.*

Securities and Exchange Commission *SEC* is acceptable on second reference.

The related legislation is the *Securities Exchange Act* (no *and*).

Security Council (U.N.) *Security Council* may be used on first reference in stories under a United Nations dateline. Use *U.N. Security Council* in other first references.

Retain capitalization of *Security Council* in all references.

Lowercase *council* whenever it stands alone.

Seeing Eye dog A trademark for a guide dog.

seesaw

self- Always hyphenate:

self-assured	self-government
self-defense	

sell out (v.) **sellout** (n.)

semi- The rules in **prefixes** apply, but in general, no hyphen. Some examples:

semifinal	semiofficial
semi-invalid	semitropical

semiannual Twice a year, a synonym for *biannual*.

Do not confuse it with *biennial*, which means every two years.

semicolon In general, use the semicolon to indicate a greater separation of thought and information than a comma can convey but less than the separation that a period implies.

The basic guidelines:

TO CLARIFY A SERIES: Use semicolons to separate elements of a series when individual segments contain material that also must be set off by commas:

He leaves a son, John Smith of Chicago; three daughters, Jane Smith of Wichita, Kan., Mary Smith of Denver, and Susan, wife of William Kingsbury of Boston; and a sister, Martha, wife of Robert Warren of Omaha, Neb.

Note that the semicolon is used before the final *and* in such a series.

Another application of this principle may be seen in the cross-references at the end of entries in this book. Because some entries themselves have a comma, a semicolon is used to separate references to multiple entries, as in: *See the* **felon, misdemeanor** *entry;* **pardon, parole, probation***; and* **prison, jail**.

See the **dash** entry for a different type of connection that uses dashes to avoid multiple commas.

TO LINK INDEPENDENT CLAUSES: Use a semicolon when a coordinating conjunction such as *and, but* or *for* is not present: *The package was due last week; it arrived today.*

If a coordinating conjunction is present, use a semicolon before it only if extensive punctuation also is required in one or more of the individual clauses: *They pulled their boats from the water, sandbagged the retaining walls, and boarded up the windows; but even with these precautions, the island was hard-hit by the hurricane.*

Unless a particular literary effect is desired, however, the better approach in these circumstances is to break the independent clauses into separate sentences.

PLACEMENT WITH QUOTES: Place semicolons outside quotation marks.

senate Capitalize all specific references to governmental legislative bodies, regardless of whether the name of the nation or state is used: *the U.S. Senate, the Senate; the Virginia Senate, the state Senate, the Senate.*
Lowercase plural uses: *the Virginia and North Carolina senates.*
See **governmental bodies**.
The same principles apply to foreign bodies. See **foreign legislative bodies**.
Lowercase references to non-governmental bodies: *The student senate at Yale.*

senator, Sen. See **legislative titles** and **party affiliation**.

senatorial Always lowercase.

send off (v.) **send-off** (n.)

senior See the **junior, senior** entry.

senior citizen Use the term sparingly. See **elderly**.

sentences Capitalize the first word of every sentence, including quoted statements and direct questions:
Patrick Henry said, "I know not what course others may take, but as for me, give me liberty or give me death."
Capitalize the first word of a quoted statement if it constitutes a sentence, even if it was part of a larger sentence in the original: *Patrick Henry said, "Give me liberty or give me death."*
In direct questions, even without quotation marks: *The story answers the question, Where does true happiness really lie?*
See **ellipsis** and **poetry**.

September See **months**.

sergeant See **military titles**.

serial numbers Use figures and capital letters in solid form (no hyphens or spaces unless the source indicates they are an integral part of the code): *A1234567.*

serviceable

service clubs See the **fraternal organizations and service clubs** entry.

serviceman, servicewoman

service mark A brand, symbol, word, etc. used by a supplier of services and protected by law to prevent a competitor from using it: *Realtor,* for a member of the National Association of Realtors, for example.
When a service mark is used, capitalize it.
The preferred form, however, is to use a generic term unless the service mark is essential to the story.
See **brand names** and **trademark**.

sesquicentennial Every 150 years.

set up (v.) **setup** (n. and adj.)

Seven Seas Arabian Sea, Atlantic Ocean, Bay of Bengal, Mediterranean Sea, Persian Gulf, Red Sea, South China Sea.

Seven Sisters The colleges are: Barnard, Bryn Mawr, Mount Holyoke, Radcliffe, Smith, Vassar and Wellesley.
Also a nickname for the world's largest privately operated oil companies: British Petroleum, Exxon, Gulf, Mobil, Royal Dutch-Shell, Standard Oil Co. of California and Texaco.

Seventh-day Adventist Church The denomination is traceable to the preaching of William Miller of New Hampton, N.Y., a Baptist layman who said his study of the Book of Daniel showed that the end of the world would come in the mid-1840s.
When the prediction did not come true, the Millerites split into smaller

groups. One, influenced by visions described by Ellen Harmon, later Mrs. James White, is the precursor of Seventh-day Adventist practice today.

The General Conference, which meets every four years, has authority to make decisions that affect the denomination worldwide. In descending order of authority come divisions for various sections of the world, union conferences for major areas within a division, and, in the United States, state conferences. Members at each level participate in electing representatives to higher levels.

The office of the General Conference, located in Washington, lists U.S. membership at 500,000 and worldwide membership at 2.5 million.

BELIEFS: The description *adventist* is based on the belief that a second coming of Christ is near. Believers hold that events leading to the coming began in the mid-1840s and will continue until the completion of a process that will identify those worthy of joining in the resurrection at the second coming of Christ.

Seventh-day derives from the contention that the Bible permits no deviation from observing the seventh day of the week as the Sabbath.

Baptism, by immersion, is reserved for those old enough to understand its meaning. Baptism and the Lord's Supper are the only sacraments.

CLERGY: The head of the General Conference holds the formal title of *president.* The formal titles for ministers are *pastor* or *elder.* Capitalize them when used immediately before a name on first reference. On second reference, use only the last name of a man; use *Miss, Mrs.* or *Ms.* before the last name of a woman, depending on her preference.

The designation *the Rev.* is not used.

See **religious titles.**

Seven-Up, 7-Up Trademarks for a brand of soft drink.

Seven Wonders of the World The Egyptian pyramids, the hanging gardens of Babylon, the Mausoleum at Halicarnassus, the temple of Artemis at Ephesus, the Colossus of Rhodes, the statue of Zeus by Phidias at Olympia and the Pharos or lighthouse at Alexandria.

sewage, sewerage *Sewage* is waste matter.

Sewerage is the drainage system.

sex changes Follow these guidelines in using proper names or personal pronouns when referring to an individual who has had a sex-change operation:

—If the reference is to an action before the operation, use the proper name and gender of the individual at that time.

—If the reference is to an action after the operation, use the new proper name and gender.

For example:

Dr. Richard Raskind was a first-rate amateur tennis player. He won several tournaments. Ten years later, when Dr. Renee Richards applied to play in tournaments, many women players objected on the ground that she was the former Richard Raskind, who had undergone a sex-change operation. Miss Richards said she was entitled to compete as a woman.

sexism See **women.**

shah Capitalize when used as a title before a name: *Shah Mohammed Reza Pahlavi of Iran.*

The Shah of Iran commonly is known only by this title, which is, in effect, an alternate name. Capitalize *Shah of Iran* in references to the holder of the title; lowercase subsequent references as *the shah.*

The practice is based on the guidelines in the **nobility** entry.

shake up (v.) **shake-up** (n. and adj.)

shall, will Use *shall* to express determination: *We shall overcome. You and he shall stay.*

Either *shall* or *will* may be used in first-person constructions that do not emphasize determination: *We shall hold a meeting. We will hold a meeting.*

For second- and third-person constructions, use *will* unless determination is stressed: *You will like it. She will not be pleased.*

See the **should, would** entry and **subjunctive mood**.

shape up (v.) **shape-up** (n. and adj.)

Shariah The legal code of Islam. It is roughly comparable to the Talmudic tradition in Judaism.

Shavuot The Jewish Feast of Weeks, commemorating the receiving of the Ten Commandments. Occurs in May or June.

she Do not use this pronoun in references to ships or nations.

Use *it* instead.

Sheet Metal Workers International Association The shortened form *Sheet Metal Workers union* is acceptable in all references.

Headquarters is in Washington.

Sheetrock A trademark for a brand of gypsum wallboard.

shell See **weapons**.

Shell Oil Co. This U.S. company, with headquarters in Houston, is part of the Royal Dutch-Shell Group of Companies. The group owns more than half of the stock in Shell Oil.

sheriff Capitalize when used as a formal title before a name. See **titles**.

ships See the **boats, ships** entry.

shirt sleeve, shirt sleeves (n.) **shirt-sleeve** (adj.)

shoeshine, shoestring

shopworn

shortchange

short-lived (adj.) *A short-lived plan. The plan was short-lived.*

short ton Equal to 2,000 pounds. See **ton**.

shot See **weapons**.

shotgun See **weapons**.

should, would Use *should* to express an obligation: *We should help the needy.*

Use *would* to express a customary action: *In the summer we would spend hours by the seashore.*

Use *would* also in constructing a conditional past tense, but be careful:

Wrong: *If Soderholm would not have had an injured foot, Thompson would not have been in the lineup.*

Right: *If Soderholm had not had an injured foot, Thompson would not have been in the lineup.*

See **subjunctive mood**.

showcase, showroom

show off (v.) **showoff** (n.)

shrubs See **plants**.

shut down (v.) **shutdown** (n.)

shut-in

shut off (v.) **shut-off** (n.)

shut out (v.) **shutout** (n.)

(sic) Do not use *(sic)* unless it is in the matter being quoted. To show that an error, peculiar usage or spelling is in the original, use a note to editors at the end of copy, after a dash:

☐ — — ☐

☐↑*Editors: The spelling cabob is in the original copy.* ←

Or:

☐↑*Editors: The spelling Jorga is correct.* ←

Sicily Use instead of *Italy* in datelines on stories from communities on this island.

side by side, side-by-side *They walked side by side. The stories received side-by-side display.*

Sierra Nevada, the Not *Sierra Nevada Mountains.* (*Sierra* means mountains.)

sightseeing, sightseer

Simoniz A trademark for a brand of auto wax.

Sinai Not *the Sinai.* But: *the Sinai Desert, the Sinai Peninsula.*

Singapore Stands alone in datelines.

single-handed, single-handedly

sir See **nobility.**

sister Capitalize in all references before the names of nuns.

If no surname is given, the name is the same in all references: *Sister Agnes Rita.*

If a surname is used in first reference, drop the given name on second reference: *Sister Clair Regina Torpy* on first reference, *Sister Torpy* in subsequent references.

Use *mother* the same way when referring to a woman who heads a group of nuns.

See **religious titles.**

sister-in-law, sisters-in-law

sit down (v.) **sit-down** (n. and adj.)

sit in (v.) **sit-in** (n. and adj.)

sizable

sizes Use figures: *a size 9 dress, size 40 long, 10½B shoes, a 34½ sleeve.*

skating, figure Scoring includes both ordinals and points.

Use a basic summary. Examples:

> **Men**
> (After 3 compulsory figures)
> 1, Sergei Volkov, Soviet Union, 19.5 ordinals, 44.76 points. 2, John Curry, Britain, 21.5, 44.96. 3, Etc.
> **Women's Final**
> 1, Dorothy Hamill, Riverside, Conn., 9.0 ordinals, 215 points. 2, Dianne de Leeuw, Netherlands, 20.0, 236. 3, Etc.

skating, speed Scoring is in minutes, seconds and tenths of a second. Extend to hundredths if available.

Use a basic summary.

skeptic See the **cynic, skeptic** entry.

ski, skis, skier, skied, skiing Also: *ski jump, ski jumping.*

Skid Road, Skid Row The term originated as *Skid Road* in the Seattle area, where dirt roads were used to skid logs to the mill. Over the years, *Skid Road* became a synonym for the area where loggers gathered, usually down among the rooming houses and saloons.

In time, the term spread to other cities as a description for sections, such as the Bowery in New York, that are havens for derelicts. In the process, *row* replaced *road* in many references.

Use *Skid Road* for this section in Seattle; either *Skid Road* or *Skid Row* for other areas.

skiing Identify events as: *Men's downhill, women's slalom,* etc. In ski jumping, note style where two jumps and points are posted.

Use a basic summary. Example:

> 90-meter special jumping—1, Karl Schnabel, Austria, 320 and 318 feet, 234.8 points. 2, Toni Innauer, Austria, 377-299, 232.9. 3, Etc. Also: 27, Bob Smith, Hanover, N.H., 312-280, 201. 29, Etc.

skillful

slang In general, avoid slang, the highly informal language that is outside of conventional or standard usage.

See **colloquialisms; dialect;** and **word selection.**

slaying See the **homicide, murder, manslaughter** entry.

sledgehammer

sleet See **weather terms.**

sleight of hand

slowdown

slumlord

slush fund

small-arms fire

small-business man

smash up (v.) **smashup** (n. and adj.)

Smithfield Ham A trademark for a ham dry-cured, smoked and aged in Smithfield, Va.

Smithsonian Institution Not *Smithsonian Institute.*

smoke bomb, smoke screen

Smokey Or *Smokey Bear.* Not *Smokey the Bear.*
But: *A smoky room.*

snowdrift, snowfall, snowflake, snowman, snowplow, snowshoe, snowstorm, snowsuit

so called (adv.) **so-called** (adj.)

socialist, socialism See the **political parties and philosophies** entry.

Social Security Capitalize all references to the U.S. system.
The number groups are hyphenated: *123-45-6789.*
Lowercase generic uses such as: *Is there a social security program in Sweden?*

social titles See **courtesy titles.**

Society for the Prevention of Cruelty to Animals *SPCA* is acceptable on second reference.
The *American Society for the Prevention of Cruelty to Animals* is limited to the five boroughs of New York City.
The autonomous chapters in other cities ordinarily precede the organization by the name of the city: On first reference, the *Philadelphia Society for the Prevention of Cruelty to Animals*; on second, the *Philadelphia SPCA* or *SPCA* as appropriate in the context.

Society of Friends See **Quakers.**

soft-spoken

solicitor See **lawyer.**

Solid South Those Southern states traditionally regarded as supporters of the Democratic Party.

soliloquy, soliloquies

song titles See **composition titles.**

son-in-law, sons-in-law

SOS The distress signal.
S.O.S (no final period) is a trademark for a brand of soap pad.

sound barrier The speed of sound, no longer a true barrier because aircraft have exceeded it. See **Mach number.**

South As defined by the U.S. Census Bureau, the 16-state region is broken into three divisions.
The four *East South Central* states are Alabama, Kentucky, Mississippi and Tennessee.
The eight *South Atlantic* states are Delaware, Florida, Georgia, Maryland, North Carolina, South Carolina, Virginia and West Virginia.
The four *West South Central* states are Arkansas, Louisiana, Oklahoma and Texas.

See **North Central region; Northeast region;** and **West** for the bureau's other regional breakdowns.

south, southern, southeast, southwest See the **directions and regions** entry.

South America See **Western Hemisphere.**

South Carolina Abbrev.: *S.C.* See **state names.**

South Dakota Abbrev.: *S.D.* See **state names.**

Southeast Asia The nations of the Indochinese Peninsula and the islands southeast of it: Burma, Cambodia, Indonesia, Laos, Malaysia, New Guinea, the Philippines, Singapore, Thailand and Vietnam.
See **Asian subcontinent** and **Far East.**

Southeast Asia Treaty Organization *SEATO* is acceptable on second reference. But use *the alliance* in some references to reduce the frequency of alphabet soup.

Southeastern Conference Alabama, Auburn, Florida, Georgia, Kentucky, Louisiana State, Mississippi, Mississippi State, Tennessee, Vanderbilt.

Southwest Conference Arkansas, Baylor, Houston, Rice, Southern Methodist, Texas, Texas A&M, Texas Christian, Texas Tech.

Soviet Union Acceptable in all references in the body of a story for *Union of Soviet Socialist Republics.* But use *U.S.S.R.* in datelines.
See the **Russia, Soviet Union** entry for guidance on using *Soviet* and for a list of the 15 republics that make up the nation.

Space Age It began with the launching of Sputnik 1 on Oct. 4, 1957.

space agency See **National Aeronautics and Space Administration.**

space centers See **John F. Kennedy Space Center** and **Lyndon B. Johnson Space Center.**

spacecraft The plural also is *spacecraft.*

spacecraft designations Use Arabic figures and capitalize the name: *Gemini 7, Apollo 11.*

spaceship

space shuttle Lowercase *space shuttle,* but capitalize a proper name.
The first American shuttle, *Enterprise,* is a reusable winged aircraft capable of carrying scientists and cargo into Earth orbit. It is designed to take off vertically with the aid of booster rockets. After an orbital mission, reentry begins with the firing of engines that send the craft back into Earth's atmosphere. The final leg of the return trip is a powerless glide to a landing strip.

Spanish-American War

Spanish and Portuguese names The family names of both the father and mother usually are considered part of a person's full name. In everyday use, customs vary widely with individuals and countries.
The normal sequence is given name, father's family name, mother's family name: *Jose Lopez Portillo.*
On second reference, use only the father's family name (*Lopez*), unless the individual prefers or is widely known by a multiple last name (*Lopez Portillo*).
Some individuals use a *y* (for *and*) between the two surnames: *Jose Lopez y Portillo.* Include the *y* on second reference only if both names are used: *Lopez y Portillo.*
In the Portuguese practice common in Portugal and Brazil, some individuals use only the mother's family name on

second reference. If the individual's preference is not known, use both family names on second reference: *Humberto Castello Branco* on first reference, *Castello Branco* on second.

A married woman frequently uses her father's family name followed by the particle *de* (for *of*) and her husband's name. A woman named *Irma Perez* who married a man named *Anibal Gutierrez* would be known as *Irma Perez de Gutierrez*. Use *Mrs. Gutierrez* on second reference.

speaker Capitalize as a formal title before a name. Generally, it is a formal title only for the speaker of a legislative body: *Speaker Thomas P. O'Neill.*
See **titles**.

special contexts When this term is used in this book, it means that the material described may be used in a regular column devoted to a specialized subject or when a particular literary effect is suitable.

Special literary effects generally are suitable only in feature copy, but even there they should be used with care. Most feature material should follow the same style norms that apply to regular news copy.

species Same in singular and plural. Use singular or plural verbs and pronouns depending on the sense: *The species has been unable to maintain itself. Both species are extinct.*

speeches Capitalize and use quotation marks for their formal titles, as described in **composition titles**.

speechmaker, speechmaking

speed of sound See **Mach number**.

speeds Use figures. *The car slowed to 7 miles per hour, winds of 5 to 10 miles per hour, winds of 7 to 9 knots, 10-knot wind.*

Avoid extensively hyphenated constructions such as *5-mile-per-hour winds*.

speed up (v.) **speedup** (n. and adj.)

spelling The basic rule when in doubt is to consult this book followed by, if necessary, a dictionary under conditions described in the **dictionary** entry.

Memory Aid: Noah Webster developed the following rule of thumb for the frequently vexing question of whether to double a final consonant in forming the present participle and past tense of a verb:

—If the stress in pronunciation is on the first syllable, do not double the consonant: *combat, combating, combated; cancel, canceling, canceled.*

—If the stress in pronunciation is on the second syllable, double the consonant: *control, controlling, controlled; refer, referring, referred.*

—If the word is only one syllable, double a consonant unless confusion would result: *jut, jutted, jutting.* An exception, to avoid confusion with *buss*, is *bus, bused, busing.*

spill, spilled, spilling Not *spilt* in the past tense.

split infinitive See **verbs**.

spokesman, spokeswoman But not *spokesperson*. Use *a representative* if you do not know the sex of the individual.

sports editor Capitalize as a formal title before a name. See **titles**.

sports titles See **titles**.

spouse Use when some of the persons involved may be men. For example: *physicians and their spouses*, not *physicians and their wives.*

spring See **seasons**.

springtime

sputnik Usually lowercase, but capitalize when followed by a figure as part of a proper name: *Sputnik 1.*

squall See **weather terms**.

square Do not abbreviate. Capitalize when part of a proper name: *Washington Square.*

squash Games are won by the first player to score 15 points, unless it is necessary to continue until one player has a two-point spread. Most matches go to the first winner of two games.

Use a match summary. Example:

Bill Davis, Boston University, def. Larry Elders, Bates, 15-8, 8-15, 17-15.

squinting modifier A misplaced adverb that can be interpreted as modifying either of two words: *Those who lie often are found out.*

Place the adverb where there can be no confusion, even if a compound verb must be split: *Those who often lie are found out.* Or if that was not the sense: *Those who lie are often found out.*

Sri Lanka Formerly Ceylon. Use *Sri Lanka* in datelines and other references to the nation.

The people may be called either *Sri Lankans* or *Ceylonese.*

Before the nation was called Ceylon, it was Serendip, whence comes the word *serendipity.*

SRO Acceptable on second reference for *standing room only.*

S.S. Kresge Co. Headquarters is in Troy, Mich.

SST Acceptable in all references for a *supersonic transport.*

stadium, stadiums Capitalize only when part of a proper name: *Yankee Stadium.*

Stalin, Josef Not *Joseph.*

stanch, staunch *Stanch* is a verb: *He stanched the flow of blood.*

Staunch is an adjective: *She is a staunch supporter of equality.*

Standard & Poor's Register of Corporations The source for determining the formal name of a business. See **company names**.

The register is published by Standard & Poor's Corp. of New York.

standard-bearer

Standard Oil Co. (Indiana) *Indiana Standard* or *Standard of Indiana* is acceptable on second reference.

Amoco is a company trademark.

Headquarters is in Chicago.

Standard Oil Co. (New Jersey) The former name of *Exxon Corp.*

Standard Oil Co. of California *Socal* is acceptable on second reference.

Headquarters is in San Francisco.

Standard Oil Co. (Ohio) *Sohio* is acceptable on second reference.

Headquarters is in Cleveland.

standard time Capitalize *Eastern Standard Time, Pacific Standard Time,* etc., but lowercase *standard time* when standing alone.

See **time zones**.

stand in (v.) **stand-in** (n. and adj.)

standing room only *SRO* is acceptable on second reference.

stand off (v.) **standoff** (n. and adj.)

stand out (v.) **standout** (n. and adj.)

"The Star-Spangled Banner" But lowercase *the national anthem.*

state Lowercase in all *state of* constructions: *the state of Maine, the states of Maine and Vermont.*

Four states — Kentucky, Massachusetts, Pennsylvania and Virginia — are legally commonwealths rather than states. The distinction is necessary only in formal uses: *The commonwealth of Kentucky filed a suit.* For simple geographic reference: *Tobacco is grown in the state of Kentucky.*

Do not capitalize *state* when used simply as an adjective to specify a level of jurisdiction: *state Rep. William Smith, the state Transportation Department, state funds.*

Apply the same principle to phrases such as *the city of Chicago, the town of Auburn,* etc.

See also **state names**.

statehouse Capitalize all references to a specific statehouse, with or without the name of the state: *The Massachusetts Statehouse is in Boston. The governor will visit the Statehouse today.*

Lowercase plural uses: *the Massachusetts and Rhode Island statehouses.*

state names Follow these guidelines:

STANDING ALONE: Spell out the names of the 50 U.S. states when they stand alone in textual material. Any state name may be condensed, however, to fit typographical requirements for tabular material.

EIGHT NOT ABBREVIATED: The names of eight states are never abbreviated in datelines or text: *Alaska, Hawaii, Idaho, Iowa, Maine, Ohio, Texas* and *Utah.*

Memory Aid: Spell out the names of the two states that are not part of the continental United States and of the continental states that are five letters or fewer.

ABBREVIATIONS REQUIRED: Use the state abbreviations listed at the end of this section:

—In conjunction with the name of a city, town, village or military base in most datelines. See **datelines** for examples and exceptions for large cities.

—In conjunction with the name of a city, county, town, village or military base in text. See examples in punctuation section below. See **datelines** for guidelines on when a city name may stand alone in the body of a story.

—In short-form listings of party affiliation: *D-Ala., R-Mont.* See **party affiliation** for details.

The abbreviations, which also appear in the entries for each state, are:

Ala.	Md.	N.D.
Ariz.	Mass.	Okla.
Ark.	Mich.	Ore.
Calif.	Minn.	Pa.
Colo.	Miss.	R.I.
Conn.	Mo.	S.C.
Del.	Mont.	S.D.
Fla.	Neb.	Tenn.
Ga.	Nev.	Vt.
Ill.	N.H.	Va.
Ind.	N.J.	Wash.
Kan.	N.M.	W.Va.
Ky.	N.Y.	Wis.
La.	N.C.	Wyo.

PUNCTUATION: Place one comma between the city and the state name, and another comma after the state name, unless ending a sentence or indicating a dateline: *He was traveling from Nashville, Tenn., to Austin, Texas, en route to his home in Albuquerque, N.M. She said Cook County, Ill., was Mayor Daley's stronghold.*

MISCELLANEOUS: Use *New York state* when necessary to distinguish the state from New York City.

Use *state of Washington* or *Washington state* when necessary to distinguish the state from the District of Columbia. (*Washington State* is the name of a university in the state of Washington.)

State of the Union Capitalize all references to the president's annual address.

Lowercase other uses: *"The state of the union is confused,"* the editor said.

state police Capitalize with a state name if part of the formal description for a police agency: *the New York State Police, the Virginia State Police.*

In most cases, *state police* standing alone is a shorthand reference for *state policemen* rather than a reference to the agency. For consistency and to avoid hairline distinctions about whether the reference is to the agency or the officers, lowercase the words *state police* whenever they are not preceded by a state name.

See **highway patrol**.

states' rights

statewide

stationary, stationery To stand still is to be *stationary*.
Writing paper is *stationery*.

station wagon

statute mile It equals 5,280 feet, or approximately 1.6 kilometers.
To convert to approximate nautical miles, multiply the number of statute miles by .869.
See **kilometer; knot; mile;** and **nautical mile.**

staunch See the **stanch, staunch** entry.

steady-state theory See **big-bang theory.**

stepbrother, stepfather Also: *stepsister, stepmother.*

steppingstone

stifling

St. John's The city in the Canadian province of Newfoundland.
Not to be confused with *Saint John, New Brunswick.*

St. Louis The city in Missouri stands alone in datelines.

stock See the **common stock, preferred stock** entry.

stockbroker

stock market prices Use fractions rather than decimals, spelling out the fraction if it is not linked with a figure: *The stock went up three-quarters of a point. The stock went up 1½ points.*

stockmen's advisory See **weather terms.**

Stone Age

stool pigeon

stopgap

storm See **weather terms.**

storyteller

straight-laced, strait-laced Use *straight-laced* for someone strict or severe in behavior or moral views.
Reserve *strait-laced* for the notion of confinement, as in a corset.

strait Capitalize as part of a proper name: *Bering Strait, Strait of Gibraltar.*
But: *the Bosporus* and *the Dardanelles.* Neither is followed by *Strait.*

straitjacket Not *straightjacket.*

Strategic Air Command *SAC* is acceptable on second reference.

Strategic Arms Limitation Talks *SALT* is acceptable on first reference. Use *the arms talks* or *the talks* in some references to avoid alphabet soup.

street Abbreviate only with a numbered address. See **addresses.**

strikebreaker

strong-arm (v., adj.)

strong-willed

student See the **pupil, student** entry.

Styrofoam A trademark for a brand of plastic foam.

sub- The rules in **prefixes** apply, but in general, no hyphen. Some examples:

subbasement   submachine gun
subcommittee   suborbital
subculture   subtotal
subdivision   subzero

subcommittee Lowercase when used with the name of a legislative body's full committee: *a Ways and Means subcommittee.*

Capitalize when a subcommittee has a proper name of its own: *the Senate Permanent Subcommittee on Investigations.*

subject See the **citizen, resident, subject, national, native** entry.

subjunctive mood Use the subjunctive mood of a verb for contrary-to-fact conditions, and expressions of doubts, wishes or regrets:

If I were a rich man, I wouldn't have to work hard.

I doubt that more money would be the answer.

I wish it were possible to take back my words.

Sentences that express a contingency or hypothesis may use either the subjunctive or the indicative mood depending on the context. In general, use the subjunctive if there is little likelihood that a contingency might come true:

If I were to marry a millionaire, I wouldn't have to worry about money.

If the bill should overcome the opposition against it, it would provide extensive tax relief.

But:

If I marry my millionaire beau, I won't have to worry about money.

If the bill passes as expected, it will provide an immediate tax cut.

See the **should, would** entry.

submachine gun See **weapons.**

subpoena, subpoenaed, subpoenaing

Sucaryl A trademark for a brand of non-caloric sweetener.

successor

suffixes See separate listings for commonly used suffixes.

Follow Webster's New World Dictionary for words not in this book.

If a word combination is not listed in Webster's New World, use two words for the verb form; hyphenate any noun or adjective forms.

suit, suite You may have a *suit* of clothes, a *suit* of cards, or be faced with a *lawsuit.*

There are *suites* of music, rooms and furniture.

Sukkot The Jewish Feast of Tabernacles, celebrating the fall harvest and commemorating the desert wandering of the Jews during the Exodus. Occurs in September or October.

summer See **seasons.**

summertime

sun Lowercase. See **heavenly bodies.**

sunbathe The verb forms: *sunbathed, sunbathing.* Also: *sunbather.*

Sun Belt Generally those states in the South and West, ranging from Florida and Georgia through the Gulf states into California.

Sunday See **days of the week.**

super Avoid the slang tendency to use it in place of *excellent, wonderful,* etc.

super- The rules in **prefixes** apply, but in general, no hyphen. Some frequently used words:

superagency	superhighway
supercarrier	superpower
supercharge	supertanker

As with all prefixes, however, use a hyphen if the word that follows is capitalized: *super-Republican.*

Super Bowl

superintendent Do not abbreviate. Capitalize when used as a formal title before a name.

See **titles.**

superior court See **court names.**

supersede

supersonic See **Mach number.**

supersonic transport *SST* is acceptable in all references.

supra- The rules in **prefixes** apply, but in general, no hyphen. Some examples:

supragovernmental   supranational

Supreme Court of the United States Capitalize *U.S. Supreme Court* and also *the Supreme Court* when the context makes the *U.S.* designation unnecessary.

The chief justice is properly the *chief justice of the United States*, not *of the Supreme Court*: *Chief Justice Warren Burger.*

The proper title for the eight other members of the court is *associate justice.* When used as a formal title before a name, it should be shortened to *justice* unless there are special circumstances: *Justice William Rehnquist, Associate Justice William Rehnquist.*

See **judge.**

supreme courts of the states Capitalize with the state name (*the New Jersey Supreme Court*) and without the state name when the context makes it unnecessary: *the state Supreme Court, the Supreme Court.*

If a court with this name is not a state's highest tribunal, the fact should be noted. In New York, for example, the Supreme Court is a trial court. Appeals are directed to the Appellate Division of the Supreme Court. The state's highest court is the Court of Appeals.

Supreme Soviet The principal legislative body of the Soviet Union.

surface-to-air missile(s) *SAM(s)* may be used on second reference. Avoid the redundant *SAM missiles.*

suspensive hyphenation The form: *The 5- and 6-year-olds attend morning classes.*

swastika

sweat pants, sweat shirt, sweat suit

swimming Scoring is in minutes, if appropriate, seconds and tenths of a second. Extend to hundredths if available.

Events in the United States normally are measured in yards. Olympic contests and other international events are measured in metric units.

Identify events as *100-yard freestyle, women's 100-meter backstroke,* etc. on first reference. Condense to *men's 100 freestyle, women's 100 backstroke* on second reference.

See the **track and field** entry for the style on relay teams and events where a record is broken.

Use a basic summary. Examples, where qualifying heats are required:

> Men's 200-meter Backstroke Heats (fastest eight qualify for final Saturday night) Heat 1—1, John Nabor, USC, 2:03.25. 2, Zoltan Verraszio, Hungary, 2:03.50 3. Etc

For diving events, adapt the format shown in the **skating, figure** entry.

Swissair Headquarters is in Zurich, Switzerland.

syllabus, syllabuses

synagogue Capitalize only when part of a formal name.

Synagogue Council of America See **Jewish congregations.**

synod A council of churches or church officials. See the entry for the denomination in question.

Tabasco A trademark for a brand of hot pepper sauce.

tablecloth

tablespoon, tablespoonfuls Equal to three teaspoons or one-half a fluid ounce.

The metric equivalent is approximately 15 milliliters.

See **liter** and **recipes**.

table tennis See **pingpong**.

tabular matter Exceptions may be made to the normal rules for abbreviations, as necessary to make material fit. But make any abbreviations as clear as possible.

tailspin

tail wind

Taiwan Use *Taiwan*, not *Formosa*, in references to the Nationalist government on Taiwan and to the island itself. See **China**.

take-home pay

take off (v.) **takeoff** (n. and adj.)

take out (v.) **takeout** (n. and adj.)

take over (v.) **takeover** (n. and adj.)

take up (v.) **takeup** (n. and adj.)

Talmud The collection of writings that constitute the Jewish civil and religious law.

Tammany, Tammany Hall, Tammany Society

tanks Use Arabic figures, separated from letters by a hyphen: *M-60*. Plural: *M-60s*.

tape recording The noun. But hyphenate the verb form: *tape-record.*

Tass The Soviet government's news agency.

tattletale

teachers college No apostrophe.

team See **collective nouns**.

teammate

teamster Capitalize *teamster* only if the intended meaning is that the individual is a member of the International Brotherhood of Teamsters, Chauffeurs, Warehousemen and Helpers of America.

Teamsters union Acceptable in all references to the *International Brotherhood of Teamsters, Chauffeurs, Warehousemen and Helpers of America.*

See the entry under that name.

tear gas Two words. See **Chemical Mace**.

teaspoon Equal to one-sixth of a fluid ounce, or one-third of a tablespoon. The metric equivalent is approximately five milliliters.

See **liter**.

teaspoonful, teaspoonfuls Not *teaspoonsful.* See **recipes**.

Technicolor A trademark for a process of making color motion pictures.

teen, teen-ager (n.) **teen-age** (adj.) Do not use *teen-aged.*

Teflon A trademark for a type of non-stick coating.

telecast (n.) **televise** (v.)

telephone numbers Use figures. The forms: *(212) 262-4000, 262-4000, (212) MU2-0400.* If extension numbers are given: *Ext. 2, Ext. 364, Ext. 4071.*

The parentheses around the area code are based on a format that telephone companies have agreed upon for domestic and international communications.

TelePrompTer A trademark for a type of cuing device.

It is no relation to *Teleprompter Corp.,* a cable television company with headquarters in New York.

Teletype A trademark for a brand of teleprinters and teletypewriters.

television program titles Follow the guidelines in **composition titles**.

Put quotation marks around *show* only if it is part of the formal name. The word *show* may be dropped when it would be cumbersome, such as in a set of listings.

Treat programs named for the star in any of the following ways as appropriate in text or listing: *"The Mary Tyler Moore Show," "Mary Tyler Moore"* or *the Mary Tyler Moore show.* But be consistent in a story or set of listings.

Use quotation marks also for the title of an episode: *"Chuckles Bites the Dust," an episode of "The Mary Tyler Moore Show."*

television station The call letters alone are frequently adequate, but when this phrase is needed, use lowercase: *television station WTEV.*

telltale

temblor See **earthquakes**.

temperature-humidity index See **weather terms**.

temperatures Use figures for all except *zero.* Use a word, not a minus sign, to indicate temperatures below zero.

Right: *The day's low was minus 10.*

Right: *The day's low was 10 below zero.*

Wrong: *The day's low was -10.*

Right: *The temperature rose to zero by noon.*

Right: *The day's high was expected to be 9 or 10.*

Also: *5-degree temperatures, temperatures fell 5 degrees, temperatures in the 30s* (no apostrophe).

Temperatures get *higher* or *lower,* but they don't get *warmer* or *cooler:*

Wrong: *Temperatures are expected to warm up in the area Friday.*

Right: *Temperatures are expected to rise in the area Friday.*

See **Fahrenheit; Celsius;** and **weather terms**.

Ten Commandments Do not abbreviate or use figures.

tenderhearted

tenfold

Tennessee Abbrev.: *Tenn.* See **state names**.

Tennessee Valley Authority *TVA* is acceptable on second reference.

Headquarters is in Knoxville, Tenn.

tennis The scoring units are points, games, sets and matches.

A player wins a point if his opponent fails to return the ball, hits it into the net or hits it out of bounds. A player also wins a point if his opponent is serving and fails to put the ball into play after two attempts (*double faults,* in tennis terms).

A player must win four points to win a game. In tennis scoring, both players begin at love, or zero, and advance to 15, 30, 40 and game. (The numbers 15, 30 and 40 have no point value as such — they are simply tennis terminology for 1 point, 2 points and 3 points.) The server's score always is called out first. If a game is tied at 40-all, or *deuce,* play continues until one player has a two-point margin.

A set is won if a player wins six games before his opponent has won five. If a set becomes tied at five games apiece, it goes to the first player to win seven games. If two players who were tied at five games apiece also tie at six games apiece, they normally play a tiebreaker — a game that goes to the first player to win seven points. In some cases, however, the rules call for a player to win by two games.

A match may be either a best-of-three contest that goes to the first player or team to win two sets, or a best-of-five contest that goes to the first player or team to win three sets.

In reporting on a match, some typical sentences might read:

—*Chris Evert won the first set from Sue Barker 6-0, lost the second 3-6 and won the third 7-6.*

—*Chris Evert won her match, defeating Sue Barker 6-0, 3-6, 7-6.*

SUMMARIES: Winners always are listed first in agate summaries. An example:

Men's Singles
First Round

Jimmy Connors, Belleville, Ill., def. Manuel Orantes, Spain, 2-6, 6-3, 6-2, 6-1.

Bjorn Borg, Sweden, def. Jim Green, New York (default).

Arthur Ashe, New York, def. James Peters, Chicago, 6-3, 4-3 (retired).

tera- A prefix denoting 1 trillion units of a measure. Move a decimal point 12 places to the right, adding zeros if necessary, to convert to the basic unit: 5.5 teratons = 5,500,000,000,000 tons.

terrace Do not abbreviate. See **addresses**.

Texaco Inc. Headquarters is in Harrison, N.Y.

Texas Do not abbreviate. Second in total land area: 262,134 square miles.
See **state names**.

texts, transcripts Follow normal style guidelines for capitalization, spelling and abbreviations in handling a text or transcript.

Use quotation marks only for words or phrases that were quoted in the text or by the person who spoke.

Identify a change in speakers by starting a paragraph with the new speaker's name and a colon. Use normal second-reference forms if the speaker has been identified earlier; provide a full name and identification if the individual is being mentioned for the first time.

Use *Q:* for *question* and *A:* for *answer* at the start of paragraphs when these notations are adequate to identify a change in speakers.

See **ellipsis** for guidelines on condensing texts and transcripts.

Thai A native or the language of Thailand.
Siam and *Siamese* are historical only.
Use *siamese* for the cat.

Thanksgiving, Thanksgiving Day The fourth Thursday in November.

that (conjunction) Use the conjunction *that* to introduce a dependent clause if the sentence sounds or looks awkward without it. There are no hard-and-fast rules, but in general:

—*That* usually may be omitted when a dependent clause immediately follows a

form of the verb *to say: The president
said he had signed the bill.*

—*That* should be used when a time element intervenes between the verb and
the dependent clause: *The president
said Monday that he had signed the bill.*

—*That* usually is necessary after some
verbs. They include: *advocate, assert,
contend, declare, estimate, make clear,
point out, propose* and *state.*

—*That* is required before subordinate
clauses beginning with conjunctions
such as *after, although, because, before,
in addition to, until* and *while:
Haldeman said that after he learned of
Nixon's intention to resign, he sought
pardons for all connected with
Watergate.*

When in doubt, include *that.* Omission
can hurt. Inclusion never does.

**that, which, who, whom (pro-
nouns)** Use *who* and *whom* in referring
to persons and to animals with a name:
John Jones is the man who helped me.
See the **who, whom** entry.

Use *that* and *which* in referring to inanimate objects and to animals without
a name.

See the **essential clauses, non-
essential clauses** entry for guidelines
on using *that* and *which* to introduce
phrases and clauses.

theater Use this spelling also in all
names: *Shubert Theater.*

theft See the **burglary, larceny, robbery, theft** entry.

their, there, they're *Their* is a possessive pronoun: *They went to their
house.*

There is an adverb indicating direction: *We went there for dinner.*

There also is used with the force of a
pronoun for impersonal constructions in
which the real subject follows the verb:
There is no food on the table.

They're is a contraction for *they are.*

theretofore Use *until then.*

Thermo-Fax A trademark for a
brand of photocopy machine.

thermos Formerly a trademark, now
a generic term for any vacuum bottle,
although one manufacturer still uses the
word as a brand name.

Lowercase *thermos* when it is used to
mean any vacuum bottle; use *Thermos*
when referring to the specific brand.

Third World The economically developing nations of Africa, Asia and
Latin America.

Do not confuse with *non-aligned*,
which is a political term. See **non-
aligned.**

three-D *3-D* is preferred.

three R's They are: *reading, 'riting
and 'rithmetic.*

threesome

throwaway (n. and adj.)

thunderstorm See **weather terms.**

Thursday See **days of the week.**

tidbit

tie, tied, tying

tie in (v.) **tie-in** (n. and adj.)

tie up (v.) **tie-up** (n. and adj.)

time element Use *today, this morning, this afternoon, tonight,* etc., as appropriate in stories for afternoon edi-
tions. Use the day of the week
elsewhere. See the **today, tonight** and
the **tomorrow, yesterday** entries.

Use *Monday, Tuesday,* etc., for days
of the week within seven days before or
after the current date.

Use the month and a figure for dates
beyond this range. See **dates** for forms
and punctuation.

Avoid such redundancies as *last Tuesday* or *next Tuesday.* The past, present
or future tense used for the verb usually

provides adequate indication of which *Tuesday* is meant: *He said he finished the job Tuesday. She will return on Tuesday.*

Avoid awkward placements of the time element, particularly those that suggest the day of the week is the object of a transitive verb: *The police jailed Tuesday.* Potential remedies include the use of the word *on* (see the **on** entry), rephrasing the sentence, or placing the time element in a different sentence.

time of day The exact time of day that an event has happened or will happen is not necessary in most stories. Follow these guidelines to determine when it should be included and in what form:

SPECIFY THE TIME:

—Whenever it gives the reader a better picture of the scene: Did the earthquake occur when people were likely to be home asleep or at work? A clock reading for the time in the datelined community is acceptable, although *pre-dawn hours* or *rush hour* often is more graphic.

—Whenever the time is critical to the story: When will the rocket be launched? When will a major political address be broadcast? What is the deadline for meeting a demand?

DECIDING ON CLOCK TIME: When giving a clock reading, use the time in the datelined community.

If the story is undated, use the clock time in force where the event happened or will take place.

The only exception is a nationwide story or tabular listing that involves television or radio programs. Always use Eastern time, followed by *EDT* or *EST*, and specify whether the program will be broadcast simultaneously nationwide or whether times will vary because of separate transmissions for different time zones. If practical, specify those times in a separate paragraph.

ZONE ABBREVIATIONS: Use *EST, CDT, PST*, etc., after a clock time only if:

—The story involves travel or other activities, such as the closing hour for polling places or the time of a televised speech, likely to affect persons or developments in more than one time zone.

—The item involves television or radio programs. (See above.)

—The item is undated.

—The item is an advisory to editors.

CONVERT TO EASTERN TIME? Do not convert clock times from other time zones in the continental United States to Eastern time. If there is high interest in the precise time, add *CDT, PST*, etc., to the local reading to help readers determine their equivalent local time.

If the time is critical in a story from outside the continental United States, provide a conversion to Eastern time using this form: *The kidnappers set a 9 a.m. (3 a.m. EDT) deadline.*

See **time zones** for additional guidance on forms.

times Use figures except for *noon* and *midnight*. Use a colon to separate hours from minutes: *11 a.m., 1 p.m., 3:30 p.m.*

Avoid such redundancies as *10 a.m. this morning, 10 p.m. tonight* or *10 p.m. Monday night.* Use *10 a.m. today, 10 p.m. today* or *10 p.m. Monday*, etc., as required by the norms in **time element**.

The construction *4 o'clock* is acceptable, but time listings with *a.m.* or *p.m.* are preferred.

See **midnight** and **time zones**.

time sequences Use figures, colons and periods as follows: *2:30:21.65* (hours, minutes, seconds, tenths, hundredths).

time zones Capitalize the full name of the time in force within a particular zone: *Eastern Standard Time, Eastern Daylight Time, Central Standard Time*, etc.

Lowercase all but the region in short forms: *the Eastern time zone, Eastern time, Mountain time*, etc.

See **time of day** for guidelines on when to use clock time in a story.

Spell out time zones in references not accompanied by a clock reading: *Chicago is in the Central time zone.*

The abbreviations *EST, CDT,* etc., are acceptable on first reference for zones used within the continental United States, Canada and Mexico only if the abbreviation is linked with a clock reading: *noon EST, 9 a.m. PST.* (Do not set the abbreviations off with commas.)

Spell out all references to time zones not used within the continental United States: *When it is noon EDT, it is 1 p.m. Atlantic Standard Time and 7 a.m. Alaska Standard Time.*

One exception to the spelled-out form: *Greenwich Mean Time* may be abbreviated as *GMT* on second reference if used with a clock reading.

tiptop

titleholder

titles In general, confine capitalization to formal titles used directly before an individual's name.

The basic guidelines:

LOWERCASE: Lowercase and spell out titles when they are not used with an individual's name: *The president issued a statement. The pope gave his blessing.*

Lowercase and spell out titles in constructions that set them off from a name by commas: *The vice president, Nelson Rockefeller, declined to run again. Paul VI, the current pope, does not plan to retire.*

COURTESY TITLES: See the **courtesy titles** entry for guidelines on when to use *Miss, Mr., Mrs.* and *Ms.*

The forms *Mr., Mrs.* and *Ms.* apply both in regular text and in quotations.

FORMAL TITLES: Capitalize formal titles when they are used immediately before one or more names: *Pope Paul, President Washington, Vice Presidents John Jones and William Smith.*

A formal title generally is one that denotes a scope of authority, professional activity or academic accomplishment so specific that the designation becomes almost as much an integral part of an individual's identity as a proper name itself: *President Carter, Gov. Ella Grasso, Dr. Marcus Welby, Pvt. Gomer Pyle.*

Other titles serve primarily as occupational descriptions: *astronaut John Glenn, movie star John Wayne, peanut farmer Jimmy Carter.*

A final determination on whether a title is formal or occupational depends on the practice of the governmental or private organization that confers it. If there is doubt about the status of a title and the practice of the organization cannot be determined, use a construction that sets the name or the title off with commas.

ABBREVIATED TITLES: The following formal titles are capitalized and abbreviated as shown when used before a name outside quotations: *Dr., Gov., Lt. Gov., Rep., Sen.* and certain military ranks listed in the **military titles** entry. Spell out all except *Dr.* when they are used in quotations.

All other formal titles are spelled out in all uses.

ROYAL TITLES: Capitalize *king, queen,* etc., when used directly before a name. See individual entries and **nobility.**

TITLES OF NOBILITY: Capitalize a full title when it serves as the alternate name for an individual. See **nobility.**

PAST AND FUTURE TITLES: A formal title that an individual formerly held, is about to hold or holds temporarily is capitalized if used before the person's name. But do not capitalize the qualifying word: *former President Ford, deposed King Constantine, Attorney General-designate Griffin B. Bell, acting Mayor Peter Barry.*

LONG TITLES: Separate a long title from a name by a construction that requires a comma: *Charles Robinson, undersecretary for economic affairs, spoke.* Or: *The undersecretary for economic affairs, Charles Robinson, spoke.*

UNIQUE TITLES: If a title applies only to one person in an organization, insert the word *the* in a construction that uses commas: *John Jones, the deputy vice president, spoke.*

ADDITIONAL GUIDANCE: Many commonly used titles and occupational descriptions are listed separately in this book, together with guidelines on whether and/or when they are capitalized. In these entries, the phrases *before a name* or *immediately before a name* are used to specify that capitalization applies only when a title is not set off from a name by commas.

See **composition titles; legislative titles; military titles;** and **religious titles.**

TNT Acceptable in all references for *trinitrotoluene.*

tobacco, tobaccos

Tobago See the **Trinidad and Tobago** entry.

today, tonight Use in direct quotations, in stories intended for publication in afternoon newspapers on the day in question, and in phrases that do not refer to a specific day: *Customs today are different from those of a century ago.*

Use the day of the week in stories intended for publication in morning newspapers and in stories filed for use in either publishing cycle.

See **tonight.**

Tokyo Stands alone in datelines.

tollhouse, tollhouse cookies

Tommy gun Alternate trademark for *Thompson submachine gun.*

See **weapons.**

tomorrow Use only in direct quotations and in phrases that do not refer to a specific day: *The world of tomorrow will need additional energy resources.*

Use the day of the week in other cases.

ton There are three different types:

A **short ton** is equal to 2,000 pounds,

A **long ton**, also known as a *British ton*, is equal to 2,240 pounds.

A **metric ton** is equal to 1,000 kilograms, or approximately 2,204.62 pounds.

CONVERSION EQUATIONS:

Short to long: Multiply by .89 (5 short tons x .89 = 4.45 long tons).

Short to metric: Multiply by .9 (5 short tons x .9 = 4.5 metric tons).

Long to short: Multiply by 1.12 (5 long tons x 1.12 = 5.6 short tons).

Long to metric: Multiply by 1.02 (5 long tons x 1.02 = 5.1 metric tons).

Metric to short: Multiply by 1.1 (5 metric tons x 1.1 = 5.5 short tons).

Metric to long: Multiply by .98 (5 metric tons x .98 = 4.9 long tons).

See **metric system.**

See **kiloton** for units used to measure the power of nuclear explosions.

See **oil** for formulas to convert the tonnage of oil shipments to gallons.

tonight All that's necessary is *8 tonight*, or *8 p.m. today.* Avoid the redundant *8 p.m. tonight.*

tornado See **weather terms.**

Toronto The city in Canada stands alone in datelines.

Tory, Tories An exception to the normal practice when forming the plural of a proper name ending in *y.*

The words are acceptable on second reference to the *Conservative Party* in Britain and its members.

total, totaled, totaling The phrase *a total of* often is redundant.

It may be used, however, to avoid a figure at the start of a sentence: *A total of 650 persons were killed in holiday traffic accidents.*

toward Not *towards*.

town Apply the capitalization principles in **city**.

town council Apply the capitalization principles in **city council**.

track and field Scoring is in distance or time, depending on the event.

Distance events in the United States are normally in feet and yards. Olympic contests and other international events are measured in metric units.

Do not use a colon before times given in seconds and tenths of a second. Use *6.0, 9.4, 10.1*, etc. Extend times to hundredths if available: *9.45*.

For longer distances, such as the mile run, it is *3:36.1* for *three minutes, 36.1 seconds*.

In running events, the first event should be spelled out as: *60-yard dash*. Others may be *100, 220, mile, 120-hurdles*, etc., except where metric distances are included in a meet otherwise run in yards. Then: *100-meters*, etc.

For field events — those that do not involve running — use these forms: *26-½* for *26 feet, one-half inch; 25-10½* for *25 feet, 10½ inches*, etc.

In general, use a basic summary. For the style when a record is broken, note the mile event in the example below. For the style in listing relay teams, note 1,000-meter relay.

Examples:

> 60-yard dash—1, Steve Williams, Florida TC, 6.0. 2, Hasley Crawford, Philadelphia Pioneer, 6.2. 3, Mike McFarland, Chicago TC, 6.2. 3, Etc.
> 100—1, Steve Williams, Florida TC 10.1. 2, Etc.
> Mile—1, Filbert Bayi, Tanzania, 3:35.1, meet record; old record 3:59, Jim Beatty, Los Angeles TC, Feb. 27, 1963. 2, Paul Cummings, Beverly Hills TC, 3:36.1. 3, Etc.
> Women's 880—1, Johanna Forman, Falmouth TC, 2:07.9. 2, Etc.
> 1,600-meter relay—1, St. John's, Jon Kennedy, Doug Johnson, Gary Gordon, Ordner Emanuel, 3:21.9. 2, Brown, 3:23.5. 3, Fordham, 3:24.1. 4, Etc.
> Team scoring—Chicago TC 32, Philadelphia Pioneer 29, Etc.

Where qualifying heats are required:

> Men's 100-meter heats (first two in each heat qualify for Friday's semifinals): Heat 1—1, Steve Williams, Florida TC, 10.1. 2, Etc.

On major meets where both metric units and feet and inches are available, use this form:

> Long jump—1, Larry Myricks, Mississippi College, 26-½ (7.94m). 2, Arnie Robinson, Maccabi Union TC, 25-10½ (7.88m). 3, Etc.

trade in (v.) **trade-in** (n. and adj.)

trademark A trademark is a brand, symbol, word, etc., used by a manufacturer or dealer and protected by law to prevent a competitor from using it: *Astroturf*, for a type of artificial grass, for example.

In general, use a generic equivalent unless the trademark name is essential to the story.

When a trademark is used, capitalize it.

Many trademarks are listed separately in this book, together with generic equivalents.

The U.S. Trademark Association, located in New York, is a helpful source of information about trademarks.

See **brand names** and **service marks**.

trade off (v.) **trade-off** (n. and adj.)

traffic, trafficked, trafficking

trampoline Formerly a trademark, now a generic term.

trans- The rules in **prefixes** apply, but in general, no hyphen. Some examples:

transcontinental   transsexual
transmigrate   transship
transoceanic   trans-Siberian

Also: *trans-Atlantic* and *trans-Pacific*. These are exceptions to Webster's New World in keeping with the general rule that a hyphen is needed when a prefix precedes a capitalized word.

transcripts See the **texts, transcripts** entry.

transfer, transferred, transferring

Transjordan Earlier name for *Jordan*.

transsexuals See **sex changes**.

Trans World Airlines A *TWA airliner* is acceptable in any reference.
Headquarters is in New York.

travel, traveled, traveling, traveler

travelogue Not *travelog*.

treasurer Capitalize when used as a formal title immediately before a name. See **titles**.
Caution: The secretary of the U.S. Department of the Treasury is not the same person as the U.S. treasurer.

Treasury bills, Treasury bonds, Treasury notes See **loan terminology**.

trees See **plants**.

tribes See the **nationalities and races** entry.

trigger-happy

TriMotor The proper name of a three-engine airplane once made by Ford Motor Co.

Trinidad and Tobago In datelines on stories from this island nation, use a community name followed by either *Trinidad* or *Tobago* — but not both — depending on where the community is located.

TriStar The proper name that Lockheed Aircraft Corp. uses for its L-1011 jetliner.

Trojan horse, Trojan War

troop, troops, troupe A *troop* is a group of persons or animals. *Troops* mean several such groups, particularly groups of soldiers.
Use *troupe* only for ensembles of actors, dancers, singers, etc.

tropical depression See **weather terms**.

Truman, Harry S. With a period after the initial. Truman once said there was no need for the period because the *S* did not stand for a name. Asked in the early 1960s about his preference, he replied, "It makes no difference to me."
AP style has called for the period since that time.

trustee A person to whom another's property or the management of another's property is entrusted.
Do not capitalize if used before a name.

trusty A prison inmate granted special privileges as a trustworthy person.
Do not capitalize if used before a name.

try out (v.) **tryout** (n.)

tsar Use *czar*.

T-shirt

tuberculosis *TB* is acceptable on second reference.

Tuesday See **days of the week**.

tune up (v.) **tuneup** (n. and adj.)

turboprop See **aircraft terms**.

turnpike Capitalize as part of a proper name: *the Pennsylvania Turnpike.* Lowercase *turnpike* when it stands alone.
See **highway designations**.

TV Acceptable as an adjective or in such constructions as *cable TV*. But do not normally use as a noun unless part of a quotation.

Twelve Apostles The disciples of Jesus. An exception to the normal practice of using figures for 10 and above.

20th Century-Fox, Twentieth Century Fund, Twentieth Century Limited Follow an organization's practice. See **company names**.

typhoons Capitalize *typhoon* when it is part of the name that weather forecasters assign to a storm: *Typhoon Tilda*.

But use *it* and *its* — not *she, her* or *hers* — in pronoun references.

And do not use the presence of a woman's name as an excuse to attribute sexist images of women's behavior to a typhoon.

See **weather terms**.

U

U-boat

UFO, UFOs Acceptable in all references for *unidentified flying object(s).*

UHF Acceptable in all references for *ultrahigh frequency.*

Ukrainian Catholic Church See **Eastern Rite churches.**

Ukrainian Soviet Socialist Republic See the **Russia, Soviet Union** entry.

ukulele

Ulster A colloquial synonym for *Northern Ireland.* See **United Kingdom.**

ultra- The rules in **prefixes** apply, but in general, no hyphen. Some examples:

ultramodern	ultrasonic
ultranationalism	ultraviolet

ultrahigh frequency *UHF* is acceptable in all references.

un- The rules in **prefixes** apply, but in general, no hyphen. Some examples:

un-American	unnecessary
unarmed	unshaven

U.N. Used as an adjective, but not as a noun, for *United Nations.*
See **United Nations.**

Uncle Sam

Uncle Tom A term of contempt applied to a black person, taken from the main character in Harriet Beecher Stowe's novel "Uncle Tom's Cabin." It describes the practice of kowtowing to whites to curry favor.
Do not apply it to an individual. It carries potentially libelous connotations of having sold one's convictions for money, prestige or political influence.

under- The rules in **prefixes** apply, but in general, no hyphen. Some examples:

underdog	undersheriff
underground	undersold

undersecretary One word. See **titles.**

under way Two words in virtually all uses: *The project is under way. The naval maneuvers are under way.*
One word only when used as an adjective before a noun in a nautical sense: *an underway flotilla.*

unemployment rate In the United States, this estimate of the number of unemployed residents seeking work is compiled monthly by the Bureau of Labor Statistics, an agency of the Labor Department.
Each month the bureau selects a nationwide cross section of the population and conducts interviews to determine the size of the U.S. work force. The *work force* is defined as the number of persons

with jobs and the number looking for jobs.

The unemployment rate is expressed as a percentage figure. The essential calculation involves dividing the total work force into the number of persons looking for jobs, followed by adjustments to reflect variable factors such as seasonal trends.

UNESCO Acceptable on first reference for the *United Nations Educational, Scientific and Cultural Organization,* but a subsequent reference should give the full name.

UNICEF Acceptable in all references for the *United Nations Children's Fund.* The words *International* and *Emergency,* originally part of the name, have been dropped.

unidentified flying object(s) *UFO* and *UFOs* are acceptable in all references.

Uniform Code of Military Justice The laws covering members of the U.S. armed forces.

uninterested See the **disinterested, uninterested** entry.

union Capitalize when used as a proper name for the Northern states during the Civil War: *The Union defeated the Confederacy.*

union names The formal names of unions may be condensed to conventionally accepted short forms that capitalize characteristic words from the full name followed by *union* in lowercase.

Follow union practice in the use of the word *worker* in shortened forms. Among major unions, all except the *United Steelworkers* use two words: *United Auto Workers, United Mine Workers,* etc.

When *worker* is used generically, make *autoworkers* one word in keeping with widespread practice; use two words

for other job descriptions: *bakery workers, mine workers, steel workers.*

See the **local of a union** entry and the individual entries for these unions frequently in the news:

> **Amalgamated Clothing and Textile Workers Union of America**
> **Amalgamated Transit Union**
> **American Federation of Government Employees**
> **American Federation of Labor and Congress of Industrial Organizations**
> **American Federation of Musicians**
> **American Federation of State, County and Municipal Employees**
> **American Federation of Teachers**
> **American Federation of Television and Radio Artists**
> **American Postal Workers Union**
> **Bakery and Confectionery Workers' International Union of America**
> **Bricklayers, Masons and Plasterers' International Union of America**
> **Brotherhood of Railway, Airline and Steamship Clerks, Freight Handlers, Express and Station Employees**
> **Communications Workers of America**
> **Hotel and Restaurant Employees and Bartenders International Union**
> **International Association of Machinists and Aerospace Workers**
> **International Brotherhood of Electrical Workers**
> **International Brotherhood of Painters and Allied Trades of the United States and Canada**
> **International Brotherhood of Teamsters, Chauffeurs, Warehousemen and Helpers of America**
> **International Ladies' Garment Workers Union**
> **International Longshoremen's and Warehousemen's Union**
> **International Longshoremen's Association**
> **Laborers' International Union of North America**
> **National Association of Letter Carriers**
> **Newspaper Guild, The**
> **Oil, Chemical and Atomic Workers International Union**
> **Retail Clerks International Association**
> **Sheet Metal Workers International Association**
> **United Automobile, Aerospace and Agricultural Implement Workers of America**
> **United Brotherhood of Carpenters and Joiners of America**

United Electrical, Radio and Machine
   Workers of America
United Mine Workers of America
United Rubber, Cork, Linoleum and
   Plastic Workers of America
United Steelworkers of America

Union of American Hebrew Congregations See Jewish congregations.

Union of Orthodox Jewish Congregations of America See Jewish congregations.

Union of Soviet Socialist Republics Use *U.S.S.R.* in datelines from all cities except *Moscow*, which stands alone in datelines.
Soviet Union is acceptable in all references in the body of a story.
See the **Russia, Soviet Union** entry for a list of the republics.

union shop See closed shop.

unique It means one of a kind. Do not describe something as *rather unique* or *most unique*.

United Airlines A subsidiary of UAL Inc.
Headquarters is in Chicago.

United Arab Emirates Do not abbreviate, even in datelines.
Use *U.A.E.* (with periods) if quoted matter requires the abbreviation.

United Automobile, Aerospace and Agricultural Implement Workers of America The shortened forms *United Auto Workers* and *United Auto Workers union* are acceptable in all references.
UAW and *Auto Workers* are acceptable on second reference.
Use *autoworker* or *autoworkers* (one word, lowercase) in generic references to workers in the auto industry.
Headquarters is in Detroit.

United Brotherhood of Carpenters and Joiners of America The shortened form *Carpenters union* is acceptable in all references.
Headquarters is in Washington.

United Church of Christ See Congregationalist churches.

United Electrical, Radio and Machine Workers of America The shortened form *Electrical Workers union* is acceptable in all references.
Headquarters is in New York.

United Kingdom It consists of Great Britain and Northern Ireland.
Great Britain (or *Britain*) consists of England, Scotland and Wales.
Ireland is independent of the United Kingdom.
See **datelines** and **Ireland**.

United Klans of America See Ku Klux Klan.

United Methodist Church See Methodist churches.

United Mine Workers of America The shortened forms *United Mine Workers* and *United Mine Workers union* are acceptable in all references.
UMW and *Mine Workers* are acceptable on second reference.
Use *mine workers* or *miners*, lowercase, in generic references to workers in the industry.
Headquarters is in Washington.

United Nations Spell out when used as a noun. Use *U.N.* (no space) only as an adjective.
The periods in *U.N.*, for consistency with *U.S.*, are an exception to the first listing in Webster's New World Dictionary.
In datelines:
UNITED NATIONS (AP) —
Use *U.N. General Assembly, U.N. Secretariat* and *U.N. Security Council* in first references not under a United Nations dateline.
General Assembly, the Secretariat and *Security Council* are acceptable in all references under a United Nations dateline and on second reference under other datelines.
Lowercase *the assembly* and *the council* when they stand alone.
See **UNESCO** and **UNICEF**.

United Presbyterian Church in the United States of America See Presbyterian churches.

United Press International A privately owned news agency formed in 1958 as a merger of United Press and International News Service.

Use the full name on first reference. *UPI* is acceptable on second reference.

The address is 220 E. 42nd St., New York, N.Y. 10017. The telephone number is (212) 682-0400.

United Rubber, Cork, Linoleum and Plastic Workers of America The shortened forms *United Rubber Workers* and *United Rubber Workers union* are acceptable in all references.

Capitalize *Rubber Workers* in references to the union or its members.

Use *rubber workers*, lowercase, in generic references to workers in the rubber industry.

Headquarters is in Akron, Ohio.

United Service Organizations *USO* is acceptable on second reference.

United States Spell out when used as a noun. Use *U.S.* (no space) only as an adjective.

For organizations with names beginning with the words United States, see entries alphabetized under U.S.

United Steelworkers of America The shortened forms *United Steelworkers* and *United Steelworkers union* are acceptable in all references.

Capitalize *Steelworkers* in references to the union or its members.

Use *steel workers* (two words, lowercase) in generic references to workers in the steel industry. (Many Steelworkers are employed in other industries and thus are not steel workers.)

Headquarters is in Pittsburgh.

United Synagogue of America Not *synagogues*. See **Jewish congregations**.

up- The rules in **prefixes** apply, but in general, no hyphen. Some examples:

upend	upstate
upgrade	uptown

-up Follow Webster's New World Dictionary. Hyphenate if not listed there.

Some frequently used words (all are nouns, some also are used as adjectives):

breakup	makeup
buildup	mix-up
call-up	mock-up
change-up	pileup
checkup	push-up
cleanup	roundup
close-up	runners-up
cover-up	setup
crackup	shake-up
follow-up	shape-up
frame-up	smashup
grown-up	speedup
holdup	tie-up
letup	walk-up
lineup	windup

Use two words when any of these occurs as a verb.

See **suffixes**.

UPI Acceptable on second reference for *United Press International*.

uppercase One word (n., v., adj.) when referring to the use of capital letters. An exception to Webster's New World in keeping with printers' practice.

upside down (adv.) **upside-down** (adj.) *The car turned upside down. She made an upside-down cake. The book is upside-down.*

upstate Always lowercase: *upstate New York.*

upward Not *upwards.*

U.S. Used as an adjective, but not as a noun, for *United States.*

U.S. Air Force See **air force; military academies;** and **military titles.**

U.S. Army See **army; military academies;** and **military titles.**

U.S. Coast Guard See **coast guard; military academies;** and **military titles.**

U.S. Conference of Mayors The members are the mayors of cities with 30,000 or more residents. See **National League of Cities.**

Use *the conference* or *the mayors' conference* on second reference.

There is no organization with the name *National Mayors' Conference.*

U.S. Court of Appeals The court is divided into 11 circuits as follows:

District of Columbia Circuit.

1st Circuit: Maine, Massachusetts, New Hampshire, Rhode Island, Puerto Rico. Based in Boston.

2nd Circuit: Connecticut, New York, Vermont. Based in New York.

3rd Circuit: Delaware, New Jersey, Pennsylvania, Virgin Islands. Based in Philadelphia.

4th Circuit: Maryland, North Carolina, South Carolina, Virginia, West Virginia. Based in Richmond, Va.

5th Circuit: Alabama, Florida, Georgia, Louisiana, Mississippi, Texas, Canal Zone. Based in New Orleans.

6th Circuit: Kentucky, Michigan, Ohio, Tennessee. Based in Cincinnati.

7th Circuit: Illinois, Indiana, Wisconsin. Based in Chicago.

8th Circuit: Arkansas, Iowa, Minnesota, Missouri, Nebraska, North Dakota, South Dakota. Based in St. Louis.

9th Circuit: Alaska, Arizona, California, Hawaii, Idaho, Montana, Nevada, Oregon, Washington, Guam. Based in San Francisco.

10th Circuit: Colorado, Kansas, New Mexico, Oklahoma, Utah, Wyoming. Based in Denver.

The courts do not always sit in the cities where they are based. Sessions may be held in other major cities within each region.

REFERENCE FORMS: A phrase such as *a federal appeals court* is acceptable on first reference.

On first reference to the full name, use *U.S. Court of Appeals* or a full name: *8th U.S. Circuit Court of Appeals* or *the U.S. Court of Appeals for the 8th Circuit.*

U.S. Circuit Court of Appeals without a circuit number is a misnomer and should not be used.

In shortened and subsequent references: *the Court of Appeals, the 2nd Circuit, the appeals court, the appellate court(s), the circuit court(s), the court.*

Do not create non-existent entities such as *the San Francisco Court of Appeals.* Make it *the U.S. Court of Appeals in San Francisco.*

JURISTS: The formal title for the jurists on the court is *judge: U.S. Circuit Judge Homer Thornberry* is preferred to *U.S. Appeals Judge Homer Thornberry,* but either is acceptable.

See **judge.**

U.S. Court of Claims This court handles suits against the federal government. It is based in Washington.

U.S. Court of Customs and Patent Appeals This court handles appeals involving customs, patents and copyrights. It is based in Washington.

U.S. Court of Military Appeals This court, not part of the judicial branch as such, is a civilian body established by Congress to hear appeals from actions of the Defense Department. It is based in Washington.

U.S. Customs Court This court, based in New York City, handles disputes over customs duties that arise at any U.S. port of entry.

U.S. District Courts There are 94. In shortened and subsequent references: *the District Court, the District Courts, the court.*

Judge is the formal title for District Court jurists: *U.S. District Judge Frank Johnson.* See **judge.**

usher Use for both men and women.

U.S. Information Agency *USIA* is acceptable on second reference.

U.S. Military Academy See **military academies.**

U.S. Navy See **navy; military academies;** and **military titles.**

U.S. Postal Service Use *U.S. Postal Service* or *the Postal Service* on first reference. Retain capitalization of *Postal Service* in subsequent references to the agency.

Lowercase *the service* when it stands alone. Lowercase *post office* in generic references to the agency and to an individual office: *I went to the post office.*

U.S. Postal Service Directory of Post Offices The reference for U.S. place names not covered in this book.

USS For *United States Ship, Steamer* or *Steamship*, preceding the name of a vessel: *the USS Iowa.*

In datelines:

ABOARD USS IOWA (AP) —

U.S. Supreme Court See **Supreme Court of the United States.**

U.S. Tax Court This is an administrative body within the U.S. Treasury Department rather than part of the judicial branch. It handles appeals in tax cases.

Utah Do not abbreviate. See **state names.**

U-turn (n. and adj.)

v. See **verbs**.

vacuum

Valium A trademark for a brand of tranquilizer and muscle relaxant. It also may be called *diazepam*.

valley Capitalize as part of a full name: *the Mississippi Valley.*
Lowercase in plural uses: *the Missouri and Mississippi valleys.*

Vandyke beard, Vandyke collar

Varig Brazilian Airlines Headquarters is in Rio de Janeiro.

Vaseline A trademark for a brand of petroleum jelly.

Vatican City Stands alone in datelines.

V-E Day May 8, 1945, the day the surrender of Germany was announced, officially ending the European phase of World War II.

vegetables See **food**.

V-8 The engine.

vendor

venereal disease *VD* is acceptable on second reference.

verbal See the **oral, verbal, written** entry.

verbs The abbreviation *v.* is used in this book to identify the spelling of the verb forms of words frequently misspelled.
SPLIT FORMS: In general, avoid awkward constructions that split infinitive forms of a verb (*to leave, to help,* etc.) or compound forms (*had left, are found out,* etc.).
Awkward: *She was ordered to immediately leave on an assignment.*
Preferred: *She was ordered to leave immediately on an assignment.*
Awkward: *There stood the wagon that we had early last autumn left by the barn.*
Preferred: *There stood the wagon that we had left by the barn early last autumn.*
Occasionally, however, a split is not awkward and is necessary to convey the meaning:
He wanted to really help his mother.
Those who lie are often found out.
How has your health been?
The budget was tentatively approved.

Vermont Abbrev.: *Vt.* See **state names**.

vernacular The native language of a country or place. A vernacular term that has achieved widespread recognition may be used without explanation if appropriate in the context.
Terms not widely known should be explained when used. In general, they are appropriate only when illustrating vernacular speech.
See **colloquialisms** and **dialect**.

verses See **poetry** for guidelines on how to handle verses of poetry typographically.

versus Abbreviate as *vs.* in all uses.

vertical takeoff aircraft See the **V-STOL** and **VTOL** entries.

very high frequency *VHF* is acceptable in all references.

Very Rev. See **Episcopal Church; religious titles;** and **Roman Catholic Church.**

Veterans Administration No apostrophe. *VA* may be used on second reference.

When referring to VA hospitals, capitalize full names: *the Boston Veterans Administration Hospital* (or *the Boston VA Hospital* if second reference), but lowercase references such as *the VA hospital.*

Veterans Day Formerly Armistice Day, Nov. 11, the anniversary of the armistice that ended World War I in 1918.

The federal legal holiday, observed on the fourth Monday in October during the mid 1970s, returns to Nov. 11 in 1978.

Veterans of Foreign Wars *VFW* is acceptable on second reference.

Headquarters is in Kansas City, Mo.

veto, vetoes (n.) The verb forms: *vetoed, vetoing.*

VHF Acceptable in all references for *very high frequency.*

vice- Use two words: *vice admiral, vice chairman, vice chancellor, vice consul, vice president, vice principal, vice regent, vice secretary.*

Several are exceptions to Webster's New World. The two-word rule has been adopted for consistency in handling the similar terms.

vice president Capitalize or lowercase following the same rules that apply to *president.* See **president** and **titles.**

Do not drop the first name on first reference.

vice versa

Victrola A trademark for a brand of record player.

videotape (n. and v.)

vie, vied, vying

vienna bread, vienna coffee, vienna sausages See **food.**

Viet Cong

Vietnam Not *Viet Nam.*

Vietnam War

village Apply the capitalization principles in **city.**

VIP, VIPs Acceptable in all references for *very important person(s).*

Virginia Abbrev.: *Va.* Legally a commonwealth, not a state.

See **state** and **state names.**

Virgin Islands Use with a community name in datelines on stories from the U.S. Virgin Islands. Do not abbreviate.

Identify an individual island in the text if relevant.

See **datelines** and **British Virgin Islands.**

viscount, viscountess See **nobility.**

vitamins Lowercase *vitamin,* use a capital letter and/or a figure for the type: *vitamin A, vitamin B-12.*

V-J Day The day of victory for the Allied forces over Japan in World War II.

It is calculated both as Aug. 15, 1945, the day the fighting with Japan ended, and as Sept. 2, 1945, the day Japan officially surrendered.

V-neck (n. and adj.)

Voice of America *VOA* is acceptable on second reference.

Volkswagen of America Inc. The name of the U.S. subsidiary of the German company named Volkswagen A.G.

U.S. headquarters is in Englewood Cliffs, N.J.

volley, volleys

volleyball Games are won by the first team to score 15 points, unless it is necessary to continue until one team has a two-point spread.

Use a match summary. Example:

> National AAU Men's Volleyball
> First Round
> New York AC def. Illinois AC 15-7, 12-15, 19-17.
> Vesper Boat Club, Philadelphia, def. Harvard 15-7, 15-8.

Volunteers in Service to America *VISTA* is acceptable on second reference.

von See **foreign particles**.

voodoo

vote-getter

vote tabulations Always use figures for the totals.

Spell out below 10 in other phrases related to voting: *by a five-vote majority, with three abstentions, four votes short of the necessary two-thirds majority.*

For results that involve fewer than 1,000 votes on each side, use these forms: *The House voted 230-205, a 230-205 vote.*

To make totals that involve more than 1,000 votes on a side easier to read, separate the figures with the word *to* and avoid hyphenated adjectival constructions. See **election returns** for examples.

V-STOL Acceptable on second reference for an aircraft capable of *vertical or short takeoff or landing.*

VTOL Acceptable on second reference for an aircraft capable of *vertical takeoff or landing.*

vulgarities See the **obscenities, profanities, vulgarities** entry.

Wac, WAC *Wac* no longer is used by the military but is an acceptable term in a reference to a woman who served in what used to be the *Women's Army Corps.*

WAC is acceptable on second reference to the corps.

Waf, WAF *Waf* no longer is used by the military but is acceptable in a reference to a woman who served in the Air Force.

WAF is acceptable on second reference to the *Women's Air Force,* an unofficial organizational distinction formerly made by the Air Force but never authorized by Congress.

waiter (male) **waitress** (female)

Wales Use *Wales* after the names of Welsh communities in datelines.

See **datelines** and **United Kingdom.**

walk up (v.) **walk-up** (n. and adj.)

Wall Street When the reference is to the entire complex of financial institutions in the area rather than the actual street itself, *the Street* is an acceptable short form.

See **capitalization.**

war Capitalize when used as part of the name for a specific conflict: *the Civil War, the Cod War, the Cold War, the Korean War, the Vietnam War, the War of 1812, World War II,* etc.

warden Capitalize as a formal title before a name. See **titles.**

wards Use figures. See **political divisions.**

warhead

war horse, warhorse Two words for a horse used in battle.

One word for a veteran of many battles: *He is a political warhorse.*

warlike

warlord

Warner Communications Inc. Headquarters is in New York.

The motion picture division is Warner Bros. Inc.

warrant officer See **military titles.**

wartime

washed-up

Washington Abbreviate the state as *Wash.*

Never abbreviate when referring to the U.S. capital.

Use *state of Washington* or *Washington state* and *Washington, D.C.,* or *District of Columbia* when the context requires a distinction between the state and the federal district.

See **state** and **state names.**

Washington's Birthday Capitalize *birthday* in references to the holiday.

The date he was born is computed as Feb. 22. The federal legal holiday is the third Monday in February.

wastebasket

water polo Scoring is by goals. List team scores. Example:

World Water Polo Championship
First Round
United States 7, Canada 1
Britain 5, France 3
Etc.

water skiing Scoring is in points. Use a basic summary. Example:

World Water Skiing Championships
Men
Overall—1, George Jones, Canada, 1,987 points. 2, Phil Brown, Britain, 1,756. 3, Etc.
Slalom—1, George Jones, Canada, 73 buoys (two rounds). 2, Etc.

waterspout See weather terms.

Wave, WAVES *Wave* no longer is used by the military but is acceptable in a reference to a woman who served in the Navy.

WAVES is acceptable on second reference to the *Women's Auxiliary Volunteer Emergency Service*, an organizational distinction made for women in the Navy during World War II but subsequently discontinued.

weak-kneed

weapons *Gun* is an acceptable term for any firearm. Note the following definitions and forms in dealing with weapons and ammunition:

anti-aircraft A heavy-caliber cannon that fires explosive shells. It is designed for defense against air attack. The form: *a 105mm anti-aircraft gun.*

artillery A carriage-mounted cannon.

automatic A kind of pistol designed for automatic or semiautomatic firing.

Its cartridges are held in a magazine. The form: *a .22-caliber automatic.*

buckshot See **shot** below.

bullet The projectile fired by a rifle, pistol or machine gun. Together with metal casing, primer and propellant, it forms a *cartridge.*

caliber A measurement of the diameter of the inside of a gun barrel except for most shotguns. Measurement is in either millimeters or decimal fractions of an inch. The word *caliber* is not used when giving the metric measurement. The forms: *a 9mm pistol, a .22-caliber rifle.*

cannon A large-caliber weapon, usually supported on some type of carriage, that fires explosive projectiles. The form: *a 105mm cannon.*

carbine A short-barreled rifle. The form: *an M-3 carbine.*

cartridge See **bullet** above.

Colt Named for Samuel Colt, it designates a make of weapon or ammunition developed for Colt handguns. The forms: *a Colt .45-caliber revolver, .45 Long Colt ammunition.*

gauge This word describes the size of a shotgun. Gauge is expressed in terms of the number per pound of round lead balls with a diameter equal to the size of the barrel. The bigger the number, the smaller the shotgun.

Some common shotgun gauges:

Gauge	Interior Diameter
10	.775 inches
12	.729 inches
16	.662 inches
20	.615 inches
28	.550 inches
.410	.410 inches

The .410 actually is a caliber, but commonly is called a gauge.

The forms: *a 12-gauge shotgun, a .410-gauge shotgun.*

howitzer A cannon shorter than a gun of the same caliber employed to fire projectiles at relatively high angles at a target, such as opposing forces behind a ridge. The form: *a 105mm howitzer.*

machine gun An automatic gun, usually mounted on a support, that fires as long as the trigger is depressed. The forms: *a .50-caliber Browning machine gun.*

Magnum A trademark for a type of high-powered cartridge with a larger case and a larger powder charge than other cartridges of approximately the same caliber. The form: *a .357-caliber Magnum, a .44-caliber Magnum.*

M-1, M-14 These and similar combinations of a letter and figure(s) designate rifles used by the military. The forms: *an M-1 rifle, an M-14 carbine.*

musket A heavy, smooth-bore, large-caliber shoulder firearm fired by means of a matchlock, a wheel lock, a flintlock or a percussion lock. Its ammunition is a musket ball.

pistol A hand weapon. It may be a *revolver* or an *automatic*. Its measurements are in calibers. The form: *a .38-caliber pistol.*

revolver A kind of pistol. Its cartridges are held in chambers in a cylinder that revolves. The form: *a .45-caliber revolver.*

rifle A firearm with a rifled bore. It uses bullets or cartridges for ammunition. Its size is measured in calibers. The form: *a .22-caliber rifle.*

Saturday Night Special The popular name for the type of cheap pistol used for impulsive crimes, often committed Saturday nights.

shell The word applies to military or naval ammunition and to shotgun ammunition.

shot Small lead or steel pellets fired by shotguns. A shotgun shell usually contains 1 to 2 ounces of shot. Do not use *shot* interchangeably with *buckshot,* which refers only to the largest shot sizes.

shotgun A small-arms gun with a smooth bore, sometimes double-barreled. Its ammunition is shot. Its size is measured in gauges. The form: *a 12-gauge shotgun.*

submachine gun A lightweight automatic or semiautomatic gun firing small-arms ammunition.

weather-beaten

weather bureau See **National Weather Service.**

weatherman The preferred term is *weather forecaster.*

weather terms The following are based on definitions used by the National Weather Service. All temperatures are Fahrenheit.

blizzard Wind speeds of 35 mph or more and considerable falling and/or blowing of snow with visibility near zero.

coastal waters The waters within about 20 miles of the coast, including bays, harbors and sounds.

cyclone A storm with strong winds rotating about a moving center of low atmospheric pressure.

The word sometimes is used in the United States to mean *tornado* and in the Indian Ocean area to mean *hurricane.* Because of the confusion that can result, use the more precise words *tornado* or *hurricane.*

degree-day A degree-day is a computation that gauges the amount of heating or cooling needed for a building. An uninsulated building will maintain an inside temperature of 70 degrees if the outside temperature is 65 degrees. A degree-day is a one-degree difference in this equilibrium for one day (a temperature of 64 degrees for 24 hours), or its equivalent such as a two-degree difference for half a day (a temperature of 63 for 12 hours).

A temperature of 10 below zero for 24 hours yields 75 degree-days. A temperature of 85 degrees for six hours yields five degree-days.

dust storm Visibility of one-half mile or less due to dust, wind speeds of 30 mph or more.

flash flood A sudden, violent flood. It typically occurs after a heavy rain or the melting of a heavy snow.

flash flood warning Warns that flash flooding is imminent or in progress. Persons in the affected area should take necessary precautions immediately.

flash flood watch Alerts the public that flash flooding is possible. Those in the affected area are urged to be ready to take additional precautions if a flash flood warning is issued or if flooding is observed.

flood Stories about floods usually tell how high the water is and where it is expected to crest. Such a story should also, for comparison, list flood stage and how high the water is above, or below, flood stage.
Wrong: *The river is expected to crest at 39 feet.*
Right: *The river is expected to crest at 39 feet, 12 feet above flood stage.*

freeze Describes conditions when the temperature at or near the surface is expected to be below 32 degrees during the growing season. Adjectives such as *severe* or *hard* are used if a cold spell exceeding two days is expected.
A freeze may or may not be accompanied by the formation of frost. However, use of the term *freeze* usually is restricted for occasions when wind or other conditions prevent frost.

freezing drizzle, freezing rain Synonyms for *ice storm.*

frost Describes the formation of thin ice crystals, which might develop under conditions similar to dew except for the minimum temperatures involved. Phrases such as *frost in low places* or *scattered light frost* are used when appropriate. The term *frost* seldom appears in state forecasts unless rather heavy frost is expected over an extensive area.

funnel cloud A violent, rotating column of air that does not touch the ground, usually a pendant from a cumulonimbus cloud.

gale Sustained winds within the range of 39 to 54 mph (34 to 47 knots).

heavy snow It generally means:
a. A fall accumulating to 4 inches or more in depth in 12 hours, or
b. A fall accumulating to 6 inches or more in depth in 24 hours.

high wind Normally indicates that sustained winds of 39 mph or greater are expected to persist for one hour or longer.

hurricane or typhoon A warm-core tropical cyclone in which the minimum sustained surface wind is 74 mph or more.
Hurricanes are spawned east of the international date line. Typhoons develop west of the line.
When a hurricane or typhoon loses strength (wind speed), usually after landfall, it is reduced to *tropical storm* status.

hurricane eye The relatively calm area in the center of the storm. In this area winds are light and the sky often is covered only partly by clouds.

hurricane season The portion of the year that has a relatively high incidence of hurricanes. In the Atlantic, Caribbean and Gulf of Mexico, this is from June through November. In the eastern Pacific, it is June through Nov. 15. In the central Pacific, it is June through October.

hurricane tide Same as *storm tide.*

hurricane warning Warns that one or both of these dangerous effects of a hurricane are expected in specified coastal areas in 24 hours or less:
a. Sustained winds of 74 mph (64 knots) or higher, and/or
b. Dangerously high water or a combination of dangerously high water and exceptionally high waves, even though winds expected may be less than hurricane force.

hurricane watch An announcement for specific areas that a hurricane or incipient hurricane conditions may pose a threat to coastal and inland communities.

ice storm, freezing drizzle, freezing rain Describes the freezing of drizzle or rain on objects as it strikes them. *Freezing drizzle* and *freezing rain* are synonyms for *ice storm.*

ice storm warning Reserved for occasions when significant, and possibly damaging, accumulations of ice are expected.

National Hurricane Center The National Weather Service's National Hurricane Center in Miami has overall responsibility for tracking and providing information about tropical depressions, tropical storms and hurricanes in the Atlantic Ocean, Gulf of Mexico and Caribbean Sea.

The service's Eastern Pacific Hurricane Center in San Francisco is responsible for hurricane information in the Pacific Ocean area north of the equator and east of 140 degrees west longitude.

The service's Central Pacific Hurricane Center in Honolulu is responsible for hurricane information in the Pacific Ocean area north of the equator from 140 degrees west longitude to 180 degrees.

nearshore waters The waters extending to 5 miles from shore.

offshore waters The waters extending to about 250 miles from shore.

sandstorm Visibility of one-half mile or less due to sand blown by winds of 30 mph or more.

severe blizzard Wind speeds of 45 mph or more, great density of falling and/or blowing snow with visibility frequently near zero and a temperature of 10 degrees or lower.

severe thunderstorm Describes either of the following:
a. Winds — Thunderstorm-related surface winds sustained or gusts 50 knots or greater.
b. Hail — Surface hail three-quarters of an inch in diameter or larger. The word *hail* in a watch implies hail at the surface and aloft unless qualifying phrases such as *hail aloft* are used.

sleet (one form of ice pellet) Describes generally solid grains of ice formed by the freezing of raindrops or the refreezing of largely melted snowflakes. Sleet, like small hail, usually bounces when hitting a hard surface.

sleet (heavy) Heavy sleet is a fairly rare event in which the ground is covered to a depth of significance to motorists and others.

snow avalanche bulletin Snow avalanche bulletins are issued by the U.S. Forest Service for avalanche-prone areas in the western United States.

squall A sudden increase of wind speed by at least 16 knots and rising to 25 knots or more and lasting for at least one minute.

stockmen's advisory Alerts the public that livestock may require protection because of certain combinations of cold, wet and windy weather, specifically cold rain and/or snow with temperatures 45 degrees or lower and winds of 25 mph or higher. If the temperature is in the mid-30s or lower, the wind speed criterion is lowered to about 15 mph.

tornado A violent rotating column of air forming a pendant, usually from a cumulonimbus cloud, and touching the ground. It usually starts as a funnel cloud and is accompanied by a loud roaring noise. On a local scale, it is the most destructive of all atmospheric phenomena.

tornado warning Warns the public of an existing tornado or one suspected to be in existence.

tornado watch Alerts the public to the possibility of a tornado.

travelers' advisory Alerts the public that difficult traveling or hazardous road conditions are expected to be widespread.

tropical depression A tropical cyclone in which the maximum sustained surface wind is 38 mph (33 knots) or less.

tropical storm A warm-core tropical cyclone in which the maximum sustained surface wind ranges from 39 to 73 mph (34 to 63 knots) inclusive.

typhoon See **hurricane or typhoon** in this listing.

waterspout A tornado over water.

wind chill index No hyphen. The wind chill index is a calculation that describes the combined effect of the wind and cold temperatures on outdoor activites. The wind chill index would be minus 22, for example, if the temperature was 15 degrees and the wind was blowing at 25 mph — in other words, the combined effect would be the same as a temperature of 22 below zero with no wind.

The higher the wind at a given temperature, the lower the wind chill reading, although wind speeds above 40 mph have little additional chilling effect.

winter storm warning Notifies the public that severe winter weather conditions are almost certain to occur.

winter storm watch Alerts the public to the possibility of severe winter weather conditions.

weather vane

Webster's New World Dictionary See **dictionaries.**

Webster's Third New International Dictionary See **dictionaries.**

Wednesday See **days of the week.**

weekend

weeklong

weightlifting Identify events by weight classes. Where both pounds and kilograms are available, use both figures with kilograms in parentheses, as shown in the examples.

Use a basic summary. Example:

Flyweight (114.5 lbs.)—1, Zygmont Smalcerz, Poland, 744 pounds (337.5 kg). 2, Lajos Szuecs, Hungary, 728 (330 kg). 3, Etc.

weights Use figures: *The baby weighed 9 pounds, 7 ounces. She had a 9-pound, 7-ounce boy.*

weird, weirdo

well Hyphenate as part of a compound modifier: *She is a well-dressed woman. She is well-dressed.*

See the **hyphen** entry for guidelines on compound modifiers.

well-being

well-to-do

well-wishers

west, western See the **directions and regions** entry.

West As defined by the U.S. Census Bureau, the 13-state region is broken into two divisions.

The eight *Mountain division* states are Arizona, Colorado, Idaho, Montana, Nevada, New Mexico, Utah and Wyoming.

The five *Pacific division* states are Alaska, California, Hawaii, Oregon and Washington.

See **North Central region; Northeast region;** and **South** for the bureau's other three regional breakdowns.

Western Airlines Use this spelling of *airlines,* which Western has adopted for its public identity. Only its incorporation papers still read *air lines.*

Headquarters is in Los Angeles.

Western Athletic Conference Brigham Young, Colorado State, New Mexico, Texas El Paso, Utah, Wyoming.

Western Hemisphere The continents of North and South America, and the islands near them.

It frequently is subdivided as follows:

Caribbean The islands from the tip of Florida to the continent of South America, plus, particularly in a political sense, French Guiana, Guyana and Surinam on the northeastern coast of South America.

Major island elements are the Bahamas, Cuba, Hispaniola (the island shared by the Dominican Republic and Haiti), Jamaica, Puerto Rico, and the West Indies islands.

Central America The narrow strip of land between Mexico and Colombia. Located there are Belize, Costa Rica, El Salvador, Guatemala, Honduras, Nicaragua and Panama.

Latin America The area of the Americas south of the United States where Romance languages (those derived from Latin) are dominant. It applies to most of the region south of the United States except areas with a British heritage: the Bahamas, Barbados, Belize, Grenada, Guyana, Jamaica, Trinidad and Tobago, and various islands in the West Indies. Surinam, the former Dutch Guiana, is an additional exception.

North America Canada, Mexico, the United States and the Danish territory of Greenland. When the term is used in more than its continental sense, it also may include the islands of the Caribbean.

South America Argentina, Bolivia, Brazil, Chile, Colombia, Ecuador, Paraguay, Peru, Uruguay, Venezuela, and in a purely continental sense, French Guiana, Guyana and Surinam. Politically and psychologically, however, the latter three regard themselves as part of the Caribbean.

West Indies The term no longer is used extensively, but it applies to the Caribbean islands east of Puerto Rico southward to South America.

Major island elements are the nations of Barbados, Grenada, and Trinidad and Tobago, plus smaller islands dependent in various degrees on:

—Britain: British Virgin Islands, Anguilla, and the West Indies Associated States, including Antigua, Dominica, St. Lucia, St. Vincent and St. Christopher-Nevis.

—France: Guadeloupe (composed of islands known as Basse-Terre and Grande-Terre, plus five other islands) and Martinique.

—Netherlands: Netherlands Antilles, composed of Aruba, Bonaire, Curacao, Saba, St. Eustatius and the southern portion of St. Martin Island (the northern half is held by France).

—United States: U.S. Virgin Islands, principally St. Croix, St. John and St. Thomas.

West Germany Use in datelines instead of the *Federal Republic of Germany*.

See **Berlin** and **East Germany**.

West Indies See **Western Hemisphere**.

West Point Acceptable on second reference to the *U.S. Military Academy*. See **military academies**.

In datelines:

WEST POINT, N.Y. (AP) —

West Virginia Abbrev.: *W.Va.* (no space between *W.* and *Va.*). See **state names**.

wheat It is measured in bushels domestically, in metric tons for international trade.

There are 36.7 bushels of wheat in a metric ton.

wheelchair

wheeler-dealer

whereabouts Takes a singular verb: *His whereabouts is a mystery.*

wherever

which See the **essential clauses, non-essential clauses** entry; the **that, which** entry; and the **who, whom** entry.

whip Capitalize when used as a formal title before a name. See **legislative titles** and **titles**.

whiskey, whiskeys Use the spelling *whisky* only in conjunction with *Scotch*. See the **Scotch whisky** entry.

white-collar (adj.)

White House Do not personify it with phrases such as *the White House said.* Instead, use a phrase such as *a White House official said.*

white paper Two words, lowercase, when used to refer to a special report.

whitewash (n., v. and adj.)

who, whom Use *who* and *whom* for references to human beings and to animals with a name. Use *that* and *which* for inanimate objects and animals without a name.

Who is the word when someone is the subject of a sentence, clause or phrase: *The woman who rented the room left the window open. Who is there?*

Whom is the word when someone is the object of a verb or preposition: *The woman to whom the room was rented left the window open. Whom do you wish to see?*

See the **essential clauses, non-essential clauses** entry for guidelines on how to punctuate clauses introduced by *who, whom, that* and *which*.

wholehearted

wholesale price index A measurement of the changes in the average prices that businesses pay for a selected group of industrial commodities, farm products, processed foods and feed for animals.

Capitalize when referring to the U.S. index, issued monthly by the Bureau of Labor Statistics, an agency of the Labor Department.

whole-wheat

who's, whose *Who's* is a contraction for *who is,* not a possessive: *Who's there?*

Whose is the possessive: *I do not know whose coat it is.*

wide- Usually hyphenated. Some examples:

wide-angle	wide-eyed
wide-awake	wide-open
wide-brimmed	

Exception: *widespread*.

-wide No hyphen. Some examples:

citywide	nationwide
continentwide	statewide
countrywide	worldwide
industrywide	

widow, widower In obituaries: A man *is survived by his wife,* or *leaves his wife.* A woman *is survived by her husband,* or *leaves her husband.*

Guard against the redundant *widow of the late.* Use *wife of the late* or *widow of.*

widths See **dimensions**.

wigwag

wildlife

Wilkes-Barre, Pa.

will See the **shall, will** entry and **subjunctive mood**.

Wilson's disease After Samuel A. Wilson, an English neurologist. A disease characterized by abnormal accumulation of copper in the brain, liver and other organs.

Windbreaker A trademark for a brand of wind-resistant sports jacket.

wind chill index See **weather terms**.

window dressing The noun. But as a verb: *window-dress*.

wind-swept

wind up (v.) **windup** (n. and adj.)

wingspan

winter See **seasons**.

wintertime

wiretap, wiretapper The verb forms: *wiretap, wiretapped, wiretapping*.

Wisconsin Abbrev.: *Wis*. See **state names**.

-wise No hyphen when it means in the direction of or with regard to. Some examples:

| clockwise | otherwise |
| lengthwise | slantwise |

Avoid contrived combinations such as *moneywise, religionwise*.

The word *penny-wise* is spelled with a hyphen because it is a compound adjective in which *wise* means *smart*, not an application of the suffix *-wise*. The same for *street-wise* in *street-wise youth*.

Woman's Christian Temperance Union Not *Women's*. *WCTU* is acceptable on second reference.

women Women should receive the same treatment as men in all areas of coverage. Physical descriptions, sexist references, demeaning stereotypes and condescending phrases should not be used.

To cite some examples, this means that:

—Copy should not assume maleness when both sexes are involved, as in *Jackson told newsmen* or in *the taxpayer . . . he* when it easily can be said *Jackson told reporters* or *taxpayers . . . they*.

—Copy should not express surprise that an attractive woman can be professionally accomplished, as in: *Mary Smith doesn't look the part but she's an authority on . . .*

—Copy should not gratuitously mention family relationships when there is no relevance to the subject, as in: *Golda Meir, a doughty grandmother, told the Egyptians today . . .*

—Use the same standards for men and women in deciding whether to include specific mention of personal appearance or marital and family situation.

In other words, treatment of the sexes should be even-handed and free of assumptions and stereotypes. This does not mean that valid and acceptable words such as *mankind* or *humanity* cannot be used. They are proper.

See **courtesy titles**; **divorcee**; the **man, mankind** entry; and **-persons**.

Women's Army Corps See the **Wac, WAC** entry.

Woolworth's Acceptable in all references for *F.W. Woolworth Co.*

word-of-mouth (n. and adj.)

words as words The meaning of this phrase, which appears occasionally in this book and similar manuals that deal with words, is best illustrated by an example: In this sentence, *woman* appears solely as a word rather than as the means of representing the concept normally associated with the word.

When italics are available, a word used as a word should be italicized. Entries in this book use italics when a word or phrase is discussed in this sense. Note, for example, the italics used on *woman* in this sentence and in the example sentence.

Italics are not available to highlight this type of word use on the news wires.

When a news story must use a word as a word, place quotation marks around it instead.

See **italics** and **plurals**.

word selection In general, any word with a meaning that universally is understood is acceptable unless it is offensive or below the normal standards for literate writing.

This stylebook lists many words with cautionary notes about how they should be used. The entries in Webster's New World Dictionary provide cautionary notes, comparisons and usage guidelines to help a writer choose the correct word for a particular context.

Any word listed in Webster's New World may be used for the definitions given unless this stylebook restricts its use to only some of the definitions recorded by the dictionary or specifies that the word be confined to certain contexts.

If the dictionary cautions that a particular usage is objected to by some linguists or is not accepted widely, be wary of the usage unless there is a reason in the context.

The dictionary uses the description *substandard* to identify words below the norms for literate writing.

The dictionary provides guidance on many idiomatic expressions under the principal word in the expression. The definition and spelling of *under way,* for example, are found in the "way" entry.

If it is necessary to use an archaic word or an archaic sense of a word, explain the meaning.

Additional guidance on the acceptability of words is provided in this book under:

Americanisms	**jargon**
colloquialisms	**special contexts**
dialect	**vernacular**
foreign words	

See also the **obscenities, profanities and vulgarities** entry.

workday

working class (n.) **working-class** (adj.)

workout

workweek

World Bank Acceptable in all references for *International Bank for Reconstruction and Development.*

World Council of Churches This is the main international, interdenominational cooperative body of Anglican, Eastern Orthodox, Protestant and old or national Catholic churches.

Roman Catholicism is not a member but cooperates with the council in various programs.

Headquarters is in Geneva, Switzerland.

World Court This was an alternate name for the *Permanent Court of International Justice* set up by the League of Nations.

See the entry for the **International Court of Justice,** which has replaced it.

World Health Organization *WHO* is acceptable on second reference.

Headquarters is in Geneva, Switzerland.

World Series Or *the Series* on second reference. A rare exception to the general principles under **capitalization.**

World War I, World War II

worldwide

worn-out

worship, worshiped, worshiping, worshiper

worthwhile

would See the **should, would** entry.

wrack See the **rack, wrack** entry.

wrestling Identify events by weight divisions.

The key words to indicate winners are *pinned* and *outpointed*.

Use a basic summary for final results of major tournaments. Use a match summary for preliminary rounds.

write in (v.) **write-in** (n. and adj.)

wrongdoing

Wyoming Abbrev.: *Wyo.* See **state names.**

XYZ

X The rating that denotes *individuals under 17 are not admitted.* See **movie ratings**.

Xerox A trademark for a brand of photocopy machine. Never a verb.

X-ray (n., v. and adj.) Use for both the photographic process and the radiation particles themselves.

yachting Use a basic summary, identifying events by classes.

yam Botanically, yams and sweet potatoes are not related, although several varieties of moist-fleshed sweet potatoes are popularly called *yams* in some parts on the United States.

Yankee Conference Boston University, Connecticut, Maine, Massachusetts, New Hampshire, Rhode Island, Vermont.

yard Equal to three feet.
The metric equivalent is approximately 0.91 meter.
To convert to meters, multiply by .91 (5 yards x .91 = 4.55 meters).
See **foot; meter;** and **distances**.

yard lines Use figures to indicate the dividing lines on a football field and distance traveled: *5-yard line, 40-yard line, he plunged in from the 2, he ran 6 yards, a 7-yard gain.*

year-end (adj.)

yearling An animal 1 year old or in its second year. The birthdays of all thoroughbred horses arbitrarily are set at Jan. 1. On that date, any foal born in the preceding year is reckoned 1 year old.

yearlong

years Use figures, without commas: *1975.* Use an *s* without an apostrophe to indicate spans of decades or centuries: *the 1890s, the 1800s.*
Years are the lone exception to the general rule in **numerals** that a figure is not used to start a sentence: *1976 was a very good year.*
See **A.D.; B.C.; centuries; historical periods and events;** and **months**.

yellow journalism The use of cheaply sensational methods to attract or influence readers. The term comes from the "Yellow Kid," a comic strip, in the New York World in 1895.

yeoman See **military titles**.

yesterday Use only in direct quotations and in phrases that do not refer to a specific day: *Yesterday we were young.*
Use the day of the week in other cases.

yesteryear

yield In a financial sense, the annual rate of return on an investment, as paid in dividends or interest. It is expressed as a percentage obtained by dividing the market price for a stock or bond into the dividend or interest paid in the preceding 12 months.

See **profit terminology.**

Yom Kippur The Jewish Day of Atonement. Occurs in September or October.

Young Men's Christian Association *YMCA* is acceptable in all references.

Headquarters is in New York.

Young Women's Christian Association *YWCA* is acceptable in all references.

Headquarters is in New York.

youth Applicable to boys and girls from age 13 until 18th birthday. Use *man* or *woman* for individuals 18 and older.

yo-yo Formerly a trademark, now a generic term.

Yukon A territorial section of Canada. Do not abbreviate. Use in datelines after the names of communities in the territory.

See **Canada.**

yule, yuletide

zero, zeros

zigzag

Zionism The effort of the Jews to regain and retain their biblical homeland. It is based on the promise of God in the Book of Genesis that Israel would forever belong to Abraham and his descendants as a nation.

The term is named for Mount Zion, the site of the ancient temple in Jerusalem. The Bible also frequently uses *Zion* in a general sense to denote the place where God is especially present with his people.

ZIP codes Use all-caps *ZIP* for *Zone Improvement Program*, but always lowercase the word *code.*

Run the five digits together without a comma, and do not put a comma between the state name and the ZIP code: *New York, N.Y. 10020.*

BIBLIOGRAPHY

Following are reference books used in the preparation of The Associated Press Stylebook. They are the accepted reference sources for material not covered by the Stylebook.

First reference for spelling, style, usage and foreign geographic names:
Webster's New World Dictionary of the American Language, Second College Edition; William Collins-World Publishing Co. Inc., Cleveland and New York.

Second reference for spelling, style and usage:
Webster's Third New International Dictionary of the English Language, Unabridged; G. & C. Merriam Co., Springfield, Mass.

Second reference for foreign geographic names:
The Columbia Lippincott Gazetteer of the World; Columbia University Press, Morningside Heights, N.Y., by arrangement with J.B. Lippincott Co., New York.

First reference for place names in the 50 states:
U.S. Postal Service Directory of Post Offices; U.S. Postal Service, Washington.

For aircraft names:
Jane's All the World's Aircraft; Jane's Yearbooks, London, and Franklin Watts Inc., New York.

For military ships:
Jane's Fighting Ships; Jane's Yearbooks, London, and Franklin Watts Inc., New York.

For non-military ships:
Lloyd's Register of Shipping; Lloyd's Register of Shipping Trust Corp. Ltd., London.

For railroads:
Official Railway Guide—Freight Service, and *Official Railway Guide—Passenger Service*, Travel Edition; Official Railway Guide, New York.

For federal government questions:
Official Congressional Directory; U.S. Government Printing Office, Washington.

For foreign government questions:
Political Handbook of the World; McGraw-Hill Book Co., New York.

For the formal name of a business:
Standard & Poor's Register of Corporations, Directors and Executives; Standard & Poor's Corp., New York.

For religion questions:
Handbook of Denominations in the United States; Abingdon Press, Nashville, Tenn., and New York.
Yearbook of American and Canadian Churches; Abingdon Press, Nashville, Tenn., and New York, for the National Council of Churches of Christ in the U.S.A., New York.

Other references consulted in the preparation of the AP Stylebook:

Bernstein, Theodore M. *The Careful Writer: A Modern Guide to English Usage*. Atheneum, 1965.

Bernstein, Theodore M. *More Language That Needs Watching*. Channel Press, 1962.

Bernstein, Theodore M. *Watch Your Language*. Atheneum, 1958.

Follett, Wilson (edited and completed by Jacques Barzun). *Modern American Usage*. Hill & Wang, 1966.

Fowler, H.W. *A Dictionary of Modern English Usage*. Oxford University Press, 1965.

A Manual of Style, 12th Edition. University of Chicago Press, 1969.

Morris, William and Morris, Mary. *Harper Dictionary of Contemporary Usage*. Harper & Row, 1975.

Shaw, Harry. *Dictionary of Problem Words & Expressions*. McGraw-Hill Book Co., 1975.

Skillin, Marjorie E. and Gay, Robert M. *Words Into Type*. Prentice-Hall Inc., 1974.

Strunk, William Jr. and White, E.B. *The Elements of Style*, Second Edition. The Macmillan Co., 1972.

Also consulted were the stylebooks of the Boston Globe, Indianapolis News, Kansas City Star, Los Angeles Times, Miami Herald, Milwaukee Journal, Milwaukee Sentinel, Newsday, New York Times, Wilmington (Del.) News-Journal, and the U.S. Government Printing Office.

LIBEL MANUAL

FOREWORD

What follows is not a textbook on libel. It is a guide for The Associated Press staff. It explains fundamental principles in libel for working writers and editors.

This manual will make no reader an expert on libel. It will, we hope, make everyone aware of what libel is and how to avoid it.

Underlying all the guidance in this book is one basic rule for the AP staff: If a legal problem develops with a story, or if guidance is needed in the handling of a story, consult the General Desk. Nothing in the manual alters this rule.

As is the case in other fields of the law, the law of libel is not static. We have seen dramatic changes in the past 13 years — not all in the same direction. And the new interpretations go on even as this is written.

What does not change is our promise to ourselves to be accurate and to be fair.

For his help with this manual we are indebted to retired General News Editor Samuel G. Blackman.

LOUIS D. BOCCARDI
Vice President and
Executive Editor
July 1977

Chapter 1

INTRODUCTION

Associate Justice John Marshall Harlan remarked that "the law of libel has changed substantially since the early days of the Republic."

And it has changed substantially since he made that observation more than a decade ago. The past 13 years have seen the Supreme Court of the United States decide several cases that made headlines and truly can be called landmarks.

But the working journalist remembers: The news stories which generate the most claims of injury to reputation — the basis of libel — are run-of-the-mill. Perhaps 95 of 100 libel suits are in that category and result from publication of charges of crime, immorality, incompetence or inefficiency.

A Harvard Nieman report makes the point: "The gee-whiz, slam-bang stories usually aren't the ones that generate libel, but the innocent-appearing, potentially treacherous minor yarns from police courts and traffic cases, from routine meetings and from business reports."

Most of these suits based on relatively minor stories result from factual error or inexact language — for example, getting the plea wrong or making it appear that all defendants in a case face identical charges.

Libel even lurks in such innocent-appearing stories as birth notices and engagements. The fact that some New York newspapers had to defend suits recently for such announcements illustrates the care and concern required in every editorial department.

Turner Catledge, retired managing editor of The New York Times, says in his book, "My Life and the Times," that he learned over the years that newspapers must be extremely careful in checking engagement announcements. He noted that "sometimes people will call in the engagement of two people who hate each other, as a practical joke."

In short, there is no substitute for accuracy. But, of course, this does not mean that accurately reporting libelous assertions automatically absolves the journalist of culpability.

Accurate reporting will not prevent libel if there is no privilege, either the constitutional privilege or the fair report privilege.

A fair and impartial report of judicial, legislative and other public and official proceedings is privileged — that is, not actionable for libel. But it is important to know, for instance, what constitutes judicial action. In many states there is no privilege to report the filing of the summons and complaint in a civil suit until there has been some judicial action.

Many libel suits occur in the handling of court and police news, especially criminal courts. Problems can arise in stories about crime and in identifying a suspect where there has been no arrest or where no charge has been made.

Don't be deluded into thinking a safe approach is to eliminate the subject's name. If the description — physical or otherwise — readily identifies him to those in his immediate area, the story has, in effect, named him.

When accusations are made against a person, it is always well to try for balancing comment. The reply must have some relation to the original charges. Irrelevant countercharges can lead to problems with the person who made the first accusation.

The chief causes of libel suits are carelessness, misunderstanding of the law of libel, limitations of the defense of privilege (including the First Amendment privilege) and the extent to which developments may be reported in arrests. These are discussed in detail in this manual, which is "must" reading for every Associated Press staff member. It should be reviewed periodically.

Chapter 2

LIBEL, DEFENSES and PRIVILEGE

Libel is injury to reputation.

Words, pictures or cartoons that expose a person to public hatred, shame, disgrace or ridicule, or induce an ill opinion of a person are libelous.

Actions for civil libel result mainly from news stories that allege crime, fraud, dishonesty, immoral or dishonorable conduct, or stories that defame the subject professionally, causing financial loss either personally or to a business.

There is only one complete and unconditional defense to a civil action for libel: that the facts stated are PROVABLY TRUE. (Note well that word, PROVABLY.) Quoting someone correctly is not enough. The important thing is to be able to satisfy a jury that the libelous statement is substantially correct.

A second important defense is PRIVILEGE. Privilege is one of two kinds — absolute and qualified.

Absolute privilege means that certain persons in some circumstances can state, without fear of being sued for libel, material which may be false, malicious and damaging. These circumstances include judicial, legislative, public and official proceedings and the contents of most public records.

The doctrine of absolute privilege is founded on the fact that on certain occasions the public interest requires that some individuals be exempted from legal liability for what they say.

Remarks by a member of a legislative body in the discharge of official duties are not actionable. Similarly, libelous statements made in the course of legal proceedings by participants are also absolutely privileged, if they are relevant to the issue. Statements containing defamatory matter may be absolutely privileged if publication is required by law.

The interests of society require that judicial, legislative and similar official proceedings be subject to public discussion. To that extent, the rights of the individual about whom damaging statements may be made are subordinated to what are deemed to be the interests of the community.

We have been talking about absolute privilege as it applies to participants in the types of proceedings described here.

As applied to the press, the courts generally have held that privilege is not absolute, but rather is qualified. That means that it can be lost or diluted by how the journalist handles the material.

Privilege can be lost if there are errors in the report of the hearing, or if the plaintiff can show malice on the part of the publication or broadcast outlet.

An exception: Broadcasters have absolute privilege to carry the broadcast statements of political candidates.

The two key points are:
1—Does the material at issue come from a privileged circumstance
   or proceeding?
2—Is the report a fair and accurate summation?

Again, the absolute privilege legislators enjoy — they cannot be sued, for example, for anything said on the floor of the legislature — affords total protection.

The journalist's protection is not as tight. But it is important and substantial and enables the press to report freely on many items of public interest which otherwise would have to go unreported.

The press has a qualified privilege to report that John Doe has been arrested for bank robbery. If the report is fair and accurate, there is no problem.

Statements made outside the court by police or a prosecutor or an attorney may not be privileged unless the circumstances indicate it is an official proceeding. However, some states do extend privilege to these statements if made by specified top officials.

Newspapers and broadcasters often carry accounts going beyond the narrow confines of what is stated in the official charges, taking the risk without malice because they feel the importance of the case and the public interest warrant doing so.

The source of such statements should be specified.

Sometimes there are traps.

In New York and some other states, court rules provide that the papers filed in matrimonial actions are sealed and thus not open to inspection by the general public.

But sometimes litigants or their lawyers may slip a copy of the papers to reporters. Publication of the material is dangerous because often the litigants come to terms outside of court and the case never goes to trial. So privilege may never attach to the accusations made in the court papers.

In one such case, the vice president of a company filed suit alleging that he was fired because the newspaper published his wife's charges of infidelity. The newspaper responded that its report was a true and fair account of court proceedings. The New York Court of Appeals rejected that argument on grounds that the law makes details of marital cases secret because spatting spouses frequently make unfounded charges. The newspaper appealed to the Supreme Court of the United States. But it lost.

Unless some other privilege applies, there is danger in carrying a report of court papers that are not available for public inspection by reason of a law, court rule or court order directing that such papers be sealed.

As stated earlier, a fair and accurate report of public and official proceedings is privileged.

There has never been an exact legal definition of what constitutes an official proceeding. Some cases are obvious — trials, legislative sessions and hearings, etc.

Strictly speaking, conventions of private organizations are not "public and official proceedings" even though they may be forums for discussions of public questions. Hence, statements made on the floor of convention sessions or from speakers' platforms may not be privileged.

Statements made by the president of the United States or a governor in the course of executive proceedings have absolute privilege for the speaker, even if false or defamatory. However, this absolute privilege may not apply to statements having no relation to executive proceedings.

President Kennedy once was asked at a news conference what he was going to do about "two well-known security risks" in the State Department. The reporter gave names when the president asked for them. This was not privileged and many newspapers and radio stations did not carry them. The Associated Press did because it seemed in the public interest to report the incident fully. No suits resulted.

After a civil rights march, George Wallace, then governor of Alabama, appeared on a television show and said some of the marchers were members of Communist and Communist-front organizations. He gave some names, which newspapers carried. Some libel suits resulted.

The courts have ruled that publishing that a person is a Communist is libelous on its face if he is not a Communist.

"The claimed charge that the plaintiff is a Nazi and a Communist is in the same category. ... The current effect of these statements is the decisive test. Whatever doubt there may have been in the past as to the opprobrious effect on the ordinary mind of such a charge ... recent events and legislation make it manifest that to label an attorney a Communist or a Nazi is to taint him with disrepute." (*Levy v. Gelber, 175 Misc. 746*)

The fact that news comes from official sources does not eliminate the concern. To say that *a high police official said* means that you are making the accusation. A statement that a crime has been committed and that the police are holding someone for questioning is reasonably safe, because it is provably true. However, there are times when the nature of the crime or the prominence of those involved requires broader treatment. Under those circumstances, the safest guide is whatever past experience has shown as to the responsibility of the source. The source must be trustworthy and certain to stand behind the information given.

Repetition of Libel

In reporting the filing of a libel suit, can we report the content of the charge? By so doing, do we compound the libel, even though we quote from the legal complaint?

Ordinarily, a fair and impartial report of the contents of legal papers in a libel action filed in the office of the clerk of the court is privileged. However, many states do not extend privilege to the filing of court actions; in such a case there is no privilege until the case comes to trial or until some other judicial action takes place.

But we have found that it is safe, generally speaking, to repeat the libel in a story based on the filing of a suit.

Fair Comment and Criticism

The publication of defamatory matter that consists of comment and opinion, as distinguished from fact, with reference to matters of public interest or importance, is covered by the defense of fair comment.

Of course, whatever facts are stated must be true.

The right of fair comment has been summarized as follows:

"Everyone has a right to comment on matters of public interest and concern, provided they do so fairly and with an honest purpose. Such comments or criticism are not libelous, however severe in their terms, unless they are written maliciously. Thus it has been held that books, prints, pictures and statuary publicly exhibited, and the architecture of public buildings, and actors and exhibitors are all the legitimate subjects of newspapers' criticism, and such criticism fairly and honestly made is not libelous, however strong the terms of censure may be." (*Hoeppner v. Dunkirk Pr. Co., 254 N.Y. 95*)

Criminal Libel

The publication of a libel may result in what is considered a breach of the peace. For that reason, it may constitute a criminal offense. It is unnecessary to review that phase of the law here because the fundamental elements of the crime do not differ substantially from those that give rise to a civil action for damages.

Chapter 3

PUBLIC OFFICIALS, PUBLIC FIGURES, PUBLIC ISSUES

In a series of decisions commencing in 1964, the Supreme Court made rulings of profound importance in establishing First Amendment protections for the press in the libel area.

More recent decisions have, in the eyes of many legal experts, weakened some of those protections.

While the impact of these later decisions is not yet clear, a review of this vital area can help explain what is evolving as this is written.

Three basic cases established important precedents. They did so in a logical progression. The cases were:

—New York Times vs. Sullivan.

—Associated Press vs. Walker.

—Rosenbloom vs. Metromedia.

In The New York Times case, the Supreme Court ruled in March 1964 that a public official cannot recover damages for a report related to his official duties unless he proves actual malice.

To establish actual malice, the official was required to prove that at the time of publication those responsible for the story knew it was false or published it with reckless disregard of whether it was true or false.

The decision reversed a $500,000 libel verdict returned in Alabama against The New York Times and four black ministers.

The court said:

"The constitutional guarantees (the First and Fourteenth Amendments) require, we think, a federal rule that prohibits a public official from recovering damages for a defamatory falsehood relating to his official conduct unless he proves that the statement was made with 'actual malice' — that is, with knowledge that it was false or with reckless disregard of whether it was false or not."

This does not give newspapers absolute immunity against libel suits by officials who are criticized. But it does mean that when a newspaper publishes information about a public official and publishes it without "actual malice," it should be spared a damage suit even though some of the information may be wrong.

The court said it considered the case "against the background of a profound national commitment to the principle that debate on public issues should be uninhibited, robust, and wide-open, and that it may well include vehement, caustic, and sometimes unpleasantly sharp attacks on government and public officials."

The ruling in The New York Times case with respect to public officials was extended by the Supreme Court in June 1967 to apply also to public figures.

In so holding, the court reversed a $500,000 libel judgment won by former Maj. Gen. Edwin A. Walker in a Texas state court against The Associated Press. The AP reported that Walker had "assumed command" of rioters at the University of Mississippi and "led a charge of students against federal marshals" when James H. Meredith was admitted to the university in September 1962. Walker alleged those statements to be false.

The court said: "Under any reasoning, Gen. Walker was a public man in whose public conduct society and the press had a legitimate and substantial interest."

The rulings in The New York Times and The Associated Press cases were constitutional landmark decisions for freedom of the press and speech. They offered safeguards not heretofore defined. But they did not confer license for defamatory statements or for "reckless disregard" of the truth.

The AP decision made an additional important distinction.

In the same opinion, the court upheld an award granted Wallace Butts, former athletic director of the University of Georgia, against Curtis Publishing Co. The suit was based on an article in the Saturday Evening Post accusing Butts of giving his football team's strategy secrets to an opposing coach prior to a game between the two colleges.

The court found that Butts was a "public figure," but said there was a substantial difference between the two cases. Justice Harlan said: "The evidence showed that the Butts story was in no sense 'hot news' and the editors of the magazine recognized the need for a thorough investigation of the serious charges. Elementary precautions were, nevertheless, ignored. . . ."

Chief Justice Warren, in a concurring opinion, referred to "slipshod and sketchy investigatory techniques employed to check the veracity of the source." He said the evidence disclosed "reckless disregard for the truth."

The differing rulings in The Associated Press and the Saturday Evening Post cases should be noted carefully. The AP-Walker case was "hot news"; the Post-Butts story was investigative reporting of which journalists are doing more and more.

Extension of the Times' rule in one case was based on a column by Drew Pearson which characterized a candidate for the United States Senate as "a former small-time bootlegger." The jury held that the accusation related to the private sector of the candidate's life. Reversing this judgment, the Supreme Court said:

"We therefore hold as a matter of constitutional law that a charge of criminal conduct, no matter how remote in time or place, can never be irrelevant to an official's or a candidate's fitness for office for purposes of application of the 'knowing falsehood or reckless disregard' rule of New York Times v. Sullivan."

Another case was brought by a Chicago captain of detectives against Time magazine, which had quoted from a report of the U.S. Civil Rights Commission without making clear that the charges of police brutality were those of the complainant whose home was raided and not the independent findings of the commission. The court described the commission's documents as "bristling with ambiguities" and said Time did not engage in a "falsification" sufficient to sustain a finding of "actual malice."

To this point, then, the important constitutional protections were extended to public officials and public figures.

Now for the third case in the important Supreme Court trilogy: Rosenbloom vs. Metromedia.

This case concerned a suit brought against a Philadelphia radio station, WIP, by a former distributor of a nudist magazine in the area. The station had referred to material seized in a police raid as obscene and referred to an injunction suit against police as an attempt to force police to "lay off the smut literature racket."

The trial jury awarded a substantial verdict to the magazine distributor. But in 1971, the Supreme Court ruled in favor of the radio station, saying private individuals have no more protection than public officials and other public figures in matters that involve the public interest. The court said:

"The community has a vital interest in the proper enforcement of its criminal laws, particularly in an area such as obscenity where a number of highly important values are potentially in conflict: The public has an interest both in seeing that the criminal law is adequately enforced and in assuring that the law is not used unconstitutionally to suppress free expression."

The Supreme Court decisions starting with The New York Times case and continuing through the Philadelphia radio case offer safeguards not heretofore defined. But it should be remembered at all times that they do not confer license for making knowingly false defamatory statements or for "reckless disregard" of the truth. As the Supreme Court has stated: "There must be sufficient evidence to permit the conclusion that the defendant in fact entertained serious doubts as to the truth of his publication. Publishing with such doubts shows reckless disregard for truth or falsity and demonstrates actual malice."

The progression of the New York Times, AP and Metromedia cases was interrupted in June 1974 with the Supreme Court's decision in the case of Gertz vs. Robert Welch Inc.

Gertz, a lawyer of prominence in Chicago, had been attacked in a John Birch Society publication as a Communist. There were additional accusations as well.

Gertz sued and the Supreme Court upheld him, ruling that he was neither a public official nor a public figure.

The decision opened the door to giving courts somewhat wider leeway in determining whether someone was a public person.

This also opened the way to giving the state courts the right to assess what standard of liability should be used in testing whether a publication about a private individual is actionable.

For instance, some state courts have established a negligence standard (whether a reasonable person would have done the same thing as the publisher under the circumstances). The New York courts follow a "gross negligence" test. And others still observe the actual malice test in suits by private individuals against the press.

Bear in mind that the significance of the Gertz decision still is being developed, as new cases arise and are adjudicated in the courts.

But at a minimum it opened the way to judgments the three earlier cases would seem to have barred.

More recently, in the case of Time vs. Firestone, the Supreme Court again appears to have restricted the "public figure" and "public issue" standards.

The case stemmed from Time magazine's account of the divorce of Russell and Mary Alice Firestone. The magazine said she had been divorced on grounds of "extreme cruelty and adultery." The court made no finding of adultery. She sued.

She was a prominent social figure in Palm Beach, Fla., and held press conferences in the course of the divorce proceedings. Yet the Supreme Court said she was not a public figure because "she did not assume any role of special prominence in the affairs of society, other than perhaps Palm Beach society, and she did not thrust herself to the forefront of any particular public controversy in order to influence resolution of the issues involved in it."

As in the Gertz case, the decision opens the way to findings within the states involving negligence, a standard less severe than the "actual malice" standard that was at the base of three earlier landmark cases.

As has been pointed out a few times, this area of the law is evolving, and it is sufficient to note now that there is a drift in a direction different from the Sullivan-Walker-Rosenbloom cases.

Some experts see a trend to more restrictive application of the constitutional privileges established earlier and to a wider role for the state courts in assessing what is to be considered negligence, rather than actual malice, on the part of the publisher.

Chapter 4

THE RIGHT OF PRIVACY

The right of privacy is a doctrine that has been developing in the past 60 years. It is recognized by statute in only a few states, including New York, but courts increasingly are taking cognizance of it. It is clearly an area to be watched.

The doctrine is based on the idea that a person has the right to be let alone, to live a private life free from publicity.

In 1890, two Boston lawyers, wrote in the Harvard Law Review:

"The press is overstepping in every direction the obvious bounds of propriety and decency."

It is of interest that one of those lawyers, who later became Justice Brandeis, said years later in one of his dissents:

"The makers of our Constitution undertook to secure conditions favorable to the pursuit of happiness. They recognized the significance of man's spiritual nature, of his feelings and of his intellect. They knew that only a part of the pain, pleasure and satisfactions of life are to be found in material things. They sought to protect Americans in their beliefs, their thoughts, their emotions and their sensations. They conferred, as against the government, the right to be let alone — the most comprehensive of rights and the right most valued by civilized men." (*Olmstead v. United States, 277 U.S. 438,478*)

When a person becomes involved in a news event, voluntarily or involuntarily, he forfeits the right to privacy. Similarly a person somehow involved in a matter of legitimate public interest, even if not a bona fide spot news event, normally can be written about with safety.

However, this is different from publication of a story or picture that dredges up the sordid details of a person's past and has no current newsworthiness.

Paul P. Ashley, then president of the Washington State Bar Association, said in a talk on this subject at a meeting of The Associated Press Managing Editors Association:

"The essence of the wrong will be found in crudity, in ruthless exploitation of the woes or other personal affairs of private individuals who have done nothing noteworthy and have not by design or misadventure been involved in an event which tosses them into an arena subject to public gaze."

Here are details of a few cases brought in the name of right of privacy:

—A leading case centering on publication of details of a person's past concerned a man who as a child prodigy in 1910 had attracted national attention. In 1937, The New Yorker magazine published a biographical sketch of the plaintiff. He alleged invasion of privacy.

The court said "he had cloaked himself in obscurity but his subsequent history, containing as it did the answer to the question of whether or not he had fulfilled his early promise, was still a matter of public concern. The article . . . sketched the life of an unusual personality, and it possessed considerable popular news interest."

The court said further:

"We express no comment on whether or not the newsworthiness of the matter printed will always constitute a complete defense. Revelations may be so intimate and so unwarranted in view of the victim's position as to outrage the community's notions of decency. But when focused upon public characters, truthful comments upon dress, speech, habits, and the ordinary aspects of personality will usually not transgress this line. Regrettably or not, the misfortunes and frailties of neighbors and 'public figures' are subjects of considerable interest and discussion to the rest of the population. And when such are the mores of the community, it would be unwise for a court to bar their expression in the newspapers, books, and magazines of the day."

—The unsavory incidents of the past of a former prostitute, who had been tried for murder, acquitted, married and lived a respectable life, were featured in a motion picture. The court ruled that the use of her name in the picture and the statement in advertisements that the story was taken from true incidents in her life violated her right to pursue and obtain happiness.

Some courts have ruled that a person who is recognizable in a picture of a crowd in a public place is not entitled to the right of privacy. But if a camera singled him out for no news-connected reason, then his privacy is invaded, some courts have ruled.

Another example of spot news interest: A child was injured in an auto accident in Alabama. A newspaper took a picture of the scene before the child was removed and ran it. That was spot news. Twenty months later a magazine used the picture to illustrate an article. The magazine was sued and lost the case, the court ruling that 20 months after the accident the child was no longer "in the news."

In another case, a newspaper photographer in search of a picture to illustrate a hot weather story took a picture of a woman sitting on her front porch. She wore a housedress, her hair in curlers, her feet in thong sandals. The picture was taken from a car parked across the street from the woman's home. She sued, charging invasion of privacy. A court, denying the newspaper's motion for dismissal of the suit, said the scene photographed "was not a particularly newsworthy incident," and the limits of decency were exceeded by "surreptitious" taking and publishing of pictures "in an embarrassing pose."

A woman took her two children to the county fair and went with them into the funhouse. A newspaper photographer took her picture just as a jet of air blew up her dress. She sued, and the Supreme Court of Alabama upheld the damages.

The rules in New York State on the right of privacy that are applicable to unauthorized publication of photographs in a single issue of a newspaper may be summarized generally as follows:

1. The plaintiff may recover damages if the photograph is published in or as part of an advertisement, or for advertising purposes.

2. There is liability if the photograph is used in connection with an article of fiction in any part of a newspaper.

3. There may be no recovery under the statute for publication of a photograph in connection with an article of current news or immediate public interest.

4. Newspapers publish articles that are neither strictly news items nor strictly fictional in character. They are not the responses to an event of peculiarly immediate interest, but though based on fact, are used to satisfy an ever-present educational need. Such articles include, among others, travel stories, stories of distant places, tales of history personages and events, the reproduction of items of past news and surveys of social conditions. These are articles educational and informative in character. As a general rule, such cases are not within the purview of the statute. (*Lahiri v. Daily Mirror Inc., Misc. Reports, N.Y. 162, p780*).

The Supreme Court of the United States ruled in January 1967 that the constitutional guarantees of freedom of the press are applicable to invasion-of-privacy cases involving reports of newsworthy matters.

The ruling arose out of a reversal by the Supreme Court of a decision of a New York court that an article with photos in Life magazine reviewing a play, "The Desperate Hours," violated the privacy of a couple who had been held hostage in a real-life incident. In illustrating the article, Life posed the actors in the house where the real family had been held captive.

The family alleged violation of privacy, saying the article gave readers the impression that the play was a true account of their experiences. Life said the article was "basically truthful."

The court said:

"The line between the informing and the entertaining is too elusive for the protection of (freedom of the press). Erroneous statement is no less inevitable in such case than in the case of comment upon public affairs, and in both, if innocent or merely negligent, it must be protected if the freedoms of expression are to have the 'breathing space' that they 'need to survive.'

"We create grave risk of serious impairment of the indispensable service of a free press in a free society if we saddle the press with the impossible burden of verifying to a certainty the facts associated in a news article with a person's name, picture or portrait, particularly as related to non-defamatory matter."

The court added, however, that these constitutional guarantees do not extend to "knowing or reckless falsehood." A newspaper still may be liable for invasion of privacy if the facts of a story are changed deliberately or recklessly, or "fictionalized." As with The New York Times and The Associated Press decisions in the field of libel, the "Desperate Hours" case does not confer a license for defamatory statements or for reckless disregard of the truth.

Chapter 5

APPLYING THE RULES

We already have defined libel and explained the defenses available to the press. Let's now look at some applications.

In a society in which standards of right living are recognized by most persons, any accusation that a member of society has violated such standards must be injurious. Members of a community establish in the minds of others an estimate of what they are believed to be. Injury to that reputation may mean business, professional or social ruin.

One court decision put the matter this way:

"The law of defamation is concerned only with injuries to one's reputation. . . .

"Embarrassment and discomfort no doubt came to her from the publication, as they would to any decent woman under like circumstances. Her own reaction, however, has no bearing upon her reputation. That rests entirely upon the reactions of others. We are unable to find anything in this article which could appreciably injure plaintiff's reputation." (*Kimmerle v. New York Evening Journal Inc., 262 N.Y. 99*)

In order to be libelous, it is not necessary that a publication impute criminal activity. The following was held to be libelous:

"Pauper's Grave For Poor Child

"Unless financial aid is forthcoming immediately, the body of a 4-year-old boy who was run over Tuesday will be interred in Potter's Field, burying ground of the homeless, friendless and penniless, who die or are killed in New York City. The parents of this youngster are in dire financial straits, and at this writing have no alternative but to let their son go to his final rest in a pauper's grave."

The court said:

"It is reasonably clear, therefore, that in some cases it may be a libel if the plaintiff has been written up as an object of pity. . . . The reason is that in libel the matter is defamatory not only if it brings a party into hatred, ridicule or contempt by asserting some moral discredit upon his part, but also if it tends to make him be shunned or avoided, although it imputes no moral turpitude to him." (*Katapodis v. Brooklyn Spectator Inc., 287 N.Y. 17*)

A publication that does not discredit a person as an individual may nonetheless damage a person's professional status.

A story stated that after a man's body had been taken from the waters in which he had been swimming, he was pronounced dead by a doctor. Later the youth was revived. The doctor sued because of the implication that he had been unable to determine whether a person was living or dead.

Similarly, a publication may affect a business.

Companies are naturally sensitive to news stories that reflect on their business prospects and practices. There have been many such news stories in the field of environmental and consumer protection. The issues are complicated, and the legal aspects not always clear. Formal charges and allegations should be reported precisely and fairly.

Likewise, there is no alternative to precision in reporting any criminal charge.

Not only what is written, but the instruments used in transmitting it, must be considered in handling news. It is safer to say *acquitted* or *innocent,* rather than *not guilty* because of the danger that the negative may be dropped in transmission.

An essential element of an action for libel is that the complainant be identifiable to a third party. Nevertheless, the omission of names will not, in itself, provide a shield against a claim for libel. As was pointed out earlier, there may be enough details for the person to be recognizable.

A story may, by the use of a general description or name, make a libelous charge against an organized group. It is possible that any member of the group could bring an action on the story.

If the material is libelous and not privileged, then the question turns to proof.

Can the substance be established by documents, by testimony from trustworthy persons or by material from privileged sources? Hearsay evidence is not enough. It is not enough to show that somebody gave you the unprivileged information. The issue turns on proof.

Another libel pitfall is the mistaken identity case. There is no complete defense when a newspaper confuses a famous individual with a person bearing a similar name who gets into a scrape. Petty thieves running afoul of the law may give the names of famous persons — often old-time athletes — in the hope of getting leniency from a judge.

A few years ago a man charged with a minor crime appeared in Magistrate's Court in New York and gave as his name that of a once-great baseball pitcher. The magistrate gave the prisoner a suspended sentence. The real baseball player was a prosperous auto salesman, who threatened multiple suits when he read the story in the newspapers.

PHOTO CAPTIONS

The art of writing captions for Laserphotos can be elusive to many journalists simply because, for the most, so little time is spent at it.

But it is no mystery. Adherence to a few basic rules, the mastery of simple mechanical preparations, and a touch of writing flair will result in readable, widely published captions.

CAPTION CONTENT

The caption's job is to describe and explain the picture to the reader.

The challenge is to do it interestingly, accurately, always in good taste.

A further challenge is to write the caption, whenever appropriate, in a spritely, lively vein.

An APME Continuing Study Committee put together Ten Tests of a Good Caption. They are:

1. Is it complete?
2. Does it identify, fully and clearly?
3. Does it tell when?
4. Does it tell where?
5. Does it tell what's in the picture?
6. Does it have the names spelled correctly, with the proper name on the right person?
7. Is it specific?
8. Is it easy to read?
9. Have as many adjectives as possible been removed?
10. Does it suggest another picture?

And rule No.11, the Cardinal Rule, never, never to be violated:

NEVER WRITE A CAPTION WITHOUT SEEING THE PICTURE.

STYLE REQUIREMENTS

Caption style rules that deal with spelling, capitalization, abbreviations, grammar, titles, etc., are precisely the same as for the news wires.

There are some mechanical style requirements for captions alone, however.

Most Laserphotos will carry a caption setup like this:

> **(NY 14) NEW YORK, Feb. 18—WANNA BUY A PUSSYCAT?—Subway riders cuddle kittens found abandoned in a cardboard box on a subway platform in New York Friday. A sign attached to the box read "Kittens For Sale, \$2 Each," but the seller was nowhere to be found. The box and its batch of six pussycats were taken to the American Society for the Prevention of Cruelty to Animals shelter in Manhattan. (AP Laserphoto) (jtm61405mbr/dns) 1976**

Figure 1

The various parts of the caption are as follows:

(NY 14) The call letters of the network station where the transmitter is located, and picture number in the station's sequence of offerings on a given day.

NEW YORK The name of the city where the picture was made. Identify the state, too, if there could be doubt about the city's location.

Feb. 18 The date the picture is transmitted. The time element of when the picture was made should be included in the body of the caption.

WANNA BUY A PUSSYCAT? The overline. Just a few bright words to put across the point of the picture, attract the reader's attention, or evoke a smile. Use verbs in overlines, avoid labels and lifeless phrases.

(AP Laserphoto) The credit immediately follows the body of the caption.

jtm The initials of the caption writer.

61405 The day of the week the picture was transmitted — in this case 6 for *Friday* — and the time the caption was written on a 24-hour clock.

mbr/dns The source of the picture — in this case a *member (mbr), The Daily News (dns)*. If the picture is from an AP staff photographer, the photographer's initials should be used. Other possible designations include *handout (ho), stringer (str)*.

1976 The year of transmission, for library reference.

There are times when the credit (*AP Laserphoto*) will be carried in a different way. For example: (*Tass photo via AP Laserphoto*), (*White House photo via AP Laserphoto*), (*Newsweek photo via AP Laserphoto*), (*Hsinhua photo via AP Laserphoto*), (*Department of Defense photo via AP Laserphoto*), (*NBC-TV photo via AP Laserphoto*), etc.

These special credit lines are carried at the insistence of the source or because we want to make clear just what the source of the photo was because of possible influence on its content.

The Undated Caption

When a picture is taken from files, regardless of where that file is — member, stringer or the AP file — use an undated caption.

> **(NY 3-Jan. 6) INDUSTRIALIST DIES—Tom Smith, president of Industrial Industries, died Tuesday in Kansas City where he was attending a convention. He was 68 years old. (AP Laserphoto) (jcy31040fls) 1977 (EDS: This is a 1974 file picture)**

Note that the caption used on this file photo does not carry a dateline, carries a reference to *files* (*fls*) as a source, and provides an editor's note telling when the photo was made.

The undated style is used so that there is no confusion about the picture being made on the day of the news event.

Captions for Advances

Many pictures we transmit on the Laserphoto network are moved in advance. As with stories, these pictures must carry word to editors regarding publication date.

Captions for AP advances should carry the date and cycle in which the picture will be printed, along with information that will connect the picture to a story in situations in which a story also is provided.

Here is a sample advance caption:

> **(ADVANCE FOR FRIDAY PMS, FEB. 18, WITH STORY SLUGGED BETS BY BURT BERLINER)**
>
> **(NY20-Feb. 12) A BET A DAY KEEPS THE BLAHS AWAY—Suzy Q. Pretty cheers her favorite horse and jockey on to what she hopes will be a first-place win Saturday at New York's Aqueduct Racetrack. Miss Pretty says betting on the horses has brought new excitement into her life. She is one of an increasing number of people who are betting more money despite America's skyrocketing cost of living. (AP Laserphoto) (rjk71600stf/bb) 1977**

TRANSMISSION PREPARATION

There are basically two sizes of captions—a long version, which runs along the 10-inch dimension of the print, and a short version which runs along the 8-inch dimension. See **Figures 2** and **3** for examples.

There will be cases in which the print you transmit will be smaller than 8×10 inches, generally for mugshots. In such cases, the caption should be measured and written to fit neatly on the picture, as in **Figure 4. Figure 5** shows improper mounting.

On occasion you will want to "combo" pictures, which means sending two small prints in one transmission. Pictures must be the same size if comboed. See **Figure 6** for correct procedure. **Figure 7** shows incorrect mounting.

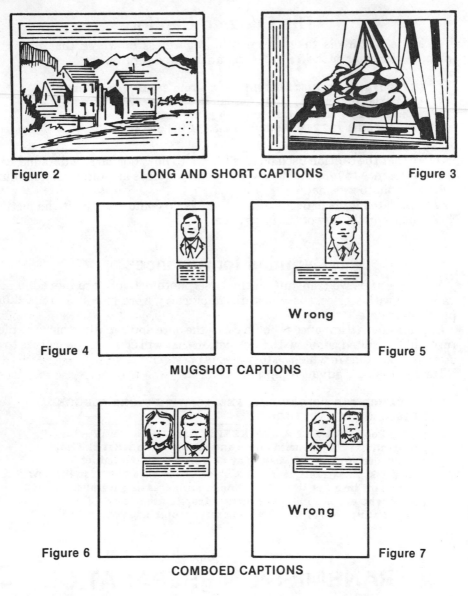

Figure 2   **LONG AND SHORT CAPTIONS**   Figure 3

Figure 4   **Wrong**   Figure 5

MUGSHOT CAPTIONS

Figure 6   **Wrong**   Figure 7

COMBOED CAPTIONS

When transmitting pictures, always place the photo in the Laser transmitter as follows: The 10-inch dimension of the picture should enter the transmitter. Do not insert the 8-inch dimension. The photo image always should face away from you as you insert the print. See **Figure 8.**

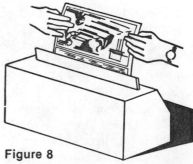

Figure 8

FILING
THE WIRE

These guidelines seek to help editors at newspapers and AP offices handle copy easily and efficiently.

The three principal objectives of the coding are:

—Assurance that stories will be routed promptly to the proper editor.

—Assurance that directories showing only the first slug line on a story will be as informative as possible.

—The ability to have a computer system automatically link leads, adds, inserts, subs, etc. to previous copy.

CODING REQUIREMENTS

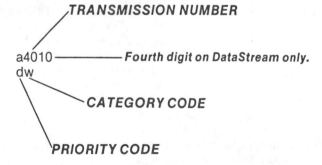

TRANSMISSION NUMBER

a4010 ————— *Fourth digit on DataStream only.*
dw

CATEGORY CODE

PRIORITY CODE

Every **transmission number** begins with a letter of the alphabet. The principal letters reserved for nationwide transmissions are:

a and **b** — Spot news and/or advances.

f — News designed primarily for financial pages.

s — Sports copy.

The letter in the transmission number is identified in some technical contexts as a **service level designator.**

Transmission numbers are placed on stories by computers. The remaining codes described in these pages must be placed on stories by staff members.

Priority codes are used by AP bureaus to assure that stories move on the wires in the order of their urgency. At newspapers, the codes can be used by computer systems to determine the order in which stories come to an editor's attention.

The principal priority codes, in order of urgency, and their use:

f — Flash, highest priority, seldom used.

b — Bulletins, first adds to bulletins, kill notes.

u — Urgent, high-priority copy, including all corrections. It must be used on all items that carry an *URGENT* slug. It also may be used on items that lack this slug but must move on an urgent basis.

r — Regular priority: digests, advisories, indexes, digest stories, other major stories that break too late for the digest, special fixtures such as People in the News.

d — Deferred priority. Used for spot copy that can be delayed if more urgent material is available.

h — The lowest spot news priority. On DataStream it usually indicates a story that will not move on the A Wire.

a — For weekday advances designed for use more than 12 hours after transmission. Hold-for-release material sent for use in less than 12 hours carries a spot news priority.

s — For Sunday advances designed for use more than 12 hours after transmission.

y — Used for internal routing among AP bureaus. When seen by a newspaper, it indicates a rerun.

Category codes are designed to help newspapers with computer systems sort copy into the electronic equivalents of putting paper copy on domestic stories in one pile, Washington stories in a second, international stories in a third, etc.

A space appears between the priority code and the category code when a story is transmitted. A space also appears between the two when a story is being edited on the screen of many AP computer terminals. However, some terminals require that there be no space between the two, although the space is inserted at the time of transmission.

The principal category codes and their use:

a and **b** — Domestic, non-Washington general news items. These two letters are used interchangeably. No separate sort is practical.

f — News copy, regardless of dateline, designed primarily for use on financial pages. When a major story of financial interest also moves as part of the general news service, editors should be advised that the same story has been routed to both financial desks and news desks.

i — International items, including stories from the United Nations, U.S. possessions, and undated roundups keyed to foreign events.

n — Stories of state or regional interest under domestic datelines. If a regional item has a Washington dateline, use the *w* category. If a regional item has an international dateline, use the *i* category. If a regional item is designed primarily for financial pages, use the *f* category regardless of the dateline.

q — Use only for the result or period score of a single sports event. The code is designed to help newspaper computer systems build a list of scores or ignore individual scores and wait for transmissions that group them.

s — Sports stories, standings, results of more than one event.

v — Advisories affecting stories that may carry any one of the four category letters (*a, b, i* or *w*) used for nationwide news stories. This code is used primarily for nationwide news digests, late news advisories, lists of transmitted advances, and indexes.

w — Washington-datelined stories. Change to the *a* or *b* category code if a subsequent lead shifts the dateline to a different city.

KEYWORD SLUG LINE

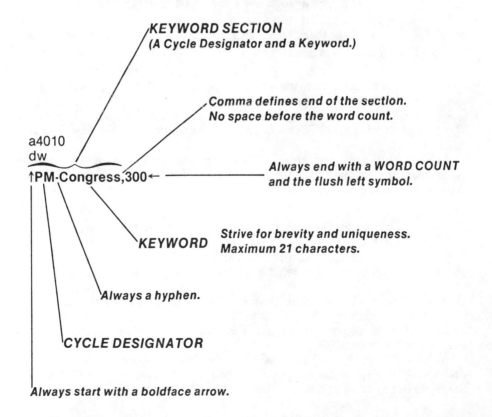

KEYWORD SECTION
(A Cycle Designator and a Keyword.)

Comma defines end of the section.
No space before the word count.

a4010
dw

↑PM-Congress,300←

Always end with a WORD COUNT and the flush left symbol.

KEYWORD *Strive for brevity and uniqueness. Maximum 21 characters.*

Always a hyphen.

CYCLE DESIGNATOR

Always start with a boldface arrow.

Every item transmitted on AP news and sports wires must begin with a **keyword slug line.** There are no exceptions.

Every keyword slug line must have at least a keyword section. Up to three other sections, as shown in examples that follow, are used when necessary.

The commas that appear in the examples are critical for operations of many AP computers. On high-speed AP circuits, the commas are replaced by spaces, and all other spaces in the line are eliminated, to conform with industrywide specifications for automatic routing of copy in newspaper computer systems.

Always end the keyword slug line with the flush left symbol (← or <).

The **keyword section** of the line consists of a cycle designator and a keyword or keywords. A boldface symbol (↑ or ∧) precedes the cycle designator. A comma marks the end of the section.

Because the keyword section provides the basic identification of a story for automatic linkup routines, it *must be repeated in exactly the same form on all subsequent leads, adds, inserts, subs,* etc. filed for a story.

There are three **cycle designators:**

↑AM- Indicates that morning newspapers have first use of the story.

↑PM- Indicates that afternoon newspapers have first use of the story.

↑BC- Indicates that the item is for use by either AMs or PMs — immediately if it is a spot item, or on the publication date if it is an advance.

The *BC-* designation is used on all Sunday advances.

The **keyword** should provide an indication of the story's content.

The following standards apply:

—Overall, the keyword should not exceed a total of 21 letters and/or figures. (Rule of thumb: *If you have to count the letters, the keyword is too long.*)

—Commonly accepted abbreviations and acronyms such as *Scotus* for Supreme Court of the United States and *Xgr* for legislature are encouraged where applicable.

Provide a **word count** estimate at the end of the keyword slug line.

When using a CRT to edit or write a story, obtain the estimate by counting the number of lines and multiplying by 10. Include lines that have only one or two words — this helps compensate for lines with more than 10 words.

When a story will run more than one take, the first take should give the word count for that take followed by a hyphen and the total wordage estimate for the story (do not use a comma if the total is more than 999 words, for example *1020*).

No take of a story should exceed an estimated 450 words.

Do not put a space before the word count or a comma after it. End with the flush left symbol and strike the return key.

VERSION SECTION

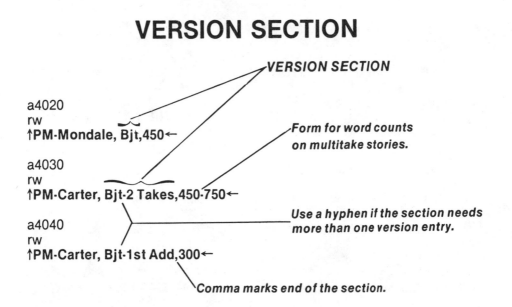

VERSION SECTION

a4020
rw
↑PM-Mondale, Bjt,450←

Form for word counts on multitake stories.

a4030
rw
↑PM-Carter, Bjt-2 Takes,450-750←

Use a hyphen if the section needs more than one version entry.

a4040
rw
↑PM-Carter, Bjt-1st Add,300←

Comma marks end of the section.

The **version section** of the keyword slug line is designed to give editors and computer systems a quick indication of whether to place an item at the top, bottom or middle of previous takes sent under the same keyword.

The terms that follow are the only ones that should appear in the version section of a keyword slug line. When more than one term is necessary, separate them with a hyphen. Use figures as indicated.

The version vocabulary is broken into two lists. Do not use more than one of the terms from this first list in a keyword slug line. If a term from the second list is needed, it must follow any term from this first list:

> **Bjt**
> **1st Ld, 2nd Ld, 10th Ld,** etc.
> **Adv 01, Adv 31,** etc.
> **Advisory**
> **KILL**
> **WITHHOLD**
> **ELIMINATION**

A term from the second list may stand alone in the version section if no term from the first list is needed. Some stories require two terms from the second list. If that is the case, the order in which the terms appear is not critical, but they must be separated by a hyphen. The second list:

> **2 Takes, 3 Takes,** etc.
> **1st Add, 2nd Add,** etc.
> **Insert**
> **Sub**
> **Correction**
> **Writethru**
> **Box** (Sports only.)

REFERENCE NUMBER SECTION

*Note that Bjt is not repeated
in filing a lead.*

REFERENCE NUMBER SECTION

a5840
uw
↑PM-Carter, 1st Ld, a4030,300←

Comma marks end of the section.

a5910
uw
↑PM-Carter, 1st Ld-1st Add, a5840,200←

a6010
uw
↑PM-Carter, 2nd Ld-3 Takes-Writethru, a5840,450-1100←

a6020
uw
↑PM-Carter, 2nd Ld-1st Add-Writethru, a6010,400←

*Note form when three terms from
the version lists are needed.*

The **reference number** is the transmission number used on a previous
take of a story. List only one in a keyword line.

Follow these norms:

—Cite the number of the most recent lead if you are sending a new lead,
sub, insert, correction, advisory, etc.

—If you are filing an add, cite only the transmission number on the immediately preceding take of the story.

—If a story has moved in many pieces and you think editors should have
more reference numbers than the one in the keyword line, list them on a line
below the keyword slug line.

DATARECAPS

a6910
uw
↑PM-Carter, 5th Ld-3 Takes, DataRecap,400-1100←

a6920
uw
↑PM-Carter, 5th Ld-1st Add, DataRecap,400←

A **DataRecap** is a high-speed transmission that puts together the pieces of an item for easier handling at a newspaper desk. It is not a new lead and should not be slugged as such.

To distinguish the *Carter 5th Ld* from the *Carter 5th Ld DataRecap*, the term *DataRecap* replaces the reference number, as in the example shown here.

Use *DataRecap* on all takes of the transmission.

Once a DataRecap has been filed, use the transmission number on it as the reference number for any subsequent leads, inserts, etc. (Even if a telegraph editor has not used the DataRecap for typesetting, it is presumed that he has kept a copy of the DataRecap.) Using the examples here, the reference number for a *PM-Carter, 6th Ld* would be *a6910,* not the number used on the original 5th Ld.

Some procedures for DataRecaps:

—Advise editors in advance that a DataRecap is planned and give an estimate of when it will move.

—Eliminate from the body of a story a first name or similar material that is superfluous because of developments in new leads.

—If some of the original paragraphs of a story have been outdated by developments, eliminate them. Tell editors in a non-publishable editor's note below the keyword slug line that some editing has been done.

—If more extensive changes are necessary in a story, go to a new lead and mark it *Writethru.*

FORMAT IDENTIFIERS

```
a6240
dabt
↑PM-Temperatures,300←

s3570
rsat
↑BC-Celts-Knicks, Box,←
```

Two additional letters, called **format identifiers**, appear after the category code if an item is intended for agate and/or contains tabular material.

Use **bt** if the item is intended to be set in body type and contains even one tabular line.

Use **at** if the item is intended to be set in agate type and contains even one tabular line.

Use **ax** if the item is intended to be set in agate type but contains no tabular lines.

Some CRT screens automatically show **bx** if the item has not been coded for agate or tabular composition.

SPECIAL NOTE TO MEMBERS

KEYWORD FORMAT — Slow-Speed

Newspapers that receive the A Wire and other circuits operating at 66 words per minute will notice that slugs appear in the form shown in these illustrations, with the commas intact.

KEYWORD FORMAT — DataStream

As indicated in the introduction on the keyword, the commas in the keyword slug line are replaced by spaces when stories are sent on DataStream at 1,200 words per minute.

Any spaces in the line as originally typed are removed automatically to meet the industry standards for the keyword line in high-speed transmissions.

In addition to the information placed in the keyword slug by editors, the computers that transmit DataStream add a four-digit filing date with a hyphen in the middle and a four-digit word count. The computer makes the word estimate by counting the number of characters in the story and dividing by six.

Here is how some of the slugs shown earlier would look on DataStream:

u w PM-Carter 2ndLd-3Takes-Writethru a5840 02-06 0455

u w PM-Carter 5thLd-3Takes DataRecap 02-06 0407

FORMAT IDENTIFIERS on DataStream

The letters *at*, *bt*, etc. shown in the examples of **format identifiers** do not appear on DataStream. However, they help generate non-printing characters that are sent in this location to convey the same information about whether the item is meant to be set in agate or body type and whether it contains tabular material.

For additional copies and information write:

THE ASSOCIATED PRESS
AP Newsfeatures Department
50 Rockefeller Plaza
New York, N.Y. 10020